Eichendorff:
The Spiritual Geometer

Contents

Introduction   1

I Early Poems   14

II Sonette   68

III Jugendandacht   100

IV Two Forces and a Song   170

V Marmorbild   201

VI Taugenichts   271

Epilogue   355

Fata Morgana

Du Pilger im Wüstensande,
Ich spiegle Wälder und Kluft,
Der Heimat blühende Lande
Dir wunderbar in der Luft.

Wer hielte in dieser Wüste
Das einsame Wandern aus,
Wenn ich barmherzig nicht grüsste
Mit Frühlingsdüften von Haus?

Und ob's auch wieder verflogen
In Luft und schien doch so nah,
Nur frisch durch die sengenden Wogen,
Wer weiss, wie bald bist du da!

(I, 107)

Introduction

In a brief but very perceptive essay, Wilhelm Emrich observes "Die Eichendorffverehrung unserer Zeit beruht zumeist auf einer fatalen Selbsttäuschung. Eine Welt, die die unbequemen Wahrheiten ihrer eigenen Dichter beiseiteräumt unter dem Vorwand, sie nicht verstehen zu können, verfehlt auch die Wahrheit der vergangenen Poesie, die sie gegen sie ausspielt."[1] A few lines further on, in speaking of the strangeness and even incomprehensibility of present-day poetic imagery, he returns to the poet and remarks: "Eichendorffs scheinbar so verständliche Dichtung war in Wahrheit ein früher, aber entscheidender Schritt in diesem Verrätselungsprozess. Dafür sprechen nicht nur seine bis heute noch nicht wirklich erschlossenen hieroglyphischen Verzauberungssymbole, sondern auch seine unmittelbaren, kritischen Äusserungen über das Verhältnis zwischen Dichtung und Zeit, Poesie und menschlicher Gesellschaft."[2] This writer has devoted more than a decade to the problem-mystery of understanding what Emrich calls the "hieroglyphischen Verzauberungssymbole." Since the publication of Emrich's thoughts no appreciable progress has been made in "decoding" the poet's emblematic language. The reason is really quite simple: no one has read the poet's works a hundred times and more (the only alternative to a concordance) in a sincere and determined effort to penetrate the seemingly disarming simplicity of his prose and poems. Emrich briefly discusses "die eigentümliche Grundmelodie. . . die jedem in tiefster Seele mitgegeben ist . . . ."[3] He is the first to understand the significance of the word "mitgegeben."

1

It originates "von einer anderen Macht, vom Schöpfer selbst zugeteilt."[4] And now, using Emrich's own words, I must point to the error in reasoning which, so it seems, prevented his insight from bearing fruit. He concludes: "Die wahre Grundmelodie ist irdisch und überirdisch zugleich."[5] This cannot be. If the "Grundmelodie" is imparted to man by God then it cannot be defined as "irdisch." It is the purpose of this study to distinguish between "die irdische und überirdische [Melodie]." The problem is that both songs seem to be the same. The mystery is grounded in the fact that man, the poet, may and does confuse one with the other. The entire structure of Joseph von Eichendorff's imagery may be visualized as "lines" passing through one point. Eichendorff himself calls them "Radien."[6] But this one point consists of X and X^1, where the latter is a reflection of the former. To the human creature, both the reality and the reflection (illusion) seem real. By way of analogy, I should like to draw upon the principle of equivalence which is a facet of the theory of relativity.

Let us imagine our earth as a box in which stands a man holding a plate. He releases this object and it falls to the ground. Each time he repeats this experiment he observes the same result. However, another observer, at a considerable distance from earth, watches and sees a different sequence of events. As the man in the box (earth) releases the plate, he sees the ground rising and striking the plate. It must seem that one observer is deceived. The fact of the matter is that there is a measure of truth or correctness in both conclusions. However, one truth is greater than the other because it explains what would otherwise remain a mystery. For all practical purposes, especially on a rather elementary level, it would seem to make no difference whether the plate falls or the ground rises. I use this example as an introduction to a later discussion of centrifugal and centripetal force. As far as the senses are concerned, they seem to have the same effect. The latter would seem to involve man in a world that grows smaller and smaller, while the former would seem to involve the creature in an ever expanding universe. Actually, this is a contradiction. Centripetal force means movement into God's "weite Welt," and centrifugal force leads to an ever smaller world of the self. This is the fundamental idea in Eichendorff's works, and it is the purpose of this book to guide the reader toward this perspective.[7] I have found nothing in Eichendorff scholarship which indicates any awareness of this noetic structure in his works.[8] This explains the absence of a bibliography. Furthermore, there is no need for an index, because the chapters are designed in such a fashion that we always refer to or return to the same point. And this point can be defined by one word: love. Human love, as discussed in this book, is a reflection or the image of divine love. These are the two forces which are always in contention.

A chapter of some fifty pages was deleted from this book. It represented an effort to demonstrate how the process of selecting only certain passages from Eichendorff's works has introduced lines of distortion into the Eichendorff "Bild." In some instances authors have deleted lines from passages which tended to contradict their conclusions. I know that this is not due to a lack of good will but reflects the tendency in literary criticism to organize patterns and "evidence" which substantiates preconceived opinions. Much space could be saved on our library shelves if scholars with an interest in the same poet would consult each other before publication. I have a bibliography of some two hundred items, and most of the articles tell me more about the author than Eichendorff. It is hoped that this book will be read with the poet's works at hand. In most instances I have presented entire poems and complete prose passages. I deem it imperative that the reader see the entire context. Furthermore, I never presume to offer what might be called a "complete" interpretation of a poem. My purpose was to organize Eichendorff's own thoughts in such fashion that the reader is guided as to how they should be read and understood. The poet is the teacher, and not the critic. The latter should seek but to do the will of the poet. This book concentrates on the young Eichendorff, up to the publication of the "Taugenichts" novella. The older Eichendorff retains the same imagery and does not change his perspective. He does, however, shift the emphasis from "Dichter und Dichtung" to man and society. Even *Dichter und ihre Gesellen,* which critics still view as a novel concerning poets, is sorely misunderstood. From the very beginning, Victor, the main figure, is no longer a poet, and the entire book concerns his spiritual evolution to that which transcends the poet. It is difficult for scholars to realize that Eichendorff is not the Romanticist we think him to be. Eichendorff is basically a critic; he judges and condemns not only his own early efforts as a poet, but the society in which he lives. There is in this man a surprising and even painful hardness. He himself says the poet is "das Herz der Welt." But Eichendorff became even more than that. He is the conscience of the nineteenth and the twentieth century. And we still ignore him, because man does not like to be reminded of what he should not be.

A useful introduction should offer the reader a statement concerning the contents of the book. I should like to mention briefly the most significant areas of departure from the Eichendorff "Bild" as critics know it.

1. Eichendorff the critic. Preconceived notions concerning criticism, creative talent, and didactic poetry have blinded us to the possibility that great poetry, even lyric poetry, may be primarily didactic and critical. Eichendorff is keenly analytical, his lyricism is highly rational, his romanticism is classical. He combines the contradictory and the paradoxical, and that is a good definition of early German Romanticism at its best. No later than 1807, Eichendorff became a critic, first of his own earlier poetry and then, very quickly, of the Romantic movement. However, he was a constructive critic. What "Poesie" was and what it should be constitute the content, the subject matter, of his own creative works. He knew that his poetry and prose works were not understood, so he turned to epic poems, drama, and literary histories to say the same thing. Eichendorff did not change. He remained consistent, and all of his work was involved in what he calls "den schönen Gottesstreit."

2. What is "Poesie"? Scholarship has mined his histories and works for statements or definitions of poetry and the poet. Unfortunately, and because scholars have not examined Eichendorff's use of words, it is not clearly known how poetry is represented in his creative works. "Poesie" is a woman. Her name may be Rosa, Romana, Bianca, Venus, Annidi, Juana, "die gnädige Frau," to cite just a few. Eichendorff insists that the poet dare not deal in abstractions but must give the idea in flesh and blood. The relationship between the poet-hero and the "woman" is a precise definition of that poetry which holds the hero enthralled. The fact that this is always presented as a love affair points to another dimension which scholarship has missed. Creativity is the manifestation of love, and the poet's words and his use of imagery are carefully designed to suggest the movement of love.

3. The Law of Love. Eichendorff tells us there are two laws in man's spiritual world. He calls them centripetal and centrifugal force. The former is divine love and draws man upward or in toward what he calls the center of all being. The other is also love, but a love which denies obedience to the first love and thus moves the creature down or away from the center. Upon these two laws or loves is based the entire noetic structure in our poet's works. This is the idea which gives form to his works. It also is the ground for the principles of deception and inversion.

4. The Movement of Love. All of Eichendorff's poetry involves movement, because love is both a seeking and a doing; therefore our poet has his characters drawn, as it were, by centripetal or centrifugal force. Depending upon which love draws the poet-hero, he moves toward an ever more restricting finiteness or seemingly infinite expansion. This is the secret of Eichendorff's use of "Raum." Whenever the poet-hero allows himself to be drawn by divine love, the nature imagery suggests expansion; if the poet's song speaks only of his own love, then that same imagery is used to imply limitation or restriction. The process continues to the point of "Erstarrung." But, and this is the theme of deception which is always present in such a development, the poet-hero may feel that his own love draws him toward an infinitely expanded existence. Eichendorff would show us that man's own love deceives him. Indeed, this is precisely what Raimund tells us. Furthermore, the entire "Marmorbild" story is based upon one question: "Ist's Liebe, ist's Andacht,/ Was so dich beglückt." This novella is also the clearest but not the only example of inversion; the poet-hero thinks he rises when he is actually sinking, he thinks his song expresses "Andacht" and it is only "Liebe."

5. The Imagery. This must be the scholar's workshop. When one investigates thousands of contexts in which specific words and phrases are used, a number of interesting facts come to light. As far as my work has gone it is highly probable that Eichendorff's imagery can be reduced to air, fire, earth, and water, the ancient insight concerning creation. This is not an idea which the poet sought to implement in later works, but can be seen in the "Jugendandacht" cycle (1808-1810). If one now combines this reduction of imagery with the principles of two laws or loves in Eichendorff's works, the mystery suddenly deep-

ens. The reference to two laws or loves means that Eichendorff
is concerned with two realities, both of which he describes
with the same imagery. That is why deception is such a significant factor in his works. The reader should not be amazed at
the emphasis placed upon deception: it is the fundamental experience of each poet-hero who will be mentioned in our book:
Friedrich, Raimund, Florio, Otto, Lothario, the "Taugenichts."
For each, the beloved is "Poesie" who becomes flesh and blood;
but because "Poesie" is their own love become visible, they are
deceived by themselves, by their own song. This is a fundamental aspect of this study. But this is not all. Eichendorff's
imagery is metamorphic. By this I mean that air becomes song
which becomes light which becomes a stream; or stream
("Fluss") becomes light which becomes song. The process is
reversible. All of Eichendorff's nature symbolism is drawn into
this reduction process. I shall demonstrate that the poet's
"Hieroglyphenschrift," which involves much of his nature
imagery, is actually a communication outlining the landscape of
the soul. That is why I call him a spiritual geometer. Criticism
has always suggested that Eichendorff is limited in his range of
themes. I suggest we consider the law of commutations and per-
mutations. Given a small number of items, let us say ten, the
number of possible combinations becomes astounding. This is the
secret of Eichendorff's variations upon a theme. The delicate
shading and subtlety which this man achieves is truly amazing.

6. Polarity. In the latest research, I have seen an attempt
to apply this to Eichendorff. Let us not confuse Eichendorff with
Goethe. The two loves which form the basis for all that Eichendorff would say to us are not opposite poles, as we usually
understand them in magnetism. It is true that he clearly describes the relationship between them as "feindlich." Centripetal
and centrifugal forces move in opposite directions. And yet
man's love, which in and of itself tends to deny God, is man's
only key to the first love. And that is what Eichendorff would
teach us. Out of denial acceptance is born, and rebellion becomes
obedience. Only a Saul could become a Paul. But this is also
the ground of man's helplessness. As I shall show in an analysis
of imagery, this new man is not man's work. "Was wahr in dir
wird sich gestalten." That is why Eichendorff throughout his
life and in all of his works is the implacable enemy of those
religions, for which he has a host of names, which imply that

man makes the new man. In his own words, man would save himself and be his own god. But this new man is always a variation of the old man. That is why in Eichendorff's works the poet-hero always is confronted with his own image. "Poesie," because it is but the movement of his own love, cannot be a Beatrice. For this we need another woman, and another "Bild" must be present in the heart of the poet.

7. "Das Bild." Eichendorff insists that in the poet's mind and heart must be a vision of Truth and Beauty which is one with his religion. Combine this with the points discussed above and we have what is tantamount to an equation: religion = Truth and Beauty = "Bild" = "Poesie" = woman. But "Dichten und Glauben," although they have a common root, are different in function. The poet tells us that faith enters the depths and is concerned with "Anschauung der Wahrheit," while "Dichten" seeks to embellish what faith has seen. That is why they are one, yet basically different. Now look at our equation and keep in mind the definitions just given. Then "Dichten" becomes a seeing and embellishing of Truth and Beauty, of "das Bild" of woman, of religion. Then what is a "Marmorbild"? It is religion-Truth-Beauty-"Poesie"-woman who has turned to stone. It is the image in Florio's heart, and she is reborn in the springtime of his love and is given life by his song.

> And now the "Taugenichts."
> Wohin ich geh' und schaue,
> In Feld und Wald und Tal,
> Vom Berg' ins Himmelblaue.
> Vielschöne gnädige Frau
> Grüss ich dich tausendmal.

This fool in Christ looks at the entire universe and sees a woman. But we have just said that Florio does this. Then what is the difference between these two? Florio's "Bild" is his word (song) become flesh. As she takes more and more life from him, he loses his. The entire novella reeks of death; its fragrance trembles in the air disguised as the essence of flowers, and the "woman" is a flower, standing for his song, his poetry, the movement of his love. And the "Taugenichts"? His image remains in his heart. The woman does not become flesh. Once, he makes a mistake; he tries to see his love. For this he pays a price. And that is why, if scholars would seek to understand these two novellas, they must learn to view them as opposite sides of the same coin. "Das Bild," a woman who is "Poesie," plays a dominant role in both stories, and her name is Venus. Each is a goddess of love and queen of the garden. The earthly Venus must learn her songs from the poet; she has none of her own because her grave is silent. The heavenly Venus teaches him her song, the song from on high which bursts into man's heart in a crescendo of light. It is the Magnificat, the "Grundmelodie" asleep in nature and in the depths of man's heart.

8. Multiplicity in Oneness. Eichendorff's poetry was studied in chronological order. It is the only way in which one can establish the poet's definition of a word and the possible shift in meaning assigned to it. This process also led to the realization that Eichendorff's enigmatic terms have a double meaning, a positive and negative aspect, which corresponds to what I have called the movement of love. The poetry chapters follow this reading pattern and introduce the poems in chronological order beginning with 1807. Another reason for this approach is to show the reader that Eichendorff uses the same key terms regardless of whether the poem comes from the section "Wanderlieder, Frühling und Liebe, Geistliche Gedichte, Sängerleben" or even "Zeitlieder." This significant vocabulary, which might be called "Chiffren," is used just as freely and in the same sense in his literary histories and prose works. The Eichendorff scholar immediately realizes that one can have two to three hundred entries for one word. It seems a reasonable assumption that one could select perhaps ten to fifteen emblematic terms, show how each is used in significant contexts, and thus arrive at an Eichendorff definition of the word. This proved to be unsatisfactory. It was discovered that one enigmatic term could not be given a full definition without bringing in other terms. For example, spring becomes a song, which becomes a flower, which becomes a woman, who is a star; and the entire constellation is part of a certain "Morgenrot" which is the symbol for a love. This is why we have called Eichendorff's imagery metamorphic; one term flows into another and the whole has a unity. It is as though the poet consciously brought to bear his superb artistry to show that all things are reduced to one. I have become convinced that this amazing unity suggested by his imagery was not only deliberate but necessary. He insists that all revolutions are basically religious in nature. This means that he judges the

value of whatever is new by the relationship with God effected by the innovation. If it brings man closer to God, it is good; if it effects denial, he rejects it. This same statement applies to his poetry; it is, after all, nothing more than a restatement of centripetal and centrifugal force, of what I have called the movement of love. And these words suggest that particular oneness or unity which I see reflected in everything the poet wrote.

9. Nature, Light and Song. At the beginning of the second book of *Ahnung und Gegenwart*, Friedrich has just entered the city and finds himself alone. "In solchen verlassenen Stunden wenden wir uns mit doppelter Liebe nach den Augen der Geliebten, aus denen uns die Natur wieder wunderbar begrüsst, wo wir Ruhe, Trost und Freude wiederzufinden wähnen" (II, 125). To the best of my knowledge this passage has never been discussed. The reader obviously does not know what the poet is talking about. At the end of the second chapter of the "Taugenichts" story, as this new minstrel decides to travel again, he reaches for his dusty and neglected violin. "Ein Morgenstrahl aber aus dem gegenüberliegenden Fenster fuhr gerade blitzend über die Saiten. Das gab einen rechten Klang in meinem Herzen. Ja, sagt' ich, komm nur her, du getreues Instrument! Unser Reich ist nicht von dieser Welt! — " (II, 368). Why should sunlight touch a violin and cause his heart to sing? One night Friedrich dreams that he is awakened in a dream — a significant sequence — and sees a beautiful child "Mitten in der Sonne zwischen den spielenden Farbenlichtern traurig an ein grosses Kreuz gelehnt." Without moving its lips the child says: "Liebst du mich recht, so gehe mit mir unter, als Sonne wirst du wieder aufgehen, und die Welt ist frei!—" (II, 166).

How is it possible to look into the eyes of the beloved and be greeted by nature? And then we recall that Rosa, for that is the beloved's name, is called a painted spring. The idea that a woman should be described in this fashion brings to mind the poem "Der Maler" in which God, using the rays of the sun which have been dipped in fragrance, paints the face of an angel upon the entire world. And of this angel the poem speaks.

> O lichte Augen ernst und mild,
> Ich kann nicht von euch lassen!
>
> . . . .
>
> Durch die verworrnen Gassen
> Führ mich, mein göttlich Bild!

But the pattern is not yet complete. Florio feels that the marble statue had entered spring, the pond was now an immense landscape, the stars in it were flowers and "der ganze Frühling ein Bild der Schönen" (II, 324). So that the reader will have some preparation for what our study attempts to clarify, I have brought together several of the enigmatic terms with which one must deal, words such as "Bild, Blume, Stern, Frühling, Weiher [water symbolism], Augen, Natur" and woman, the common denominator. If one were to draw a line between all these "points-terms," one would have a sketch of two faces, one superimposed upon the other. With these words I paraphrase what Eichendorff would reveal when Florio experiences the presence of Bianca and Venus, and the blinded youth cannot distinguish between them. Let us see how Eichendorff metamorphoses his imagery and imparts a sense of mystery and deception.

In Rosa's eyes Friedrich seems to see nature. But when she is described as a painted spring, then we must conclude that she is, somehow, artificial. As a consequence, the nature "seen" in her eyes is as *false* as the spring which she represents. And then we come to a spring which is an image of Venus, a marble statue. Even nature is mysteriously suspect because a pond has been changed into an entire region. If we examine all of Eichendorff's words which concern water, such terms as "Fluss, Strom, Meer, Quelle," then we slowly realize, and I shall show this, that the water symbolism is designed to suggest the poet's song. With this in mind we recall that Venus arises from the pond. Clearly, the pond must be related to the song which "contains" Venus. Thus guided, we are not surprised to read that a certain song courses like blood through Venus' body, giving her life. Therefore the pond is the deep within the poet from which arises "Das Bild," his version of Truth and Beauty, which is his religion and which he embellishes with song; his flowers. But the pond also becomes "eine unermessliche Landschaft!" It must follow that this nature is not nature as critics have, with remarkable obstinacy, continued to describe it. The pond is a veritable world in which a certain song is sung, and in that world nature is not nature because the trees are not trees, the birds are not birds, the flowers not flowers, and the fountains are not fountains. It is a world which exists within Florio, and it is exactly what Raimund in "Die Zauberei im Herbste" calls "ein wunderbares, dunkles Reich der Gedanken" (II, 983).

In the eyes of his beloved, Friedrich is greeted by nature where he thinks he can find peace, consolation, joy. Neither woman nor nature can give him that for which he yearns. Given the proper perspective, this statement is both clear and necessary. We shall show that woman "is" poetry, that which the creator brings into being. And whatever the artist makes can never be that for which he searches. Eichendorff repeatedly asserts this truth. Nature, he tells us, is both mute and blind; man is the eye and most powerful voice in the hierarchy of created things. Consequently, he informs us that nature cannot speak to man of God unless He is already within man. This means that nature is to man what he is to himself. This means, furthermore, that the song asleep in all things will not be released until the poet sings the same song. And that song is a hymn of praise to the Lord God on high. Nature, which obeys the Law, knows no other song. And this same song is produced by the sunbeam as it touches the string of the violin which is the love of the "Taugenichts." That is why their kingdom is not of this world. The "Taugenichts" is the minstrel of our Lady; he sings her song, the Magnificat. It is written that man is to love God above all and his neighbor as himself. Man disobeys. He does not seek the will of the Lord, nor work to get it done. That is why Christ tells Friedrich in a dream: Love me and the world will be free. Free of what? Free of man's love which is a seeking of his own will. Love, not intelligence, is man's most precious gift. It is also the most dangerous. I accept, as the most workable definition of man, that he is the one creature on earth filled with a consuming desire to be more than he is. Power for this expansion is provided by love, a seeking of his own will. That is precisely why the poet says it leads down to "Absonderung, zur Zerstörung und zum Hasse" (IV, 1069).

I have presented this brief summary of what the book would clarify in detail for a very personal reason. After years of reading and tracing words and phrases in thousands of contexts I am certain that I have listened to Eichendorff and heard him correctly. I am quite confident that the Eichendorff "Bild" is not distorted by original thoughts of my own. And yet the genius of the poet is such that he utterly transcends my capacity to delineate and organize effectively. This admission causes me no embarrassment, but I fear for the poet. My own ineptitude and awkwardness of expression must not become another veil which conceals the poet's noetic structure. For this reason I have presented a brief discussion of the most important conclusions. If the reader will keep them in mind he should be able to test the correctness or reasonableness at each step in their development. It should be pointed out that the opening chapters concentrate on the poetry that is employed to isolate the emblematic terms. In the "Jugendandacht" chapter, a first effort is made to bring the material together. The last two chapters, which deal with "Das Marmorbild" and the "Taugenichts" story, are designed to present the final proof of my theory. If a theory is properly grounded in correct observation, it must of necessity explain what has been ignored or not understood. The perspective which, as I would insist, Eichendorff has taught me to adopt, allows one to see these novellas in a new and more revealing light. Furthermore, and I have attempted to test this rigorously, the conclusions reached do not contradict what Eichendorff says in his later works, critical or creative. As stated before, there is a oneness about his entire productivity. I hope the book engenders conversation which will lead beyond the present horizon of "Dichtung and Dichter" toward Eichendorff, the critic of society, philosophy and religion. Readers have "typed" this man and must learn to understand that his essential concern is man's relationship with his God, and the function of religion in the total spectrum of existence. In *Dichter und ihre Gesellen* he gives a picture of the twentieth century; the nations of the world united against the common enemy, God. The evil one shows mankind the splendor of the world and exclaims: "Seid frei und alles ist euer!"

Here is the negation of Christ's words heard by Friedrich: "Be mine and the world is free." These two statements voiced by the first and the second morning star are the song sung by the first and the second Venus, and they define the movement of the two loves which we see in the poet's works. Both loves seem to offer what is the hunger of the soul: to be more than one is. But the human creature must decide wisely. "Denn mitten in unserer Welt liegt eine wunderbare Sphinx, die dem, der unberufen die Lösung ihrer ewigen Rätsel wagt, den Hals bricht" (IV, 1078).

Notes

1. Wilhelm Emrich. *Protest und Verheissung: Studien zur klassischer und moderner Dichtung* (Frankfurt am Main, Bonn: Athenäum, 1960), p. 104. I am particularly grateful to Emrich for this astute and critical observation; particularly in view of the fact that Eichendorff made the same observation concerning the reception of his own poetry in 1810-12. "Wenn unserer Altvordern Herzen wohl mit dreifachem Erz gewappnet waren, das vor dem rechten Strahle erklang, wie das Erz von Dodna; so sind die unsrigen nun mit sechsfacher Butter des häuslichen Glückes, des guten Geschmacks, zarter Empfindungen und edelmütiger Handlungen umgeben, durch die kein Wunderlaut bis zu der Talggrube hindurchdringt. Zieht dann von Zeit zu Zeit einmal ein wunderbarer, altfränkischer Gesell', der es noch ehrlich und ernsthaft meint, wie Don Quixote, vorüber, so sehen Herren und Damen nach der Tafel gebildet und gemächlich zu den Fenstern hinaus, stochern sich die Zähne und ergötzen sich an seinen wunderlichen Kapriolen, oder machen wohl gar auch Sonette auf ihn, und meinen, er sei eine recht interessante Erscheinung, wenn er nur nicht eigentlich verrückt wäre" (II, 293). Eichendorff, like Hölderlin, had to wait nearly a full century for his "discovery."

2. Emrich, p. 104.

3. Emrich, p. 107.

4. Ibid.

5. Emrich, p. 109.

6. Joseph von Eichendorff, *Werke* ed. by Seigfried Grosse and Gerhart Baumann, 4 vols., (Stuttgart: Cotta, 1953-57), II, 75. Subsequent volume and page references to this edition will be made in the text.

7. I would have the reader realize that Eichendorff's works rest upon the principle of the paradox. And that is also the cornerstone of Christianity.

8. In a later context I shall mention the one scholar who has revealed his awareness of the problem. It concerns the concept of "Raum."

I

Early Poems

Das Zaubernetz

Fraue, in den blauen Tagen
Hast ein Netz du ausgehangen,
Zart gewebt aus seidnen Haaren,
Süssen Worten, weissen Armen.

Und die blauen Augen sprachen,
Da ich waldwärts wollte jagen:
"Zieh mir, Schöner, nicht von dannen!"
Ach, da war ich dein Gefangner!

Hörst du nun den Frühling laden? —
Jägers Waldhorn geht im Walde,
Lockend grüssen bunte Flaggen,
Nach dem Sänger alle fragen.

Ach, von euch, ihr Frühlingsfahnen,
Kann ich, wie von dir, nicht lassen!
Reisen in den blauen Tagen
Muss der Sänger mit dem Klange.

Flügel hat, den du gefangen —
Alle Schlingen müssen lassen,
Und er wird dir weggetragen,
Wenn die ersten Lerchen sangen.

Liebst du, treu dem alten Sange
Wie dem Sänger, mich wahrhaftig:
Lass dein Schloss, den schönen Garten,
Führ' dich heim in Waldesprachten!

Auf dem Zelter sollst du prangen,
Um die schönen Glieder schlanke
Seide, himmelblau, gespannet,
Als ein süssgeschmückter Knabe.

Und der Jäger sieht uns fahren,
Und er lässt das Wild, das Jagen,
Will nun ewig mit uns wandern
Mit dem frischen Hörnerklange.

Wer von uns verführt den andern,
Ob es deine Augen taten,
Meine Laut', des Jägers Blasen? —
Ach, wir können's nicht erraten;

Aber um uns drei zusammen
Wird der Lenz im grünen Walde
Wohl ein Zaubernetze schlagen,
Dem noch keiner je entgangen.

(I, 182; 1807)

Eichendorff was not yet twenty years old when he began to revise his ideas concerning poetry and the poet. The process must have been initiated sometime between 1805 and 1807. A singular characteristic of many poems and the early prose works led to this conclusion: They hark back to an experience prior to the time level of the poem itself. The above poem offers the first concrete evidence of this shift in Eichendorff's thinking. We are told that in "den blauen Tagen" (sometime in the past) the woman had hung out a net consisting of silken hair, sweet words, white arms. The third strophe reveals that spring now ("nun") invites him and, although the minstrel is obviously drawn to the woman, he clearly feels compelled to follow spring. The inner tension is not denied, as we can see from the fourth strophe, but the decision, considering the force of the verb "müssen," is never in doubt. If he is to remain a minstrel, he must be part of this spring.

The third and fourth strophe introduce spring and reveal that it is a complex term. It refers not only to the resurgence of color in nature ("bunte Flaggen"), but also to the sound of the hunter's horn. Although spring seems to consist of colors and song, the poem informs us that the minstrel must travel with "dem Klange." This suggests that the song ("Waldhorn") is the vital essence of spring and distinct from the colors. Precisely because the poem stresses this, we are encouraged to wonder what would happen if the minstrel could not distinguish between colors and the song. Although this poem does not allow the reader to answer the question, one can say that the colors remain stationary while the song moves ("reisen"), and the minstrel must be involved in movement. This is underscored by the fifth strophe which tells us that the "Sänger" has wings and must not remain in the magic net. He should be like the lark, the dawn bird, which "senses" the coming light, and is the first to greet the sun, "Aurora."

In the sixth strophe we see that the woman may travel with the minstrel if she loves him and is faithful to him as well as "dem alten Sange." What would happen if the woman loves the poet but is not faithful to the song? I suggest that this is a basic problem from this poem to *Dichter und ihre Gesellen.* Also, if the minstrel falls in love with the woman, he "dies." Their togetherness, alone, is a perversion of what both of them should be. The woman is told that she must leave the castle and garden. Raimund and Florio find and would stay in her realm. The former dies to the living and the latter must be rescued by "dem alten Sange." That is why in this poem the hunter "mit dem frischen Hörnerklange" accompanies them and "Will nun ewig mit uns wandern." These three remain together and "Lenz" envelops them in a "Zaubernetze." Seeing this word in the last strophe, one remembers that the poem is called "Das Zaubernetz," and suddenly suspects that the magic net fashioned by this "Lenz" is what the poet had in mind in the first stanza. The very next stanza refers to the woman's blue eyes which ask him not to leave. And then he was her prisoner. Eichendorff always imputes a mysterious power to the eyes. In them is reflected the very essence of a person; it is as though they were the window of the soul. In this poem, therefore, the physical charms of the woman, the net, have no real power over the minstrel. He is imprisoned not by what he sees but by what he hears. The same pattern can be found in that complex term, *spring.* It consists of "bunte Flaggen" (colors) and "Jägers Waldhorn" (song). But the poet must pursue the song. He must follow what he hears and not what he sees.

The second strophe offers a further thought which is very perplexing. The woman's eyes speak to the minstrel as he is on the verge of moving ("jagen") toward the forest (waldwärts"). The woman detains him. And yet the last strophe depicts the three of them (hunter, woman, minstrel) together "im grünen Walde." Clearly, from the beginning, that had been his goal. The progression of events in the poem instructs us that spring calls to him. This seems to remind him that he has wings. Then he informs the woman that, if she loves him and will be faithful to him and the ancient song,[1] he will lead her "heim in Waldes-prachten." I cannot escape the conclusion that the splendor of the forest is home. If one could understand "in Waldesprach-ten" as "in a splendid forest," I would not give the phrase a second thought. Paying careful heed to the poem's imagery, we are confronted with what seems to be a deliberately structured pattern. Not the physical charms of woman, but her eyes, draw him toward her. Not the colorful opulence of spring, but its song, seems to attract him. Likewise, it is not the forest as such which lures him, but its splendor. In each instance the poet is drawn not by the thing itself but by its meaning, essence, or spiritual quality. As I shall demonstrate, this always involves light and song. In this poem the song ("der alte Sang") leads to light or splendor. We shall discover that light may lead to song. And in both instances, woman is involved.

I have made no effort to interpret this first poem, but have used it to isolate significant emblems and imagery. It must be clear that whatever the poem conveys is hidden in the unknown: woman, spring, castle and garden, song, and the forest. We also could ask why the woman must ride on a horse disguised "Als ein süssgeschmückter Knabe." Why must her identity be kept a secret? and from whom? Also, why does the minstrel say of himself: " . . . er *wird* dir weggetragen" (italics mine)? I cannot doubt that the song "Klang = der alte Sang" is responsible for this movement. In the "Marmorbild" story Fortunato sings the song "Götterdämmerung." The first strophe reads as follows:

> Was klingt mir so heiter
> Durch Busen und Sinn?
> Zu Wolken und weiter
> Wo trägt es mich hin?

The song is the minstrel's wings which carry him up beyond the clouds. Furthermore, the song is instrumental in bringing the minstrel and the woman "heim in Waldesprachten." Then just where is the splendor of the forest? How can one arrive there on a horse? Interestingly enough, the poet has given us a poem, "Das Flügelross" (1816, I, 238), which is a continuation of the poem "Das Zaubernetz." The time structure of the latter refers to the past and moves to the present, while the last five strophes concern the future. We are told what will happen if the woman is faithful to the song. The "Flugelross" poem describes, in greater detail, the same relationship between "Sänger" and "Liebste." Together they soar toward "Aurora." I wonder if perhaps "Aurora" is the splendor of the forest ("Waldesprachten"). The woman in the "Zaubernetz" poem may be called an enchantress because she is a magic net. Now what would happen if we were to delete "Pracht = Aurora" from the compound "Waldesprachten"? Then we might have a "Zauberin im Walde." As it happens, this is the title of a very important poem (1808; I, 323). In this song the movement is toward darkness ("zum dunklen Grunde"). This invites the assumption that the beloved may dwell in the forest with the minstrel only if light ("Aurora") is present. Delete this "Pracht" and the "Sänger" is no longer the lark who rises to greet the dawn, but a trapped bird who "falls" toward darkness.

The "Zaubernetz" poem offers further opportunity to indulge in constructive speculation. We are instructed that the minstrel wishes to leave neither spring nor the woman. The last strophe informs us that woman, song, spring, and minstrel are mysteriously one in a magic net. What if the delicate relationship were disturbed? Because spring is such a fragile union of song and colors, the minstrel could be confused and assume that the song is in the colors. Furthermore, because the poet is clearly drawn to both the woman and spring, he may, in his anxiety, feel that her words ("don't leave me") are a part of spring's colors. In the "Jugendandacht" cycle we find, in the third poem, the lines: " . . . dieser Farben heimlich spreiten/Deckt einer Jungfrau strahlend reine Glieder." In the "Zaubernetz" poem we read that the woman's "schöne Glieder" are covered with "Seide, himmelblaue." The difference is absolutely definitive.

My purpose in this "game of combinations" has been to alert the reader. In 1807 Eichendorff appeared upon the literary scene and communicated largely in terms of unknowns. It is absolutely impossible to interpret the "Zaubernetz" poem unless the read-

er can define the emblems which have been isolated. Neither
the form nor the content offer us a clue as to the identity of
the woman. In one way or another, her presence is felt in scores
of poems and all of the prose works. If we do not know who she
is, we really cannot claim to understand Eichendorff.

Die Nonne und der Ritter

Da die Welt zur Ruh' gegangen,
Wacht mit Sternen mein Verlangen;
In der Kühle muss ich lauschen,
Wie die Wellen unten rauschen.

"Fernher mich die Wellen tragen,
Die ans Land so traurig schlagen.
Unter deines Fensters Gitter,
Fraue, kennst du noch den Ritter?"

Ist's doch, als ob seltsam' Stimmen
Durch die lauen Lüfte schwimmen:
Wieder hat's der Wind genommen!
Ach, mein Herz ist so beklommen!

"Drüben liegt dein Schloss verfallen,
Klagend in den öden Hallen
Aus dem Grund der Wald mich grüsste —
's war, als ob ich sterben müsste."

Alte Klänge blühend schreiten!
Wie aus lang versunknen Zeiten
Will mich Wehmut noch bescheinen,
Und ich möcht' von Herzen weinen.

"Uber'm Walde blitzt's vom weiten,
Wo um Christi Grab sie streiten;
Dorthin will mein Schiff ich wenden,
Da wird alles, alles enden!"

Geht ein Schiff, ein Mann stand drinne —
Falsche Nacht, verwirrst die Sinne,
Welt', Ade! Gott woll' bewahren,
Die noch irr' im Dunkeln fahren.

(I, 337; 1807/08)

Again we are confronted with a conversation: a nun and
a knight exchange "words" without really seeing or hearing each

other. In fact, the woman does not actually speak to him, and if he had not said, "kennst du noch den Ritter," we would have no grounds for assuming that a relationship existed. This "noch" repeated again by the woman in the fifth strophe is the key to a very strange communication. The poet informs us of the real conversation via three concepts of symbolic content: water, the song, and light. They are repeated like major and minor themes of a composition, brought together in the fifth strophe and then suddenly given a different sign or meaning. The first two strophes are united by the water motif. The nun hears the waves and these same waves seem to bear the knight toward land. Waves that strike the shore sadly can no longer be understood as merely waves. Either the poet imputes to them a subjective mood or they represent something else. The same strophes also introduce the notion of sound. It is the action of these waves given by the words "rauschen" and "schlagen." In the third and fourth strophes the sounds "Stimme" and "Klagen" dominate the conversation without, however, discarding the water motif because these words swim through the air. The "Stimmen" heard by the woman has a counterpart in the "greeting" heard by the man. Their reaction to these sounds is similar: she is almost moved to tears and he feels as though he must die. The fifth strophe combines the themes of water and sound, explains them, and introduces the final significant term, *light*.

What has been heard by the nun and the knight is defined as "alte Klänge." It is the same word which we saw in the previous poem. At first glance one might assume that "das alte Lied" should be equated with the song suggested by "alte Klänge," but the speaker in "Das Zaubernetz" makes it clear that his song is associated with wings and freedom; it carries him up to the heights. The song presently under discussion moves in the opposite direction. The nun, we must assume, is somewhere above, on the heights, and the water or waves are below. The waves bring this man to her. The "Stimmen," merely another reference to "Klänge," merge with the water; indeed, they are in the water, because they must "swim" to her. When we read that "Alte Klänge blühend schreiten," it is as though the song had assumed a form and were walking toward her. And the knight is a part of this song that approaches her. With the word "blühend" the poet invokes the power of spring, the insinuation of rebirth and resurrection. If we now combine this with the next two lines in the fifth strophe, which inform us that "Wehmut aus lang versunken Zeiten" once again seeks to exercise its power over the nun,[2] the full structure of the imagery comes into focus. The unknowns of the spiritual equation are given in the fifth strophe: the song ("Alte Klänge"), spring ("blühend"), water ("versunknen Zeiten"), and light ("bescheinen"). These four words describe a reality which will be presented to us, ten years later, in "Das Marmorbild." As Florio speaks of a certain movement of love, he remarks: "Ach! das ist alles wie ein Meer von Stille, in dem das Herz vor Wehmut untergehen möchte" (II, 338). Knowing that Florio's heart does enter the immersed garden of Venus, where he finds the light and song of love associated with her name, we begin to see what the nun experiences.

Our poet thinks of time as a moving river or a vast ocean upon which man sails his small ship (himself). The human being is always capable of entering these "waters" and infusing new life into what is submerged by giving it his love. This is precisely what Florio does when he sings his song "Liebe in der Fremde." The nun, too, approaches a similar temptation. She tells us that her desire watches with the stars, now that the world is still and at peace. But everything that the word *Ruhe* suggests is categorically denied by the rest of the poem. This being so, we are faced with the possibility that the mysterious movement, the waves, voices, and song are not outside but within her. In the depths of her heart, the *deep* that is in every human breast, the love song of long ago calls to her. And yet, because she is behind bars and has willed to be Christ's bride, she cannot enter these depths as Florio or numerous other figures in Eichendorff's poems will, but must listen "in der Kühle." This delightfully opaque expression is not uncommon in Eichendorff's works. Such "coolness" always implies a disassociation from the fire that destroys, but it is intimately one with the light that is cool. I shall have more to say of this later. My concern is the simple fact that the woman does not know peace but listens to the song. To suggest the precise nature of "die alten Klänge," I quote four lines from a song sung by Romana.

Von der Welt kann ich nicht lassen,
Liebeln nicht von fern mit Reden,

Muss im Arm lebendig fassen! —
Lass mich lieben, lass mich leben!

(II, 138)

Here is the love that speaks within her heart when the knight says, "do you still know me?" Flesh and blood would, indeed, seek to know him still, but she had promised to stand guard with the stars over her desires. Love is a vast spectrum that embraces heaven and hell, and its mystery will remain of central significance in Eichendorff's life. We shall see it in the poem "Jugendandacht" as well as in those two verses which could serve as a subtitle for "Das Marmorbild": "Ist's Liebe, ist's Andacht/Was so dich beglückt." It is instructive to note that Romana's words suggest her inability to give her love a spiritual connotation — only the sensual can satisfy her. That is why her love is associated with the fire and not light. She consigns her body and her past to the flames. With the power of his love man may destroy himself. Unlike the God in whose image he is made, he deceives and can be deceived by himself. And this deception is so beautiful that the sixty-five-year-old poet can write about it with all the passion of youth: "Ach vor Liebe todeswund" (I, 228). And yet this love seems to illuminate creation and fill the world with song. That is why it is so much like another love. What these two loves mean to man is "des Lebens wahrhafte Geschichte"; we say love, but it is better to speak of light because that is the pertinent term in the poem "Die Nonne und der Ritter." The nun had spoken of "Wehmut" which still seeks to shine upon her. The knight responds, as it were, by referring to another light, the light associated with Christ's grave, and he now decides to join the crusades. The implementation of this decision involves turning his ship "dorthin." With this term we must eliminate the possibility that the water represents a stream because this simply cannot be done on a river. This leaves us with another interesting problem. The knight remarks, "Drüben liegt dein Schloss verfallen." The fact that it is in ruins poses no difficulty. In the previous poem, woman was asked to leave her castle, her former way of life, and follow "dem Sänger." What should we do with the word "drüben?" This is a thought or idea in the poet's mind which is not easily identified. We shall encounter it several times, especially in Florio's song when he addresses the maiden

(Venus) "jenseits überm Fluss." One thing is clear; her castle or former life are on one side of the "river" and her present existence is on the other. This river separates two realities or modes of existence.

Many similarities may be seen in the poem "Frau Venus" (I, 225) which I shall discuss later. Both women speak of being called, of a "sunken" existence, and of a "Wehmut" which gives no peace. What the knight says must be compared with Florio's thoughts in "Liebe in der Fremde" (II, 310 and 317). Both men are part of a stream. It is startling that a poem concerning a nun and a knight should present imagery which tends to define Venus and Florio. We know that Raimund should be a knight and that Friedrich is depicted as one.[3] Can there be the insinuation of a similar relationship between Venus and the nun? The figure of a nun almost disappears from the poet's works. We note, however, that Diana in "Die Entführung" becomes a religious. Just who is this nun, this woman, who has placed herself behind bars and no longer knows the knight who obviously appeals to a past relationship? It is clear that the woman was not a nun when she "knew" the knight. The poem suggests a willed and deliberate separation, as though each had elected to serve God; and yet, this resignation seems forced and unnatural; it carries the stigma of death and not joy. Within the context of Eichendorff's early poetry, and we shall see this in the next poem, there is a questioning, probing, and evaluating, a constant reappraisal of the poet's role and the functional relationship between talent and faith. In a word, how can creativity be obedient to the will of the Father? Young Eichendorff's imagery instructs us that he sees this not as a problem involving a contradiction but as a mystery based upon a paradox. That is why freedom and love must be viewed as the foundation of the noetic structure in his works. The knight, in our poem, is the poet; but the woman? I suggest that the nun may be "Poesie."[4] To show the full dimension of the problem, let it be understood that "Poesie" may also "be" a harlot!

Aufgebot

Waldhorn bringt Kund' getragen,
Es hab' nun aufgeschlagen
Auf Berg und Tal und Feld
Der Lenz seine bunten Zelt'!

Ins Grün ziehn Sänger, Reiter,
Ein jeglich Herz wird weiter,
Möcht' jauchzend übers Grün
Mit den Lerchen ins Blaue ziehn.

Was stehst du so alleine,
Pilgrim, im grünen Scheine?
Lockt dich der Wunderlaut
Nicht auch zur fernen Braut?

"Ach! diese tausendfachen
Heilig verschlungnen Sprachen,
So lockend Lust, wie Schmerz,
Zerreissen mir das Herz."

"Ein Wort will mir's verkünden,
Oft ist's als müsst' ich's finden,
Und wieder ist's nicht so,
Und ewig frag' ich: Wo?" —

So stürz' dich einmal, Geselle,
Nur frisch in die Frühlingswelle!
Da spürst du's im Innersten gleich,
Wo's rechte Himmelreich.

Und wer dann noch mag fragen:
Freudlos in blauen Tagen
Der wandern und fragen mag
Bis an den Jüngsten Tag!

(I, 77-78; 1807-08)

Once again color-filled spring is introduced by the "Waldhorn" and "Sänger und Reiter" surge through the new green. It is important to note the words, "Ein jeglich Herz wird weiter." The much discussed "Räumlickkeit" in our poet's works must be traced to the heart and its desires. Spring has the power to expand the heart and, as we have seen, imparts wings to man's movement. And now the conversation begins in the poem. "Sänger und Reiter" are filled with the burst of new joy, but the Pilgrim stands confused and alone. He is asked if this miracle of song, "der Wunderlaut," does not lure him to the distant bride. The thrust of new life, the sounds of spring, is a veritable chorus, "verschlungene Sprachen," which seeks to convey a message. But there is an interesting discrepancy between the question and the initial answer in the fourth strophe above. The questioner speaks of "Wunderlaut" and the pilgrim responds with the word "Sprachen." The staggering multiplicity of the response to spring should have about it a oneness, a unity. The pilgrim shows his awareness of this in the next strophe when he speaks of "Ein Wort," which we must equate with "Wunderlaut." Fortunato, in "Das Marmorbild," will tell Florio, "Jeder lobt Gott auf seine Weise . . . und alle Stimmen zusammen machen den Frühling" (I, 307). Exactly the same magnificent variety yet singleness of intent! Spring is supposed to mean something which the pilgrim does not understand, and he is somewhat misguided in his search for a goal. The last two strophes offer a correction. He is told to immerse himself in spring, the wave of new life. A few years later, in *Ahnung und Gegenwart*, Eichendorff has Christ say to Friedrich, "Liebst du mich recht, so gehe mit mir unter" ("Immerse yourself in Me")! With this thought we encounter a perplexing ambiguity. In the conversation between the nun and the knight it seemed clear that water, song, and spring represented a complex which drew man from God. In the present poem, especially the sixth strophe, he suggests that spring and water are combined in a positive sense, and he exhorts the pilgrim to plunge into these "waters" to find "das rechte Himmelreich." The moment that he says "das rechte," the poet implies that there is a false one which, perhaps, is defined by spring, water, light, and song. This, of course, is the purpose of our analysis: to suggest that the poet deals in two realities which confuse the wounded human creature. Here is the spiritual problem which concerns Eichendorff. How is man to tell them apart? The pilgrim is told that he will perceive the truth within himself; and yet, I have suggested that the nun hears a false night within! Much misunderstanding, discernible in criticism, is due to misinterpretation of this point.

The fourth strophe offers one further thought for our consideration. It seems to the pilgrim that both "Lust und Schmerz" lure him, and his indecision as to which he should pursue leaves him painfully divided. The word "Lust" is a broad spectrum which hardly rises to the spiritual connotation of joy; it remains bound to what is of this earth. At least that is how Eichendorff uses it in scores of contexts. On the other hand, and keeping in mind that we are talking about a pilgrim, the renunciation of all that is associated with "Lust" fills this man with pain. To the flesh and blood pilgrim, a creature incompletely spiritual, both seem desirable. Spring, as a duality, consists of a thousand voices or songs delicately interwined and, in a certain sense, both "Lust und Schmerz" have a positive spiritual connotation. Thus the final exhortation. The word that all these languages say is not anywhere that man can see; it is everywhere and only thus can it be "Ein Wort." Only within can the human creature know where it is! Man must always be "on his way," to tarry, to find a castle, and, yes, to find a woman to whom he gives his love; these are dangerous. What man does with his love is the key to heaven or hell. The next poem, "Die Zauberin im Walde" (I, 323; 1808), was written at about the same time that "Die Zauberei im Herbste" began to take form. It is not surprising, therefore, that there should be many interesting similarities. Rather than quote the entire poem,[5] which contains nineteen strophes, I would like to point out the continued use of certain themes. This will lead us into a brief discussion of the novella. The central part of the poem, some six strophes, will not be considered here; they will be taken up in a later chapter.

The poem is divided into two parts; the first fourteen strophes are written in the first person and the last five identify a person. The "ich" understands, has experienced, and feels the temptation of the problem-mystery, but will not allow itself to be overpowered. It is almost as though the poet had been speaking of the self and then disassociates himself from the movement of events which lead to the final imprisonment. It is Florimunde who, in the fifteenth strophe, leaves the castle and "falls" into "dem dunkelgrünen Grunde" where "alles Leben weit versunken." Like Florio, he is below the waters of time, in the past, and is lost to the father. For each man there is "eine Zauberin"; Florimunde, one ancestor of Florio, found his and disappeared from among the living. The first strophe informs us that the "ich," many years ago, had been on the other shore. Once again it is water that separates two worlds or realities. The wording also informs us that he is no longer over there. The speaker experienced the temptation but came back. Now we know why the last song sung by Florio is called "Der Umkehrende." Just what did he experience over there? The answer is given in clear and simple terms: a dream. It all began long ago when, as a child, he heard a bird which sounded like a "Waldhorn" heard in a dream. An integral part of this dream-reality are "seltsam hohe Blumen, Schlünde," a stream speaking dark words which he seems to understand and a powerful desire ("Gelüsten") to fall into the depths. He is drawn down and not up. The fifth strophe suggests what this "down" is and who is there. "Sah ich auf kristallnem Nachen,/Tief im Herzensgrund erschrocken,/Eine wunderschöne Frau,/Ganz umwallt von goldnen Locken." I know that the first and second verse are separated by a comma and that the syntactical structure militates against my view, and yet, this beautiful woman is deep within him, "tief im Herzensgrund." In later poems this will be much clearer, but we can see it in "Zauberei im Herbste." Raimund pursues a song and a woman, "das Fräulein, *das alle meine Gedanken meinten.*" (II, 977, italics mine.) His thoughts were directed toward this woman and he gave her life. Florimunde, too, hears a song and sees a woman, and both are in the depths of his soul. Florio looks at a mutilated stone statue but "sees" a vision of loveliness and delight. In each instance, beginning with 1807-08, this woman is in man's mind and heart before she becomes flesh and blood.[6] Our poet began early to wrestle with the power and mystery of "Gedanken" and love.

The child in the poem grew up and "Schlummert oft und träumte golden/In dem schwülen Waldesgarten." Already the young Eichendorff has finalized in his mind the spiritual danger of "schwül, schlummern" and dreaming. His call to man is "Seid wach, hütet euch!" Nothing is more dangerous than to fall asleep and dream in a sultry forest garden. Is this really a forest? Man's dreams become his reality. It has always been thus, for the fool and the genius, the saint or the sinner. Man's mind is at home wherever the heart takes up its abode. And thus, although the garden has been washed away by time, and the flowers as well as the region have disappeared, Florimunde still lives a dream. "In der Fern' liegt jetzt mein Leben,/Breitend sich wie junge Träume." This dream is a veritable light ("Schimmert stets so seltsam lockend"), which shines upon him now and blinds him to the reality which surrounds him. And did not the nun say: "Wie aus lang versunknen Zeiten/Will mich Wehmut noch bescheinen?"

It is the same light, or the same love. And now we approach two very confusing strophes.

Jetzt erst weiss ich, was der Vogel
Ewig ruft so bange, bange,
Unbekannt zieht ew'ge Treue
Mich hinunter zu dem Sange.

Wie die Wälder kühle rauschen,
Zwischendurch das alte Rufen,
Wo bin ich so lang gewesen? —
O, ich muss hinab zur Ruhe!"

(I, 324)

The first strophe in the poem indicates that he, the speaker, had once been on the other shore and now there is a call from the depths: "Where have you been so long?" Of course, this suggests that he should come back. The poem "Aufgebot" speaks of the call, the summons, of being lured "zur fernen Braut." The very first poem that we discussed, "Das Zaubernetz," informs us that the eyes of the woman seem to say "don't leave me!" Come back or don't leave me; are they not the same call? And now our poet's imagery becomes even more perplexing. In the first strophe we are instructed that, unknown to the speaker, or subconsciously, eternal faithfulness draws him down to the song. But in "Das Zaubernetz" a man, "der Sänger," accepts the woman only if she is faithful to "dem alten Sange." This song gives man wings; it enables him to escape the "Schlingen." The word *song*, as a concept, is involved in both freedom and slavery. I have taken these poems in chronological order. They come from sections of the collected poems called "Sängerleben," "Frühling und Liebe" and "Romanzen." Their point of origin is clearly irrelevant; the poet uses the same imagery, and the constellation of ideas is almost a constant. We are confronted with woman, spring, water, and the song, and to this we must add deception. We have suggested that spring is a duality; the same is true of the song. Man must be faithful to a song, but which song? Who sings the song? Surely the dark words, the call or song which seems to come from below, cannot be the same old song which seems to give man wings; and yet, Florimunde says "ew'ge Treue" draws him down to the song. If one examines Eichendorff's entire works, looking for his understanding or definition of the word "Treue," the combination of ideas given us in the poem seems to be an enigma. This faithfulness in conjunction with the adjective eternal is always positive, that is, it has a positive spiritual connotation. Despite this, the "ich" is drawn down. Why? It seems that this happens without his awareness, it is "unbekannt." How can a man move toward the depths, be lost to the living (which happens to Florimunde), and still feel that he is being faithful? That is the problem of love. It is the same profound spiritual problem toward which Goethe points. This may call to mind *Faust I* and Gretchen. She had been seduced by Faust and remarks, in effect, that everything which had driven her to do this was so good. Was it? She listened to her heart. And what song did it sing? Florimunde, the nun, and the pilgrim all hear a song. Is it, perhaps, a song from the depths of the heart, a song of love in the light of which all is beautiful and good? Perhaps it is possible that man intends to move in one direction and yet, almost unwittingly ("unbekannt"), is drawn in the opposite direction. In other words, he is deceived. The fact that man's love may deceive him is the very heart of the problem-mystery. I am not yet prepared to provide substantial evidence, but already Eichendorff has offered several clues. Let us turn to the "Zauberei" novella and, keeping in mind the emblematic terms thus far suggested, trace the imagery of deception.

Raimund, the youth in the "Zauberei" novella, should be a knight. Since early childhood he and his friend Ubaldo have had but one desire: to go to that land "wo Gottfried und die anderen Helden in lichtem Glanze des Ruhmes lebten und stritten. — Aber wie bald verwandelte sich alles in mir!" (975).[7] What had induced the youth to change his goal? We are told that a young woman

> "die Blume aller Schönheit, die ich nur einigemal gesehen und zu welcher ich, ohne dass sie davon wusste, gleich von Anfang eine unbezwingliche Liebe gefasst hatte, hielt mich in dem stillen Zwinger dieser Berge gebannt. Jetzt, da ich stark genug war, mitzukämpfen, konnte ich nicht scheiden und liess meinen Freund allein ziehen" (Ibid).

Insight into the progression and shift in Eichendorff's thinking is gained when we realize that this first attempt to structure the problem is an autumn novella, while the "Marmorbild" story concerns spring. Also, Raimund speaks of entering a prison ("Zwinger"), while Florio feels as though released from a prison ("Gefängnis"). And there is good reason for this change. The novella deals with a problem but does not develop it clearly. And yet, the first attempt demonstrates the direction of Eichendorff's thinking. At the end of the story, just before Raimund sinks back into madness, he calls out in utter despair, "meine Liebe und mein ganzes Leben eine lange Täuschung"! (984). Love can be deception! This is the heart of the matter. Inherent in this statement is the proposition that not the created, the other, *any* object of man's love, is the source of deception, but man himself. Love blinds, which is why Florio is called "der Blöde." At the same time, love may be defined as a certain form of seeing and doing; indeed, we could call it a mode of being. Consequently, love is paradoxical. And because this is so, it may become a contradiction. The young Eichendorff's inability to give a structured definition to this matter induced him, I am sure, to suppress his first attempt in prose. Let us seek to isolate the defect.

Raimund does not serve his God because he falls in love. He admits this. In fact, one could make the same statement about all of Eichendorff's poet-heroes. In other words, the movement of their own love stands between them and God. But this love, in prose and poems, is presented in the flesh and blood as a woman, a Venus figure. Who is she? After Ubaldo leaves him, Raimund is filled with an overpowering yearning and aloneness, a veritable void which he seeks to fill by hunting. Taking his falcon he rides into the mountains, crosses a "Heide" (the word has a double meaning here) where "die herbstlichen Gespinste . . . wie Schleier durch die heitere blaue Luft flogen." (In a later context I shall discuss this veil.) High above him birds are singing "Abschiedslieder." Suddenly he hears "Waldhörner" and several voices singing a song which "der Wind zwischen den Klängen herüberwehte" (976). The poet seems to make a distinction between the song and the sound of the horns. No sooner did the falcon hear this song than he became "scheu, schwang sich wildkreischend auf, hoch in die Lüfte verschwindend, und kam nicht wieder." Raimund could not resist — obviously he should have — and pursues the "verlockende Waldhornsliede." He comes upon a garden where the colors are far more intense than elsewhere, and notices that the "Waldhornklänge" come from here. And there "mitten in diesem Glanze unter wilden Weinlaubranken sah ich, innerlichst erschrocken —

das Fraulein, das alle meine Gedanken meinten, zwischen den Klängen, selber singend, herumwandeln" (977). Part of our question is answered. This woman is the object of his thoughts. As she sees him, she falls silent, but the sound of the horn continues. Raimund, we are told, flies through the gold-covered gate and falls at the feet of this woman who is dressed in red and whose golden hair is covered by "lange Schleier, durchsichtig wie die Sommerfäden des Herbstes." Just a moment ago this same veil covered an entire region.[8] This "Blume aller Schönheit" is more than woman.

At this point the woman speaks "mit einer rührenden, wie von Liebe und Schmerz gebrochenen Stimme," and admits that she had long loved him. And then she observes: "Unglücklicher! Wie bist du denn in den Kreis meiner Klänge gekommen? Lass mich und fliehe!" The young Eichendorff already has imparted emblematic weight to two features which characterize his works: the circle motif and the warning uttered by the Venus figure. They walk along in silence for a moment, and then she continues: "So wisse denn," dein Jugendfreund, der heute von dir geschieden ist, ist ein Verräter. Ich bin gezwungen seine verlobte Braut. Aus wilder Eifersucht verhehlte er dir seine Liebe. Er ist nicht nach Palästina, sondern kommt morgen, um mich abzuholen und in einem abgelegenen Schlosse vor allen menschlichen Augen auf ewig zu verbergen. — Ich muss nun scheiden. Wir sehen uns nie wieder, wenn er nicht stirbt" (978). It would seem that two men are in love with the same woman, but she loves only Raimund, the knight who would not serve his God. This strange woman cannot be called evil because she warns the victim. But she also lies. Ubaldo, the man he is to kill, tells us that he had left for Palestine immediately after the farewell festivities described on page 975. Raimund could not kill him because he is not there. The girl both of them love is Berta, but she never sees Raimund again. In fact, Ubaldo tells Raimund that everything "was du da erzähltest, ist eitel Phantasie" (984). Thus "das Fräulein, das alle meine Gedanken meinten," as Raimund says, is not Berta, and the man he kills is not Ubaldo. Who are they? Let us go back to the story.

The woman's words are like poison in his veins (978), and her parting kiss burns "mit fast schauerlicher Wollust durch alle meine Adern." She leaves him and he falls asleep still hearing the sound of the "Waldhörner." The next day he goes hunting without his falcon. He sees a beautiful bird and prepares to shoot it, but the bird flits away and gradually leads him to a scene borrowed from Greek mythology. He peers through a thicket and sees his lady and her maidens bathing in a pool. At the sight his very body is "filled" with fire and he runs madly to escape "jene Bilder" (979). The youth carefully avoids all possible contact with human beings — he sinks more and more within himself — and, as a storm-filled night settles upon the hills, he finds himself high upon a peak and under him, upon a rock, sits his friend "der Bräutigam meiner Geliebten" (980). Like a falcon he hurls himself upon the figure, wrestles in silence with it, and casts it into the depths. "Da wurde es auf einmal still in der Tiefe und rings umher, nur der Strom unten rauschte stärker, als wäre mein ganzes voriges Leben unter diesen wirbelnden Wogen begraben und alles auf ewig vorbei." The storm without is but an echo of the storm within. Now that the deed is done, all is quiet. And whom did he kill? Ubaldo and Raimund are one; they represent the two possibilities, and there are only two, open to human love. Man is a knight (and Friedrich is one), whose love is given first to his God; or man is like Raimund and allows love to seek any other goal. In killing Ubaldo he buries his former life in a stream, and his former life had been filled with one thought, to serve God (974). That thought is now dead![9]

As he leaves the place where he died to God, he sees the bird which had taken him to his lady, sitting in a tree top. Hurrying through the forest he comes to her castle, pounds upon the door screaming, "mach auf, ich habe meinen Herzensbruder erschlagen! Du bist nun mein auf Erden und in der Hölle." But not in heaven. And so he lives with this woman amidst the fragrance of "ausländischer Blumen und Bäume" and remains immersed in "den Wogen von Licht und Musik." Gradually fall becomes winter, the sound of the "Waldhörner" dies away and he falls, almost against his will, into a deep dreamlike sleep. When he awakens it is night, the woman has turned to stone and he flees in fright. Ancient memories return to his "ausgebrannte Herz" — the fire of his love had destroyed the temple — and behold, in the real world it is spring. I should like to use Eichendorff's own words to suggest what Raimund has purchased with the death of his "Herzensbruder." In his

History of the German Novel, Eichendorff insists that art ("Kunst") cannot remain neutral especially during periods of contention and strife. Even an anti-Christian movement will and must have its own poetry. "Darum wollen wir indes die Kunst selbst nicht verkennen und verschmähen, weil jene sie zu teuer mit ihrer Seele erkauft und missbraucht haben; denn sie ist ein von Gott bestimmtes Gefäss himmlischer Wahrheiten." (IV, 858-859). The word "jene" refers to poets, and the Raimund-Ubaldo figure is intended to be a poet, or what a poet should be and what he can become if his love is not guarded. "Dichten" is dangerous! In a later context I shall return to this "Gefäss himmlischer Wahrheiten" and show that the vessel is also a chalice, the calyx of a flower, which conceals a woman. And this woman has two faces.

Raimund decides to live as a hermit and do penance before returning to "die heitere, schuldlose Welt" (983). Observe that the world, which includes nature, is called innocent. Neither evil nor sin are to be found in nature because only the free spirit of man can give his love to denial. Nearly all professional criticism rests upon a distortion of nature in our Eichendorff's works. The young man lives for a year this way but makes very little spiritual progress.

Und als nun der Herbst wieder sein wunderlich farbiges Netz über Berg und Tal ausspreitete, da schweiften von neuem einzelne wohlbekannte Töne aus dem Walde in meine Einsamkeit und dunkle Stimmen in mir klangen sie wider und gaben ihnen Antwort, und im Innersten erschreckten mich noch immer die Glockenklänge des fernen Doms, wenn sie am klaren Sonntagsmorgen über die Berge zu mir herüberlangten, als suchten sie das alte, stille Gottesreich der Kindheit in meiner Brust, das nicht mehr in ihr war. — Seht, es ist ein wunderbares, dunkles Reich von Gedanken in des Menschen Brust, da blitzen Kristall und Rubin und alle die versteinerten Blumen der Tiefe mit schauerlichem Liebesblick herauf, zauberische Klänge wehen dazwischen, du weisst nicht, woher sie kommen und wohin sie gehen, die Schönheit des irdischen Lebens schimmert von draussen dämmernd herein, die unsichtbaren Quellen rauschen wehmütig lockend in einem fort und es zieht dich ewig hinunter — hinunter! (Ibid).

The word "Netz" should bring to mind the word "Schleier" because they refer to the same phenomenon. The first poem to be mentioned, "Das Zaubernetz," clearly defines the net as consisting of "seidnen Harren,/Süssen Worten, weissen Armen." A certain woman is the trap into which the poet falls. This quotation then speaks of well-known tones, a song, to which he gives answer. Turning to Raimund's description of "des Menschen Brust," we must conclude that the "versteinerten Blumen" refer to "die Blume aller Schönheit" whom the youth sees at the farewell festival. Like "Das Marmorbild" the stone image has come to life. The flowers seem to grow in what I would call the devil's garden, but we are also told that "zauberische Klänge wehen dazwischen." I have pointed out that the woman seen by Raimund is consistently described in this manner. The word "Quellen" cannot be defined by evidence offered within the novella; we shall have to consult other poems for a definition. Everything experienced by Raimund is defined by the word "hinunter." Remembering that he had hurled Ubaldo into the depths of a stream, I can reiterate my previous conclusion that Ubaldo is Raimund who, like Lucifer, falls from the heights into the depths where "Kristall und Rubin," the devil's flowers, grow. The entire passage makes it clear that this reality, woman, song, and garden are within man; all is fashioned by his love and thoughts and they represent the depths into which he is drawn. On the other hand, the logic of the quotation dictates that "wohlbekannte Töne" come from the outside, are independent of him, and he gives answer to them. Let us pursue this song, these "Klänge," and trace the imagery in the novella.

> Aus der Kluft treibt mich das Bangen,
> Alte Klänge nach mir langen —
> Süsse Sünde, lass mich los!
> Oder wirf mich ganz darnieder,
> Vor dem Zauber dieser Lieder
> Bergend in der Erde Schoss!
>
> Gott! Inbrünstig möcht' ich beten,
> Doch der Erde Bilder treten
> Immer zwischen dich und mich,
> Und ringsum der Wälder Sausen
> Füllt die Seele mir mit Grausen,
> Strenger Gott! Ich fürchte dich.

Ach! So brich auch meine Ketten!
Alle Menschen zu erretten,
Gingst du ja in bittern Tod.
Irrend an der Hölle Toren,
Ach, wie bald bin ich verloren!
Jesus, hilf in meiner Not!

(II, 972)

Eichendorff did not include this song in his collection of poems. The first strophe was discarded and the last two were modified and called "Das Gebet." In a later chapter we shall turn again to these two strophes, but it is apparent that the stress laid upon "der Erde Bilder" leaves open the possibility that other images are the object of his prayer. The manner in which "der Wälder Sausen" is worked into the structure of the thought guides me to the conviction that the storm is associated with God. This can be documented in many prose passages and will be discussed in the "Marmorbild" chapter. The last strophe speaks of the gates of hell which may refer to the devil's garden, man's love, and thoughts which have embraced denial. The reference to chains brings us to the first strophe, a constellation of thoughts which Eichendorff himself rejects. The last three verses insinuate a willingness to surrender, a lack of courage and faith for which our poet has only the sternest words. If we now inspect the first three verses it is apparent that "alte Klänge," a song, seems to reach for him. And this song is equated with "süsse Sünde." We recall that Raimund was led by a mysterious bird to a secluded glade where he saw his beloved bathing in a pool. He runs to escape the temptation, but the further he flees "desto lebendiger gaukelten jene Bilder vor meinen Augen, desto verzehrender langte der Schimmer jener jugendlichen Glieder mir nach" (979). The imagery associates the song with a woman. Indeed, they are one. Now let us look at the song which seems to be so intimately associated with "Waldhörner," a song sung by his "Fräulein."

Golden meine Locken wallen,
Süss mein junger Leib noch blüht —
Bald ist Schönheit auch verfallen,
Wie des Sommers Glanz verglüht,
Jugend muss die Blüten neigen,
Rings die Hörner alle schweigen.

> Schlanke Arme zu umarmen,
> Roten Mund zum süssen Kuss,
> Weisse Brust, dran zu erwärmen,
> Reichen, vollen Liebesgruss
> Bietet dir der Hörner Schallen,
> Süsser! komm, eh sie verhallen!
>
> (II, 976)

I do not see how we can fail to sense what Eichendorff's imagery seeks to convey. The song *is* a lovely woman with whom he has fallen in love and who, in turn, seems to seek him and will yield to the lover, but at a price. She is a song, the flesh and blood personification of "dem Zauber dieser Lieder." The song is the "woman" who reaches for him. We also know that the stone flowers in his breast look at him with "schauerlichem Liebesblick" and that Raimund falls in love with "das Fräulein, das alle meine Gedanken meinten." Consequently, the flower, the woman, and the song really are all one, traced back to "Gedanken"; that is what the poet has in mind when he says, "Süsse Sünde, lass mich los." And this sin is, so to speak, a falling in love with one's own thoughts, thoughts expressed in song, which is a woman, the "Blume aller Schönheit," which grows in what we have called the devil's garden, the soul that denies God its love. This denial was consumated when Raimund "kills" Ubaldo. Just before he sinks into final madness, Raimund returns to his own partially destroyed "Burg." He walks into the garden which is now "wüst und zerstört" — the garden is his soul — and sitting upon one of the few remaining flowers is a beautiful bird. The bird sings a lovely song which fills his heart "mit unendlicher Sehnsucht." And then:

> "Mit Schrecken erkannte er auch nun den schönen, goldgelben Vogel aus dem Zauberwalde wieder. — Hinter ihm aber, hoch aus einem Bogenfenster des Schlosses schaute während des Gesanges ein langer Mann über die Gegend hinaus, still, bleich und mit Blut besprizt. Es war leibhaftig Ubaldos Gestalt" (985) .

In his own castle the bloody apparition appears as a final warning. He has killed what he should be. Raimund speaks to Ubaldo[10] and observes,

> "ich betrachte Eure feste, freudige, männliche Gestalt mit wahrer Scheu und Ehrfurcht, wie Ihr Euch, unbekümmert

durch Leid und Freud, bewegt und das Leben ruhig regier-
et, während Ihr Euch demselben ganz hinzugeben scheint,
gleich einem Schiffer, der bestimmt weiss, wo er hinsteu-
ern soll, und sich vom dem wunderbaren Liede der Sirenen
unterwegens nicht irre machen lässt. Ich bin mir in Eurer
Nähe schon oft vergekommen wie ein feiger Tor oder wie
ein Wahnsinniger. — Es gibt vom Leben Berauschte — Ach,
wie schrecklich ist es, dann auf einmal wieder nüchtern zu
werden!" (973-74).

The scene is carefully structured by Eichendorff. Raimund
stands in the garden and looks at his castle. The line of sight
passes from the bird to the figure in the window. It is as though
the song leads to death. But the youth, who calls himself a
fool and a coward, disregards the warning. He deliberately turns
his back to the vision. "Da sprengte plötzlich unten auf einem
schlanken Rosse das schöne Zauberfräulein, lächelnd, in üppiger
Jugendblüte, vorüber. Silberne Sommerfäden flogen hinter ihr
drein, die Aster von ihrer Stirne warf lange grünlich-goldene
Scheine über die Heide" (985). If he had had the courage, and
that is precisely what is needed, to examine his life, he would
not have seen her. But now, "In allen Sinnen verwirrt, stürzte
Raimund aus dem Garten, dem holden Bilde nach." As he follows the bird, its song gradually changes into "das alte Waldhornlied, das ihn damals verlockte." With this, Raimund has
come full circle. He has failed to utilize the period of freedom
granted him and we are told "Sein Schloss, die Berge und die
ganze Welt versank dämmernd hinter ihm." Pertinent imagery
allows me to state with absolute confidence that this "Bild" is,
so to speak, a creature of his own making. I can thus assert
that "Bild, Blume, Lieder, Vogel, Süsse Sünde," all have a common denominator: "woman." Therefore, Raimund's decision not
to serve his God means that he has elected to exist, as it were,
in her realms. As this discussion develops, I shall show that
there are always two realms or kingdoms in the spiritual world
which Eichendorff structures for us, and Raimund has rejected
God's "weite Welt." He has confined himself to the world of the
circle. This much our novella allows me to say, but Eichendorff
was dissatisfied with his own labors, and I should point to the
defects which, in my understanding, caused him such concern.

The farewell festival takes place at the beginning of the story,
and it is here that he sees Berta. It is insinuated that she is

his "Fräulein" and yet it is obvious that he never sees Berta again until near the end just before he sinks into final darkness. Berta and the "Fräulein" are really one — they are "Poesie." And "Poesie" is a woman always described in terms of man's relationship with God which, in turn, is answered by the question: What is the movement of the poet's love? According to Eichendorff, every poet gives the answer in his works. Our artist confronted himself with a most formidable task when he sought to structure for us the two extremes of "Dichter und Dichten." That is why the story involves four people but only two possibilities: Raimund-Ubalda, and Berta-"das Fräulein." In view of the fact that our book concerns this question, I cannot give a detailed discussion here; however, I can say that Eichendorff wrote two novellas to deal with this mystery, "Das Marmorbild" and the "Taugenichts" story. The Berta-"Fräulein" figure becomes Bianca-Venus and Raimund becomes Florio. In "Der Taugenichts," the Berta-"Fräulein" figure becomes "die schöne Frau" who is a duality, and Ubaldo, with certain modifications, becomes our good-for-nothing. Also, the season is poorly chosen and Eichendorff, while yet working on this novella, already had decided that spring was a far more appropriate season to insinuate the rather complex concept which he had in mind. Eichendorff originally selected fall because it is the season of burning colors which conceals the encroaching death, and Raimund, we must remember, elected to die to God. Because of this the principle of deception as voiced by Raimund is poorly developed. When we hear him say that he could not serve his God because he loved "das Fräulein" (975), it no longer seems proper to speak of deception, but of error based upon a deliberate choice. Furthermore, a denial expressed in such terms is a problem, and Eichendorff's real concern is with mystery. The novella remained unpublished because the poet had acquired a different perspective. Based upon a remarkable awareness of self as well as a keen analysis of the Romanticism in which he was immersed, he rephrased his own question: how could poets and poetry seemingly express a concern for Christianity and yet remain ignorant of the Law and even deny it? In his literary histories, he comes back again and again to the same statement: man wishes to emancipate himself, create his own religion, be a law unto himself. But, and this is the crux of the matter, man is deceived by his own love. That is what Eichendorff wanted to give us with Raimund's words: "Meine Liebe und mein ganzes Leben eine lange Täuschung." Our poet insinuated that with the clearly suggested distinction between "das Waldhornlied" sung by the woman and the sound of the "Waldhörner." In "Das Marmorbild" the question will be asked: "Ist's Liebe, ist's Andacht/Was so dich beglückt?" That is the heart of the matter. And now, as an introduction to the next poem, we should look once more at the mysterious bird in our novella.

The first time that Raimund sees the bird, he observes how its *"hellgoldenen* Schwingen reizend im Sonnenschein glänzten" (II, 978, italics mine). And in the final scenes it is referred to as "der schöne, goldgelbene Vogel" (II, 985). The garden of Venus is "vom Herbste viel kräftiger gefärbt als anderswo" (II, 977) and the colors are "purpurrot, goldgelb und feuerfarb." The gate by which he enters the garden is covered with gold. The woman herself has golden hair. Everything, it seems, is golden, the color of fire. Ubaldo informs us that "irdische Sehnsucht" bursts forth "Aus den irre flammenden Augen des Mannes (Raimund)" (II, 973). Everything comes from Raimund: the garden, the woman, the fire and the bird. When we include the woman in this, we have not forgotten that she is supposed to be Berta, the intended of Ubaldo. The truth of the matter is that Raimund has changed her. The very first encounter in the garden, he looks at "das Fräulein, das alle meine Gedanken meinten" (II, 977). What "woman" means to him is the essence of this novella. His love, his fire, has made her into what she must not be to man. Eichendorff will make this clearer for us. And it is in a later novella that we find an answer to our question concerning the bird. As Florio enters the garden of Venus he walks among the high trees, "zwischen denen goldene Vögel wie abgewehte Blüten hin und wieder flatterten" (II, 321). There can be no doubt that these are the same kind of birds, strange birds which seem to have lost the power of flight and song. Something has been taken from them. They seem to float down, like blossoms shaken from a fading flower. A bird that cannot fly is a prisoner. We cannot escape the conviction that these birds are Venus' prisoners. Let us now examine a poem written in 1808.

Der Knabe

Es war ein zartes Vögelein,
Das sass in Lieb' gefangen,
Ein Knabe hegt' und pflegt' sich's fein
Wohl hinter goldnen Stangen.

Und draussen hört's auf grünem Plan
Verschiedner Vögel Weisen,
Sah Tag und Nacht den Knaben an,
Mocht' nicht mit ihnen reisen.

Und als der Frühling weit und breit
Von neuem schien und schwärmte,
Da tat dem Knaben's Vöglein leid,
Dass es kein Strahl erwärmte.

Da nahm er aus dem stillen Haus
Das Vöglein fromm und treue
Und schweift' mit ihm durchs Feld hinaus
Ins himmelblaue Freie.

Er setzt' es vor sich auf die Hand,
Da wend't und putzt sich's feine,
In bunten Farben spielt' und brannt'
Sein Kleid im Sonnenscheine.

Doch aus dem Wald ein Singen rief,
Bunt' Vöglein ziehn und reisen,
Das lockt so hell, das lockt so tief
In wundersüssen Weisen.

Das Vöglein frisch die Flügel rührt —
Er ruft: Kommst du nicht balde? —
Das hat das Vögelein verführt,
Fort flog's zum grünen Walde —

Nun muss der Knabe einsam gehn,
Klagt über Tal und Hügel:
"Süss' Lieb', süss' Lieb', wie bist du schön:
Ach, hätt'st du keine Flügel!" —

(I, 336; 1808)

The bird is a prisoner, guarded and cared for gently by the
youth behind golden bars. We recall that the nun, too, is behind
bars and that the gate leading to Venus' garden is gold-covered.

Although the bird hears the song of its own kind on the out-side, it pays this no heed and is content to look fully into the face of the lad.[11] Whenever Eichendorff invokes this rapt atten-tive and almost hypnotic gaze at something or someone, it seems to suggest the movement of a spiritual or psychic energy be-tween object and beholder, as though nothing else existed but what is seen. At this point in the poem, the youth reaches a fateful decision. He decides to let his bird experience the warmth of spring and, leaving the quiet house with the bars, he goes through the fields "ins himmelblaue Freie." We see the verb "schweifen," and wherever this is found the context suggests that the individual is moving without direction, as though he were straying from a designated path. And, indeed, this is what the youth has done; he should never have left the house with bars. We can imagine that he has left a prison, and that is precisely what Florio will tell us. Now this little bird is "fromm und treue." It is the first time that we have encountered the word "fromm" in a poem, although it was used in reference to Raimund in the "Zauberei" novella. "Treue" is familiar to us from our dis-cussion of "Die Zauberin im Walde." This bird will suffer the same fate as Florimunde. Exposed to the bright sunlight, it sits in the lad's hands, preens itself, and "In bunten Farben spielt' und brannt'/Sein Kleid im Sonnenschein." Once again we are told of the burning colors, the fall colors, and the insinuation of gold. Surely it is the same kind of bird as those in Venus' garden and the one that Raimund saw.

And now we approach a most surprising sequence of events. The singing in the forest and the passage of other colorful birds seems to be a wondrously sweet song which "lockt hell und tief." These words insinuate with a certain nicety the dream-reality which Raimund experiences: a world that is colorful, bright, and in the depths of his heart. This brings us to the next to last strophe, and three times the poet uses the "Gedankenstrich" which, as Oskar Seidlin knows, speaks volumes in the hands of our poet. The sweet song causes the bird to stir its wings; it begins to fly. At this the youth calls out, "Kommst du nicht balde? —" The movement of ideas in the poem prepares one for a: "Stay with me! Don't leave!" The youth, we may assume, is prepared to return to the house and the security of the bars, but the bird misunderstands his words. It interprets his call as an invitation to fly away and join the others of its kind. We

must realize, because it is highly important, that not the singing from the forest but the youth's words "seduced" it. We are
forced to accept this understanding by the demonstrative
"Das."[12] The pious little bird is not led astray by the song of
the external world but by the call of the one whom it loves, he
who cares for it and whom it never tires of seeing. It is so
intimately and exclusively his and yet it flies away and escapes
from him. It seems to obey, and in doing so it rebels. The good
which it would do, it does not; but the evil which it would not
do, it does. I cannot overemphasize the importance of this inversion; as a fundamental principle it is an instrument which
opens up the enigmatic quality of Eichendorff's imagery.

And what does the bird represent? The last strophe clearly
tells us that it is *love*. For Eichendorff, it is the love song
that gives man wings and enables him to fly to those heights
where divine grace supports his wings. On the other hand, it
is love that draws man down into depths where he is a stranger
to himself and lost to his God. We shall see the same problem
in various poems and in "Das Marmorbild" as well as in the
"Taugenichts" novella. The youth in our poem is now alone
and searches for his love. He does not return to the quiet house
with the bars. And how can he? Man must follow wherever his
love takes him. The little bird, love, took Raimund to his beloved,
to the one toward whom his thoughts were directed. The "Waldhörner" are the call "Kommst du nicht balde?—" Raimund had
made the decision not to live for Christ. He is being called to
come back, just as the bird is called. The Venus figure has
nothing to do with the "Waldhorn"; she sings words to its melody and walks among "die Klänge," but is not really part of
them. It seems that woman, song, and minstrel are united in a
relationship which Eichendorff seeks to define. From 1807 until
Ahnung und Gegenwart was finished in 1812, he wrestled with
this problem. We have seen that the "Waldhorn" frees the
"Sänger" in "Das Zaubernetz." In a dream, the song of a bird
seems to sound like a "Waldhorn" ("Die Zauberin im Walde");
and in the "Zauberei" novella, the song of the bird and the
"Waldhorn" are so delicately intertwined that they seem to
merge with woman. But we must remember Raimund's words
that love and life were "eine lange Täuschung." It seems that
Eichendorff had two songs in mind: the "Waldhorn" and another
song which sounds like a "Waldhorn," but only in a dream. But

the word *dream* is associated with "die Zauberin" and Raimund's "Fräulein." The latter is linked by Eichendorff's imagery with the bird, the garden and castle (which the "Zauberin" in the "Zaubernetz" poem had to leave before the minstrel would accept her), and the woman who seems to be an embodiment of song. But the song-woman turns to stone, which identifies her with the stone flowers "in" Raimund's breast. The "nun and the knight" poem indicates that song ("Klänge") and woman must be associated with water and movement. And finally, it is "der Sänger" who stands at the center of this constellation of emblems: woman, song, spring, water, movement, flower, bird, and forest.[13] He is the minstrel who both sings and hears a song. All things speak to him of "Die Eine, Deine." In the "Zauberei" novella the woman-song is his, but at the price of madness and even "murder." It is still 1808-09.

Jugendsehnen

Du blauer Strom, an dessen duft'gem Strande
   Ich Licht und Lenz zum ersten Male schaute,
   In frommer Sehnsucht mir mein Schifflein baute,
   Wann Segel unten kamen und verschwanden.

Von fernen Bergen überm weiten Lande
   Bracht'st du mir Gruss und fremde frohe Laute,
   Dass ich den Frühlingslüften mich vertraute,
   Vom Ufer lösend hoffnungsreich die Bande.

Noch wusst' ich nicht, wohin und was ich meine,
   Doch Morgenrot sah ich unendlich quellen,
   Das Herz voll Freiheit, Kraft der Treue, Tugend;

Als ob des Lebens Glanz für mich nur scheine,
   Fühlt' ich zu fernem Ziel die Segel schwellen,
   All' Wimpel rauschten da in ew'ger Jugend!
                      (I, 70-71; 1808)

Much of what we have seen and will continue to see in the early poems concerns the concept of "Jugend." As all of Eichendorff's significant terminology, the word has a dimension, a positive and negative aspect. *Ahnung und Gegenwart*, on the very first page, informs us: "Unsere freudigen Gedanken werden niemals alt und die Jugend ist ewig" (II, 9). On the other hand, a young man hopelessly in love with a girl who has no real regard for him is told: "Lass doch die Jugend fahren!" (II, 151). There is a certain facet of youth which man must outgrow or it will destroy him. The poem is uncomplicated, but offers certain imagery which becomes important for Eichendorff. Again we are by a stream where the child builds its ship, that is, becomes what it is to be. Our poet understands the almost definitive significance of childhood. It is difficult to redesign the "ship" later in life. Although he speaks of a stream or river we should be careful before accepting a literal interpretation. The movement of a river determines one's course, but the second strophe suggests that the youth gives himself, his ship, to the movement of the spring air and this, as seems reasonable, means that the ship moves wherever the winds blow. The same problem was encountered in "Die Nonne und der Ritter." The possibilities are infinite. This seems substantiated by the third strophe which clearly admits that youth does not yet know where he means to go. The words "was ich meine" add an unexpected depth to the idea of movement. The poet seems to suggest that his entire existence and movement in time is to have a meaning, and yet the youth is unsure as to what it is. Despite the uncertainty he sees "Morgenrot . . . unendlich quellen." For the first time we see this word *morning-red* combined with a verb generally associated with water. In a later context we shall have to discuss "die Quelle." The term "Morgenrot" always has a positive connotation in Eichendorff imagery. When it is offered in conjunction with the verb "quellen" we are urged to think of a place of origin and of inexhaustible plenitude. One thinks of light welling forth from the East, the Orient, which is another name for Christ. The insinuation of light is continued in the last strophe when the poet speaks of "des Lebens Glanz." The impact of this light, somehow, fills the sails of his ship (himself) and engenders the movement toward a distant goal. The last verse of the poem becomes very specific. The treetops rustle in the breeze, but this breeze is really a light which causes the treetops to rustle in "ew'ger Jugend." Are they really trees, in the conventional sense? The light seemingly envelops them in eternal youth. We recall the poet's words that our joyful thoughts never become old and that this youth is eternal. Combine this with the last verse of the poem and we are left with the impression that thoughts are trees! If the imagery is properly combined we are guided to this conclusion. But our poet offers us help. In a poem written in 1809 we find two pertinent strophes.

So verschlingen in Gedanken
Sich zwei Stämme wundertreu,
Andre dran sich mutig ranken
Kron' an Krone immer neu.

Prächt'ger Wald, wo's kühl zu wohnen,
Stille wachsend Baum an Baum,
Mit den brüderlichen Kronen
Rauschend in dem Himmelsraum![14]

(I, 116)

Note that the imagery is the same as is the poem written a
year earlier! The rustling of the trees takes place "im Himmelsraum." Is this not the light, the Orient, the breeze which causes
the sails to swell and moves man to his goal? The most significant part of the tree is the crown which rustles in the breeze; it
sings like a minstrel. And up there is the "Himmelsraum." Living here in this "Wald," these thoughts, is described as cool.
Not the fire, but the cool light rules in God's "Raum." In the
first poem considered, "Das Zaubernetz," the youth leads the
woman "Heim in Waldesprachten." One may recall that the blue
eyes of the woman speak to him "da [er] waldwärtz wollte
jagen." Are we not incredibly naive if we persist in the understanding that this woman does not want him to move "toward"
a forest? I submit that the entire poem loses in mystery and
significance if we assume that they will live in a forest. This
conclusion does not do our poet justice and leaves the poem
almost meaningless. I shall return to this. My present purpose
is fully served if I have left the reader with some slight awareness of what must be done with Eichendorff's nature imagery.
He is not a "nature" poet!

Rettung

Ich spielt', ein frohes Kind, im Morgenscheine,
Der Frühling schlug die Augen auf so helle,
Hinunter reisten Ström' und Wolken schnelle,
Ich streckt' die Arme nach ins Blaue, Reine.

Noch wusst' ich's selbst nicht, was das alles meine:
Die Lerch', der Wald, Lüfte blaue Welle.
Und träumend stand ich an des Frühlings Schwelle,
Von fern rief's immer fort: Ich bin die Deine!

(I, 61; 1808)

Once again the poet begins with childhood. It is instructive to compare the above strophes with "Die Zauberin im Walde." The latter expresses a dreamy phantasy which the poet later will call the "Liebeskupplerin." The above verses have about them a pristine purity, a sense of expectation and even wonder, which suggests a soul filled with the loveliness of beauty but not yet committed to the painful search for its source. Man, as the imagery suggests, is constantly subject to the movement of life about him; he is always called by something or someone. In the poem "Aufgebot," the pilgrim is asked: "Lockt dich der Wunderlaut/Nicht auch zur fernen Braut?" The last verse above voices the same enigmatic reference without, however, offering an identification. "Die Braut und die Deine," one is inclined to suggest, surely must be the same. This we know: ten years later Florio will stand before two woman, both of whom are called "ein Bild des Frühlings." One looks at him and the other always casts down her eyes. The main body of the poem consists of forty-four uninterrupted verses. There is a heaviness here which is quite compatible with the subject. We are told that the child is kidnapped by an old man, hurried across the land while nature calls and reaches out for him, and brought into an old house.

> Da wogt' es unten in Nacht und Graus,
> Da war ein Hämmern, ein Schachern und Rumoren,
> Als hätte das Chaos noch nicht ausgegoren.
> Hier hielt der Alte würdig und breit:
> Mein Sohn, sprach er zu mir, das ist die Nützlichkeit!
> Die haben wir so zum gemeinen Besten erfunden.
>
> (I, 61)

He is left alone and tied, barely able to look out of the window at the movement of life below. It is suggested that what man does belongs to chaos, the unformed; whatever he does in his own name will be touched by death.

> Ach! weiss denn niemand, niemand um mein Trauern?
> Wie alle Fernen mir prophetisch singen
> Von meinem künft'gen wundervollen Leben!
>
> Von innen fühlt' ich blaue Schwingen ringen,
> Die Hände konnt' ich innigst betend heben —
> Da sprengt' ein grosser Klang so Band wie Mauern.

Da ward ich im innersten Herzen so munter,
Schwindelten alle Sinne in den Lenz hinunter,
Weit waren kleinliche Mühen und Sorgen,
Ich sprang hinaus in den farbigen Morgen.

(I, 62)

The raising of the hands in prayer is an interior action, a movement of the mind, a thought. I have presented the poem primarily because of this significance. The word "Gedanken" will be used more and more frequently in his works. Not only man's personal (subjective) reality, but even the concept of self as well as the world without, depend upon his thoughts.[15] The Christian, because he has no more precise way of referring to divine creativity and his own absolute dependence upon the Creator, frequently says he is the thought of God and the Father's thoughts are clothed in a reality that we call creation. Eichendorff gives to man a similar power. The thoughts of the human creature become his reality; he even gives them flesh and blood. In this poem there are also two realities: "Nützlichkeit," which is the chaos of human values and doing, and life "in den farbigen Morgen." The former is man's reality; the latter is an introduction to God's reality.

Der Fromme

Es sass ein Kind gebunden und gefangen,
   Wo vor der Menschen eitlem Tun und Schallen
   Der Vorzeit Wunderlaute trüb verhallen;
   Der alten Heimat dacht' es voll Verlangen.

Da sieht es draussen Ströme, hell ergangen,
   Durch zaubrisch Land viel' Pilger, Sänger wallen,
   Kühl rauscht der Wald, die lust'gen Hörner schallen.
   Aurora scheint, so weit die Blicke langen. —

O lass die Sehnsucht ganz dein Herz durchdringen!
   So legt sich blühend um die Welt dein Trauern
   Und himmlisch wird dein Schmerz und deine Sorgen.

Ein frisch Gemüt mag wohl die Welt bezwingen,
   Ein recht Gebet bricht Banden bald und Mauern:
   Und frei springst du hinunter in den Morgen.

Willkommen, Liebchen, denn am Meeresstrande!
Wie rauschen lockend da ans Herz die Wellen

Und tiefe Sehnsucht will die Seele schwellen,
Wenn andre träge schlafen auf dem Lande.

So walte Gott! — Ich lös' des Schiffleins Bande,
Wegweiser sind die Stern', die ewig hellen,
Viel' Segel fahren da und frisch Gesellen
Begrüssen uns von ihrer Schiffe Rande.

Wir sitzen still, gleich Schwänen zieht das Segel,
Ich schau' in deiner Augen lichte Sterne,
Du schweigst und schauerst heimlich oft zusammen.

Blick auf! Schon schweifen Paradiesesvögel,
Schon wehen Wunderklänge aus der Ferne,
Der Garten Gottes steigt aus Morgenflammen.

(I, 279-80; 1808)

It is significant that many of Eichendorff's early endeavors possess a common denominator, namely, the concern for freedom. This will remain as a cornerstone of his "Weltanschauung." There are two prisons which the poet fears: the world and the self, and both do violence to the essential nature of man. The child is imprisoned and bound and, because of man's riotous doing, is unable to hear "die Wunderlaute der Vorzeit." This must refer to what we now might call the age of faith. And the child thinks with longing of "der alten Heimat." There can be no doubt, even at this early stage, of what the young poet means with this phrase. The human being, the essence of what man is, comes from above, from the Father. Man is not at home here on earth; he is the native of another land. A passage in *Ahnung und Gegenwart* contains the same imagery. Eichendorff speaks of a friend whom he addresses personally in the novel.

Aus dem finstern Erker siehst du durch bunt und phantastisch gemalte Scheiben über das niedere, emsig wimmelnde Land unten weg in ein anderes, ruhiges, wunderbares, ewig freies Land. Alle die wenigen, die dich kennen und lieben, siehst du dort im Sonnenscheine wandeln und das Heimweh befällt auch dich. Aber dir fehlen Flügel und Segel, und du reissest in verzweifelter Lustigkeit an den Saiten der alten Laute, dass es mir oft das Herz zerreissen wollte. Die Leute gehen unten vorüber und verlachen dein wildes Geklimper, aber ich

sage dir, es ist mehr göttlicher Klang darin, als in ihrem ordentlichen, allgepriesenen Geleier (II, 101).

I shall have more to say about the musical instrument and the song; at the moment, my interest concerns the description of the landscape. It is a reasonable and even accurate paraphrase of the second strophe above. Here nature is filled with the movement of light and song. The land is enchanted and, borrowing from the prose passage, is called "ruhig . . . ein ewig freies Land." *Quiet, peaceful,* and *free* are words which must be associated with light and song, but only if the latter comes from above. In this land of light and song, minstrels and pilgrims wander home. The rustling of the "trees" is cool, because the light is cool. The horn sounds joyously and even the streams disport themselves brightly. To my mind, the structure of this strophe is most provocative; one feels that streams, forest, and sun mean something other than the usual connotation. I suggest that the streams are the songs of many men and the trees are man's thoughts bathed in that cool light of which Florio sings and Friedrich speaks — divine grace! In this land of the "hunter, the streams, and the trees" man is free;[16] in the other land, man, the child, is a prisoner. The strophe is initiated by the word "Da" which flows from the statement that the child thought longingly of "der alten Heimat," and the second strophe ends with a dash. This sets these four lines apart and indicates that the universe is under a different sign. Just to think of the eternal immerses the world in a different light.

Yearning must permeate man's heart, and then the sadness, which every reflective and contemplative being feels, becomes a veritable spring. This is the light which works in the darkness even before the day has begun and needs only man's *Amen* to bring forth the flowers of heavenly fragrance. This spring may come at any season and it works its miracle to free man from that pain and care which incarcerate the creature within the self and the world. He then can leap into the morning, the flowing stream of light from the Orient, and begin the journey which all must undertake if they would seek the kingdom that is not of this world. On the shores of the ocean the youth is joined by the beloved. Theirs is a rather strange realtionship. As they journey, the pious child gazes into her eyes and time, somehow, does not exist because the next strophe suggests that God's garden is visible on the horizon. This silent woman is an intriguing mystery. Eichendorff takes the word "Augenstern," breaks it assunder, modifies the "Stern" component with the word *light* so that the woman's eyes may be like the light of the eternal stars. It is as though the child, in looking into her eyes, sees the heavenly firmament and the stars which are "Wegweiser." We shall see the same curious imagery in "Jugendandacht." Now why do we read in the fifth strophe that the woman is welcome "denn am Meerestrande?" Surely "denn" is more than a filler. As the sequence of ideas implies, springing into the morning is equivalent to being on the shore of the ocean. Here, in the morning or on the shore where the journey to "der alten Heimat" begins, she is welcome. Would she be welcome in the valley, "im Grunde," in the forest, by a pond, in the stream, in his dreams, in the garden? The Eichendorff scholar knows that she is found in all of these places. Who is she? If we will grant that this woman can join him only on the shore of ocean, then we have the same pattern as in "Das Zaubernetz" where the woman can join the minstrel only if she loves the ancient song. Let us go one step further. The woman in "Die Zauberei im Herbst" makes Raimund choose between herself and joining the Crusades. The youth kills the self who is Ubaldo who, as it were, serves Christ. The woman in the poem "Die Zauberin im Walde" lures Florimunde away from life and he remains a prisoner in a "Venusberg." Raimund sees "das Fräulein, das alle meine Gedanken meinten." If we equate "im Walde" with "Gedanken" then we would seem to suggest that the enchantress is really in his mind. Our "Taugenichts" will sing a song called "Heimweh" which begins with the lines, "Wer in die Fremde will wandern,/Der muss mit der Liebsten gehen." Who is "die Liebste" through whose eyes one seems to see heaven? Raimund and Florio also find a beloved, but her eyes are hollow and empty, the eyes of death. Woman is associated with flowers, light, and song, and it is suggested that the poet who is attracted to her may be in great danger. It must not be assumed that we are speaking of just one woman. Raimund says that his entire life and love were "eine lange Täuschung." There are two women who represent two loves, that is to say, two laws: the law by which the old man lives and the law whereby the new man is to be. Within the breast of every Christian, who seeks more and more to be a Christian, the divisiveness of this inner struggle is a fearful

battle which our poet describes for us. Man must be separated
from all that he thinks he is and all that the flesh can understand and love. For it is written: "Think ye, that I am come to
give peace on earth? I tell you, Nay; but rather division" (Luke
12: 51). Friedrich, in *Ahnung und Gegenwart,* is separated
from woman, friends, worldly possessions and even his own brother. Indeed, in order that we might not misunderstand his intention, the poet says that Friedrich is declared dead: he has
died to the world. This is the struggle, the movement of divine
love seeking to free man from himself and the world, which
Eichendorff structures again and again. Man resists and love
woos him. And so must we understand the poem:

An A . . .

1

Die Klugen, die nach Gott nicht wollten fragen,
Den heil'gen Kampf gern irdisch möchten schlichten,
Zum Tod kein Herz, nicht Lieb', sich aufzurichten,
Verzehren sich nur selbst in eitlen Klagen.

Sind alle eure Schiffe denn zerschlagen:
Sieht man die heil'ge Flagge d i c h aufrichten,
Vom Liebessturm, der jene musst' vernichten,
Dein junges Schiff siegreich hinweggetragen.

Südwinde spielen lau um Laut' und Locken,
Im Morgenrot des Hutes Federn schwanken,
Und Gottes Atem macht die Segel schwellen.

Wen noch die alten Heimatklänge locken,
Dem füllt der Segel wie der Töne Schwellen
Die Brust mit jungen, ewigen Gedanken.

(I, 123; um 1809)

Man has emancipated himself from God's love, which is the
law, and feels the strength to pursue his own salvation. This
is what is meant by "irdisch schlichten." The ship, once again,
is a symbol for man and his mode of life, his movement toward
eternity on the stream of time; and this ship must be destroyed
— by love. Divine love is a veritable storm which reduces what
man makes of himself. In "Das Marmorbild" we shall see how
man, Florio, builds a temple which is destroyed in three days
and then built anew by God. The last two strophes are an in-

teresting and instructive study of the poet's technique; the meaningful content is found in those terms which we have sought to isolate: "Morgenrot, Segel, Heimatklänge, Töne, Gedanken."[17] Everything is movement, but it is a movement caused by God and not man. Man must travel in God's light ("Morgenrot"), and then the sail, merely a variation of the ship symbol, is filled with divine grace that moves/draws the creature toward the Creator. The first line of the last strophe expresses what is elsewhere called "heilige Sehnsucht." The word *holy* should be stressed because not all of man's yearning can be thus defined. When the human being is filled with this desire then his thoughts are young and eternal. It is the Psalmist who said that God is the joy of my youth; and he who walks with God is always young. It is said so easily! A few strokes of the pen and this impossible thought is on paper — to walk with God. Our poet knows both the joy and terrible loneliness of this resolve, the dark night of faith when there is not light and the Hand seems withdrawn.

3

> Es will die Zeit mit ihrem Schutt verdecken
> Den hellen Quell, der meiner Brust entsprungen,
> Umsonst Gebete himmelan geschwungen,
> Sie mögen nicht das Ohr der Gnade wecken.
>
> So lass die Nacht die grausen Flügel strecken,
> Nur immerzu, mein tapfres Schiff, gedrungen!
> Wer einmal mit den Wogen hat gerungen,
> Fühlt sich das Herz gehoben in den Schrecken.
>
> Schiesst zu, trefft, Pfeile, die durchs Dunkel schwirren!
> Ruhvoll um Klippen überm tück'schen Grunde
> Lenk' ich mein Schiff, wohin die Sterne winken.
>
> Mag dann der Steuermann nach langem Irren,
> Rasch ziehend alle Pfeile aus der Wunde,
> Tot an der Heimatküste niedersinken!

(I, 124)

Much of what Eichendorff has to say concerns water. We have encountered thus far "Fluss, Strom, Welle, schwimmende Stimmen, Frühlingswelle, Meeresstrand, Segel und Schiff." This poem adds another one, "heller Quell." The adjective "hell" insinuates an association with light. This spring wells forth from the breast, and his age seems bent upon suppressing the spring. Eichendorff did not become a critic when he began to write histories of literature; he was one from the very beginning. One must assume that the spirit of his age was incompatible with "den hellen Quell." More evidence is needed for a definition.

It would be an error to conclude that "die Nacht" (first line, second strophe) refers to night in the conventional sense. Man is in darkness and must continue to wage the battle, armed only with faith, a faith entrusted to a fragile vessel and subject to attack by arrows, waves, reefs, and treacherous deeps, that is, a world which rages against the man who would believe. The entire poem is a magnificent rebuttal to those who have called him a "Biedermeier." The scholar who espouses this conclusion could never agree with Eichendorff that Christianity is the greatest challenge that we can experience. It is the discovery of a new world fraught with dangers that man cannot truly measure. It is not an extension of the known, as all voyages of discovery are, but a movement into a universe where the instruments of human measurement do not apply. However we define this word "Biedermeier" it does not apply to our poet. The stature of a man is measured not by what he has but by what he does not have, and what he will do to find and possess it. Eichendorff understands finiteness and yet he would have God; the cup dares to hold the ocean! The last line of the poem above tells us that man does err, but if he follows the stars he will die the death of a hero — at home. We would grant that a given mind could call all this foolishness; brand it a vision that no practical man would follow. But such love demands great courage and absolute dedication. It requires that a man give of himself utterly and completely, holding nothing in reserve. And how difficult it is for man to say, "Not my will but yours!" We do not speak of those whom life has crippled and even broken, but of those who would master it. Let such a man *live* those words. Do we not have the Garden of Olives which suggests how painful it is for flesh to heed the will of the Father? We may reject the "absurdity" of his love, but we must recognize its heroic and uncompromising thrust. So much has been written about this poet which misses the mark because he has not been read carefully and readers have failed to grasp his Christianity. But Eichendorff, even in his youth, understood his position, as may be seen in his prayer below.

Gebet

Was soll ich, auf Gott nur bauend,
Schlechter sein als all' die andern,
Die, so wohlbehaglich schauend,
Froh dem eignen Nichts vertrauend,
Die gemeine Strasse wandern?

Warum gabst du mir die Güte,
Die Gedanken himmelwärts,[18]
Und ein ritterlich Gemüte,
Das die Treue heilig hüte
In der Zeit treulosem Scherz?

Was hast du mich blank gerüstet,
Wenn mein Volk mich nicht begehrt,
Keinen mehr nach Freiheit lüstet,
Dass mein Herz, betrübt, verwüstet,
Nur dem Grabe zugekehrt? —

Lass die Ketten mich zerschlagen,
Frei zum schönen Gottesstreit
Deine hellen Waffen tragen,
Fröhlich beten, herrlich wagen,
Gib zur Kraft die Freudigkeit!

(I, 131-32; 1810)

Eichendorff accuses the creature of wishing to save itself. It trusts in its own nothingness. Man no longer walks in faithfulness but mocks the ancient truths. In this atmosphere the heart of the speaker is disconsolate and laid waste. These feelings are his chains. He does not presume to make man free, but he must be free if he is to wage God's battle. He can pray and dare splendidly and wield God's weapons. Just what weapon does Eichendorff have in mind? In the poem "Heimkehr" (I, 129; 1810) we find a rather strange reference to a sword which critics have not discussed. The son comes home and finds the father's estate in ruins. In the moonlight he sees a vision in the courtyard which seems to take his breath away. All of his ancestors stand there silently, and in the father's folded hands is a bright sword: "Tat die Blicke niemals wenden,/Ewig auf den Stahl gekehrt." The son calls out: "Was das Schwert mit seinen Scheinen,/Rede, was dein Schauen will." Suddenly it is morning and he sees that he had been looking at stones.

Nur der Degen blieb da droben
Einsam liegen überm Grab;
"Sei denn Hab und Gut zerstoben,
Wenn ich dich, du Schwert, nur hab'!"
Und ich fasst' es. — Leute wühlten
Über'n Berg, hinab, hinauf,
Ob sie für verrückt mich hielten —
Mir ging hell die Sonne auf.

(I, 131)

The sword, it seems, is passed on from generation to generation.
It is filled with light and is priceless beyond all treasure. The
mountain is covered, crawling, with humanity; he alone has the
bright sword, holds fast to it, even though others think him
insane. What is this strange sword that others disregard? In
Ahnung und Gegenwart Friedrich comes upon the ruins of his
childhood castle and discovers an unusual sepulcher.

Es stellte nämlich eine junge, schöne, fast wollüstig gebaute,
weibliche Figur vor, die tot über den Steinen lag. Ihre Arme
waren mit künstlichen Spangen, ihr Haupt mit Pfauenfedern
geschmückt. Eine grosse Schlange, mit einem Krönlein auf
dem Kopfe, hatte sich ihr dreimal um den Leib geschlungen.
Neben und zum Teil über dem schönen Leichnam lag ein alt-
geformtes Schwert, in der Mitte entzwei gesprungen, und
ein zerbrochenes Wappen. Aus dieser Gruppe erhob sich ein
hohes, einfaches Kreuz, mit seinem Fusse die Schlange er-
drückend (II, 250-251).

This picture, and it is "ein Bild," is a visual representation of
significant threads, indeed, the very lives of several characters
in the novel. Again we encounter the sword. Now it is no longer
bright, and whatever it represents has been broken. Near the
end of the novel, Leontin speaks disparagingly and even con-
temptuously of his age and observes:

Das alte grosse Racheschwert haben sie sorglich vergraben
und verschüttet, und keiner weiss den Fleck mehr, und darüber
auf dem lockern Schutt bauen sie nun ihre Villen, Parks,
Eremitagen und Wohnstuben, und meinen in ihrer vernünf-
tigen Dummheit, der Plunder könne so fortbestehn. Die Wälder
haben sie ausgehauen, denn sie fürchten sich vor ihnen, weil
sie von der alten Zeit zu ihnen sprechen und am Ende den

Ort noch verraten könnten, wo das Schwert vergraben liegt. (II, 293).

Again the sword! The intent of this passage is precisely the same as in the poem "Heimkehr." Man does not want this sword; indeed, he has gone to considerable trouble to rid himself of it. Despite this, it is the ground of his existence; he builds upon it but will have nothing to do with it. He is even afraid that, somehow, it might come to light. The sword that is bright in the hands is hidden, broken, discarded, feared! It is written: "Think not that I am come to send peace on earth: I come not to send peace, but a sword. For I am come to set a man at variance against his father, and the daughter against her mother, and the daughter-in-law against her mother-in-law" (Math. 10;34-35). I have spoken of separation; it is the intent of the sword to divide, to separate those who belong to the Father from those who belong to the earth. In the same sequence of verses the apostle goes on to speak of cold water; we shall come to this in a little while. Man is to put on the whole armour of God. It is written: "Above all, taking the shield of faith, wherewith ye shall be able to quench the fiery darts of the wicked. And take the helmet of salvation, and the sword of the spirit, which is the word of God" (Eph. 6, 16-17). "And he had in his right hand seven stars: and out of his mouth went a sharp two-edged sword: and his countenance was as the sun shineth in his strength" (Rev. 1,16). And again in Rev. 19, 15, the great one is called the Word of God out of whose mouth goeth a sharp sword, that with it he should smite the nations. Can there be any question that Eichendorff's sword is the word of God uttered by the Man who come to divide, to bring pain and suffering, the voice of the shepherd who would not deceive us by promising peace?

Why does man destroy the forests because he fears that they might reveal the presence of the sword? Surely we cannot be so naive as to assume that our poet is a conservationist who is loathe to see trees cut down. Then why this charge, this indictment, as though man were guilty of a transgression? In the mouth of a fool, Eichendorff places the following observation.

"Die Burgen sind geschleift, die Wälder ausgehauen, alle Wunder haben Abschied genommen, und die Erde schämt sich recht in ihrer fahlen, leeren Nacktheit vor dem Kruzifixe, wo noch eines einsam auf dem Felde steht; aber die Heiden hantieren und gehen hochmütig vorüber und schämen sich nicht" (II, 253).

Eichendorff uses the word "Burgen" instead of "Schlösser"; he is interested in a word which suggests defense against an enemy. It is the heathen who razes these defenses and decimates the forests. The fact that the heathen does this reminds us that the forests are destroyed because man fears they might reveal where the sword is buried. Can we, indeed, remain content with the motion that *trees* might lead man to the word of God? We have suggested that, in certain contexts, trees must be equated with thoughts. We shall see later that the "Taugenichts," at certain critical moments, climbs trees. That is not irrelevant. In 1848 the older Eichendorff looked at his world and observed: "Thron, Burg, Altar, es hat sie all' verschlungen/Ein wilder Strom entfesselter Gedanken" (I, 172). Man's thoughts can be a mighty stream which destroys. Thoughts are also trees which rise up "zum Himmelsraum" and stir their branches in prayer. Again, the older Eichendorff looks at his own life and describes the growth and seasons of a tree.

> Jetzo sinkt die Abendröte,
> Blüte fallt, es schweigt der Sang,
> Und ich rausch' wie im Gebete
> Mit den Zweigen: Gott sei Dank!
>
> (I, 174)

In the year 1849, as our poet laments the death of freedom, he writes:

> 's war ein mächt'ger Wald da droben,
> Treulich Stamm in Stamm verwoben,
> Mir zum grünen Dom erhoben.
>
> Weh', du schönes Land der Eichen!
> Bruderzwist schon, den todbleichen,
> Seh' ich mit der Mordaxt schleichen.
>
> Und in künft'gen öden Tagen
> Werden nur verworrne Sagen
> Um den deutschen Wald noch klagen.
>
> (I, 174)

Thirty years before, Eichendorff had used the same imagery. Man destroys the forest or perhaps we should say he tops the trees ("aushauen"). He behaves like a heathen and does not let his thoughts soar up to God! Going back to 1810, one finds a series of "Zeitlieder" all written in the same year that Napoleon divided Tirol. Such poems as "Der Tiroler Nachtwache" and "An die Meisten" clearly reveal that thoughts of freedom are a veritable forest which the poet calls "Ein' feste Burg, Trutz der Gewalt." The sword is the word of God which father should pass on to son. Man decided to hide the sword deep in the forest of his thoughts, which is to say, he sought to emancipate himself from God. And then even the thought of God was banished from his mind. The creature was utterly independent, indeed, he was his own God. Our poet saw the spiritual, intellectual, and artistic thrust of an age in which this apostasy become a way of life. To him, German Romanticism was a last effort to bring God back into the lives of man. He became the severe critic of his movement, not so much because it failed, but because it lost its care for man and its love for God. This is the real substance of his first novel, *Ahnung und Gegenwart*. Friedrich passes through his own "poetischer Rausch," dedicates himself to the cause of freedom which the poet calls "lebendig eindringen," and then learns that man must give himself to God before he can work for human freedom. Thus the novel consists of three books which portray the three paths that confront the young man at the very beginning of the story. The poet began writing the novel in 1810, and by then he had begun to under stand the nature of his personal growth. The mystery of love merged with the problem of human freedom. He learned that freedom for man is utterly dependent upon the movement of his love. That is why Friedrich is told that the world will be free if man immerses himself in Christ.

The poems selected for this analysis are among the first that the poet deemed worthy of inclusion in the collections that were published periodically during his lifetime. This qualifying statement is necessary because I have no reliable information as to how many earlier efforts were destroyed by the author. The highly personal imagery, the symbols, themes, and motifs which I have discussed, were destined to become the structural elements of his creative production and even of his criticism. The Eichendorff of 1807-1810 can be seen best in two cycles of poems written between 1808 and 1810. Everything that I have sought to iso-late is now combined in these poems. Before turning to them I should like to deal briefly with one item that has not been properly investigated, namely, the poet's use of "Quellen." In the poem "Jugendsehnen" the poet speaks of seeing "das Mor-genrot unendlich quellen," and in "Sonette An A . . ." he says "Es will die Zeit mit ihrem Schutt verdecken/Den hellen Quell, der meiner Brust entsprungen." What manner of spring could this be that has its source in his breast? In a poem "Auf dem Rhein," (1808) the word is used in a context that clarifies one facet of its meaning.

Auf Dem Rhein

Kühle auf dem schönen Rheine,
Fuhren wir vereinte Brüder,
Tranken von dem goldnen Weine,
Singend gute deutsche Lieder.
Was uns dort erfüllt die Brust,
Sollen wir halten,
Niemals erkalten,
Und vollbringen treu mit Lust!
Und so wollen wir uns teilen,
E i n e s Fels verschiedne Quellen,
Bleiben so auf hundert Meilen
Ewig redliche Gesellen!

(I, 136)

We now have this fountain welling forth from a rock. The fact that all these springs have their origin in a particular or single rock creates a brotherly bond between them. Clearly Eich-endorff uses "Quelle" as a synonym for human beings. Even though these people are separated they are still one. In the poem "An meinen Bruder" (1813), exactly the same imagery is em-ployed.

Auf E i n e m Fels geboren,
Verteilen kühlerauschend sich zwei Quellen,
Die eigne Bahn zu schwellen.
Doch wie sie fern einander auch verloren:
Es treffen echte Brüder
Im ew'gen Meere doch zusammen wieder.

(I, 141)

The poem "Trost," written about 1810, offers a far more complex structure.

> Sag an, du helles Bächlein du,
> Von Felsen eingeschlossen,
> Du rauschst so munter immerzu,
> Wo kommst du hergeflossen?
>
> "Dort oben steht des Vaters Haus
> Still in den klaren Lüften,
> Da ruhn die alten Helden aus
> In den kristallnen Klüften.
>
> Ich sah den Morgen freudig stehn
> Hoch auf der Felsenschwelle,
> Die Adler ziehn und Ströme gehn
> Und sprang hinaus ins Helle."
>
> Sag an, du königlicher Strom,
> Was geht mein Herz mir auf,
> Seh ich dich ziehn durch Waldes Dom?
> Wohin führt dich dein Lauf?
>
> "Es treibt und rauscht der Eisenquell
> Noch fort mir durch die Glieder;
> Die Felsenluft, so kühl und hell,
> Lockt zu mir alle Brüder."

(I, 137)

Eichendorff once again designs the poem in the form of a conversation, this time between the brook, a mighty river, and a person. The brook is asked where it comes from and the answer is delightfully ambiguous. Everything in the second strophe is quite in order; one expects that a brook should have its origin among the ice fields, the father's house. It is the third line that destroys the logic of our assumption. That ancient heroes should dwell in the house of the father is utterly incongruent with ice fields. We must entertain the possibility that the rivulet is a person. If it is a *someone*, then the reference to the Father's house and the ancient heroes becomes meaningful. Our poet's "nach Hause und Heimweh" has been documented in his earliest poems. Man's native country is the Kingdom of God. In such a context the third strophe repeats the theme we have seen several times: "in den hellen, farbigen Morgen hinausspringen." In the fourth strophe the small brook has merged with many others

until it has become "ein königlicher Strom." Remaining faithful
to my suggestion, this mighty stream would have to be seen as
a collection of individuals involved in a particular movement and
action. As a matter of fact, although so much of Eichendorff's
imagery involves the movement of water, a stream, brook, river,
or ocean, the titles of his poems reveal a striking lack of interest
in these bodies of water, as such. Our understanding of the poet
will grow if we concentrate on what they mean and not what they
are. Our poet prefers the less specific word "Strom" because he
is interested in movement, and we can find "Strom" or "strömen"
used in conjunction with "Bilder, Leute, Zeit, Leben, Gedanken,
Lieder, Licht" and many more. Furthermore, although another
poet might ask a river where it is going, Eichendorff would
not. But he does ask this of man. In the body of his prose
and poetry this question is asked rather frequently, but it is
rarely answered. This is only natural because the movement of
the heart and soul is the mystery of a relationship between
God and the individual. Only under certain conditions is our poet
that specific. In *Dichter und ihre Gesellen,* Otto, a Florio figure,
meets a child in the mountains and asks her where she is taking
him. " 'Nach Hause,' entgegnete das Kind. — Ihm schauerte unwillkürlich bei dem Doppelsinn der Antwort." (II, 694). An angel
guides Otto home. But in our poem, "der königliche Strom" is
not guided but rather influenced by something else. The last
strophe provides the necessary information. Rather than answer
the question as to where it is going, the river tells us about itself. Within the large body of its movement there is a certain
invigorating component, "Der Eisenquell." This is a veiled yet
clear reference to "das Bächlein." Now this little brook comes
from the Father's house which is situated "in den klaren Lüften."
Eichendorff's imagery compels the mind to reach ever higher
until it finds the mystery that the poet would not name. When
we look at the last two lines of the strophe we see that the
significant function of the brook is to lure "alle Brüder" to the
river. And yet, it is not the water which entices, but "die Felsenluft," and this word brings us back to the second strophe. The
ancient heroes are resting in the cool air of the Father's House,
which can refer only to the Father's Kingdom where there are
many mansions. This cliff-air is cool and bright, it is the significant and essential constituent of the brook, "der Eisenquell."
In other words, what the mighty river feels in its members,

"Glieder," is the spirit of the brook. This combination of ideas can be found in an impressive number of passages which convey their meaning by the use of words suggesting light, water, movement and the song. In Eichendorff's mind it is this spirit of the brook, "Die Felsenluft so kühl und hell," that comes from above, which lures the poet, "den Sänger," to sing his song of praise. If the reader would look again at the poem "Auf dem Rhein" he will find that our analysis gives deeper meaning to its imagery, especially that the singers are "E i n e s Fels verschiedenen Quellen."[19] We should also consider that the poem has a title which we dare not regard as an arbitrary and irrelevant factor in our considerations. Eichendorff, as one who sings of man's secret hunger for God, can say that the ideas in the poem constitute a consolation —"Trost" — to him. He hears others, although very few, in the constant progression of singers, who strike a true chord which is one with the eternal hymn of praise that streams from the created to the Creator.

During this period, 1810, Eichendorff's mind was involved in the writing of his first novel, *Ahnung und Gegenwart*. It should not be surprising then, that what we have seen in his poetry is also reflected in his prose. At the very end of the novel, the main characters express in song the characteristic movement of their deepest desires. It is at this point that Friedrich sings his song "An die Dichter" which is discussed elsewhere. Just before this Faber observes: "Es ist seltsam . . . wie sich unser Gespräch nach und nach beinah in einen Wechselgesang aufgelöst hat. Der weite, gestirnte Himmel, das Rauschen der Wälder ringsumher, der innere Reichtum und die überschwengliche Wonne, mit welcher neue Entschlüsse uns jederzeit erfüllen, alles kommt zusammen; es ist, als hörte die Seele in der Ferne unaufhörlich eine gross, himmlische Melodie, wie von einem unbekannten Strome, der durch die Welt zieht, und so werden am Ende auch die Worte unwillkürlich melodisch, als wollten sie jenen wunderbaren Strom erreichen und mitziehen" (II, 295-296). The little "Bächlein, der Eisenquell," is a note from this "grosse, himmlische Melodie, der unbekannte Strom, der durch die Welt zieht." Faber says "die Worte werden unwillkürlich Melodisch," they become a song of praise and join that river of love. The "Quell [e]," then, is that bursting forth of a song of love and praise from the breast of man. And that is exactly what the poet says in "Sonette An A . . . ": "Es will die Zeit mit ihrem Schutt verdecken/Den *hellen Quell,* der meiner Brust entsprungen." But, as always with our poet, it is dangerous to assign a value to a word, to solve for the unknown, and assume that one has established or found a constant. A given datum must always be inspected for a positive and negative connotation, a seemingly minor yet demonstrable difference which can be gleaned only from a particular context. The "Quell" that we have sought to define is also described by Christ. It is written: "If any man thirst, let him come to me, and drink. He that believeth in me, as the scripture saith, Out of his belly shall flow rivers of living water. Now this he said of the Spirit which they should receive, who believed in him" (John 7:37-39). Living waters, "Eines Fels verschiedene Quellen." Eichendorff has given us a short poem, which the modern critic quotes often when writing about Eichendorff. "Schläfft ein Lied in allen Dingen,/Die da träumen fort und fort,/Und die Welt hebt on zu singen,/Triffst du nur das Zauberwort." It is remarkable that not one scholar has looked at the title of this poem and wondered why it is called "Wünschelrute." Now with a divining rod one looks for water. Can we doubt that in Eichendorff's mind there dwelt the vision of living waters? The water that wells forth from the rock, the corner stone that was rejected! It is this water which Eichendorff has in mind when he spoke of "Den hellen Quell, der meiner Brust entsprungen." By following the logic inherent in this progression of ideas and heeding Eichendorff's implicit suggestion when he insists that a short poem about "das Lied" must be called "Wünschelrute," we cannot fail to arrive at the conclusion that living waters,[20] the brook in the poem "Trost," is really a song of love. What is the Book of Psalms, but a vast outpouring of praise and love, a magnificent act of homage and adoration by men who believed, and out of whose belly flowed living waters? And what is the magic word that sets the world to singing? Our biblical quotation speaks of "him that believeth in me" (Christ); but it would be an error to equate faith with the magic word. Faith is the first gift given to man and after that comes yet another gift which transcends the first. Faith is the "Wünschelrute," persisting until it finds the rock. But the second miracle is greater than the first because faith can only believe what charity, love, would do. Now this word *do* is the sum and substance of the movement in Eichendorff's universe. Very early in his career as a writer, Eichendorff selected such terms as "der Frühling, der Garten, der Quell, (water symbolism), das Licht, das Lied, das Bild" and the role of woman to reveal the essence of man's doing. But "der Sänger" is free to love what he will love; it might be said that he pursues his will or the Creator's. For this reason "die Quelle" is both positive and negative. A check of every context in which "Quellen und Bronnen" can be found will reveal some are "verwirrt" and "verführend;" they run through strange and magic forests or thoughts. Some "Quellen" do not become cool and bright like "Felsenluft," they remain water and cover the earth. The "Zauberwort" is love, and human love may create a magic world which has nothing to do with the law of love. With this thought we approach the mystery that is Eichendorff's essential concern. The two rather long poems which I promised to discuss will provide an introduction to the mystery of love and also present a final argument in behalf of my attempt to define the significance of "der Quell."

Notes

1. "Das Zerbrochene Ringlein" (I, 346; um 1810) has long been a favorite in anthologies. And yet, because literary critics have never sought to trace imagery in the poet's works, readers may have no idea of what the poem conveys. The "Zaubernetz" poem states that the woman must be faithful. The second stanza of the "Ringlein" poem informs us: "Sie hat mir Treu' versprochen,/Gab mir ein'n Ring dabei,/Sie hat die Treu' gebrochen,/Mein Ringlein sprang entzwei." This "Liebste" is the same person as "die Frau" in the poem. Furthermore, the first stanza contains the well-known lines: "In einem kühlen Grunde/Da geht ein Mühlenrad." This same "Mühlenrad" plays a role in the "Taugenichts" story. And the "Taugenichts" speaks of a woman who had appeared to him "im kühlen Grunde." Eichendorff's imagery instructs us if we will listen and work.

2. In this strophe "Wehmut" is associated with both water and light, two of the most important concepts in his emblematic vocabulary. Despite the early date, 1807, Eichendorff already had made a definitive decision concerning the imagery which would convey meaning in his works.

3. Raimund is the poet figure in the early novella, "Zauberei im Herbste."

4. The poem "Der Kämpe" (I, 339; 1807-08) offers the same basic theme as the poem first discussed. It was the figure of the nun which determined its inclusion. If we can grant that she is "Poesie," then we may speculate that the young Eichendorff considered putting her "behind bars." But the artist's creative thrust cannot be denied. And thus the problem. If she is "free," will he not become her prisoner?

5. "Der Gefangene" (I, 347; um 1810) treats the same theme as this poem. The minstrel rides his horse into a forest and dwells with the woman in "ein kristallnes Schloss," which is surrounded by a stream. The last strophe states that no ship can bring him "Aus böser Zauberei." The poet rides his horse (life) into the depths of the forest (thoughts) where he becomes the prisoner of woman, "Poesie." Furthermore, the nature imagery in this poem has nothing to do with nature.

6. I use this term consistently to suggest Eichendorff's tendency to objectify a concept. I am in the process of proving that woman is "Poesie" or is love.

7. References to Volume II of the Cotta Edition will cite only the page number. The page number is not repeated for successive quotations from the same page.

8. Note that the theme of expansion is always associated with this woman and love. Florio will say Venus is an entire season ("Frühling").

9. Eichendorff, the youth, had dreams of being an Ubaldo, God's knight. And he discovered "Poesie." He could not keep her behind bars ("Die Nonne und der Ritter"). He "asked her" to be faithful to "dem alten Sange"; but the muse is free, an enchantress so lovely that he could not let her be. At this point, 1808, he began writing the novella.

10. There are moments, especially after rereading Eichendorff's poems to his brother, when I feel that the Ubaldo figure is a brother image. Much could be offered to substantiate the conclusion, but I can find no proof.

11. By tracing Eichendorff's imagery one may discover his intent. The nun was placed behind bars, and now is a bird. They cannot be equated because bird does not "become" woman. Hovewer, the bird leads the poet to woman. The poet has given us an equation; we must solve it.

12. This means that Eichendorff was not "deceived" by the poetry (song) of contemporary poets, but by his own song. Also, this poem concerns a "Knabe." The man must not allow his love to escape.

13. With this remark I suggest the surprising fact that the emblems which Eichendorff will use for the rest of his life are already largely established.

14. The last strophe of this poem suggests an explanation of the phrase "heim in Waldesprachten" in the "Zaubernetz" poem. The splendor of the forest must be associated with "ew'ger Jugend" which seems to refer to thoughts. Consequently, the woman in "Das Zaubernetz" may dwell only in thoughts which are eternally young. This is her "heim." It is written: "God is the joy of my youth." The poem seems to be saying that woman ("Poesie," muse) may be with him when the minstrel's thoughts soar up like a lark. If it seems that I have taken unwarranted liberties with Eichendorff's imagery, then let us remember Raimund. He loves the woman "das all meine Gedanken meinte." But they lead "hinunter . . . hinunter." He did not lead her "heim in Waldesprachten," but lived in her castle.

15. I would have this understood in the sense that Eichendorff rejects Fichte's subjectivism.

16. In the "Zaubernetz" poem, the minstrel and the woman are joined by the hunter. His presence separates and unites them. But this use of the word "Jäger" is discarded by Eichendorff. After 1807 "dër Jäger" and "das Jagen" have both a positive and negative connotation. Venus is a huntress. The "Taugenichts" is chided for wishing to hunt. Donati would hunt on Sunday. "Hunting" is spiritually improper, because man hunts the wrong game.

17. The fourth strophe of "Jugendsehnen" suggested that light causes the trees to rustle and fill the sails of the ship (man). Our poem speaks of "alte Heimatklange" which fill the same sails and man's breast "mit jungen, ewigen Gedanken." The pattern is the same. Light and song fill man's thoughts and cause him to move "heim." And the minstrel must lead the woman "heim in Waldesprachten."

18. These lines describe how Eichendorff would have "Gedanken" understood. They are filled with light and song, are eternally young, and move the minstrel toward God, because they come from him. This is the ideal. The poet knows he also has other thoughts.

19. Eichendorff himself used letterspacing as in "E i n e s" as a form of emphasis.

20. On pages 25 and 58, I translate Christ's words "gehe mit mir unter" as "immerse yourself in me." In the novel (II, 166), Eichendorff uses sun imagery and one should say "set" or "die with me." The significance of the water symbolism induced me to select "immerse." Similar reasoning prompted me to deviate from Eichendorff's own discussion of "Zauberwort" and "Wünschelrute" (IV, 26).

II

Sonette

Leid Und Lust

Euch Wolken beneid' ich
In blauer Luft,
Wie schwingt ihr euch freudig
Über Berg und Kluft!

Mein Liebchen wohl seht ihr
Im Garten gehn,
Am Springbrunnen steht sie
So morgenschön.

Und wäscht an der Quelle
Ihr goldenes Haar,
Die Äugelein helle,
Und blickt so klar.

Und Busen und Wangen
Dürft ihr da sehn. —
Ich brenn' vor Verlangen
Und muss hier stehn!

Euch Wolken bedaur' ich
Bei stiller Nacht;
Die Erde bebt schaurig,
Der Mond erwacht:

Da führt mich ein Bübchen
Mit Flügelein fein,
Durchs Dunkel zum Liebchen,
Sie lässt mich ein.

Wohl schaut ihr die Sterne
Weit, ohne Zahl,
Doch bleiben sie ferne
Euch allzumal.

Mir leuchten zwei Sterne
Mit süssem Strahl,
Die küss' ich so gerne
Viel tausendmal.

Euch grüsst mit Gefunkel
Der Wasserfall,
Und tief aus dem Dunkel
Die Nachtigall.

Doch süsser es grüsset
Als Wellentanz,
Wenn Liebchen hold flüstert:
"Dein bin ich ganz."

So segelt denn traurig
In öder Pracht!
Euch Wolken bedaur' ich
Bei süsser Nacht.

(I, 226)

Sonette 1

So viele Quellen von den Bergen rauschen,
   D i e brechen zornig aus der Felsenhalle,
   Die andern plaudern in melod'schem Falle
   Mit Nymphen, die im Grün vertraulich lauschen.

Doch wie sie irrend auch die Bahn vertauschen,
   Sie treffen endlich doch zusammen alle,
   E i n Strom, mit brüderlicher Wogen Schwalle
   Erfrischend durch das schöne Land zu rauschen.

An Burgen, die vom Felsen einsam grollen,
   Aus Waldesdunkel, zwischen Rebenhügeln
   Vorübergleitend in die duft'ge Ferne,

Entwandelt er zum Meer, dem wundervollen,
Wo träumend sich die sel'gen Inseln spiegeln,
Und auf den Fluten ruhn die ew'gen Sterne.

(I, 67-70; 1808-10)

The title "Sonette" embraces a group of six sonnets designed to reveal certain aspects of "Dichter und Dichten." The first poem above should sound very familiar because it repeats the content of the poem "Trost" just discussed. "Der Quell" represents the individual poet and the "der Strom" symbolizes the stream of poetry, the poet's unique contribution to the song of life. Seemingly, poets are divided into two basic groups; those who are angry and those who exercise their gift because they derive pleasure from it. Perhaps I should say that the latter group does not take issue with life as they find it. And then these poets exchange roles, an action modified by the word "irrend." I can state with confidence that it is an error for the poet not to come to grips with life as man lives it. This is Eichendorff's position as man and artist. Despite this tendency on the part of the poet to disregard or forget his high calling of being "das Herz der Welt," the influence of this "Strom" is given by the word "erfrischend." It refreshes because it contains "den Eisenquell." The last strophe portrays this stream of song moving toward eternity, "zum Meer, dem wundervollen." I would take special note of the word "träumend" in the last two lines. "Die sel'gen Inseln" are reflected on an ocean upon which the eternal stars rest; they do not simply shine upon the waves. This suggests that the surface of the ocean and the firmament intersect at an "infinite" distance, at the ultimate horizon, where time returns to eternity. And here, as in a dream, man "sees" the reflection of the blessed land. Frequently in his poems and specifically in "Das Marmorbild" we shall find another ocean, "ein Meer von Stille," which has no stars; or, as in the poem "Götterdämmerung," man may convert the flower into a star, the symbol for what is eternal. If my interpretation seems to extend the imagery beyond the reasonable, I shall have ample opportunity in a later chapter to provide further documentation. In fact, my understanding of the adverb "träumend" fits very well into the above analysis. Just as the word *ocean* has a dual connotation, so does the significance of the dream. In eternity man sees reflected, so to speak, a blessed existence in the Fa-

ther's house, "die sel'gen Inseln." Now it is man's destiny, as intended by God, that this dream is to become his reality. On the other
hand, the life that man leads is frequently depicted by our poet
as a dream, that is to say, it is an illusion and is divorced from
the reality that is mankind's dream. As I have suggested before,
it is this quality inherent in a given term which can easily em-
barrass the reader who assumes the constancy of a given datum.

Sonette 2

So eitel künstlich haben sie verwoben
　　Die Kunst, die selber sie nicht gläubig achten,
　　Dass sie die Sünd' in diese Unschuld brachten:
　　Wer unterscheidet, was noch stammt von oben?

Doch wer mag würdig jene Reinen loben,
　　Die in der Zeit hochmüt'gem Trieb und Trachten
　　Die heil'ge Flamme treu in sich bewachten,
　　Aus ihr die alte Schönheit neu erhoben!

O Herr! gib Demut denen, die da irren,
　　Dass, wenn ihr' Künste all' zuschanden werden.
　　Sie töricht nicht den Gott in sich verfluchen!

Begeisterung, was falsch ist, zu entwirren,
　　Und Freudigkeit, wo's öde wird auf Erden,
　　Verleihe denen, die Dich redlich suchen! 　　　　(I, 68)

The second poem begins with criticism and ends with a prayer.
The words "eitel und gläubig" instruct us as to how the gift
of poetry, the talent given to man, may be used. These words
suggest two extremes for what we have encountered in the first
poem where Eichendorff speaks of the two kinds of "Quellen":
some "plaudern in melod'schem Falle" ("eitel") and others
"brechen zornig aus der Felsenhalle" ("gläubig"). Because the
poet has lost a certain pious or devout regard for the talent
given him he has introduced sin into the innocence that poetry
should reflect. The word *sin* may strike the reader as a stern
thought in this context; after all, is the creature not free to
use what he is as he wishes? Eichendorff consistently grants
man this freedom, in fact, his entire works revolve about this
problem of freedom. And yet, if man works to embrace the
reality intended for him by the Father then he must abide by
the law. This is only just and fair. And that is our poet's position.

Freedom is possible only within the law. But how does innocence fit into this discussion? Sin is properly defined as that movement of man's mind and deeds, human doing, which transgresses God's law. "Unschuld" seeks to express its very opposite, namely, a human existence which does not wish to know good and evil and be like God. In other words, it is Eichendorff's contention that art must seek to dwell in this innocence. The reader may feel that the writer has given too much of his own mind and has gone well beyond the demonstrable as far as the poem is concerned. Let us turn to *Ahnung und Gegenwart* and listen to a conversation between Leontin, Friedrich and Faber.

> Wenn wir von einer inneren Freudigkeit erfüllt sind, welche, wie die Morgensonne, die Welt überscheint, und alle Begebenheiten, Verhältnisse und Kreaturen zur eigentümlichen Bedeutung erhebt, so ist dieses freudige Licht vielmehr die wahre göttliche Gnade, in der allein alle Tugenden und grossen Gedanken gedeihen, und die Welt ist wirklich so bedeutsam, jung und schön, wie sie unser Gemüt in sich selber anschaut.[1] Der Missmut aber, die träge Niedergeschlagenheit und alle diese Entzauberungen, das ist die wahre Einbildung, die wir durch Gebet und Mut zu überwinden trachten sollen, denn diese verdirbt die ursprüngliche Schönheit der Welt." "Ist mir auch recht," erwiderte Leontin lustig. — "Graf Friedrich," sagte Faber, "hat eine Unschuld in seinen Betrachtungen, eine Unschuld" ... (II, 41).

The innocence of Friedrich is defined in precisely those terms needed to document this interpretation. This innocence is the world of grace, divine grace; it is the world of the morning sun, God's love which illuminates, renders perceptible to our finite minds the true, unique significance of all that is. Only in His light do we see reality as it was intended to be. Only in this light, this love, can human virtues and the productive movement of the human mind achieve that excellence for which it was intended. This is reality. The reverse of the coin is perversion, illusion, "Einbildung"; it comes from man. In this passage we also find the negative aspect of our discussion concerning "das Zauberwort." If human existence is devoid of this light, this love, then it is "entzaubert." The world is filled with magic, but first man must say "I believe," and then, if love becomes flesh within him, he grows in knowledge of that original beauty, "ursprüngliche

Schönheit," which was the intent of the Creator. Because the human creature is so excrutiatingly finite and sees so darkly, he has much need of prayer and courage. He needs prayer, because innocence is no longer his, and he needs courage because the challenge and the enemy are not found in the boundless universe — it is child's play to contend with that which is outside of ourselves — but within man's own breast. Man is filled with an almost irresistible need to defend and perpetuate what he thinks he is. The "self" that man has made dies slowly and with reluctance, but die it must, if man is to be reborn as the new man, in Christ.

The last line of the first strophe echoes the truth which we tried to glean from the poem "Trost." What the river felt in its members, the cool spirit of the brook, "der Eisenquell," is, indeed, that which comes from above. This also introduces the second strophe which praises those, who in times of man's proud endeavors, "Die heil'ge Flamme treu in sich bewachten." Here we have evidence for the theme of light which is of primary importance in this discussion. The verb "bewachen" is of key significance because it insinuates that the flame is given to man by God and it is incumbent upon the creature that he guard it faithfully. Not all are capable of this dedication. The first strophe speaks of "die Kunst, die selber sie [most of the poets see the poem "An die Meisten" (I, 134)] nicht gläubig achten," while the third strophe refers to these same poets and "ihr' Künste." Eichendorff clearly suggests a difference; it is almost as if these poets were not really practicing their art, as if they were charlatans, guileful panderers who do not possess that "Auful" integrity which Eichendorff demands of the artist. This point is the subject of a conversation between Faber and Friedrich in *Ahnung und Gegenwart.* Faber in reference to one of his own poems remarks: "Dem einen ist zu tun, zu schreiben mir gegeben" (II, 31). He goes on to say that:

> Poetisch sein und Poet sein, . . . das sind zwei sehr verschiedene Dinge, man mag dagegen sagen, was man will. Bei dem letzteren ist, wie selbst unser grosser Meister Goethe eingesteht, immer etwas Taschenspielerei, Seiltänzerei usw. mit im Spiele. — "Das ist nicht so," sagte Friedrich ernst und sicher, "und wäre es so, so möchte ich niemals dichten. Wie wollt Ihr, dass die Menschen Eure Werke hochachten, sich daran erquicken und erbauen sollen, wenn Ihr Euch

selber nicht glaubt, was Ihr schreibt, und durch schöne
Worte und künstliche Gedanken Gott und Menschen zu
überlisten trachtet? Das ist ein eitles, nichtsnutziges Spiel,
und es hilft Euch doch nichts, denn es ist nichts gross, als
was aus einem einfältigen Herzen kommt. Das heisst recht,
dem Teufel der Gemeinheit, der immer in der Menge wach
und auf der Lauer ist, den Dolch selbst in die Hand geben
gegen die göttliche Poesie. Wo soll die rechte, schlichte Sitte,
das treue Tun, das schöne Lieben, die deutsche Ehre und
all die alte herrliche Schönheit sich hinflüchten, wenn es
ihre angebornen Ritter, die Dichter, nicht wahrhaft ehrlich,
aufrichtig und ritterlich mit ihr meinen? Bis in den Tod ver-
hasst sind mir besonders jene ewigen Klagen, die mit weiner-
lichen Sonetten die alte schöne Zeit zurückwinseln wollen
und, wie ein Strohfeuer, weder die Schlechten verbrennen,
noch die Guten erleuchten und erwärmen" (II, 31-32).

Faber's words are indeed a most appropriate definition of the
word "Künste." Such poetry may glitter, be profound, brilliant
in conception, and most exquisitely executed, but it is not art
as our poet would have it understood. I am particularly interested in Friedrich's final thought concerning a poetry so inef-
fective that it is like a straw fire which neither consumes "die
Schlechten" nor provides inspiration, the effect of "erleuchten
und erwärmen," for "die Guten." Notice these verbs "erleuchten
und erwärmen" and compare them with the "Erstarrungsmotiv"
which always suggest that which is cold, rigid, lifeless, uninspired.
And also compare the word "Strohfeuer" with the "Heil'ge Flamme" in the second strophe above. The strawfire is man's light
and the holy flame, the Holy Spirit, is God's light. The human
creature has the potential to receive this light but spends most
of his life evading it. That is why the last two strophes are a
prayer for those poets whose pride prevents them for saying, in
effect; "more light — not mine, but yours!" The poet who errs,
"die da irren," deals in "schöne Worte und künstliche Gedanken." The word "künstlich," as we have seen, implies that the
thoughts are artificial, unreal. We shall return to the problem
of "Gedanken" and what is real.

Although we have outgrown that incredible myopia of scholar-
ly opinion which held Eichendorff's poetry to be beautiful but
without intellectual substance, it is well to observe how the last

two strophes define the function of the poet. He is to disentangle the confusion of false opinions and bring joy to the wasteland of human existence. And all this is part of searching for God. Eichendorff is didactic in the best sense of the word. He seeks to live and sing what he feels and knows man must be. Indeed, these words merely paraphrase his own statement. There is one thought in the third strophe which cannot be found in his later works — the thought that God is in man becomes repugnant to the poet as he matures. I am convinced he became so sensitive to the spiritual rebellion which he saw in the literature of his time, that it seemed judicious to avoid a specific reference to the immanence of God. Furthermore, such a bold designation contradicts his usual preference for metaphore and simile to create the image and suggest the mystery. To speak of God being in man also tends to obscure what becomes the poet's favorite reference to the relationship between God and his creatures, namely, the growth of God in man.

3

Ein Wunderland ist oben aufgeschlagen,
　　Wo goldne Ströme gehn und dunkel schallen,
　　Gesänge durch das Rauschen tief verhallen,
　　Die möchten gern ein hohes Wort dir sagen.

Viel' goldne Brücken sind dort kühn geschlagen,
　　Darüber alte Brüder sinnend wallen —
　　Wenn Töne wie im Frühlingsregen fallen,
　　Befreite Sehnsucht will dorthin dich tragen.

Wie bald läg' unten alles Bange, Trübe,
　　Du strebtest lauschend, blicktest nicht mehr nieder,
　　Und höher winkte stets der Brüder Liebe:

Wen einmal so berührt die heil'gen Lieder,
　　Sein Leben taucht in die Musik der Sterne,
　　Ein ewig Ziehn in wunderbare Ferne!

(I, p. 68-69)

Surely the imagery of the first two strophes is now familiar to us. In his own way the poet shows us the house in which there are many mansions. However, the important aspect of his picture is the insistence upon a communication that exists between the house of the Lord and man's house. Characteristically,

what is said is conveyed in song. The tones of this melody are
thought of as a spring rain, so necessary if the seed is to grow.
And man's yearning is the seed which would grow into heaven.
But our poet speaks of "befreite Sehnsucht." What if it is not
freed? In his works Eichendorff has given us numerous examples
of how man's yearning remains the slave of concupiscence. His
most common reference to this mode of existence is found in the
term "irre Lieder" which the heart of man sings, a song that
is man's own song and has nothing to do "Mit dem unbekannten
Strom der durch die Welt zieht." In the third strophe we are
told that man strives to hear the faintest note of adoration,
which is the golden song from above. The words "Bange, Trübe"
tell us clearly what existence would be for this poet if this careful listening for the song should cease. In the last line of the
third strophe we have an insinuation of what it is that gives
yearning its persistence. It is interesting to observe that the
words chosen by the poet to describe love could apply very well
to a flame burning higher and higher. Is this not "die heil'ge
Flamme" which man should guard and preserve? I would think
so. And finally, in the last strophe is a paraphrase of what
has been read in prose form, that is, the mighty, unknown river
that flows through the universe. The music of the stars, "das
alte, fromme Lied," the eternal song of love and praise, all this
is a movement "in wunderbare Ferne," which of course, was described for us in the first two strophes. The preposition *in* is
provocative. The person thus touched seems to participate, here
and now, in the glory of "das Wunderland"; he is immersed in
the music and flows with it. Before moving on to the fourth poem
in this group it is expedient for us to make a comparison. The
poem just described is used in *Ahnung und Gegenwart,* but the
context is totally different from the spiritual atmosphere of the
poems we have been discussing. Despite this, the poet uses the
same poem, but with some changes. What he has changed affords
an interesting insight into the working of his mind. By way of
setting the stage I should like to offer the comment that follows the poem in the novel.

> "Er [a would-be-poet] las noch ein Haufen Sonette mit
> einer Art von priesterlicher Feierlichkeit. Keinem derselben
> fehlte es an irgend einem wirklich aufrichtigen kleinen Ge-
> fühlchen, an grossen Ausdrücken und lieblichen Bildern.

Alle hatten einen einzigen, bis ins Unendliche breit aus-
einandergeschlagenen Gedanken, sie bezogen sich alle auf den
Beruf des Dichters und die Göttlichkeit der Poesie, aber
die Poesie selber, das ursprüngliche, freie, tüchtige Leben,
das uns ergreift, ehe wir darüber sprechen, kam nicht zum
Vorschein vor lauter Komplimenten davor und Anstalten
dazu. Friedrich kamen diese Poesierer in ihrer durchaus
polierten, glänzenden, wohlerzogenen Weichlichkeit wie der
fade, unerquickliche Teedampf, die zierliche Teekanne mit
ihrem lodernden Spiritus auf dem Tische wie der Opferaltar
dieser Musen vor (II, 134) .

And now the poem read by this man:

"Ein Wunderland ist oben aufgeschlagen,
  Wo goldne Ströme gehn und dunkel schallen
  Und durch ihr Rauschen tief' Gesänge hallen,
  Die möchten gern ein hohes Wort uns sagen.

Viel goldne Brücken sind dort kühn geschlagen,
  Darüber alte Brüder sinnend wallen
  Und seltsam' Töne oft herunterfallen —
  Da will tief Sehnen uns von hinnen tragen.

Wen einmal so berührt die heil'gen Lieder:
  Sein Leben taucht in die Musik der Sterne,
  Ein ewig Zieh'n in wunderbare Ferne.

Wie bald liegt da tief unten alles Trübe!
  Er kniet ewig betend einsam nieder,
  Verklärt im heil'gen Morgenrot der Liebe."

This poem is defined "als fader unerquicklicher Teedampf,"
generated by a small flame under a tea kettle. The comparison
is magnificent, because the imagery compels one to think of the
song generated by "die heil'ge Flamme," that particular love
which grows higher and higher. Let us see why the above poem,
so much like the other sonnet, should be called "Dunst." The
poem previously discussed will be called A, the poem above, B.
The second line of A ends with a comma; in B the punctuation
mark is deleted and the thought flows without interruption into
the third verse. Also, the poet reversed the sequence of ideas
in the third verse, confused the function of the preposition

"durch" and changed an adverb into an adjective. Furthermore, he no longer speaks of "das Rauschen" in reference to the streams, but *"ihr* Rauschen." What does all this suggest? When "das" is changed to "ihr" we lose the unambiguous singularity of what "Rauschen" should mean, and invite a confusing plurality. I have already quoted Fortunato's rejoinder to Florio that all the songs form one spring. One spring, one song, one love, one will: that is how it must be. The mighty movement of song that flows from the mystical rose is a song of praise, adoration, and love. Faber spoke of one stream that encircles the universe. This song-stream is exquisitely simple, unencumbered as only heavenly joy can be and magnificently one in the pristine purity of its intent. The adverb "tief" modifies the verb "verhallen" and suggests that the song must descend to the created so that he who has ears may hear the word it utters. In version **B** it modifies the noun "Gesänge" and gently insinuates that the songs come from the depths. In other words, whereas in version **A** the song clearly comes from on high, in version B it comes from below. It is no longer the song of heaven but of earth! All this is an important facet of our spiritual geometry; man thinks he hears the eternal song while, in fact, all he really hears is the echo of his own song. The last line of the first strophe actually implies this but so delicately that it could be easily ignored. In poem A "die Gesänge" speak to "dir," while in version B they address themselves to "uns." This simple change makes version B suspect from the standpoint of Christianity. The entire relationship between the song of love and the creature is now distorted. The "dir" is highly directional and most personal. If one analyzes Christ's words in the Bible it is quite clear that, although he may be speaking to hundreds, the import of His words is directed to the individual. Because human beings are so absolutely and even violently distinct, separate and alone, the hand of Christ touches each heart uniquely and in a different way. We would like to say that Christianity is singular and not plural. Even though the aggregate of souls to which it is offered is a veritable infinity, the ultimate essence of Christianity is a oneness in the Mystical Body, the head of which is Christ.[2] How is this relevant to the problem of changing a "dir" to an "uns"?

Friedrich had been invited to a literary soiree, and had observed the antics of these people. Two young men seem to dom-

inate the discussion. One of them, literally glowing with "wohe-
behaglicher Selbstgefälligkeit . . . schien ein wütend Begeisterter
von Profession . . . Es fehlte ihm dabei nicht an einer gewissen schlauen Miene, womit er niedere, nicht so saftige Naturen
seiner Ironie preiszugeben pflegte. Friedrich wusste gar nicht,
wohin dieser während seiner Deklamationen so viele Liebesblicke
verschwende, bis er endlich ihm gerade gegenüber einen grossen
Spiegel entdeckte" (II, 132). Magnificent! Here we have a rare
fowl preening its feathers and admiring its own reflection. (We
shall see Venus in the same posture.) The second young man
wrote the poem which we are discussing. "Er hatte sich während
der ganzen Zeit, ohne sich um die Verhandlungen der andern
zu bekümmern, ausschliesslich mit der Frau von Haus unterhal-
ten, mit der er eine Seele zu sein schien. Ihre Unterhaltung
musste sehr zart sein, wie man von dem süssen, zugespitzten
Munde beider abnehmen konnte, und Friedrich hörte nur manchmal einzelne Laute, wie: 'mein ganzes Leben wird zum Roman, — 'überschwengliches Germüt' — 'Priesterleben' —
herüberschallen. Endlich zog auch dieser ein ungeheures Paket
Papiere aus der Tasche und begann vorzulesen, unter andern
folgendes Assonanzenlied" (II, 133). My point, quite obviously,
is the complete isolation of these two. The other people do
not exist for them. They are animated by a pseudo-spiritual
rapture which occasionally bursts forth in a pious exclamation
testifying to the solemnity and holiness of the poet's calling.
These two, isolated from the rest of the group, glowing with
their own inner light, and trembling sweetly with exotic ardor,
are the "uns" in version B of our sonnet. The context suggests
this, but the poem which this man reads just prior to the one
which we are analyzing makes this most clear.

> "Hat nun Lenz die silbern'n Bronnen
>   Losgebunden:
> Knie ich nieder, süss beklommen,
>   In die Wunder.
>
> Himmelreich so kommt geschwommen
>   Auf die Wunden!
> Hast du einzig mich erkoren
>   Zu den Wundern?
>
> In die Ferne süss verloren,
>   Lieder fluten,

Dass sie, rückwärts sanft erschollen,
Bringen Kunde.

Was die andern sorgen wollen,
Ist mir dunkel,
Mir will ew'ger Durst nur frommen
Nach dem Durste.

Was ich liebte und vernommen,
Was gelungen,
Ist den eignen, tiefen Wonnen
Selig Wunder!"

(II, 133)

Much could be drawn from these verses which would reveal Eichendorff's carefully structured sarcasm and which, I am sure, is not lost even to the casual reader. Just what is wrong here can be expressed most simply: everything is literally backwards. The movement of ideas is not up toward the eternal mystery but down into the darkness of the self. The third strophe tells us clearly what we have deduced from our analysis of version B. This man sings his own song and hears its echo. He is completely deaf and oblivious to the "Gesänge" which want to tell us "ein hohes Wort." This man does not have ears with which to hear. I have mentioned the significance of "der Quell und der Fels" as well as the living waters, the water that does, indeed, quench man's thirst. But this man thirsts for the sake of thirsting. In other words, the desire is sufficient for him; he does not have that courage, love, and faith to empty himself so that he might receive (drink) Him. The last strophe sternly and bluntly tells us that this would-be poet has experienced only himself. Like the first poet, this man looks at the world and sees it as only a mirror which always reflects the self. The entire poem expresses that very significance which we saw as Eichendorff's intent in changing the *dir* to *uns*. It speaks of isolation, separation from both the other and God.

An analysis of the first strophe of version B is not complete without one further consideration. Let us place side by side the two pertinent lines. (A) "Gesänge durch das Rauschen tief verhallen"; (B) "Und durch ihr Rauschen tief Gesänge hallen." In version A, as I understand the line in the total context of this poem and Eichendorff's imagery in general, the murmuring of the golden stream initiates — the preposition "durch" suggests a causative agent — "Rauschen," a song on high which moves into the depths of the created, but also dies away or fades as its loving urgency is more and more lost to a world that has ears only for its own song. We would say that "verhallen" describes this beautifully. This movement from on high toward the created is repeated in the third verse of the second strophe. Whenever music falls like spring rain, "Befreite Sehnsucht will dorthin dich tragen." The golden stream falls like rain and gives life to man's yearning so that it may rise up, and not 'down! In version B the imagery of this line says something else. "Tief' Gesänge" do not originate from the golden stream but well up from below and they mingle with "ihr Rauschen." I would insist the function of "durch" has been changed. If we turn to the same third verse in the second strophe of version B we read, "Und seltsam Töne oft herunterfallen." The poet deliberately avoids reference to the stream given by the word "Frühlingsregen."[3] This music is now "seltsam," a word which always suggests the spiritually improper and disallowed. As a consequence, "Rauschen und Gesänge" are two separate entities. The speaker really hears the echo of his own song. And this, I suggest, is the proper understanding of the verb "hallen"; it is precisely what we saw in the "Assonanzlied." Does not this very word suggest the same idea?

> In die Ferne süss verloren,
> Lieder fluten,
> Dass sie, rückwärts sanft erschollen,
> Bringen Kunde.[4]

I submit there can be no doubt concerning the poet's intent. The minstrel who sings this song knows only the self with its love, thirst and desires. His love is a deception and he is alone. If the reader will recall, we detected the same distinction between "Waldhornlied" and the song of "das Waldhorn" in "Die Zauberei im Herbste." Now let us turn to the second strophe.

The first alteration is the dash, "ein Gedankenstrich," which in version A separates the two worlds, "das Wunderland" above and man's world below. In version B they flow together because they are the same. The notes of the song are now "seltsam" and the words "tief Sehnen" are but a variation of "tief Gesänge" because they are really one and the same. Yearning is not freed but still part of the depths. Once again we encounter the unfortunate "uns," and then we see the real error of this song. In version A the movement of the song is clearly suggested by the word "dorthin," and the direction is specific. In version B we are left with a vague and inconclusive "von hinnen." The magnitude of this spiritual error can be appreciated only if we consider that one of the most important questions constantly asked in our poet's works is where one is going. It is Eichendorff's life-long criticism of his age that men do not have sufficient care for where they are going. Even the "Taugenichts" is embarrassed by this question and must suffer the consequences. We see that the poet has reversed the position of the third and fourth strophes in the two versions of our poem. In version A the third strophe is a proper introduction to the final mystery, a dedication of life to the song of love. We note that the verb "liegen" is in the subjunctive mood. All below would be "Trübe, Bange," if — and this is so important — man's yearning were not separated from everything the poet calls "Plunder." Eichendorff has an astounding genius for imparting to the word and his imagery a sense of Christian mystery. One line: "Du strebtest lauschend, blicktest nicht mehr nieder." (Oh Lord, give me grace to hear your song! Oh Lord, turn your face to me, do not hide from me but recognize my existence.) Florio will say: "O Vater du erkennst mich doch/Und wirst nicht von mir lassen." The word "streben" says so much of Eichendorff's religious convictions. The word suggests care, desire, understanding; the creature strives to hear the faintest note of love which the heavens may utter. And finally, the poem speaks of those brothers in Christ, the saints, who becken man and urge him on to move ever higher toward the source of love.

Now what has the poet done in version B? First of all, he has reversed the order of the last two strophes. In A the imagery suggests the ascending movement of love; the individual in the last strophe is drawn upward to the very stars. In B this seems to happen in the third strophe, but the final scene depicts him as kneeling "ewig betend einsam." Eichendorff deliberately revokes the principle of movement which is the final thought in version A. In effect, the poet has contradicted the implication of "ewig Zieh'n in wunderbare Ferne" which is given in the third strophe. Now this is quite logical. Our discussion of the first two strophes of B sought to demonstrate that what is called "die heil'gen Lieder" is simply man's own song. As the

"Assonanzlied" informs us, man hears but the echo, as it were, of his own song. Therefore, when version B implies that the singer is transfigured in the holy "Morgenrot der Liebe," we must conclude that this light is his own love. His love "shines" upon the self and he is "einsam." The significance of this word can be judged by looking at version A where man is urged ever higher, to become one with a host of loving spirits, the communion of saints, who sing the praises of God. That, and that alone, is "die Musik der Sterne." This theme of isolation has another facet. In version B no reference is made to "Du," man, who strives to hear love's song. Again this is logical. The Lord does not listen because the song is not perceived by him. The third strophe of A which is the last strophe of B reveals yet another difference. We find no reference to fear, "Bange," and fear of the Lord is the beginning of wisdom. The verb "liegen" is not in the subjunctive. This man "rises" on the wings of his own song and everything below is, indeed, "Trübe." This is the direct opposite of Eichendorff's thinking as revealed countless times in prose and poetry. The song from above is light and spring, the eternal touching the mundane and transfiguring it in its glory. The world is, indeed, "so bedeutsam, jung und schön, wie sie unser Gemüt in sich selber anschaut" (II, 41). Our would-be-poet in version B is not immersed in the light of divine love but his own. Like a moth, the soul flutters about the flame of its own spiritual endowment, and instead of being "verklärt," it is blind to the glorious light that is hidden in creation. And yet, the soul feels that it possesses light!

Thus far we have concentrated on the changes which the poet effected, but the principle of deception — and we are discussing how love deceives man — demands similarity. The entire structure of Eichendorff's imagery, from his very first poems, rests upon the proposition that man is drawn. Looking at strophe four in A and three in B we see that, with the exception of two punctuation marks, they are exactly alike. The individual, the singer, in both instances feels that he is drawn "in wunderbare Ferne." However, whereas man in A is drawn upward, the individual in B really remains within the depths of the self. The song from above and the song that man sings seem to have the same effect upon the individual! This simple statement, a spiritual equation which seems to be reversible, is the cornerstone of our investigation. This spiritual dilemma, where *a* seems to equal *a'*, is the definition of duality as we employ the term. Most of Eichendorff's complex imagery, his "Hieroglyphenschrift," revolves around the symbol of light, which is love, which is a song. Turn where you will in our poet's prose works and the song which a person sings clearly reveals which love draws him. The older Eichendorff will offer a discussion of centripetal and centrifugal force which provides further clarification of what I mean with the statement that man is *drawn*. We shall return to this later.

There can be no doubt that Eichendorff gave careful thought to the changes which he effected in the two versions of our poem. He obviously screened his own poems and selected that one which would seem to express the highest ideals of the religiously oriented poet and yet be a perfect contradiction of those aspirations. That is actually explained for us by Friedrich's thoughts upon hearing the poem read, especially the delightful analogy of "der fade, unerquickliche Teedampf" and "die zierliche Teekanne mit ihrem lodernden Spiritus." As I have suggested, the careful analysis offers one a rare opportunity to study the poet's use of metaphor and imagery; it also serves as a reminder that our poet must be read with consumate attention. We now return to the fourth poem of the cycle we are investigating.

> Wer einmal tief und durstig hat getrunken,
>> Den zieht zu sich hinab die Wunderquelle,
>> Dass er melodisch mit zieht selbst als Welle,
>> Auf der die Welt sich bricht in tausend Funken.
>
> Es wächst sehnsüchtig, stürzt und leuchtet trunken
>> Jauchzend im Innersten die heil'ge Quelle,
>> Bald Bahn sich brechend durch die Kluft zur Helle,
>> Bald kühle rauschend dann in Nacht versunken.
>
> So lass es ungeduldig brausen, drängen!
>> Hoch schwebt der Dichter drauf in goldnem Nachen,
>> Sich selber heilig opfernd in Gesängen.
>
> Die alten Felsen spalten sich mit Krachen,
>> Von drüben grüssen schon verwandte Lieder,
>> Zum ew'gen Meere führt er alle wieder.

(I, 69)

It is appropriate that the "Assonanzlied" should contain the words, "Mir will ew'ger Durst nur frommen/Nach dem Durste."

The poem above speaks of the artist who has drunk deeply from the well of living waters. I have discussed "Den hellen Quell, der meiner Brust entsprungen" and have sought to understand the word as a reference to the spiritual quality of the poet's song, that is, it is a song of love. He who has tasted of this love is drawn to it, becomes one with it as the wave is part of the stream. "Melodisch mitziehen" is an expression no longer new to us; we have seen it before, especially in Faber's reference to the great unknown stream that flows through creation. The last line of the first strophe is truly an enigma. The imagery suggests that the wave, the individual, has a most surprising firmness which resists the surging (one again thinks of water) movement of the world and causes the whole, the world's thrust, to break assunder in a brilliant display of light. If we reflect for a moment on the internal relationship of the poet's imagery, we see that he brings together three symbolic concepts; water, light, and song. All three have an intimate relationship, a one-ness, which almost suggests a trinity. They are the same in essence but different in manifestation. I believe that the accumu-lated evidence offered thus far enables us to entertain this idea. To be sure, and we must not forget this, the spiritual energy for which they stand can also have its source in man. This last line of the first strophe suggests to us that the artist, "die Welle der Wunderquelle," suffers the impact of being in the world in such a manner that the confrontation results in a burst of love (light), but not his own. And it is, indeed, a confrontation because man must be hard to resist the world. Eichendorff has no patience with those poets who would seek a compromise. We know that Florio is called "weich . . . ein träumendes Mädchen." Our poet says and believes, "man muss die Welt bezwingen." He objects to the "polierten, glänzenden, wohlerzogenen Weichlichkeit" of his contemporaries.

The action depicted in the second strophe must be understood as taking place within man. All the verbs and adverbs of the first two lines portray the growth and movement of the fountain of flame into which the poet is incorporated as he gives him-self more and more to the divine intent. Deep within man's breast, "Labyrinth des Herzens," the fiery stream works its will, sometimes breaking forth in a song of joy and love and then, again, moving in a dark and mysterious manner ("in Nacht ver-sunken") so that man has no real awareness of its labors. But,

and this is vitally important, the creature must let it be; that
is to say, man's essential participation in the working of love's
stream is, "lass es brausen, drängen." Do not confound the will
of the Divine Artist who would take this creature, man, and reveal in all its blinding splendor the Image in which he is made!
Once again, the reader may conclude that too much has been deduced from words in the poem which do not reveal explicitly the
content ascribed to them. Let us examine just one strophe from
the poem "*An die Dichter*" included in Eichendorff's first novel.

> Den lieben Gott lass in dir walten,
> Aus frischer Brust nur treulich sing'!
> Was wahr in dir, wird sich gestalten,
> Das andre ist erbärmlich Ding. —
>
> (II, 299)

Friedrich's words in this poem, it seems to me, express most
succinctly what we have deduced from the other poem. "Lass
es ungeduldig braussen, drängen" must be equated with "Den
lieben Gott lass in der walten." The rationale of both statements
is simply that the Lord will form what He will form.[5] Do not
stay the working of His hand! When the poet is exhorted to
sing "treulich aus frischer Brust" we are not far removed from
the thought "Hoch schwebt der Dichter drauf in goldnem Nachen." We know that our poet frequently uses the ship as a symbol for the individual human life sailing on the stream of life.
This ship, "Nachen," is golden because it is immersed in love,
and its thrust upward is given by "die heil'ge Quelle." This is
the song, the light in man which he should not hide under a
bushel. It is given to him to reveal to all of mankind.

> Da soll er singen *frei* auf Erden,
> In Lust und Not auf Gott vertraun,
> Dass aller Herzen freier werden,
> *Eratmend in die Klänge schaun.*
>
> (Ibid, italics mine)

Because all this is given to man and what he does is God's
doing, our poet says: "Was wahr in dir wird sich gestalten."
If we follow the logic of this thought we must come, inexorably,
to the conclusion that nothing else is truly worthy of man's time.
Only His will moves in terms of the eternal and man is fettered

to the transient and sees only a reflection, as it were, of things eternal. Thus the poet dares to say that anything other than His will is "erbärmlich Ding." Eichendorff deliberately demands that the poet sacrifice himself in song. Then he is greeted from the other side by "verwandte Lieder." The other side can refer only to the heavenly kingdom which is closer to man than his own heart beat.[6] And in this kingdom the only song heard is the Alleluia sung by the saints. The adjective "verwandt" declares imperatively that the poet must seek to sing the same song. Eichendorff's poet is the spiritual Pied Piper; he and his song are "das Bächlein" filled with the cool air, "Felsenluft" from on high, which the great stream of life feels in its "Glieder." He brings the light that is not his and the song that is given him, the truth that is formed within him. He is the heart of the world that beats with longing for the living waters. He has a mission and a terrible responsibility.

And what of "die alten Felsen?" The movement of ideas in this sonnet and the group of which it is a part preclude the possibility of accepting a literal interpretation. The towering cliffs resist the movement of the spring that is now a stream as it pursues its way to eternity. In this context the cliffs can only be man's resistance to that Divine Love which would draw all things to the Father. The cliffs are called old because man's will has always resisted the love of the Creator. The fact that the hard rock is breaking assunder would suggest that the "hardness of the heart" succumbs to the impact of that fiery stream of love which draws all to the eternal ocean. The last word in the strophe, the simple word *wieder,* instructs us that whoever has been alone and separate in stiff-necked stubborness is once more involved in the movement of Divine Love. This, then, is the poet's high ideal of the minstrel, the singer of joy, freedom and love. But this lovely vision and profound conviction are a heady wine, and the young Eichendorff indulges himself in a note of arrogance which is to cause him great concern.

5

Nicht Träume sind's und leere Wahngesichte,
    Was von dem Volk den Dichter unterscheidet.
    Was er inbrünstig bildet, liebt und leidet,
    Es ist des Lebens wahrhafte Geschichte.

Er fragt nicht viel, wie ihn die Menge richte,
   Der eignen Ehr' nur in der Brust vereidet;
   Denn wo begeistert er die Blicke weidet,
   Grüsst ihn der Weltkreis mit verwandtem Lichte.

Die schöne Mutter, die ihn hat geboren,
   Den Himmel liebt er, der ihn auserkoren,
   Lässt beide Haupt und Brust sich heiter schmücken.

Die Menge selbst, die herbruast, ihn zu fragen
   Nach seinem Recht, muss den Beglückten tragen,
   Als Element ihm bietend ihren Rücken.

(I, 69-70)

The last two poems in this group of sonnets present a rather disturbing complex of ideas. In the middle of 1808, Wilhelm and Joseph Eichendorff returned home and assisted on the family estate. In 1809 our poet became engaged. In 1810 the two brothers decided to study law in Wien and enter government service. These two years were a period of significant and far-reaching decisions, but Joseph Eichendorff left precious little evidence which would enable me to speak clearly of what transpired within the family. The preponderance of "Zeitlieder" during this period do indicate, however, that the young man's horizons expanded quite suddenly. Our two sonnets express remarkable confidence and even truculence, most of which is repudiated within a year or two. The young man feels he has been chosen by heaven, but Rudolf, Friedrich's brother in *Ahnung und Gegenwart*, will say that heaven does not want him. Just as Romana represents a potential rebelliousness within the poet, so Rudolf depicts an aspect of pride which Eichendorff knows is in every man, including himself. The very humility of which the second sonnet speaks is conspicuously absent. The glowing optimism and confidence that he is heaven's chosen one soon is sorely tested and then discarded by our poet. He very quickly learns that he does not think God's thoughts nor sing God's song. The rest of mankind, "die Menge," is almost cast as inferior creatures. It is many years before Eichendorff can come back and specifically correct this monumental arrogance. We refer to Otto, in "Dichter und ihre Gesellen" who, very much like Eichendorff, returns to the "farm" from the university "um sich zu seiner Anstellung vorzubereiten" (II, 516). The youth feels utterly out of place on the estate. His closest relatives, being simple and hard working people, look with suspicion and even disdain upon the poet. His verses may be amusing and entertaining, but on the whole, the poet's labors make no real contribution to essential human welfare. Otto senses this attitude and upon being goaded reacts violently.

> Lieber Schweine hüten, . . . als so zeitlebens auf der Treckschuite gemeiner Glückseligkeit vom Buttermarkt zum Käsemarkt fahren. Der liebe Gott schafft noch täglich Edelleute und Pöpel, gleichviel, ob sie Adelsdiplome haben oder nicht. Und ich will ein H e r r sein und bleiben, weil ich's b i n, und jene Knechte sollen mich speisen und bedienen, wie es ihnen zukommt! — (II, 530).

These words are but a step removed from the last strophe of our poem. The artist who, even vaguely, feels his superiority and the inferiority of his contemporaries wanders perilously close to pride. Our poet is consciously aware of this satanic contempt that lurks in his own heart. He knows that to voice his love for God and then to depise God's creature is a contradiction of this love. He says that to sing one song and be something else is the mark of a fool. But the thorn is in his flesh. To be more than one is and more than the other is a facet of love. So our poet places words of utter contempt for the world on the lips of those who do not believe or love their God. Romana observes:

> Die Welt, der grosse Tölpel, der niemals gescheiter wird, wäre freilich der Mühe wert, dass man ihm höflich und voll Ehrfurcht das Gesicht streichelte, damit er einen wohlwollend und voll Applaus anlächle. Es ist ja doch nichts als Magen und Kopf, und noch dazu ein recht breiter, übermütiger, selbstgefälliger, eitler, unerträglicher, den es eine rechte Götterlust ist aufs Maul zu schlagen (II, 157-58).

A moment later, and from the depths of her soul she admits,

> "wenn ich mich einmal recht verliebe, es würde mich gewiss das Leben kosten!" (ibid).

Of course! Love, as our poet will have it understood, seeks the will of the other; Romana is called "unbänding" for she "toys" with others and recognizes no will but her own. This same cold contempt fills the heart of Rudolf. Our poet knew of this feeling within his breast and had to wrestle with it for many years.

The lines in the poem "Sommerschwüle" will serve as well as any others.

> Ich klimm' zum Berg und schau' zur niedern Erde,
> Ich klimm' hinab und schau' die Berge an,
> Süss' melancholisch spitzt sich die Gebärde,
> Und gift'ge Weltverachtung ficht mich an;
> Doch will aus Schmerz und Hass nichts Rechtes werden.
>
> (I, 99)

Our sonnet also speaks of the difference between the poet and "dem Volk." This attitude, modified somewhat, will be retained. But the young poet has woven a fallacy into his thinking which only bitter experience will reveal to him. The last strophe of the third sonnet and the first strophe of the fourth repeat the word "einmal." To hear the "song" once and to drink once of the "waters" is but an introduction, a first invitation, to what man can and must be. It is a baptism which, but for a moment, frees man; the next moment he again may be in darkness and a prisoner of the self. Less then two years later Eichendorff will have shifted the emphasis. Friedrich is told to immerse himself in Christ, and he dies to the world so that he may be born to Him. The Eichendorff of 1808-1810 is still too much influenced by early German Romanticism and puts the poet on an impossible pedestal. But the change comes quickly. After all, in his two great novels he does not give us a poet but a priest, a man who dedicates himself absolutely and completely to his God. And in both instances, the intital phase of the development begins on the level of poetry, of being a poet. Friedrich tells us

> Die Poesie, seine damalige, süsse Reisegefährtin, genügte ihm nicht mehr, alle seine ernstesten, herzlichsten Pläne waren an dem Neide seiner Zeit gescheitert, seine Mädchenliebe musste, ohne dass er es selbst bemerkte, einer höheren Liebe weichen, und jenes grosse, reiche Geheimnis des Lebens hatte sich ihm endlich in Gott gelöst (II, 226).

This word "Mädchenliebe" brings us to the sixth sonnet.

6

> Ihm ist's verliehn, aus den verworrnen Tagen,
> Die um die andern sich wie Kerker dichten,
> Zum blauen Himmel sich empor zu richten,
> In Freudigkeit: Hie bin ich, Herr! zu sagen.

Das Leben hat zum Ritter ihn geschlagen,
  Er soll der Schönheit neid'sche Kerker lichten;
  Dass nicht sich alle götterlos vernichten,
  Soll er die Götter zu beschwören wagen.

Tritt erst die Lieb' auf seine blühnden Hügel,
  Fühlt er die reichen Kränze in den Haaren,
  Mit Morgenrot muss sich die Erde schmücken;

Süsschauernd dehnt der Geist die grossen Flügel,
  Es glänzt das Meer — die mut'gen Schiffe fahren,
  Da ist nichts mehr, was ihm nicht sollte glücken!

(I, 70)

The moment that the young Eichendorff dwells upon his dependency he is on safer grounds. The movement of the poet's mind and heart is caught in the phrase "Hier bin ich Herr!", words uttered by Florio as he turns from the deception of his love to the light that penetrates the tired breast. This light was mentioned in the second strophe of the fifth sonnet. The kind of poet our Eichendorff has in mind looks at creation and is greeted "mit verwandtem Lichte." This repeats the thought conveyed in the last strophe of the fourth sonnet, in which the poet is greeted from the heavenly kingdom by a song similar to his. The emphasis given the word "verwandt" suggests that both light and the song originate from "drüben." But the young Eichendorff did not pursue the thought far enough and created his own pitfall. We look again at two lines: "Denn wo begeistert er die Blicke weidet,/Grüsst ihn der Weltkreis mit verwandtem Lichte." We know what Eichendorff wants. Friedrich, as we have seen, speaks of "einer inneren Freudigkeit . . . die Morgensonne . . . dieses freudige Licht" which is "die wahre göttliche Gnade." Seen in this light the world appears "bedeutsam, jung und schön." This describes the word "be-geistert" in our poem. The light is divine grace, and the human being thus chosen to see in this fashion is greeted "mit verwandtem Lichte," by what we would call "die ursprüngliche Schönheit der Welt." Let us specifically note that the world is as we ourselves see! Our poet would have us understand that we must learn to see as God would have us see. In His light all things are seen truly and in their proper significance. But how can man be sure that he does not, indeed, see darkly as in a mirror?

It is truly fascinating that a man could express thoughts as revealed in the last two sonnets, and at the same time write a long study, "Jugendandacht," which tends to contradict many of those same thoughts. The word "begeistert" is of fundamental significance in our discussion because it is involved in a proper definition of light or love. The first time that Friedrich sees Romana we are told "Ihre Bewegungen waren feurig, ihre grossen, brennenden durchdringenden Augen, denen es nicht an Strenge fehlte, bestrichen Friedrich wie ein Magnet" (II, 135). Almost without exception, whenever the movement of events include Romana, we find the themes of fire and death. A certain magnetism is imputed to the fire in her eyes. She draws man to her to destroy them precisely as another love draws man to magnify him. This fire or love bursts forth violently in another scene which would do justice to Kleist's Penthesilea. Her last attempt to win Friedrich is accompanied by these significant words:

> Du kennst noch nicht mich und jene unbezwingliche Gewalt der Liebe, die wie ein Feuer alles verzehrt, um sich an dem freien Spiele der eigenen Flammen zu weiden und selber zu verzehren, wo Lust und Entsetzen in wildem Wahnsinn einander berühren. Auch die grünblitzenden Augen des buntschillernden, blutleckenden Drachen im Liebeszauber sind keine Fabel, ich kenne sie wohl und sie machen mich noch rasend. O, hätte, ich Helm und Schwert wie Armida! — Rosa kann mich nicht hindern, denn ihre Schönheit ist blöde und dein nicht wert. Ja, gegen dich selber will ich um dich kämpfen. Ich liebe dich unaussprechlich, bleibe bei mir, wie ich nicht mehr von dir fort kann! (II, 205).

Here is that love-fire which warms the individual but also destroys him. It is a terrible energy which moves to subdue, possess and destroy the other. It seeks its own will and is the fire from which "begeistern" may draw its energy.

The last time that Friedrich sees Romana he speaks to her of nature's terrible forces and of their obedience to the Law and offers this same nature as an example to man who must subdue his own titanic forces. Then he concludes:

> Denn es gibt etwas Festeres und Grösseres, als der kleine Mensch in seinem Hochmute, das der Scharfsinn nicht begreift und die Begeisterung nicht erfindet und macht, die, ein-

mal abtrünnig, in frecher, mutwilliger, verwilderter Willkür
wie das Feuer alles ringsum zerstört und verzehrt, bis sie über
dem Schutte in sich selber ausbrennt — Sie glauben nicht
an Gott! (II, 223).

We should take special note of the movement imputed to the
concept "Begeisterung" — a movement given by the words
"frecher, mutwilliger, verwilderter Willkür." In other words, man's
natural ability to enthuse himself is arbitrarily used and directed
toward any goal which he desires. When we see the word "abtrünnig" in the same context, there can be no doubt concerning Eichendorff's intent: man rebels against God. All the adjectives which describe the word "Willkür" imply that man is
disobedient and rejects the Law. The word "wild" is a favorite
term which always suggests the opposite of "sich bewahren wollen." Human intellectual excellence, given by the word "Scharfsinn," is energized and led astray by a rebellious love. That is
why Friedrich seeks to remind her of a power which transcends
man. Romana, we are told, lives "so schwindlich hoch" (II, 157).
She is called "eine reiche Witwe" not because of material wealth
but because of the talents given her. Her own mother had told
her that she had been given wings and must, therefore, remain
within the garden (II, 124). But of course she does leave this
garden and must admit, shortly before her death: "Ich habe
mich *hier oben verirrt,* ich weiss den Weg nicht mehr nach
Hause" (II, 222, italics mine). We always find the same pattern
in Eichendorff's spiritual pychology. Man's love enables him to
fly just so high, and then he loses his way. The individual cannot break the force that draws him to the created and the
self. His own desires, the movement of his own love, are the
chains which hold him a prisoner. Thus, after Romana is dead,
we are told: "Der müde Leib ruhte schön und fromm, da ihn
die heidnische Seele nicht mehr regierte. Er kniete neben ihr
hin und betete für sie aus Herzensgrunde" (II, 224). What God
had made, the body, is called "fromm"; the human spirit which
refused to love its God is called "heidnisch." The body is tired
because the spirit has abused it; the body has peace because
the spirit has left it. "Das Schloss sank wie ein dunkler Riese in
dem feurigen Ofen zusammen, über der alten, guten Zeit hielt
das Flammenspiel im Winde seinen wilden Tanz; es war, als ginge
der Geist ihrer Herrin noch einmal durch die Lohen. —" (ibid).

I have dwelt on the problem of being enthused because the last of the six sonnets offers a clear example of that exhilirating upward thrust so characteristic of love. These groups of poems represent Eichendorff's first longer attempt to analyze the nature of the poet and his function. It is, of course, an effort to understand himself. He feels the movement of "die heilige Quelle" within him, and his "ship" rides high on the crest of its upward surge. He knows that freedom is given him, whereas others create their own prison. The pattern or structure of Eichendorff's imagery reveals that his mind contemplates certain concepts and finds different ways of saying the same thing. Man hides the "sword" because he would not be reminded of its command. Man imprisons or despises any other who would remind him of what he should be. Beauty is placed in an envious prison because the world would have its own concepts of beauty. In short, the world prefers to forget God. That is why, as we see in the second strophe above, the poet must shed light upon original beauty and speak of things divine. This is "der heilige Kampf, der schöne Gottestreit," which is always the same yet always new because each generation fights the same battle. This is Eichendorff's "ewige Alte und ewige Neue." The Word seeks to become Flesh in man and we would have none of Him because we pursue our own love wherever it takes us ("Der Knabe"). Let us look briefly at this love before turning to the second series of poems.

Love is illumination, magnification, transcendence, creativity, all of which may effected by either light or fire.[7] In the aurora of either love all things become colorful, the created bursts forth in glory and it is spring. Both God and man may say: "Let it be spring." Thus the song, "Frische Fahrt," which is a perfect characterization of Romana, begins with the lines; "Laue Luft komm blau geflossen,/Frühling, Frühling soll es sein!" Her spring, as we have seen, is the fire that destroys. But this same spring, the fire of human love, is always associated with water. Even Romana first sees the strange hunter, with whom she celebrates the marriage ritual, on a pre-spring day when the world is flooded. She lives on an "island," and is told not to leave this garden. Love is movement, like the flowing of a stream, and yet it must not become water, as it were. This stream of love is fed first by the well-spring within. It must surge up and seek to merge with that other stream of song which embraces the universe. Thus light, springtime, the well or fountain, the stream, and the song are part of a rational and carefully-organized system of communication which the poet employs to convey the spiritual thrust of the soul. If we now substitute fire for light and retain the other factors, then it becomes clear how Eichendorff achieves the principle of deception. We have, in effect, two loves which define a reality conveyed to us by the same terms or emblems. One spiritual equation seems to be the equal of the other. When we insert into this complex such other items as the garden, flowers, stars, seasons, time of day, to name just a few, and realize that each may be illuminated by either the light or the fire, then we can understand how criticism, when it fails to see that everything may, in principle, have a double meaning, can come to see a remarkable sameness in Eichendorff's works. But this implied limitation does not rest with the poet; we are the ones who have neither seen nor heard. The explanation for our limitation can be bound in a passage quoted above. Friedrich speaks of "jenes ewige Gefühl . . . das uns in den Mittelpunkt alles Lebens versenkt, wo alle die Farbenstrahlen; gleich Radien ausgehen und sich an der wechselnden Oberfläche zu dem schmerzlich-schönen Spiele der Erscheinung gestalten." The word "Erscheinung" is in the singular. Yes, all is the same. But we have failed to consider "das schmerzlich-schöne Spiel." The substance of Eichendorff's works is a play of imagery, a beautifully wrought succession of "Bilder" which seek to convey the source of that mysterious illumination — light or fire — which renders them visible and assigns them their meaning. And, strangely enough, the key to a proper understanding is given to us on the surface, "der wechselnden Oberfläche" of his works. In our poet's prose and poetry we can find, quite literally, hundreds of lines and passages which criticism has not touched upon. To the untutored ear and eye, all looks and sounds the same. This has always been the case. We see only what we know. That is why I offered an interpretation of the two sonnets with diametrically opposed meanings.[8] Our poet changed a few words, some punctuation, and the sequence of the ideas. A casual glance and one assumes they are the same, and yet one song speaks of heaven and the other of just man. As a final thought, let us look again at the first two strophes of the "Assonanzlied."

> Hat nun Lenz die silbern'n Bronnen
>   Losgebunden:
> Knie ich nieder, süss beklommen,
>   In die Wunder.
>
> Himmelreich so kommt geschwommen
>   Auf die Wunden!
> Hast du einzig mich erkoren
>   Zu den Wundern?

(II, 133)

The word "Bronnen" can be understood as a synonym for "die Quelle." I have examined the latter in various contexts and concluded that it refers to the song welling forth from the breast of man. The second strophe informs us that the heavenly kingdom "kommt geschwommen." This imagery, already used in "Die Nonne und der Ritter," suggests that heaven is brought by the flowing stream of song. In other contexts this might be correct; witness Faber's reference to the stream of heavenly music. Here, as has been demonstrated, the song has nothing to do with heaven. But that is not our problem. The complete lines read, "Himmelreich so kommt geschwommen/Auf die Wunden." Suddenly we must entertain the possibility that this stream of song is to be equated with wounds. On these wounds, this stream of song, heaven is brought to the singer! Why did Eichendorff use the word *wounds?* If we look at the rhyme scheme we see that "Wunden" are "losgebunden." This is not a surprising conclusion, because Eichendorff uses precisely that imagery in the poem "Jugendandacht." The last strophe of this poem, as I have explained, instructs us that this singer has loved and perceived or heard ("vernommen") only "den eignen, tiefen Wonnen/Selig Wunder." Man's wound, Eichendorff seeks to tell us, is the human capacity to measure all things by the self, to see them in our own light, in terms of our own love. No matter where man goes or whatever he touches he always encounters the self. Rudolf, who is haunted by his "Doppelgänger," describes his own life as a desparate effort "die Schranken durchzubrechen und aus mir selber herauszukommen" (II, 274). He admits that deep within him is "ein dunkler, harter Fleck . . . der keine Farben annahm und doch mein eigentlicher, innerster Kern war" (II, 268). Color can appear only in the presence of light and Rudolf has hardened his heart to divine love. And because of this, his is the spirit which "Schauet mit dem starren Sinne/In das wesenlose Meer." Rudolf is an absolute extreme. Most of the figures which Eichendorff gives us render the world golden with their love. Rudolf is no longer "verliebt"; all is dead to him. At one time Rudolf was wounded. As Friedrich finds him again we are told "eine Narbe über dem rechten Auge enstellte ihn seltsam" (II, 260). The wound is healed. No love song wells forth from his breast. He admits that he is hard, cold, sterile. Now we can turn to "Jugendandacht." We shall find a youth who is just the opposite of Rudolf; and yet, he too becomes a prisoner, frozen, as it were, in the fading colors of his own love.

Notes

1. Again we see that thoughts must be touched by God's light. In a later context we shall show that man's thoughts are really shadows. Man is free to think what he will, but only God, so it seems, can give them substance.

2. Eichendorff's works are filled with so many "Bilder" that, in this introductory study, I must despair of offering even a reasonably adequate discussion. However, I should like to show that my reference to Christ, the head, comes from Eichendorff. In *Ahnung und Gegenwart*, Leontin and Friedrich ride into a dense forest and come upon a strange, utterly uninhabited and untended temple. "Ihre Augen konnten sich bei dem ersten verwirrenden Anblick durchaus nicht aus dem labyrinthischen, höchst abenteuerlichen Gemisch dieses Tempels herausfinden, so unförmlich, obgleich klein, war alles über- und durcheinander gebaut. Den Haupteingang nämlich bildete ein griechischer Tempel mit zierlichem Säulenportal, welches sehr komisch aussah, da alles überaus niedlich und nur aus angestrichenem Holze war. Sie traten hinein und fanden in der Halle einen hölzernen Apollo, der die Geige strich, und dem der Kopf fehlte, weil nicht mehr Raum genug dazu übrig geblieben war" (II, 248). This temple, obviously a caricature, represents the electicism of the age, as Eichendorff understood it. It is called "ein Surrogat- Tempel für allen Geschmack auf Erden" (ibid.) Everything seems to be in miniature, and thus reflects man's finiteness. The temple is of wood (transitory) and not stone (eternal). The Apollo figure is headless because room was lacking. Now Eichendorff insists that all great religions had one dream in common. This dream became reality with Christ's life and passion. In other words, the ancient religions all pointed to Christ. But the religions of his time were all man-made and had no room for the head, the Christ.

3. In this early poem Eichendorff imparts a positive connotation to the imagery. What he calls "die heil'gen Lieder" falls like spring rain upon the seed of yearning. But this imagery is soon discarded, because song and light must not become "water." "Zur Erde geht, was feucht und schwer,/Was klar, zu ihr [die Sonne] hinauf" (I, 83; 1815).

4. Examining the logic of these lines, we see that Eichendorff carefully contradicts what the minstrel who sings them feels. Songs which flow "in die Ferne," and are lost, can never return. He thinks he hears "Kunde" but hears only himself.

5. But Eichendorff insists that man is free. Consequently, God is "helpless" unless his creature voluntarily participates in the making of the new man. And this work demands all of man: "Gefühl, Phantasie und Verstand" (IV, 26).

6. In the poem "Wunder über Wunder" (I, 154; 1819), Eichendorff speaks of an "unermessliches Revier" for which man has no concept and in which the human being is "das grösste Wundertier." We shall expand upon this later.

7. In *Ahnung und Gegenwart* Rosa was Friedrich's first love. During the period that he was in love, he was a creative poet. But

she was not true to him (she represents the woman in "Das Zauber-netz" who was asked to remain faithful to "dem alten Sange"). Rosa portrays Eichendorff's early love affair with "Poesie." In the novel she leaves Friedrich and goes to the "Residenz." Friedrich receives one letter from her, and we quote his reaction. "Habe ich es oben auf der Höhe nicht gesagt, dass du in dein Grab hinabsteigst? Wenn die Schönheit mit ihren frischen Augen, mit den jugendlichen Gedanken und Wünschen unter euch ritt, und, wie sie die egiene, grössere Lebenslust treibt, sorglos und lüstern in das liebewarme Leben hinaus-langt und sprosst — sich an die feinen Spitzen, die zum Himmel streben, giftig anzusaugen und zur Erde hinabzuzerren, bis die ganze, prächtige Schönheit, fahl und ihres himmlischen Schmuckes beraubt, unter euch dasteht wie euresgleichen — die Halunken!" (II, 107-08). We see that man tends to be a vampire, who lusts for the spiritual quality of beauty. This can be clear only to those who believe with Eichendorff and Novalis that poetry is a heavenly but not an "ird'sche Blume."

8. Oskar Seidlin, in his *Versuche über Eichendorff,* Göttingen, 1965, says of these two sonnets. "[sie] weisen einige abweichungen auf, die aber unbeträchtlich sind" (297). It must be apparent that the scholar who cannot see the definitive difference between these two poems would have great difficulty understanding Eichendorff's imagery. Des-pite Seidlin's failure to identify Eichendorff's emblematic language, his remarkably sensitive and intelligent observations have provided recent critics with a solid base for research. Where Seidlin and I differ may be viewed best in my "Marmorbild" and "Taugenichts" chapters. Some-where, Seidlin says "Schen ist alles." At this point he and I become a confrontation of opposing convictions.

III

Jugendandacht

Lockung

Hörst du nicht die Bäume rauschen
Draussen durch die stille Rund'?
Lockt's dich nicht, hinabzulauschen
Von dem Söller in den Grund,
Wo die vielen Bäche gehen
Wunderbar im Mondenschein
Und die stillen Schlösser sehen
In den Fluss vom hohen Stein?

Kennst du noch die irren Lieder
Aus der alten, schönen Zeit?
Sie erwachen alle wieder
Nachts in Waldeseinsamkeit,
Wenn die Bäume träumend lauschen
Und der Flieder duftet schwül
Und im Fluss die Nixen rauschen —
Komm herab, hier ist's so kühl.

(I, 96)

Jugendandacht 10

Durchs Leben schleichen feindlich fremde Stunden,
  Wo Ängsten aus der Brust hinunterlauschen,
  Verworrne Worte mit dem Abgrund tauschen,
  Drin bodenlose Nacht nur ward erfunden.

Wohl ist des Dichters Seele stumm verbunden
  Mit Mächten, die am Volk vorüberrauschen;

Sehnsucht muss wachsen an der Tiefe Rauschen
Nach hellerm Licht und nach des Himmels Kunden.

O Herr! du kennst allein den treuen Willen,
Befrei ihn von der Kerkerluft des Bösen,
Lass nicht die eigne Brust mich feig zerschlagen!

Und wie ich schreibe hier, den Schmerz zu stillen,[1]
Fühl' ich den Engel schon die Riegel lösen,
Und kann vor Glanze nicht mehr weiter klagen.

(I, 278-279)

A problem of considerable significance in these poems is called to our attention by a rather startling fact. The reader's mind is given an initial set by the title "Jugendandacht," and yet the last poem of this cycle contains a prayer that the speaker be freed from "der Kerkerluft des Bösen." Somehow it would seem devotion has undergone a terrible persersion, and the soul is caught in the grip of evil which may even have been embraced from the very beginning. Perhaps it had seemed a good worthy of man's devotion, since the same strophe states that only God truly knows man's will. The individual seeks to do good yet works evil. This is Pauline doctrine. The second half of the prayer implores God's aid that the speaker would not destroy himself in despair. It seems that the prayer is answered, for the pain is lifted by the very act of calling for help. The imagery, as is so frequently the case, suggests that man is freed. But just where is this "Kerkerluft des Bösen"? The question of freedom is basic to the "Marmorbild" discussion; however, I should like to span twenty-five years and listen to Victor-Lothario-Vitalis speak to Otto, a would-be poet.

"Und red' mir nicht von Poesie, von Dichterberuf," fuhr er fort, "du hast nicht mehr davon als ein verliebtes Mädchen. Es gibt nur wenige Dichter in der Welt, und von den wenigen kaum einer steigt unversehrt in diese märchenhafte, prächt'ge Zaubernacht, wo die wilden, feurigen Blumen stehen und die Liederquellen verworren nach den Abgründen gehen, und der zauberische Spielmann zwischen dem Waldesrauschen mit herzzerreissenden Klängen nach dem Venusberg verlockt, in welchem alle Lust und Pracht der Erde entzündet, und wo die Seele wie im Traum frei wird mit ihren dunklen Gelüsten" — (II, 656-657).

Compare these words with Raimund's description of his soul (II, 983). No, Raimund does not speak of his soul but of "das dunkle Reich von Gedanken in des Menschen Brust." As I have sought to point out, the garden in which he finds his beloved is, indeed, this "Reich von Gedanken." Turning again to Lothario's description of "Poesie," is it not abundantly clear that the "prächtige Zaubernacht" must be equated with "das Reich von Gedanken"? We find the same fiery flowers, the "Quellen" which do not rise to join the great stream of heavenly music but sink into the abyss, and the minstrel whose song is heard "zwischen dem Waldesrauschen." The beautiful woman seen by Raimund was described as "zwischen den Klängen herum-wandeln." It is the same picture. Man's thoughts are "die Zauber-nacht," the prison which he creates for himself. The poet's work is dangerous!

Let me, at this point, offer one facet of Raimund's story which was reserved for this context. He tells us that he had gone hunting with his falcon, an ancient symbol used in earlier Chris-tian art to represent man's thoughts. A tame falcon represents good thoughts, and a wild one, evil thoughts. With the first notes of the seductive song, the falcon "wurde scheu, schwang sich wildkreischend auf, hoch in den Lüften verschwindend, und kam nicht wieder" (II, 976). But it did! The falcon returned twice as a bird of paradise with burning colors and lured him to the woman. In other words — and I now employ the substance of poems already discussed — man has been given wings (thoughts); he must guard them or they may become wild and not move toward the heights but the depths.[2] Instead of saying "Hier bin ich Herr," man remains concerned with the self and "sinks away" from God. Now, it is not "Scharfsinn," the human intel-lect, which lures man into the "Venusberg" but love. Love gen-erates life, gives it flesh and blood as in "Das Marmorbild." The Christian says that divine love sustains creation. The same power is given the creature made in His image. We shall see that Venus' castle rests upon "jugendliche Gedanken," but when Florio withdraws his love the castle and grounds revert to ruins. With Romana the symbolism is similar but negative. She muti-lates the pictures of her ancestors and destroys her "Stamm-schloss" because, as we see in the person of her mother, they were pious God-fearing people. She destroys what is God-oriented because it reminds her of her own denial and rejection. We always find the same pattern. Eichendorff speaks of the towers of "der Residenz. Sie stehen wie Leichensteine des versunkenen Tages" (II, 62). They stand, but they bear witness to what has died in time. This is the same imagery which Eichendorff employs to describe the love represented by Venus and her sunken realm.

The entire cycle of poems concerns the mystery of love which for Eichendorff is an essential constituent of "Dichten." Lothario insists, not without reason, that Otto has no more of a calling for the "Dichterberuf" than "ein verliebtes Mädchen." This girlish love is insufficient for the poet. Why? Near the end of *Ahnung und Gegenwart* Leontin addresses Julie whom he had just married.

> Und du . . . wirst du ganz ein Weib sein, und, wie Shakespeare sagt, dich dem Triebe hingeben, der dich zügellos ergreift und dahin oder dorthin reisst, oder wirst du immer Mut genug haben, dein Leben etwas Höherem unterzuordnen? Und dämmert endlich die Zeit heran, die mich Gott erleben lasse! wirst du fröhlich sagen können: Ziehe hin! denn was du willst und sollst, ist mehr wert, als dein und mein Leben? (II, 294).

Woman, as Eichendorff suggests, gives herself to "Triebe" which dictate her erratic movement. In our "Marmorbild" discussion we shall see that Florio thinks of himself as "ein schwaches vom Winde verwehtes Lerchenstimmlein" (II, 307). The structure of the thought is the same. And we know that Florio is called "verliebt" and "ein Mädchen"; he does not know where he is going. "Er hat keine Geschäfte" (ibid). Even the "Taugenichts" is guilty of the same error. Now what is Julie's response to Leontin? She sings a song called "Von der deutschen Jungfrau." The married woman sings the song of a virgin! The bare substance of the poem will be sufficient for our purpose. Her castle is in flames and a "röm'scher Rittersmann," a splendid heathen, has been captivated by her eyes. He offers her life, honor and wealth if she will be his. Her answer is to hurl him, her "Liebsten," as well as herself "ins heisse Grab." Julie is Leontin's wife, but her love must also be dedicated to what transcends both of them. There is a startling similarity between this ideal presented in Julie's song and Romana's final end. Both die in the flames of their own castle. Romana, however, is the very embodiment of this love-fire, while Julie is infinitely above it. Eichendorff has prepared us for this.

One evening, the summer home in which Julie's family resides bursts into flames. Two incidents occur which are of fundamental significance. A strange "weisse Frau" appears to encourage the fire fighters, and Leontin rushes into the burning building to save Julie. He carries her outside, cradles her in his arms, and both of them watch as the flames sink back into themselves. Julie's heart was full,

> wie noch niemals in ihrem ganzen Leben. Im Innersten aufgeregt von den raschen Begebenheiten dieser Nacht, war es ihr, als hätte sie in den wenigen Stunden Jahre überlebt; was lange im stillen *geglommen,* war auf einmal *in helle Flammen ausgebrochen.* Müde lehnte sie ihr Gesicht an seine Brust und sagte, ohne aufzusehen: "Sie haben mir mein Leben gerettet. Ich kann es nicht beschreiben, wie mir damals zumute war. Ich möchte Ihnen nun so gern aus ganzer Seele danken, aber ich könnte es doch nicht ausdrücken, wenn ich es auch sagen wollte. Es ist auch eigentlich nicht das, dass Sie mich aus dem Feuer getragen haben." — Hier hielt sie eine Weile inne, dann fuhr sie wieder fort: "Die Flamme ist nun verloschen. Wenn der Tag kommt, ist alles wieder gut und ruhig, wie sonst. Jeder geht wieder gelassen an seine alte Arbeit und denkt nicht mehr daran. Ich werde diese Nacht niemals vergessen" (II, 95, italics mine).

Let us not be deceived and assume that the girl speaks of an ordinary fire. She had fallen in love with this man, had attempted to paint a picture of him, and the purpose of the entire scene is to show us that "Die Flamme" is "nun verloschen." He attempts to kiss her but she does not permit it. As Aurora rises (Eichendorff's constant reminder of Christ) and stands high above the forest, we are told, "Der Rausch der Nacht war verflogen" (ibid). The end of the chapter depicts Leontin lifting "das schöne, verschlafene Kind hoch vor sich hin in den frischen Morgen hinein" (II, 95). Surely this is intended to be more than an empty gesture. Leontin raises her into the morning, the aurora; before she can be his, he must first give her to the light, the color of blood and water, which fills the sky and heralds the coming of the sun, the source of all life.

Julie has risen above the limitation of her "Mädchenliebe," that same girlish love described by Eichendorff as he portrays the gradual estrangement between Rosa and Friedrich. The young man grows away from her because he feels that very few women "begreifen der Männer Liebe in ihrem Umfange, sondern messen ungeschickt das Unermessliche nach Küssen und eitlen Versicherungen. Es ist, als wären ihre Augen zu blöde, frei in die göttliche Flamme zu schauen, sie spielen nur mit ihrem spielenden Widerscheine" (II, 168). Keeping in mind that Florio is called "verliebt, ein träumendes Mädchen" and "der Blöde," we begin to see that Florio embraces the reflection of "der göttlichen Flamme."³ Now before this thought escapes us, let us return to the very page where Friedrich describes Rosa's love. Just prior to that passage we find this observation.

> Die strebende, webende Lebensart schien Friedrich einigermassen von Rosa zu entfernen, denn jede grosse innerliche Tätigkeit macht äusserlich still. Es schien aber auch nur so, denn eigentlich hatte seine Liebe zu Rosa, ohne dass er selbst es wusste, einen grossen Anteil an seinem Ringen nach dem Höchsten. Sowie die Erde in tausend Stämmen, Strömen und Blüten treibt und singt, wenn sie der alles belebenden Sonne zugewendet, so ist auch das menschliche Gemüt zu allem Grossen freudig in der Sonnenseite der Liebe (II, 168).

Here is absolutely irrefutable evidence for Eichendorff's basic position. Friedrich had fallen in love with Rosa, and this love for her is intimately associated with his "Ringen nach dem Höchsten." The capacity to love, grounded in man's physical nature, is the human creature's point of departure for his flight to God. But only the point of departure! If man would, indeed, fly to the Father and sing the eternal Alleluia he must, as we have said, first return this love to the Giver. All by himself man cannot truly reach the heights, as Romana has told us. Rudolf, another rebel, speaks clearly to this point.

> Und wie er dehnt die Flügel aus,
> Und wie er auch sich stellt:
> Der Mensch kann nimmermehr hinaus
> Aus dieser Narrenwelt."⁴

(II, 259)

This, to be sure, is the voice of the sceptic, a man who is convinced that heaven does not want him, a man who admits that he no longer loves, which is the crucial point in our consideration. A minor episode in the poet's first novel will clarify what we have in mind. Marie, a camp follower, had given herself to a traitor. The man is captured and attempts to kill Friedrich. He is thwarted by an alert companion who shoots him. Soon thereafter Friedrich is informed that a strange girl is fighting with two of his soldiers.

> . . . Das Mädchen sei gegen Morgen allein mit verwirrtem Haar und einem Degen in der Hand an dem Schlosse herumgeirrt, als suchte sie etwas. Als sie dann auf den erschossenen Offizier gestossen, habe sie ihn schnell in die Arme genommen, und den Leichnam mit einer bewunderungswürdigen Kraft und Geduld in das Gebirge hinaufgeschleppt. Zwei Schützen, denen ihr Herumschleichen verdächtig wurde, waren ihr bis zu diesem Felsen gefolgt, den sie nun wie ihre Burg verteidigte.
> Als Friedrich näher kam, erkannte er in dem wunderbaren Mädchen sogleich Marie, sie kam ihm heute viel grösser und schöner vor. Ihre langen, schwarzen Locken waren auseinandergerollt, sie hieb nach allen Seiten um sich, so dass keiner, ohne sich zu verletzen, die steile Klippe ersteigen konnte. Als dieselbe Friedrich unter den fremden Männern erblickte, liess sie plötzlich den Degen fallen, sank auf die Knie und verbarg ihr Gesicht an der kalten Brust ihres Geliebten. Die bärtigen Männer blieben erstaunt stehn. "Ist in dir eine solche Gewalt wahrhafter Liebe," sagte Friedrich gerührt zu ihr, "so wende sie zu Gott, und du wirst noch grosse Gnade erfahren!" (II, 218-219) .

Marie, a Magdalene figure, is a harlot who has given herself to various men and, in a moment of despair, had attempted suicide. We must compare the picture of her fighting with enemy soldiers with Julie's song of "der deutschen Jungfrau." The virgin and the harlot have much in common. Eichendorff selects the prostitute, the kept woman, who is used and abused in our society, and imputes to her "wahre Liebe." Marie's total concern, in this context, is for the other, a man whom Friedrich had called worthless. It is her willingness to intercede and even sacrifice herself for the one she loves, however worthless he may be or how futile the gesture remains, which transfigures her and transforms "Mädchenliebe" into something more serious and substantial. That is why Friedrich calls her "viel schöner und grösser." Eichendorff's lifelong preoccupation with the mystery of "Dichten und Dichter" provides unambiguous and irrefutable evidence that care for the other grounded in obedience to God's law is the fundamental characteristic of the ideal poet. The poet sings, "Das aller Herzen freier werden,/Eratmend in die Klänge schaun." This word "Eratmend" should remind us of the "Bächlein" within the body of the great stream. It suggests "Felsenluft," the clean, cool, bright air which is the very opposite of "die Kerkerluft des Bösen." The latter concerns the prison mentioned by Rudolf when he discusses his own abortive efforts in art. "So schmückt sich wohl jede tüchtige Seele einmal ihren Kerker mit Künsten aus, ohne deswegen zum Künstler berufen zu sein" (II, 268). Notice that the soul fashions its own prison. It is the same prison which almost destroys Florio and Otto. Love is concerned with itself and digs its own grave, an expression we shall hear from the "Taugenichts"! Now let us see how a poem which begins with "Andacht" can end in a prayer that the soul be freed "von der Kerkerluft des Bösen." In the process we shall gain some insight as to why the poet's soul is "stumm verbunden/Mit Mächten, die am Volk vorüberrauschen."

Jugendandacht 1

Dass des verlornen Himmels es gedächte,
Schlugen ans Herz des Frühlings linde Wellen,
Wie ew'ger Wonnen schüchternes Vermuten.
Geheimer Glanz der lauen Sommernächte,
Du grüner Wald, verführend Lied der Quellen,
Des Morgens Pracht, stillblüh'nde Abendgluten,
Ihr fragt: wo Schmerz und Lust so lange ruhten,
Die süss das Herz verdunkeln und es hellen?
Wie tut ihr zaubrisch auf die alten Wunden,
Dass losgebunden in das Licht sie bluten!
O sel'ge Zeit entflossner Himmelsbläue,
Der ersten Andacht solch inbrünst'ger Liebe,
Die ewig wollte knien vor der Einen!
Demütig in der Glorie des Maien
Hob sie den Schleier oft, dass offen bliebe
Der Augen Himmel, in das Land zu scheinen.

> Und stand ich still, und musst' ich herzlich weinen;
> In ihrem Blick gereinigt alle Triebe:
> Da war nur Wonne, was ich musste klagen,
> Im Angesicht der Stillen, Ewigreinen
> Kein Schmerz, als solcher Liebe Lieb' ertragen!
>
> (I, 274)

A brief study of these lines reveals that the meaning is conveyed by light, spring, water, time, love, pain, and the wound.
Let us begin with "Liebe" and thread our way through the in-
tricately intertwined imagery. In the center of the poem we find
the lines: "O sel'ge Zeit entflossener Himmelsbläue,/Der ersten
Andacht solch inbrünst'ger Liebe." There is no question in my
mind that the repetition of motifs, themes, imagery, and their
subtle variation which characterizes Eichendorff's works is due
in large measure to his habit of examining most carefully what
he had written and actually building upon it. In "Das Marmorbild" Florio is asked in song by Fortunato, "Ist's Liebe, ist's
Andacht/Was so dich beglückt?/Rings Frühling dich an-
lacht,/Du sinnest entzückt-" (II, 312). One need only inspect
the first poem of "Jugendandacht" to conclude that the same
question could be asked of the speaker. And that is precisely
the point which concerns this group of poems: Is it love or devotion which governs the soul? The word "Andacht" seems justified by the seemingly unmistakable reference to the Queen of
Heaven, "die Stille Ewigreine." We must look carefully at the
one action imputed to her.

> Demütig in der Glorie des Maien
> Hob sie den Schleier oft, dass offen bliebe
> Der Augen Himmel, in das Land zu scheinen.

In that wondrous springtime which is the "Glorie des Maien"
the woman frequently raises a veil. Poem one offers no clue as
to what Eichendorff wishes to convey with the veil; we only
know it is raised so that a heaven may shine upon creation, "in
das Land." Considering that our poet uses the verb "scheinen,"
we must conclude that this heaven is manifested by a form
of light. The woman raises the veil, "dass offen bliebe/der
Augen Himmel, in das Land zu scheinen." The conceptualization
is rather unusual and conceals a vaguely disturbing thought.
When we read "Im Angesicht der Stillen" and combine this

with "Der Augen Himmel" we feel the suggestion that heaven means looking into her eyes. Something is amiss here; it is as though "die Wonne" of which the youth speaks were the direct result of seeing her. It is instructive to recall that the "Taugenichts" attempts to spy upon "die gnädige Frau" and from that moment on his troubles begin. The last ten lines of "Jugendandacht" 1 suggest and contradict what is a firmly established tradition of Eichendorff's Christianity: The humble maid, the second Eve, stands before the throne of the Father, and through her son works her gentle will for the children in darkness. In 1823, a period when Eichendorff was writing the "Taugenichts" story, we find a "Kirchenlied" which touches on this point.

> Wo Verlass'ne einsam weinen,
> Sorgenvoll in stiller Nacht,
> Den' vor allen lässt Du scheinen
> Deiner Liebe milde Pracht,
> Dass ein tröstend Himmelslicht
> In die dunklen Herzen bricht.
>
> Aber wütet wildverkehrter
> Sünder frevelhafte Lust:
> Da durchschneiden neue Schwerter
> Dir die treue Mutterbrust;
> Und voll Schmerzen flehst du doch:
> Herr! Vergib, o schone noch!
>
> (I, 283)

The splendor of her love is that Christ-like sacrificial care for the other, a love which is, indeed, "ein trötsend Himmelslicht." The imagery in the first strophe repeats the ideas found in Florio's song "Der Umkehrende". The love of the Queen seeks to effect man's return to God. It is this problem of returning which compels one to look with some suspicion at the line, "O sel'ge Zeit entflossener Himmelsbläue." These words introduce the last ten verses of the poem and clearly refer to the past. Let me tentatively venture a possibility. Sometime in the past, in childhood perhaps, a beautiful lady raised a veil, and through her eyes the child was introduced to a heavenly light.[5] The gaze of the quiet, eternally chaste woman purified the desires of the small heart and the child felt transfigured in the powerful surge of devotion and love, which it felt to be one. The very being of this child — and for how long we are not told — was filled only with love for this heavenly woman. All this is in the past. The child is now a youth, and the first ten verses of the poem speak of the present. What is the relationship between the speaker and this woman? The past and the present, as we shall see, are strangely telescoped. And now to the beginning of the poem.

Spring, like a shy insinuation of eternal rapture, surges gently against the heart so that man might be reminded of heaven. Spring is the return of light and warmth which presages the bursting forth of new life. But this light is rendered suspect by the imagery which likens it to the movement of water. If this seems to be a contradiction we must remind ourselves that Florio's entire "Marmorbild" experience takes place beneath the waters. As the young man for the first time seemingly by chance comes upon the garden of Venus "war es ihm, als sei das alles lange versunken, und *über ihm ginge der Strom der Tage mit leichten, klaren Wellen,* und unten läge der Garten gebunden und verzaubert und *träumte von dem vergangenen Leben*" (II, 321, italics mine). The significant components of this imagery will be found in the succeeding poems of the "Jugendandacht" group. The fact that Eichendorff introduces the movement of error in the first three lines is quite characteristic of him. Many of his poems which are dialectical (even though this is usually concealed by disarming imagery), and most of his prose works employ this technique. In "Das Marmorbild," for example, the first line tells us it is summer, but the entire story concerns spring. Not until divine grace destroys the garden of Venus are we told that it is summer again. In this way, the true season is like a frame which contains the dream brought to life by Florio. This is not quite correct. What Venus represents is indeed real and tangible; it seems to call to man, and this notion of the call is introduced in lines four through six of our poem.

We have been told that spring seeks to remind man of the heaven he had lost. On the one hand, this spring with its "linde Wellen" is thought of as "water," and this points to "O sel'ge Zeit entflossener Himmelsbläue." It is clearly in the past, but still it beats against the heart. That is not all. Lines three through five are also a definition of spring. Spring is a mysterious gleaming of the balmy summer night; it is the green forest, as well as the fountain of song which leads astray, the splendor of the morning and the quiet glow of an evening light which seems to blossom as a flower might. All this is spring! This entire constellation, a beautiful example of the poet's "Hieroglyph-enschrift," calls to man. It is the purpose of this call to re-mind him of heaven. Consider that "Jugendandacht" 10 speaks of "der Kerkerluft des Bösen" and one begins to grasp what Eichendorff has undertaken in this study. Man feels, has the sen-sation, that heaven calls, but he gives himself to Evil. Is that not a perfect description of Florio's love and the poem "Götterdäm-merung," especially the last two strophes (II, 313)? The ele-ments of deception are concealed in the three lines which de-fine spring. The summer night is called "lau" and this is one of the few words in Eichendorff's vocabulary which always has a negative connotation. It insinuates the very opposite of that mode of existence for which our poet is the ideal protagonist. All that is spiritually tepid or indifferent is utterly detested by this passionate man. The word also suggests a certain sooth-ing or lulling influence which places it within the context of another important Eichendorff word, "schlafen." Man may be "asleep" in Christ, but Eichendorff's song is frequently addressed to the man who is asleep in the world and in himself. How often he calls to his readers, "Wake up, there is danger near; gird your loins and prepare to battle evil, for the world would have you for itself!" Line four concerns these sounds that man hears: "Du grüner Wald, verführend Lied der Quellen." So many times the word "Rauschen" is coupled with the forest. The forest, the community of trees, is a thrusting upward from the earth to-ward light. It is uplifted arms beseeching and adoring. The tree:

> Er träumt von künft'ger Frühlingszeit,
> Von Grün und Quellenrauschen,
> Wo er im neuen Blütenkleid
> Zu Gottes Lob wird rauschen.

> (I, 309)

The song of the green forest is always a positive note in Eichendorff's symphony. "Das Lied der Quellen," however, the song of man, can be misleading. These two songs "touch" the speaker in the poem. The next line, "Des Morgens Pracht, still-blüh'nde Abendgluten," presents the duality of light. The word "Morgen," in various compounds and with its insinuation of light and a new day, occurs over two hundred times in our poet's works. The morning light is always a delicate reference to God's light, to His love. Guided by Eichendorff's metaphors, one would say that man must bathe in this stream of the eternal, "das fliessende Licht der Gottheit," and through grace, rise above the waters that would drown the soul. This particular concept of light is countered by its opposite, "stillblüh'nde Abendgluten." Instead of the resplendent glory suggested by "Pracht," we now find a source of illumination that is vaguely and disquietingly different. The word "Glut" refers to a fire, to a glowing produced by that which burns. But the fire dies out and then man is cold and in darkness. This will happen to the youth in "Jugendandacht."

Poem one contains twenty-one lines. At the geometric center of the poem, the eleventh line, we read: "O sel'g Zeit enflossener Himmelsbläue." If we inspect the rhyme scheme we see that this line stands alone; the word "bläue" will not combine with any other word. It is as though the poet wished to suggest that this does not belong here, and yet, this enigmatic line with its insinuation of light, water, and time points toward the woman who is the subject of the entire cycle of poems. This mysterious "Eine" is immersed in the time of "entflossner Himmelsbläue" and the mind and heart conspire to see the image. Florio and our "Taugenichts" are involved in the same process. These youths as well as the young man in our poem must learn that love and devotion may be synonymous terms for the child, but the youth, the young man, must learn that the light and the fire are not the same. The yearning which he now feels cannot be equated with the yearning experienced as a child, and this brings us to our final consideration of poem one. We must review two lines: "We tut ihr zaubrisch auf die alten Wunden, /Dass losgebunden in das Licht sie bluten!" Let us compare these words with the beginning verses of the "Assonanzlied."

> "Hat nun Lenz die silbern'n Bronnen
> Losgebunden:
> Knie ich nieder, süss beklommen,
> In die Wunder.
>
> Himmelreich so kommt geschwommen
> Auf die Wunden!"

Reflecting on our previous discussion of these lines as well as what has been said of "Jugendandacht" 1, there can be very little doubt concerning Eichendorff's intent; the young man in our poem, quite unwittingly, begins to experience the same move-

ment of love as the ludicrous poet in *Ahnung und Gegenwart.*
The song flows like a stream which explains why the poet can
say, "losgebunden in das Licht sie bluten." We should not be
disturbed by the insinuation of blood. A "Marmorbild" scene will
instruct us that the song which Florio sings "courses" through
the limbs of a marble statue and brings it to life. The youth's
song is Venus' lifeblood. From man's wound flows the song which
gives life to what must not be. The word "losbinden" is not used
in conjunction with unbandaging a wound; its basic connotation
suggests a release of what had been held in restraint. There is
a pattern to the structure of this thought which is matched by
Florio's words at the beginning of the "Marmorbild" story. "Ich
habe jetzt . . . das Reisen erwählt und befinde *mich wie aus
einem Gefängnis erlöst,* alle *alten Wünsche* und *Freuden* sind
nun auf einmal in *Freiheit* gesetzt" (II, 307-308), italics mine).
The enigmatic aspect of the two lines in "Jugendandacht" cannot be clarified unless "alte Wunden" are equated with "alte
Wünsche und Freuden" and "losgebunden" is understood as
"in Freiheit gesetzt." Christianity is, in a sense, a prison, and
Florio feels released from this prison which, in turn, gives free
reign to human desire. That is why the Christ child tells Friedrich, "Gehe mit mir unter," be my prisoner. When man is the
prisoner of Christ then the world is free. St. Paul twice begins
his epistles with the words: "I, a prisoner in Christ" (Eph. 3, 1).
Spring, once again, is not a season, but a disposition of the
heart. It is the awakening of love; thus it is always associated
with "Jugend," and love is the energizing agent of man's movement to the heights or the depths. Man's freedom to love what
he will and reject the Creator moves Eichendorff to speak of
the wound which is called old precisely as Florio's joys and desires are called old! In both instances we are concerned with a
youth and the adjective *old* is meaningless unless we think of
man's nature. To sum up then: Since the Fall, man's nature is
wounded, or no longer whole. And his love may "flow" to the
depths or the heights. In Eichendorff's works we find spring
as a trinity. There is the spring of the year, "Frühlingszeit,"
the spring of the human heart and the spring of divine love.
Nature's spring is but a reminder to man that he, too, must
blossom forth. But toward which light does the flower turn?
In "Trauriger Frühling" we see that nature's spring is not sufficient for the heart.

Mir ist's im Kopf so wüste,
Die Zeit wird mir so lang,
Wie auch der Lenz mich grüsste,
Mit Glanz und frischem Klang,
Das Herz bleibt mir so wüste.
Mir ist so sterbensbang.

Viel' Vöglein lockend sangen
Im blühenden Revier,
Ich hatt' mir eins gefangen,
Jetzt ist es weit von mir,
Viel' Vöglein draussen sangen,
Ach, hätt' ich meins nur hier!

(I, 215; 1837)

The reader will recall our discussion of the poem "Der
Knabe."[6] The youth had lost the little bird; his love had escaped him. That is why the speaker in the above poem feels "sterbensbang." Nature is filled with light and song but the speaker
cannot respond. What was elsewhere called "das verwandte
Licht und Lied" is not in him. He cannot sing the praises of the
Lord as nature would. Let us go back almost twenty years to
another poem, "Trauriger Winter."

Nun ziehen Nebel, falbe Blätter fallen,
Öd' alle Stellen, die uns oft entzücket!
Und noch einmal tief' Rührung uns beglücket,
Wie aus der Flucht die Abschiedslieder schallen.

Wohl manchem blüht aus solchem Tod Gefallen:
Dass er, nun eng ans blühnde Herz gedrücket,
Von roten Lippen holdre Sträusse pflücket,
Als Lenz je beut mit Wäldern, Wiesen allen.

Mir sagte niemals ihrer Augen Bläue:
"Ruh auch aus! Willst du ewig sinnen?"
Und einsam sah ich so den Sommer fahren.

So will ich tief des Lenzes Blüte wahren,
Und mit Erinnern zaubrisch mich umspinnen,
Bis ich nach langem Traum erwach' im Maie.

(I, 214; 1808)

There is much in this poem which reminds us of "Die Zauberei
im Herbste." Although it is winter, the heart seems to hear

and respond to the "Abschiedslieder" of the birds which fly
away at summer's end (II, 975). And this song of late summer
is translated into a spring awakened by the lips of woman.
Here man finds "flowers" even more beautiful, it would seem,
than another spring can offer. But this spring of a dying summer is associated with death. The eyes of this woman, upon whose
lips the flowers of "death" are found, do not speak of peace.
With her there is eternal restlessness, incompleteness; no whole-
ness is found with her. And so he decides to stay alone. He will
guard, preserve, not let escape, the blossom of "spring." (We
shall see later that Florio's rose escapes "aus grüner Klause.")
The blossom is his love; it must bloom in the May, in another
spring. He will remember,[7] his thoughts will be directed toward that other spring, he will wrap himself, as in a cocoon, in the
memory of another light in which the blosson, "des Lenzes
Blüte," may burst forth in glory. There is in all this the hint
of the butterfly, an ancient symbol of resurrection. The present
which he experiences, the summer which is a winter, is but a
dream. For Eichendorff there is but one true season. He is
not the nature poet we think him to be. It can be spring in
any season. And nature's spring is pointless unless that other
spring fills the heart.

Frühlingsklage

Ach, was frommt das Wehen, Sprossen
In der schönen Frühlingszeit:
Ist des Liedes Born verschlossen
Und der Seele Freudigkeit,
Die erst Blüten bringt den Sprossen
Und den Frühling in die Zeit.

Gib den alten Frieden wieder,
In der Brust den Sonnenschein,
Gib die Laute mir und Lieder,
Dann lass blühen oder schnein,
Selbst weck' ich den Lenz mir wieder,
Sollt' es auch der letzte sein!

(I, 103; um 1820)

"Born, Brunnen, Quelle;" it is all the same. The stream of
song must well forth from the heart filled with the light of the
sun, that cool light which penetrates the tired breast when man

says, "Hier bin ich Herr!" Observe that it is joy, Friedrich's "innere Freudigkeit," which is the "wahre göttliche Gnade" which causes the vine to blossom and brings the spring into time.[8] Now his song may rise and join the mystical stream of which Faber speaks.

> Da hebt die Sonne aus dem Meer
> Eratmend ihren Lauf;
> *Zur Erde geht was feucht und schwer,*
> *Was klar,* zu *ihr hinauf.*
>
> (I, 83, italics mine)

If man's song contains the alleluia, it rises to the sun; if it speaks only of man himself, it sinks back and covers the earth. Only what is done in His name lives; all else dies. The "sun" draws man's love from the waters.

An . . .

> *Was lebte rollt' zum Himmel aus dem Tale,*
> Des Ritters Mut, *Gesanges feur'ge Zungen,*
> Und aus den *Felsen Münster* kühn geschwungen,[9]
> Das Kreuz erhebend hoch im Morgenstrahle.
>
> Versunken sind die alten Wundermale,
> Nur eine Waldkapelle unbezwungen,
> Blieb einsam stehen über Niederungen,
> Die läutet fort und fort hinab zum Tale.
>
> Was frägt die Menge, ob's der Winde verwehe, —
> Nur ein'ge trifft der Laut, die stehn erschrocken,
> Und mahnend lockt's wie Heimweh sie zur Höhe.
>
> (I, 126, italics mine)

Very few have the humility to listen and feel touched by the call to adore what transcends man and his works. Man is the great leveler; he reduces everything so that he may seem to be above all. Man touches all with his light so that his world may seem "grösser, schöner und gewaltiger," but it only seems thus. Whatever, even that which was once sacred, is touched by the mind and heart of man who forgets his God is described as "versunken." This is the second deluge worked by the rebellion of man who is the instrument of his salvation and damnation. Our poet consistently employs the imagery in this sense: all is immersed in the waters of time, that ocean formed by man's "Lust und Leid, alte Freuden und Wünsche." This is the ocean that the Christian must cross and the waves with which he must contend.

Spruch

Drüben von dem sel'gen Lande
Kommt ein seltsam Grüssen her,
Warum zagst du noch am Strande?
Graut dir, weil im falschen Meer
Draussen auf verlornem Schiffe
Mancher frische Segler sinkt
Und von halbversunknem Riffe
Meerfey nachts verwirrend singt?
Wagst du's nicht draufhin zu stranden,
Wirst du nimmer drüben landen!

(I, 74, 1835)

Schifferspruch

Wenn die Wogen unten toben,
Menschenwitz zuschanden wird,
Weist mit feur'gen Zügen droben
Heimwärts dich der Wogen Hirt.
Sollst nach keinem andern fragen,
Nicht zurückschaun nach dem Land,
Fass das Steuer, lass das Zagen!
Aufgerollt hat Gottes Hand
Diese Wogen zum Befahren
Und die Sterne, dich zu wahren.

(I, 310; 1839)

Glückliche Fahrt

Wünsche sich mit Wünschen schlagen,
Und die Gier wird nie gestillt.
Wer ist in dem wüsten Jagen
Da der Jäger, wer das Wild?
Selig, wer es fromm mag wagen,
Durch das Treiben dumpf und wild
In der festen Brust zu tragen
Heil'ger Schönheit hohes Bild!

Sieh, da brechen tausend Quellen
Durch die felsenharte Welt,
Und zum Strome wird ihr Schwellen,
Der melodisch steigt und fällt,
Ringsum sich die Fernen hellen,
Gottes Hauch die Segel schwellt —
Rettend spülen dich die Wellen
In des Herzens stille Welt.

(I, 74; 1835)

We have returned to the stream of song composed of a thousand "Quellen," those poets whose song rises and falls. Our Eichendorff "sails" upon this stream, but it is God's breath which gives him movement and direction and not the stream. (Eichendorff knows that he stands aside from the main-stream of poetry. See "Berliner Tafel" [I, 91], especially the fourth strophe.) This stream works its will on the hardness of the world and moves toward light. The waves of this stream gently convey the self into the quiet world of the heart in which, as the first strophe tells us, he carries "ein Bild." This journey, and the poem is called "Glückliche Fahrt," is described by the word "rettend," and the individual who moves in this direction is called "selig und fromm." When we look at these words or even the entire poem the reader familiar with Eichendorff should see a rather accurate description of the "Taugenichts" who is "der frohe Wandersmann." His marching song is "Wem Gott will rechte Gunst erweisen,/Den schickt er in die weite Welt." Combine this with the poem "Glückliche Fahrt" and we must suggest that "die weite Welt," in a sense, is "die stille Welt des Herzens." The imagery of the poem clearly suggest that the self moves inward toward the ideal which is called "Heil'ger Schönheit hohes Bild." This poem, written in 1814, reflects a wisdom and spiritual insight which the younger Eichendorff had to earn. The reader is requested to look carefully at the last four verses of the first strophe. What would happen if the poet does not *dare* to keep this "Bild in der festen Brust?"[10] What if he wants to see?

Jugendandacht 2

Wie in einer Blume himmelblauen
Grund, wo schlummernd träumen stille Regenbogen,

Ist mein Leben ein unendlich Schauen,
Klar durchs ganze Herz Ein süsses Bild gezogen.

Stille sass ich, sah die Jahre fliegen,
Bin im Innersten dein treues Kind geblieben;
Aus dem duft'gen Kelche aufgestiegen,
Ach! wann lohnst du endlich auch mein treues Lieben!

(I, 275)

In our own minds we must pursue the pattern, retrace the coalescence of imagery, which enables us to understand the unfolding noetic structure. The youth's life consists of a looking into the sky-blue depths of a flower. This is a covert allusion to "sel'ge Zeit entflossener Himmelsbläue." Combine this with "der Augen Himmel" and "Im Angesicht der Stillen" and we have the impression that the youth has been gazing at the woman who is now identified as a flower. The verb "ist," used in its own right and as an auxiliary verb, tends to unite the first two verses with the last two. This leads us to speculate that woman, flower, image are really one. The last line states that the "Bild" moves through his heart; we thus become suspicious as to where this "Grund und Blume" really are. "Zeit der Himmelsbläue" is, as we know, "entflossen;" a similar pattern is given to us by the words "Ein süsses Bild (ist) gezogen." Is the original image still in his heart or has it been replaced by a flower? Considering poem one, the reader tends to assume that this "Bild" refers to the Virgin Mary, "die Ewigreine." Spritually speaking, the youth views himself as her child. Can we equate flower with the Virgin? If this were our intent, we would have no difficulty "proving" the point. One of the songs in the group called "Lieder," written about 1808, contains the following strophe:

Maria, schöne Rose!
Wie stünd' ich freudelose,
Hätt' ich nicht dich ersehn
Vor allen Blumen schön.

(I, 281)

The ideas of flower and seeing are nicely reproduced in this strophe, and we might be tempted to ignore the last strophe which makes a disconcerting reference to other flowers. If we pursue this matter and inspect the strophe just prior to the one quoted, we are given a different impression.

> Im Garten zu spazieren
> Die Blumen mich verführen,
> Die Augen aus dem Grün,
> Die Quellen und das Blühn.

We would be most ill-advised to assume that Eichendorff speaks of a conventional garden with flowers and a babbling brook. Everything in this seemingly simple little poem has a figurative meaning. Every man is a garden, and the flowers he cultivates tend to tell us who he is. Our "Taugenichts" also sings a song called "Der Gärtner."

> In meinem Garten find' ich
> Viel' Blumen, schön und fein,
> Viel' Kränze wohl draus wind' ich
> Und tausend Gedanken bind' ich
> Und Grüsse mit darein.
>
> Ihr darf ich keinen reichen,
> Sie ist zu hoch und schön,
> Die müssen alle verbleichen,
> Die Liebe nur ohnegleichen
> Bleibt ewig im Herzen stehn.

(I, 199-200)

Young "Taugenichts" is a highly unorthodox person. He is appointed "Zolleinnehmer" and immediately throws out all the vegetables in his garden and replaces them with flowers, an utterly useless item for man's bodily needs. It becomes his custom to pick a bouquet every evening and place them on a table for his lady fair, whom he never sees. The poem above, however, tells us that he dare not, must not, give her any of these flowers. All these flowers must die; in effect, the bouquet, which could be understood as an expression of his respect, love, veneration, is simply unacceptable. Why? What is wrong with these flowers? In the poem "An die Freunde," which introduces the selection of poems "Frühling und Liebe," our poet provides us with an interesting variation of the flower theme.

> Der Jugend Glanz, der Sehnsucht irre Weisen,
> Die tausend Ströme durch das duft'ge Land,
> Es zieht uns all' zu seinen Zauberkreisen. —
> Wem Gottesdienst in tiefster Brust entbrannt,

Der sieht mit Wehmut ein unendlich Reisen
Zu fernen Heimat, die er fromm erkannt;
Und was sich s p i e l e n d wob als ird'sche Blume,
Wölbt still den Kelch zum e r n s t e n Heiligtume.

(I, 179)

What is the essential content of the poem? The first three
lines refer to life into which man is drawn, a veritable magic
circle that encompasses the individual. The human being has
become a prisoner. The next three verses describe the man burning with desire to do God's will. The last two lines speak of the
effect which this desire has upon life. I believe I have found
a logical and workable definition for one aspect of "die Blume";
"die ird'sche Blume" concerns "Jugend Glanz, Sehnsucht irre
Weisen, tausend Ströme, das duft'ge Land." When life is dedicated
to the Father, a spiritual metamorphosis occurs and the flower
becomes "ein ernstes Heiligtum." One strophe in the poem "Götterdämmerung" informs us: "Und was hier versunken/Als
Blume zum Spiel,/Siehst oben du funkeln/Als Sterne nun
kühl." In other words, the radiance of youth, the confused song
of human yearning, streams of poetry, and even the beauty of
creation may be for man's enjoyment but must not become an
end for him. His own joys and desires cannot be the star which
guides him to eternity. That is why the "vielschöne gnädige
Frau" does not accept his bouquet. As we shall see in a later discussion, when these flowers are rejected, the "Taugenichts" has
forgotten that "die ird'sche Blume" must become "ein ernstes Heiligtem." At the time that he gives her these flowers,
"Gottesdienst" does not burn in his heart because he has become a "Zolleinnehmer," a publican.

If we now look at the first strophe of "Jugendandacht" 2
we can make one important statement about this flower. The
speaker in the poem is seemingly transfixed in literally staring
into its depths. The lines suggest a hypnotic attentiveness. This
same soulful gazing is a significant feature of Florio's first encounter with "das Bild." "Florio stand wie eingewurzelt im
Schauen,[11] denn ihm kam jenes Bild wie eine langsgesuchte,
nun plötzlich erkannte *Geliebte* vor, wie eine *Wunderblume,* aus
der Frühlingsdämmerung und träumerischen Stille seiner frühesten *Jugend* heraufgewachsen" (II, 318, italics mine). Here we
find the same hypnotic gaze, the same reference to "Bild und

Blume," the same confusion of time. The reference to "Stille" and "frühester Jugend" is a perfect explanation of what transpires in the heart of the youth in "Jugendandacht." The evidence provided by Eichendorff's imagery tends to insist that the flower into which the youth gazes is not *the* rose but another flower that grows in his garden. In order to suggest how man must see, let us call upon the "Taugenichts" and the first strophe of "Der Gartner."

> Wohin ich geh' und schaue,
> In Feld und Wald und Tal,
> Vom Berg' ins Himmelsblaue,
> Vielschöne gnäd'ge Fraue,
> Grüss' ich dich tausendmal!

(II, 353)

We observe that this is, as it were, a free seeing; it is not a hypnotized gazing or staring. In this poem the "Taugenichts" does not see his "vielschöne gnädige Frau"; his seeing, which embraces heaven and earth, is a greeting of her. The difference is crucial. The very description of the action insinuates movement while the phrase "ein unendlich Schauen" connotes rigidity. His seeing is a spiritual penetration of the "Erscheinung," which is not an end in itself. Although poem two contains other aspects to which we shall return, we must turn to poem three and pursue our discussion of the veil.

Jugendandacht 3

Was wollen mir vertraun die blauen Weiten,
  Des Landes Glanz, die Wirrung süsser Lieder,
  Mir ist so wohl, so bang! Seid ihr es wieder
  Der frommen Kindheit stille Blumenzeiten?

Wohl weiss ich's — dieser Farben heimlich Spreiten
  Deckt einer Jungfrau strahlend reine Glieder;
  Es wogt der grosse Schleier auf und nieder,
  Sie schlummert drunten fort seit Ewigkeiten.

Mir ist in solchen linden, blauen Tagen,
  Als müssten alle Farben auferstehen,
  Aus blauer Fern' sie endlich zu mir gehen.

So wart' ich still, schau' in den Frühling milde,
Das ganze Herz weint nach dem süssen Bilde,
Vor Freud', vor Schmerz? — Ich weiss es nicht zu sagen.

(I, 275)

In strophe one the created seems bent upon revealing a mystery to man, but the human creature is uncertain as to what nature says. The youth then asks his own question, and what he wants to know has to do with a way of life or a spiritual orientation toward the created, described by the words "frommen Kindheit stille Blumenzeiten." What this phrase suggests is seen best in a conversation between Rosa and Friedrich who tells her about his childhood. He speaks of certain books that he had read and of their impact upon him.

Ich weiss nicht, ob der Frühling mit seinen Zauberlichtern in diese Geschichten hineinspielte, oder ob sie den Lenz mit ihren rührenden Wunderscheinen überglänzten, — aber Blumen, Wald und Wiesen erschienen mir damals anders und schöner. Es war, als hätten mir diese Bücher die goldenen *Schlüssel zu* den Wunderschätzen und *der verborgenen Pracht der Natur* gegeben. Mir war noch nie so fromm und fröhlich zu Mute gewesen" (II, 54, italics mine).

We can see that the essential and most significant aspect of the passage is the constant and varied reference to a light which seems to bathe all in a transcendental glory, enhancing the significance of all things. Those years are "still" and not yet characterized by that blind and restless reaching into the created in search of "des verlornen Himmels." The compound, "Blumenzeiten," combines significant facets of poems one and two. "O sel'ge Zeit entflossener Himmelsbläue" is merged with "ein unendlich Schauen in den himmelblauen Grund einer Blume." The word "Blumenzeiten" exemplifies what we have deduced from the imagery; the youth unites and treats as one what must be kept separate, namely, "Liebe und Andacht." And, once again, this is the same question Fortunato puts to Florio. A similar progression can be seen in the poet's use of the word *blue*. In poem one we saw "Himmelsbläue" which then became associated with the "himmelblauen Grund einer Blume" and now reappears as "die blauen Weiten." With one word, *blue*, we have moved from that which is associated with heaven to that which is of this earth. Eternity has become time and time is now a place. The movement of Florio's own springtime will become the "Venusberg." In both instances "Andacht" has become "Liebe," or to speak more precisely as the imagery instructs us, the youth thinks they are synonymous. But, and this is a factor in the spiritual equation which Eichendorff always includes, man feels the error of his movement and is touched by fear, thus, "Mir ist so wohl, so bang!" The youth questions if he still lives within the time of pious childhood. This note of fear introduces the next strophe.

Colors are capable of a mysterious extension, a spreading out as it were, from a center. This movement of the colors constitutes the veil, a veritable kaleidoscope, which conceals "einer Jungfrau strahlend reine Glieder." White light, broken into its components, contains all the colors of the rainbow; and yet we cannot say of the red, green, and blue light that it is white. To approach this problem of light and colors let us recall Friedrich's reference to "jenes ewige Gefuhl . . . das uns wie in den Mittelpunkt alles Lebens versenkt, wo alle die Farbenstrahlen, gleich Radien, aus-gehn und sich an der wechselnden Oberfläche zu dem schmerz-lich-schönen Spiele der Erscheinung gestalten" (II, 75). We have in this passage a remarkable summary of the rational struc-ture which we detected in the imagery of "Jugendandacht." But we also discern a most significant difference which concerns the verb "spreiten." If the artist, instead of being concerned with the center of being, the light, from which all colors emerge, should feel that the play of the colors is the proper domain of artistic creativity, what then? Raimund in "Die Zaüberei im Herbste" has given us part of the answer. After his experience with the wom-an he had regained a measure of freedom and felt that the Lord had turned his countenance to him.

> Und als nun der Herbst wieder sein wunderlich farbiges Netz über Berg und Tal ausspreitete, da schweiften von neuem einzelne wohlbekannte Töne aus dem Walde in meine Ein-samkeit und dunkle Stimmen in mir klangen sie wider und gaben ihnen Antwort, und im Innersten erschreckten mich noch immer die Glockenklänge des fernen Doms, wenn sie am klaren Sonntagsmorgen über die Berge zu mir herüberlang-ten, als suchten sie das alte, stille Gottesreich der Kindheit in meiner Brust, das nicht mehr in ihr war (II, 983).

This passage, very much like Friedrich's words, reflect the thoughts in "Jugendandacht" 3. Friedrich is drawn to the center of light while Raimund and the youth in our poem are drawn to the colors. In these colors, both of them hear a call, a song. Raimund offers us an explanation of what had driven him to seek this lovely madness. "Es gibt vom Leben Berauschte — ach, wie schrecklich ist es, dann auf einmal wieder nüchtern zu werden" (II, 974). This word "Leben" brings us to Faber, the maker of illusions, who defends himself and what he represents. "Ein fröhlicher Künstler mag sich vor euch hüten. Denn wer die Gegenwart aufgibt, wie Freidrich, wem die frische Lust am Leben und seinem überschwenglichen Reichtume gebrochen ist, mit dessen Poesie ist es aus. Er ist wie ein Maler ohne Farben" (II, 297). The poet's thoughts, we are told, must be directed toward "die Gegenwart" or life because this constitutes the "colors" of existence. But the very title of the novel, *Ahnung und Gegenwart,* implies that there is a more which is not really inherent in the visible. We must combine this with another Eichendorff premise, namely, that in man's breast rests the dream of a reality which transcends all that his sense-conditioned awareness can reveal. This is "Ahnung." In "Jugendandacht" 2 this is suggested by the sky-blue ground "wo schlummernd träumen stille Regenbogen." This is the bridge to the beyond, a bridge which the poet may seek to build with colors. Many poems could be cited which provide evidence for our conclusion, but I should like to use a wonderful passage which is found in "Dichter und ihre Gesellen." A stranger, who is really Victor the poet, explains a garden to Fortunat:

> Jetzt standen sie an dem Abhange des Berges, dessen obere Fläche das Schloss und der eigentliche Ziergarten einnahmen. Von der mit Efeu umrankten Felsenwand sah man hier plötzlich in tiefe Schluchten und Wiesenplätze hinab, wo in kühlen Schatten uralter Bäume Rehe und Damhirsche weideten, die scheu die Köpfe nach ihnen emporhoben und dann pfeilschnell im tieferen Dunkel verschwanden. — "Sehen Sie da", rief Fortunatos Begleiter aus, "das Grossartige und Kühne dieser Komposition. Ich betrete diesen Ort nie ohne Ehrfurcht vor dem seltenen Genius dieses Dichtergrafen — oder sagen wir es nur lieber grad heraus Dichterkönigs! besonders muss ich Sie hier auf jene leicht geschwungenen Brücken aufmerksam machen. Sie führen, wie Sie

sehen, über die Wipfel der Bäume hinweg nach einzeln stehenden, hohen, abgerissenen Felsen hinüber, die, mit ihren
bunten Gärtchen auf den Wipfeln, wie funkelnde Blumenzinnen über Waldeseinsamkeit emporragen. Diesen Einfall
hat der liebenswürdige Graf vor dem lieben Gott voraus,
er legte diese hängenden Gärten an; das waren die Blocksberge seiner Phantasie. Hier pflegte er als Knabe, wenn
ein Gewitter heraufzog und im Schlosse alles ängstlich durch-
einanderlief, vor der unermesslichen Aussicht zu sitzen,
mit den Beinen über dem Abgrunde baumelnd, bis ihm die
ersten dicken Regentropfen an die seidenen Strümpfe klatsch-
ten." — "Es freut mich" — erwiderte Fortunat, der,
ganz in den Anblick des wunderbaren Grundes versunken,
die letzten Worte fast überhört hatte — "es freut mich
recht, dass Sie Victors poetische Erscheinung so hoch halten" (II, 518-519) .

In these lines all is figurative rather than literal. Ancient
trees are God-oriented thoughts among which not deer but the
faithful dwell. "Das Reh" is an old symbol for the faithful of the
church. This is the garden, which represents the intent of the
poet-king who is the Creator. And in this garden the poet, who
is Victor, has created bridges which represent his own efforts to
transcend his finiteness. Victor now mocks the futility of his own
creative endeavors by employing imagery which reminds us of the
hanging gardens of Babylon, the glory of a heathen world. The
riot of color inherent in the words "funkelnde Blumenzinnen"
are really "die Blocksberge seiner Phantasie." The cold satire in
Victor's words is still a passionate cry of despair on Raimund's
lips who admits "meine Liebe und mein ganzes Leben eine lange
Täuschung" (II, 984) . All that should be said about "Leben," as
we would want the word understood, is given to us in the poem
"Frische Fahrt" which heads the selection of "Wanderlieder," the
song which characterizes Romana's own existence.

> Laue Luft kommt blau geflossen,
> Frühling, Frühling soll es sein!
> Waldwärts Hörnerklang geschossen,
> Mut'ger Augen lichter Schein;
> Und das Wirren bunt und bunter
> Wird ein magisch wilder Fluss,
> In die schöne Welt hinunter
> Lockt dich dieses Stromes Gruss.

Und ich mag mich nicht bewahren!
Weit von euch treibt mich der Wind,
Auf dem Strome will ich fahren,
Von dem Glanze selig blind!
Tausend Stimmen lockend schlagen,
Hoch Aurora flammend weht,
Fahre zu! Ich mag nicht fragen,
Wo die fahrt zu Ende geht!

(I, 9)

Poetry is a sweet traveling companion; but there is another, a more serious and splendid "Reisegefährtin" whose image is in the heart of our "Taugenichts." "Mädchenliebe" is on the same plane of love as "Poesie," Faber's "Poesie." That is why he and his counterpart, Dryander, in *Dichter und ihre Gesellen,* are depicted as falling in love with young girls who make sport of them. Indeed, Dryander, on a lovely moonlight night, is convinced that he is kneeling before the Virgin Mary. These comments are all facets of the line most important for our purpose: ". . . was einem zu dem Liede verführte." This thought or its equivalent is frequently voiced in Eichendorff's works. What he really would do is impossible. He has to use "das Sinnliche" to suggest what transcends the sensual. He has to use "Bilder" to insinuate what cannot be seen, and yet he detests "die leere, willkürliche, sich selbst zerstörende Schwelgerei in Bildern" (II, 142). Sensations and feelings are utterly unreliable because they are conditioned by flesh and blood and speak only of the self; yet he must refer to "das ewige Gefühl" which, so to speak, places man in the center of existence. To my knowledge, no other German poet uses the "als ob, als wie" construction quite the same way or as profusely as Eichendorff. On every page he suggests that experiences have an *as if* quality about them. The very "colors" which he distrusts he has to use. He insists "Die Poesie liegt vielmehr in einer fortwährend begeisterten Anschauung und Betrachtung der Welt und der menschlichen Dinge" (II, 142). True, but easily said. Life is "Gegenwart," a spectrum of color, a veritable stream which carries the human creature "in die Ferne." But, because they are only his sensations, he never in truth escapes from himself. This principle of extension, actually a basic law in physics, is given us by the word "spreiten." Man's sensations emanate from the center, himself, which implies that he is the light which defines, renders visible, his reality. It requires but a simple substitution of one word, *love* instead of *light*, and we can say that man sees in terms of his own love. This is not an arbitrary step but is dictated by the poet's imagery. Let us return to the poem and the woman.

The woman who sleeps below must be Venus. We have pointed out Florio's observation as he enters her garden for the first time; her realm is immersed in the enchanted waters and dreams only of the past, that love which must not be since Christ has lived and died. Venus also sings her song which contains the line; "So mich auch ruft ihr aus dem stillen Hause" (II, 322). She is called and asked to arise from the grave. Poem two has already told us this. "Aus dem duft'gen Kelche aufgestiegen,/Ach! wann lohnst du endlich auch mein treues Lieben!" The perplexing imagery of this second poem now can be seen more clearly. What is called "Ein süsses Bild" is in a "flower" which "grows" in his heart. We recall Raimund's description of his own heart in which "alle die versteinerten Blumen mit schauerlichem Liebesblick heraufblitzen." It follows, then, that the youth sees in terms of his own love and everything which now transpires will be a sinking into the self. The poet is a gardener who cultivates flowers which seem to contain or become a woman. This enables our poet to speak, as he does so frequently, of the beloved. Is she Venus or the Virgin? With one woman the poet rises, with the other he sinks. Once again we turn to "Das Marmorbild" to inspect how Eichendorff uses this idea ten years later. Florio meets Bianca (whose name means white light) at the beginning of the story, is drawn to her and then, unable to resist the bright beauty of the moonlight, wanders into the melodious mystery of the night and sings his song "Liebe in der Fremde" (even the title is instructive). After singing this song he admits to himself that he really wasn't thinking of Bianca. "Die Musik bei den Zelten, der Traum auf seinem Zimmer und *sein* die Klänge und den Traum und die zierliche Erscheinung des Mädchens *nachträumendes Herz* hatten ihr Bild unmerklich und wundersam verwandelt in ein viel schöneres, grösseres und herrlicheres, wie er es noch nirgends gesehen" (II, 317-318, italics mine). The purity of Bianca had been changed "unmerklich und wundersam" — precisely the same process is insinuated in "Jugendandacht" — into something else. The next morning Fortunato warns him of what is transpiring in his heart and soul, but

Florio rejects all counsel. "Ich lasse mich von Euch nicht irre-machen, es gibt noch *sanfte und hohe Empfindungen,* die wohl schamhaft sind, aber sich nicht zu schämen brauchen, und ein stilles *Glück,* das sich vor dem lauten Tage verschliesst und nur dem Sternenhimmel den heiligen Kelch öffnet wie *eine Blume,* in der ein Engel wohnt" (II, 319, italics mine). These two passages bring together woman, the heart, and the flower; they substan-tiate the conclusion expressed above, that the heart, man's love, is the matrix for the earthly flower defined as "Jugend Glanz, der Sehnsucht irre Weisen, ein stilles Glück," and which, in turn, becomes the temple of Venus. In short, man's heart is Venus' temple. Let us not forget that Florio comes upon a small pond on the shores of which stands a mutilated statue surrounded by ancient ruins into which Florio's "alte Wünsche und Freuden" breathe new life. He "rebuilds" the temple and pays court to the ancient goddess after having resurrected her from the grave. In order that some of the emblems which we have been discus-sing may be viewed in one context, I offer for consideration the tableau vivant which Friedrich witnesses. The passage is rather long but we would not wish to delete even one line although certain aspects cannot receive comment in this context.

Man sah nämlich sehr überrascht ins Freie, überschaute statt eines Theaters die grosse, wunderbare Bühne der Nacht selber, die vom Monde beleuchtet draussen ruhte. Schräge über die Gegend hin streckte sich ein ungeheurer Riesenschatten weit hinaus, auf dessen Rücken eine hohe, weibliche Gestalt erhoben stand. Ihr langes weites Gewand war durchaus blendendweiss, die eine Hand hatte sie ans Herz gelegt, mit der andern hielt sie ein Kreuz zum Him-mel empor. Das Gewand schien ganz und gar von Licht durchdrungen und strömte von allen Seiten einen milden Glanz aus, der eine himmlische Glorie um die ganze Ge-stalt bildete und sich ins Firmament zu verlieren schien, wo oben an seinem Ausgange einzelne wirkliche Sterne hindurch-schimmerten. Rings unter dieser Gestalt war ein dunkler Kreis hoher, traumhafter, phantastisch ineinander ver-schlungener Pflanzen, unter denen unkenntlich verworrene Gestalten zerstreut lagen und schliefen, als ware ihr wun-derbarer Traum über ihnen abgebildet. Nur hin und her endigten sich die höchsten dieser Pfanzengewinde in ein-zelne Lilien und Rosen, die von der Glorie, der sie sich zuwandten, berührt und verklärt wurden und in deren Kelchen goldene Kanarienvögel sassen und in dem Glanze mit den Flügeln schlugen. Unter den dunklen Gestalten des untern Kreises war nur eine kenntlich. Es war ein Ritter, der sich, der glänzenden Erscheinung zugekehrt, auf beide Knie aufgerichtet hatte und auf ein Schwert stützte, und dessen goldene Rüstung von der Glorie hell beleuchtet wurde. Von der andern Seite stand eine schöne, weibliche Gestalt in griechischer Kleidung, wie die Alten ihre Göttinnen abbildeten. Sie war mit bunten, vollen Blumengewinden umhangen und hielt mit beiden aufgehobenen Armen eine Zimbel, wie zum Tanze, hoch in die Höh', so dass die ganze regelmässige Fülle und Pracht der Glieder sichtbar wurde. Das Gesicht erschrocken von der Glorie abgewendet, war sie nur zur Hälfte erleuchtet; aber es war die deutlichste und vollendetste Figur. Es schien, als wäre die irdische, lebenslustige Schönheit von dem Glanze jener himmlischen berührt, in ihrer bacchantischen Stellung plötzlich so erstarrt (II, 128-29).

We are told the woman with the cross represents "die himmlische Schönheit." The figure clothed in the Greek costume represents "die irdische, lebenslustige Schönheit" or "die lebenslustige, vor dem Glanz des Christentums zu Stein gewordene Religion[12] der Phantasie" (II, 130). This thought explains Eichendorff's "Erstarrungsmotif." Christianity did not destroy that human thrust of mind and heart which Eichendorff calls die "Religion der Phantasie"; it did, however, declare it lifeless because it is not from on high. Christianity is the living Word of God and other religions are the word of man. The tableau symbolically presents the two religions, the revealed and the man made, in the person of two women. A gentle light comes from the woman with the cross, whose very being is resplendent in a glory that is not hers. She reflects the light into the created, as does "die Stille" in the poem "Jugendandacht." A further delicate touch in the symbolic structure is the insinuation that all light comes from the moon. An older Christianity, much concerned with understanding everything in terms of its faith, saw in the moon, which only reflects the light of the sun, a perfect symbol for the Mediatrix, the Mother of God.

After several rereadings of this passage one begins to see a definite structure, a structure which seems almost Dantesque. The organization of the picture is vertical. It extends out, or up, to where real stars are visible and reaches down into the darkness and depths of the earth. We also note levels or plateaus. The woman with the cross stands between the infinite and the finite. Below her we find a vast circle of vegetation, a fantastically intertwined sea of plants. Below or among these plants is an unrecognizable and confused array of human forms, sleeping figures, for whom the woman with the cross is but a dream. Eichendorff's "phantastisch und Phantasie" generally have a pejorative connotation. As we have seen in our quotation concerning the Greek goddess in the tableau, these words must suggest what is both undedicated and undisciplined; it is a free soaring of the imagination fed by the sensation of the spirit experiencing itself. It delights in the creation of "Bilder" but cares nought for their ground. But let us have Eichendorff define his own terms.

> In wem die Religion zum Leben gelangt, wer in allem Tun und Lassen von der Gnade wahrhaft durchdrungen ist, dessen Seele mag sich auch in Liedern ihrer Entzucküng und des himmlischen Glanzes erfreuen. Wer aber hochmütig und schlau diese Geheimnisse und einfältigen Wahrheiten als beliebigen Dichtungsstoff zu überschauen glaubt, wer die Religion, die nicht dem Glauben, dem Verstande oder der Poesie allein, sondern allen dreien, dem ganzen Menschen, angehört, bloss mit der Phantasie in ihren einzelnen Schön-heiten willkürlich zusammenrafft, der wird ebenso gern an den griechischen Olymp glauben, als an das Christentum, und eins mit dem andern verwechseln und versetzen, bis der ganze Himmel furchtbar öde und leer wird" (II, 141).

Religion must *be* man's life; it demands *all* of man, heart and mind, "Glaube und Verstand." This thought is of the utmost importance. Literary critics have recognized the faith in our poet's works, but have almost no awareness of his mind or intellectual thrust. This is the manifestation of an ancient prejudice which has generated considerable momentum in the last few centuries. We accept, with a rather condescending tolerance, that man may reach for God with his heart but certainly not with his mind. Eichendorff rejects this categorically. If mind and and heart do not complement each other,[13] then religion becomes the product of human phantasy and *that* man "wird ebenso gern an den griechischen Olymp glauben, als an das Christen-

tum, und eins mit dem andern *verwechseln* und versetzen."
To confuse the one with the other is the central problem in
"Jugendandacht" and "Das Marmorbild." That is why in the
tableau the plants and the flowers which are the product of
human fantasy are between the sleeping figures and the woman
on high. Man lives a dream, and only dreams of life! The vast
mass of vegetation, the great garden of human yearning, desire
and doing, is an unrecognizable and seemingly pointless confusion with the exception of two symbolic flowers, the rose and
the lily. There are very few of them and they are drawn to
the light which apparently touches and transfigures them. These
flowers are the common symbols for love and purity. At the
risk of being overly repetitious, let me say it once more: human
love is to be divested of earthly affiliation, purified of confusing attachments, and, retaining that innocence of which we have
spoken, be given to the Father. Then it may return, transfigured, to the created. This is precisely what the Christ child had
told Friedrich. As we shall see now, the tableau reiterates this.

Of all the figures scattered about among the plants, only one
is recognizable; it is the figure of a knight on bended knee
with sword in hand. We know what the sword is; we also recall
that the youth in "Jugendandacht" kneels "vor der Einen." As
now must be apparent, the youth kneels before the wrong woman. The golden armour that the knight wears is the armour
of God, which reflects the light emanating from the woman toward whom he is turned. The reflected light plays upon the
confusion of man's desires; the flowers, and even the leaves of
the trees tremble in ecstasy as the glory touches them. From
the Mediatrix,[14] divine love moves to the created, and using
the Christian soldier, a human being, as its instrument, the light
pierces the darkness of deception that is man's finite vision.
In another context, Friedrich tells his irascible and caustic
friend Leontin: "Es ist leicht und angenehm, zu verspotten, abér
mitten in der Täuschung den grossen, herrlichen Glauben an
das Bessere festzuhalten und *die andern* mit feurigen Armen
emporzuheben, das gab Gott nur seinen liebsten Söhnen" (II,
74, italics mine). The other is raised toward the light; this is
precisely what Leontin does to Julie (II, 95). The other woman
in this tableau will bring us back to our poem "Jugendandacht."
She is called "die irdische, lebenslustige Schönheit" — Eichendorff could have said "irdische Blume" — whose dance is sud-

denly arrested by the coming of Christianity. Her head, unlike
the knight's, is turned away from the light as though in fright.
(In the "Marmorbild" novella, both Donati and Venus are frightened at a reference to Christianity.) The imagery describing
the Greek goddess suggests the natural order of perfection but
leaves half of her figure in darkness. The garlands of flowers
which twine about her have their origin in the dark circle of
"hoher, traumhafter, phantastisch ineinander verschlungenen
Planzen." This woman is of the earth and she is bound to the
created. The fact that the Greek goddess seems to emerge from
a vast circle of plants and flowers suggests that she is the fairest flower of all, of all "die irdischen Blumen." As Florio approaches Venus in her palace, "erhoben sich hin und her schöne
Mädchen, wie aus Mittagsträumen erwachend, *aus den Blumen,*
schüttelten die dunkeln Locken aus der Stirne" (II, 335, italics
mine). We can now see to better advantage why the youth in
"Jugendandacht" 2 says: "Wie in einer Blume himmelblauen
Grund . . . ist mein Leben ein unendlich Schauen." According
to the text, the Christian poet stands before two women, as
it were, each representing a love, a way of life, a particular
orientation toward the created. The "Taugenichts" faces exactly the same problem. Just after being sent into the world he
is suddenly aware that he is being followed by a coach occupied
by two beautiful ladies intently listening to his song. "Die eine
war besonders schön und jünger als die andere, aber eigentlich gefielen sie mir alle beide" (II, 350). Chronologically, Venus
was before the Virgin is, for the former "schlummert drunten
fort seit Ewigkeiten." The "Taugenichts," ideal Christian minstrel that he is, is nevertheless troubled by the same wound
which afflicts every human being; which love will he embrace?
And Eichendorff says the woman "kennt den sänger an den
Gruss." That is the mystery.

Before returning to "Jugendandacht," I must call attention
to one more significant facet of this tableau. We are told that
the longer one looks at it, "je mehr und mehr wurde das Zauber-
bild von allen Seiten lebending." The structure of this thought
has its exact counterpart in the pond scene of "Das Marmorbild."
The longer Florio looks at the statue the more it seems that its
eyes are opening and the lips wish to greet him, "als blühe
Leben wie ein lieblicher Gesang erwärmend durch die schönen
Glieder herauf." In the tableau the force or energy which seem-

ingly brings life must be the light from the woman with the
cross, that is, divine love; in the pond scene, Florio's love imparts life to the stone. His eyes are the source of life-giving
light, while "die Eine," we are told, raises the veil, "das offen
bliebe/Der Augen Himmel, in das Land zu scheinen." And our long
passage ends with the thought that the entire region, the world,
seems to be awaiting and even celebrating the coming of a splendid morning, a new day, "der das geheimnisvoll gebundene Leben
in herrlicher Pracht lösen soll." Eichendorff demands careful
reading. Heathen life is called "gebunden" because it knows not
the freedom of Christianity; but the new life of Christianity is
also "gebunden" because it is held in chains by man's denial.
Venus' garden dreams of "dem vergangenen Leben" and creation
awaits the life of the future. That is why freedom, described as
both old and new, is given such a confusing structure in our
poet's works.

> Mir ist in solchen linden, blauen Tagen,
> Als müssten alle Farben auferstehen,
> Aus blauer Fern' sie endlich zu mir gehen.

These lines are in the third strophe of "Jugendandacht" 3.
The pronoun "sie" in the last line must refer to "Farben," a reference that seems somewhat awkward when we note the action
"gehen." When we look at poem three in its entirety, however,
it becomes apparent that "sie" equals "Farben" equals "Jungfrau" and the verb "auferstehen" is perfectly plausible when
we consider the last verse of strophe two: "Sie (die Jungfrau)
schlummert drunten fort seit Ewigkeiten." The verb "schlummern" would seem to call for any verb which would suggest a
mere awakening, but the poet chose "auferstehen." In other
words, he prefers the insinuation of a resurrection rather than
a simple awakening. This conforms to our general interpretation,
that what is spiritually dead is brought back to life, a reasoning
clearly substantiated by the imagery in the tableau. But this
strophe in the context of the cycle has another dimension. The
fact that the days are "linde und blau" brings us back to "Jugendandacht" 1 where these words are associated with "Wellen"
and "Zeit entflossener Himmelsbläue." Water and time are telescoped, brought together, and if we combine this with the word
"auferstehen" we are given the impression that the youth would
see what he felt long ago. Is that not what Florio does? It is

almost as though something were to emerge from the depths.
Now if we pursue the adjective *blue* to the last line of this
strophe we seem to be told that this "sie" comes to him from
a great distance. When we consider the force of the word "endlich" one is instructed that he had been waiting for her for a
long time. She belongs in the past and yet she is his future. (See
"Die Zauberin im Walde" [I, 323; 1808] and observe the startling similarity of ideas.)

What does the poet mean with the strange suggestion that
colors are to be resurrected? In our previous discussion we have
identified the various factors of this complex term and concluded that colors are to be equated with "Leben," that particular
"Leben" of which Faber speaks. And does not Venus' garden
dream of "dem vergangenen Leben?" Fortunato explains to
Florio that each spring "das Andenken an die irdische Lust"
calls her "Aus der erschrecklichen Stille des Grabes" (II, 344).
In "Jugendandacht" 1 spring asks the youth "wo Schmerz und
Lust so lange ruhten,/Die süss das Herz verdunkeln und es
hellen?" This youth remembers what he felt as a child and now
lives this feeling. He should be a knight willing to fight for
God's kingdom, but he fails like Raimund. God's warrior is turned toward the Virgin, the very heart beat of Christianity, whose
"Gewand schien ganz und gar von Licht durchdrungen und
strömte von allen Seiten einen milden Glanz aus." The young man
in our poem, however, is turned toward another woman, the one
who represents "die Religion der Phantasie," the woman who is
arrested in her dance, "so dass die ganze regelmässige Fülle
und Pracht der Glieder sichtbar wurde." He moves toward the
depths and sees "einer Jungfrau strahlend reine Glieder." The
knight sees the woman above; the youth sees the woman below. I cannot accept that this careful interweaving of significant imagery is not without design; I must conclude that our
poet has so structured his ideas to suggest that very confusion
of which Friedrich speaks when he observes that human fantasy "wird . . . eins mit dem anderen verwechseln und versetzen," that is, Venus and the Virgin are one and the same.

We left the young man in "Jugendandacht" 3 gazing "in
den Frühling milde" and yearning with tearful heart "nach dem
süssen Bilde." It is the same "Bild" which "Jugendandacht"
2:1 depicts as being in his heart and which in the next strophe
emerges "aus dem duft'gen Kelche." "Jugendandacht" 3 speaks

of the woman who has been sleeping "drunten fort seit Ewig-keiten," and is about to emerge from the colors. We now shall continue our investigation of the significant imagery which describes the resurrection of the "Jungfrau."

Jugendandacht 4

Viel' Lenze waren lange schon vergangen,
   Vorüber zogen wunderbare Lieder,
   Die Sterne gingen ewig auf und nieder,
   Die selbst vor grosser Sehnsucht golden klangen.

Und wie so tausend Stimmen ferne sangen,
   Als riefen mich von hinnen sel'ge Brüder,
   Fühlt' ich die alten Schmerzen immer wieder,
   Seit Deine Blicke, Jungfrau, mich bezwangen.

Da war's, als ob sich still dein Auge hübe,
   Langst sehnsuchtsvoll nach mir mit offnen Armen,
   Fühlst selbst den Schmerz, den Du mir süss gegeben. —

Umfangen fühl' ich innigst mich erwarmen,
   Berührt mit goldnen Strahlen mich das Leben,
   Ach, dass ich ewig Dir am Herzen bliebe!

(I, 275-276)

The first strophe reiterates the passage of time, but a time measured in terms of "Lieder" sung in a certain spring. It is a period filled with yearning and even the stars seem to echo the desire in his heart and sing a golden song. The second strophe offers an interesting study in cause and effect. Since the glances of the "Jungfrau" subdued him, the singing of a thousand voices — the song of contemporary poetry experienced by the young Eichendorff — it like the call of "sel'ge Brüder," and he constantly feels the "alten Schmerzen." The structure of this thought may remind us of sonnet three and its modified version discussed in the previous chapter. The song of the "brothers" carries or calls him "von hinnen" and not "dorthin," that is, "das Wunderland oben." The insinuation is precisely as previously described; the youth feels the song is from on high when, in truth, it is the same song as presented in the "Assonanz-lied." The last verse in the second strophe is a clear reference to "Jugendandacht" 1 with its lines: "In ihrem Blick gereinigt alle Triebe." But this referred to "Die Stille, Ewigreine" and the word "Jungfrau," in its context, is associated with "strahlend reine Glieder." The reference to "Schmerzen" seeks to suggest that pain felt "im Angesicht der Stillen"; her love caused this pain. But look at strophe two and it must be clear that the pain which our youth feels has nothing to do with "die Ewigreine." His sensations, his feelings, are pious, but he is deceived. And now briefly: In man's heart are desires, which are flowers, and in these flowers a woman dwells. Eichendorff also refers to her as "das Bild." This image is a duality and represents the two possibilities of love; it will rise to the Creator or remain bound to the created. One woman is flesh and blood but must remain an image in the heart; the other seeks to become flesh and blood and would possess the heart. Eichendorff's imagery dictates that there is a third woman, and her name is poetry. It is best to call her "Dichten" because she is so intimately one with the creative act. The song Frau Venus speaks of "ein wunderbares Wehen" which spreads across the land. This should remind us of "Jugendandacht" 3 and the lines which refer to "dieser Farben heimlich Spreiten." Something is being born or reborn. The same delightfully mysterious movement of birth or resurrection is suggested in the second half of "Götterdämmerung":

> Wenn Frühlingslüfte wehen
> Hold über'm grünen Plan,
> Ein leises Auferstehen
> Hebt in den Tälern an.
>
> (II, 342)

The poet's love determines what is to be "born." Eichendorff's imagery suggest the singular concept that a love affair exists between the poet and the woman called "Dichten." She is a bride whom he woos, but woe to him if his love is not innocent and chaste. That which is born will then be Venus; flesh of his flesh, song of his song, the image created in the name of his desires, the "Wunderblume" who draws life from him as he becomes ever paler, fills with thoughts of death, and then sinks into madness. And Venus is so lovely because she seems to possess all the characteristics of the Queen of Heaven, the Mediatrix who introduces the child to that ineffable loveliness and beauty which is the hunger and deepest yearning of the man. At this point I should like to examine those strophes of "Die Zauberin im Walde" which I reserved for this context.

Und von ihrem Hals behende
Tät' sie lösen eine Kette,
Reicht' mit ihren weissen Händen
Mir die allerschönste Perle.

Nur ein Wort von fremden Klange
Sprach sie da mit rotem Munde,
Doch im Herzen ewig stehen
Wird des Worts geheime Kunde.

Seitdem sass ich wie gebannt dort,
Und wenn neu der Lenz erwachte,
Immer von dem Halsgeschmeide
Eine Perle sie mir brachte.

Ich barg all' im Waldesgrunde,
Und aus jeder Perl' der Fraue
Sprosste eine Blum' zur Stunde,
Wie ihr Auge anzuschauen.

Und so bin ich aufgewachsen,
Tät' der Blumen treulich warten,
Schlummert' oft und träumte golden
In dem schwülen Waldesgarten.

(I, 323-324)

The woman who gives him a pearl is a "wunderschöne Frau"
whom he finds "tief im Herzensgrund." And this pearl! Eichendorff always, so it seems, confuses the issue. Pearls are tears (I,
355). In the Eastern rite the pearl represents the eucharistic
species distributed in communion. It is the "pearl of great price."
In the West, the same pearl suggests salvation and the Word
of God. But Venus is portrayed in the pearl oyster and at her
feet are pearls. What the pearl means in our context depends
upon which woman gives it to the youth. This woman speaks a
mysterious word which has a foreign ("fremden") sound, which
is the opposite of "heimatlich," the word used in conjunction
with the appearance of Fortunato (II, 326). This is really all we
need to identify her, but let us go on. Since then (strophe three
above), he seems imprisoned there, and each spring she brings
another pearl. Now this spring, as we should know, has nothing
to do with the seasons. These are moments of fruition, the blos-
soming forth of what had been in darkness and needed but the
light of love to reveal itself. The poet, as we see in the next

strophe, very carefully avoids the suggestion that the pearl changes into a flower, but states that the flower sprouts from the pearl shortly after it is given to him, "zur Stunde," and it looks like the eye of the "Zauberin." Of course, one is tempted to think of the "Ewigreine" who raises the veil "so dass offen bliebe/Der Augen Himmel, in das Land zu scheinen." But she is not the enchantress. The fifth strophe of the "Zauberin" poem, which comes prior to the five quoted above, reads as follows:

> Und wie ich so *sinnend atme*
> *Stromes*kühl' und *Waldesdüfte,*
> Und ein wundersam Gelüsten
> Mich hinabzog nach den Klüften:
> . . . .

(italics mine)

This is a remarkable formulation, to breathe reflectively the fragrance of thoughts and the cool stream of song (I reject as meaningless that the youth thinks of forests and streams in the literal sense) of one's environment. This poem, although written when Eichendorff was only twenty, already is an analysis of an earlier interior process. It begins with the words, "Schon vor vielen, vielen Jahren,/Sass ich drüben an dem Ufer. . . ." He looks back to where he had been and seeks to understand himself in a time when he did not realize that his love was capable of a movement which as a child he could not comprehend. Although evidence is scant, it seems clear that Eichendorff was very young when he first began to write poetry. His early education was in the hands of Bernhard Heinke and Paul Ciupke. Some of the earlier "Tagebücher" were embellished with his own drawings and paintings and, in a sense, he remained a painter of "Bilder." In short, art and religion were an early and formative experience in the life of the growing youth. This helps us to understand the surprisingly numerous references to the child and poetry, especially the child held prisoner by the thoughts of others. He lived in an atmosphere filled with the songs of poets and thoughts of poetry, painting, and even the theater. The words "Waldesdüfte" and "Stromeskühl" seek to suggest this early influence. A passage in *Ahnung und Gegenwart* offers further evidence. We turn to the conversation between Rosa and Friedrich where he describes his early childhood. He speaks of

reading many religious stories which had made a deep impression upon him. And then he was discovered.

Mein Hofmeister, ein aufgeklärter Mann, kam hinter meine heimlichen Studien und nahm mir die geliebten Bücher weg. Ich war untröstlich. Aber Gott sei Dank, das Wegnehmen kam zu spät. Meine Phantasie hatte auf den waldgrünen Bergen, unter den Wundern und Helden jener Geschichten gesunde, freie Luft genug eingesogen, um sich des Anfalls einer ganzen nüchternen Welt zu erwehren. Ich bekam nun dafür Campes Kinderbibliothek. Da erfuhr ich denn, wie man Bohnen steckt, sich selber Regenschirme macht, wenn man etwa einmal, wie Robinson, auf eine wüste Insel verschlagen werden sollte, nebstbei mehrere zuckergebackene, edle Handlungen, einige Elternliebe und kindliche Liebe in Scharaden. Mitten aus dieser pädagogischen Fabrik schlugen mir einige kleine Lieder von Matthias Claudius rührend und lockend ans Herz. Sie sahen mich in meiner prosaischen Niedergeschlagenheit mit schlichten, ernsten, treuen Augen an, als wollten sie freundlichtröstend sagen: 'Lasset die Kleinen zu mir kommen!' Diese Blumen machten mir den farb- und geruchslosen, zur Menschheitssaat umgepflügten Boden, in welchen sie seltsam genug verpflanzt waren, einigermassen heimatlich. Ich entsinne mich, dass ich in dieser Zeit verschiedene Plätze im Garten hatte, welche Hamburg, Braunschweig und Wandsbeck vorstellten. Da eilte ich denn von einem zum andern und brachte dem guten Claudius, mit dem ich mich besonders gerne und lange unterhielt, immer viele Grüsse mit. Es war damals mein grösster, innigster Wunsch, ihn einmal in meinem Leben zu sehen. Bald aber machte eine neue Epoche, die entscheidende für mein ganzes Leben, dieser Spielerei ein Ende. Mein Hofmeister fing nämlich an, mir alle Sonntage aus der Leidensgeschichte Jesu vorzulesen. Ich hörte sehr aufmerksam zu. Bald wurde mir das periodische, immer wieder abgebrochene Vorlesen zu langweilig. Ich nahm das Buch und las es für mich ganz aus. Ich kann es nicht mit Worten beschreiben, was ich dabei empfand. Ich weinte aus Herzensgrunde, dass ich schluchzte. *Mein ganzes Wesen war davon erfüllt und durchdrungen,* und ich begriff nicht, wie mein Hofmeister und alle Leute im Hause, die doch das alles schon lange wussten,

nicht ebenso gerührt waren und auf ihre alte Weise so ruhig fortleben konnten" (II, 55f., italics mine).

I include this rather long passage for several reasons. An ethic which is described as "sweet" ("zuckergebackene") is hardly appropriate. The Law is always hard and bitter in the beginning. Claudius' songs are called "Blumen," but the soil, the "Christianity," in which they thrive has been altered to receive man's thoughts (the seed) and not God's. The reference to the garden informs us that it becomes something else in the child's mind. This practice, initiated by the child's fantasy, is to become a poetic device. When the child speaks of sending greetings, it refers to its poems and songs which Eichendorff deliberately defines as a form of greeting. This is true of both Florio and the "Taugenichts." Perhaps of greatest significance for our purpose is the expressed amazement that adults who know of Christ's life should go on living as before. In a very special way this insight felt by the child embraces our poet's entire life and works. To know with the mind is utterly useless unless the truth is lived by the body. This, I am sure, contributed to an idea expressed years later, that the poet should not deal in abstractions but cloak the idea in flesh and blood. "Poesie," Venus, the Queen of Heaven, God, and the devil walk the pages of his works. In this context let me offer one example of how poetry is personified. The lines are taken from "Abschiedstafel," written about 1813.

> Zu dir nun, heitre Schöne,
> Wend' ich mich voll Gedanken.
> Wie sie zu dir sich wenden,
> Muss ich so fröhlich sein.
> So weit Poeten wohnen,
> So weit der Wälder Kronen,
> So weit kunstreiche Töne
> Die heiteren Gedanken
> Und Himmelsgrüsse senden:
> Ist alles mein und dein.
>
> Lass nie die Schmach mich sehen,
> Dass auch dein Herz, der Lüge
> Des andern Volks zum Raube,
> Bereuend feig und hohl,
> An Licht und Schmuck mag zagen!

Nicht wahr ist, was sie sagen:
Dass Lieb' und Lust vergehen,
Nicht wahr, dass uns betrüge
Der schöne, freud'ge Glaube,
Und also lebe wohl!

(I, 140)

Poetry is a "heitre Schöne," a lovely woman, who must not fall victim to the disbelief of others. It is man who robs her of the beauty and light which should be and is hers. Eichendorff, the poet, is joyous when his thoughts are directed toward her. With this woman he inhabits a vast realm in which other poets dwell. And observe what defines the reaches of this empire. I would paraphrase the basic idea as follows: wherever there are poets, there will be found the tops of forests, and wherever they are found a song sends forth joyous thoughts and greetings toward heaven. In our discussion of the sword we discovered that man first hid it in the forest (his thoughts) and then topped the trees ("aushauen") so that he no longer would feel the restraint of the Law, God's words. In other words, his thoughts were no longer directed toward God. I therefore suggest that poetry, "die heitre Schone," dwells wherever a poet's thoughts soar up and, as Faber's imagery suggests, seek to join the secret and mysterious stream of song. But poetry, as a gift, is to be used, and she will be to man, the poet, whatever he is to himself.[15] As an introduction to this we should listen to Friedrich's warning.

O lasst unedle Mühe fahren,
O klinget, gleisst und spielet nicht
Mit Licht und Gnad', so ihr erfahren,
Zur Sünde macht ihr das Gedicht!

(II, 299)

When the creative power, "Dichten," is given to one who abuses "Licht und Gnade," then "die heitre Schöne" takes on the form of the rebellious spirit in which it finds its abode. Thus, to cite a less familiar example in Eichendorff's works, Romana (and her very name is suggestive) sings a song called "Die wunderliche Prinzessin." When she is finished one of the listeners feels sure that the princess represents "Poesie," and others

. . . hielten die Prinzessin im Gedicht für die Venus, andere nannten sie die Schönheit, andere nannten sie die Poesie des

Lebens. Es mag wohl die Gräfin selber sein, dachte Friedrich. — "Es ist die Jungfrau Maria als die grosse Welt-Liebe", sagte der genialische Reisende, der wenig acht gegeben hatte, mit vornehmer Nachlässigkeit. "Ei, dass Gott behüte!", brach Friedrich, dem das Gedicht der Gräfin heidnisch und übermütig vergekommen war, wie ihre ganze Schönheit, halb lachend und halb unwillig aus . . . (II, 140 f).

Eichendorff anticipates our confusion by suggesting possible identifications of the woman. What or whom does she represent? In this particular instance, we know that Romana portrays "die Religion der Phantasie," she is "die lebenslustige Schönheit" which is an identifying phrase for Venus. But Romana is also a poetess. She writes letters which her friends call the "Grundrisse zu einem Romane" (II, 189). Her poems are read by a village priest who is so impressed by their spiritual quality that he places them in his prayer book. But Romana is really "heidnisch." Sin disguises itself quite cleverly as a love song to the Creator. Romana represents that danger which Eichendorff himself feels to use poetry, "die heitre Schöne," to prostitute her and compel her to bend to his will and sing his earthly desires (flowers). The poet must live by a law: "Den lieben Gott lass in dir walten." and then, if man sings faithfully, "Was wahr in dir wird sich gestalten,/Das andere ist erbarmlich Ding." Let us see how Romana speaks of herself, the poetess.

> 'Wie so anders war es damals,
> Da mich, bräutlich Ausgeschmückte,
> Aus dem heimatlichen Garten
> Hier herab der Vater schickte!
> Wie die Erde frisch und jung noch,
> Von Gesängen rings erklingend,
> Schaudernd in Erinnerungen,
> Helle in das Herz mir blickte,
> Dass ich, schamhaft mich verhüllend,
> Meinen Ring, von Glanz geblendet,
> Schleudert' in die prächt'ge Fülle,
> Als die ew'ge Braut der Erde.
> Wo ist nun die Pracht geblieben,
> Treuer Ernst im rüst'gen Treiben,
> Rechtes Tun und rechtes Lieben
> Und die Schönheit und die Freude?

Ach! ringsum die Helden alle,
Die sonst schön und helle schauten,
Um   m i c h   in den lichten Tagen
Durch die Welt sich fröhlich hauten,
Strecken steinern nun die Glieder,
Eingehüllt in ihre Fahnen,
Sind seitdem so alt geworden,
Nur   i c h   bin so jung wie damals. —
Von der Welt kann ich nicht lassen,
Liebeln nicht von fern mit Reden,
Muss mit Armen warm umfassen! —
Lass mich lieben, lass mich leben!'

Nun verliebt die Augen gehen
Über ihres Gartens Mauer,
War so einsam dort zu sehen
Schimmernd Land und Ström' und Auen.
Und wo ihre Augen gingen:
Quellen aus der Grüne sprangen,
Berg und Wald verzaubert standen,
Tausend Vögel schwirrend sangen.
Golden blitzt es überm Grunde,
Seltne Farben irrend schweifen,
Wie zu lang entbehrtem Feste
Will die Erde sich bereiten.

(II, 138-139 f.)

Romana speaks of poetry in terms of what she herself is. The princess is poetry, a poetry which has become a bride of the earth just as Romana has. Wherever poetry "looks" it seems that "Quellen," poets, emerge from the green and all is golden and enchanted, filled with the song of birds and ablaze with light and color. Surely the reader recognizes this imagery which we have discussed at such length. Eichendorff shows us the poet's interior world, the workshop of creativity; and woe betide the creator who becomes lost in this interior world where "flowers" are golden, fountains sing of the self, and everything is the self because that is *all*, the summation of his reality. Then, as Raimund says, how utterly annihilating if one suddenly awakens, if the intoxication of self, this "be-geistern," is lost and one is sober. Then the Christian poet must call out: "Herr Gott, lass mich nicht verloren gehen in der Welt." Not in the outside world, but in the world within!

In "Jugendandacht" 4:3, the woman who raises her eyes evolves from the flowers which are the youth's desires concealed in the pearl given to him, not by poetry, but by what poetry has become in his "dunkle Reich von Gedanken" (II, 983). Filled with desire she now reaches for him. As Raimund flees the intoxicating loveliness of the nude bathers he feels as if "der Schimmer jener jugendlichen Glieder" were reaching for him (II, 979). The song which this woman sings speaks of "Schlanke Arme zu umarmen,/Roten Mund zum süssen Kuss,/Weisse Brust, dran zu erwarmen, . . ." (II, 976). And Raimund's song refers to "Alte Klänge nach mir langen —/Süsse Sünde, lass mich los!" (II, 972). If we look at this imagery and then turn to the last strophe of "Jugendandacht" 4 we cannot fail to see the startling similarity. "Die Farben" are resurrected, the woman embraces him, and life's golden rays touch him. It is life as described by Romana-"Poesie": "Golden blitzt es überm Grunde/Seltne Farben irrend schweifen." That the colors are "irrend" must be equated with Raimund's "Meine Liebe und mein ganzes Leben eine lange Täuschung." Our youth states that the woman herself feels the pain which she had given him. With this thought Eichendorff invokes the insinuation of the "Ewigreine." In "Jugendandacht" 1 the youth had said of her: "Kein Schmerz, als solcher Liebe Lieb' ertragen." In other words, our young man still thinks that "Liebe und Andacht" are one and fails to understand that he has separated them. The next poem in this cycle will make this clear for us.

Jugendandacht 5

Wann Lenzensstrahlen golden niederrinnen,
    Sieht man die Scharen losgebunden ziehen,
    Im Waldrevier, dem neu der Schmuck geliehen,
    Die lust'ge Jagd nach Lieb' und Scherz beginnen.

Den Sänger will der Frühling gar umspinnen,
    Er, der Geliebteste, darf nicht entfliehen,
    Fühlt rings ein Lied durch alle Farben ziehen,
    Das ihn so lockend nimmer lässt von hinnen.

Gefangen so, sitzt er viel' sel'ge Jahre;
    Des Einsamen spottet des Pöbels Scherzen,
    Der aller Glorie möchte Lieb' entkleiden.

Doch er grüsst fröhlich alle, wie sie fahren,
   Und mutig sagt er zu den süssen Schmerzen:
   "Gern sterb' ich bald, wollt ihr von mir je scheiden!"

(I, 276)

In the very middle of "Jugendandacht" 1 we find the lines
"O sel'ge Zeit entflossener Himmelsbläue." In the middle sonnet,
number five, we again encounter water. The light of a spring
courses down like golden water. "Zur Erde geht, was feucht
und schwer,/Was klar zu ihr (die Sonne) hinauf." The eternal
spring knows nought of the hunt for "Liebe und Scherz." This
is the world of the "Schäfer" who will appear later, but it is not
for the "Hirt" or the "Jäger." We must not imagine that Eichendorff envisions some "Waldrevier" in which foolish men play the
game of love. Man's thoughts are the forest and this forest is
newly embellished — the beauty is really just loaned to it and
will fade again — with the gold of man's love. The game is in the
mind! The very first lines of the entire cycle of poems told us
that the gentle waves of spring beat against the heart to remind
it of a heaven lost. We now see ever more clearly that this
heaven is below, immersed in the waters of forgetfulness. It is
Florio's world. Spring opens the old wounds, "Dass losgebunden
in das Licht sie bluten." The second verse of the first strophe
says "die Scharen" are "losgebunden." Everyone is free, but not
"der Sänger." He is spring's beloved and "darf nicht entfliehen."
Why? We must return to our first poem and review two strophes.

Hörst du nun den Frühling laden? —
Jägers Waldhorn geht im Walde,
Lockend grüssen bunte Flaggen,
Nach dem Sänger alle fragen.

Ach, von euch, ihr Frühlingsfahnen,
Kann ich, wie von dir, nicht lassen!
Reisen in den blauen Tagen
Muss der Sänger mit dem Klange.

(I, 183)

Spring invites, seeks, the minstrel because he must utter the
magic word which releases the song inherent in the created.
This is the function of Eichendorff's "Sänger," to whom the
word has been given, and he dare not flee this responsibility.
In our "Jugendandacht" cycle the youth feels, "in den blauen

Tagen," that the woman will come to him; and he waits with yearning heart. The "Sänger" in the above poem must travel "in den blauen Tagen," and the woman may come with him if she is faithful to "dem alten Sange." And this woman is poetry. Using the imagery found in Romana's poem, "Poesie" must leave her castle and garden and come with the minstrel. If he pursues her he eventually finds her castle and garden. That is the story of Raimund and Florio. Romana invites Friedrich to her home, the same kind of castle and grounds discovered by the afore-mentioned youths. Romana acutally appears before Friedrich in her naked splendor and Friedrich finds her "verführerisch." It is the same pattern, the same imagery, in every instance. Poetry, "die heitre Schöne," can become the poet's Venus. And what does the youth, "der Sänger," in the above two strophes suggest to poetry? He will lead her home in "Waldesprachten." Once again, are we to remain content with the utterly meaning-less notion that they will live together in the forest? Of course not! "Der Wald" represents his thoughts, but thoughts which are splendid, glowing, as it were, with heavenly light. Here she can dwell dressed in sky-blue silk. The poet will cloth her in the raiment of the sky and even of the sun.

The young man in "Jugendandacht" is not free but is trapped by "die Schlingen" mentioned in "Das Zaubernetz." We see in the third strophe of the fifth poem that he has been a prisoner for many years. The mockery of others he wears like a badge of honor. Then Eichendorff reveals, with remarkable nicety, the movement of error in the heart of the youth "Der aller Glorie möchte Lieb, entkleiden." "In der Glorie des Maien" the "Ewigreine" raises her veil; delete the "Glorie" and one has but a human spring. The minstrel would lead poetry home in "Waldes-prachten"; void this splendor and man has only his own thoughts which know nothing of heaven. "Entkleiden"! To take this light ("Glorie") away from love is to see a woman's "strahlend reine Glieder." And when the light from the other woman touches "die lebenslustige Schönheit" her dance is arrested but still re-veals "die ganze regelmässige Fülle und Pracht der Glieder." It needs but man's love and the dance begins again. The youth in our poem is so enthralled by the sweet pain of love that he would rather die than be separated from it. He does not realize that his "Dichten" is a gazing into the self and that all which he feels he does to himself. His life has become "ein unendlich

Schauen" into the mirror of his soul, and what he beholds is beautiful, indeed.

Jugendandacht 6

Wann frisch die buntgewirkten Schleier wallen,
Weit in das Land die Lerchen mich verführen,
Da kann ich's tief im Herzen wieder spüren,
Wie mich die Eine liebt und ruft vor allen.

Wenn Nachtigall'n aus grünen Hallen schallen,
Wen möchten nicht die tiefen Töne rühren;
Wen nicht das süsse Herzeleid verführen,
Im Liebesschlagen tot vom Baum zu fallen? —

So sag' auch ich bei jedem Frühlingsglanze:
Du süsse Laute! Lass uns beide sterben,
Beklagt vom Widerhallen zarter Töne,

Kann unser Lied auch nie den Lohn erwerben,
Dass hier mit eignem, frischem Blumenkranze
Uns endlich kröne nun die Wunderschöne! —

(I, 276-77)

The colors are "in" the veil which conceals the woman, and through those colors, as the previous sonnet instructs, a song seems to move ("ziehen"). This is the same verb as found in "Jugendandacht" 2: "Klar durch's ganze Herz/Ein süsses Bild gezogen." The cycle of poems simply called "Lieder" must be seen again. We quote the most pertinent strophe.

Viel' Lenze sitz' ich schon da oben,
Ein Regenbogen steht im Land erhoben
Und durch die Täler, Wiesen, Wogen
Still, wie ein fernes Lied, gezogen,
Schifft immerfort dein himmlisch Bild —
Doch Strom und Schiff nie stille hielt.

(I, 280)

The cycle from which this strophe is taken is addressed to the Virgin Mary. In the above verses everything is, so to speak, externalized. It represents an effort on Eichendorff's part to show that her "himmlisch Bild" is not of his making. It is there, everywhere, even though he, the poet, is never still. Clearly the intent

is the same as in the song of the "Taugenichts," "Wohin ich
geh' und schau," (II, 353). However, in the case of "Jugendandacht," the colors, the song, "das Bild" and the rainbow are all
in his heart. The call which he hears in the colors, the movement of his life, is really a conversation with the self, an immersion in his own world of "Gedanken." In this interior world
is "der Abgrund" surrounded by "hohe, seltsame, ausländische,
brennende Blumen," the poems of imprisoned desire.[16] And
the call generated by his own sensations and feelings is "den
eignen, tiefen Wonnen/Selig Wunder!" (II, 133).

The second strophe presents what at first glance may seem
to be a very surprising admission. "After all," the words suggest,
"who would not be deceived, led astray, by the pain of love nor
touched by the heartfelt longing in the nightingale's song?" We
even find the words "die tiefen Töne," which are the equivalent
of "tief Gesänge" found in "Sonette" 3 and its modified version. The youth tells us he knows that the song comes from
below, that it is not the heavenly music which he hears. In other
words, this entire cycle of poems is a carefully reasoned structure, or exposition, of how the heart is deceived. Now it is clear
why "Jugendandacht" 3 can begin with the words, "Wohl weiss
ich's —." We are being guided, and deliberately, into that "Labyrinth des Herzens" where human love, even with the best of intentions, enters and breathes "die Kerkerluft des Bösen." I offer
one further consideration which literally compels acceptance of
this conclusion. The "Lieder" cycle contains four poems which
were completed in 1809. The last poem in this group which speaks
so clearly of the Virgin Mary is precisely the same as the
second poem in the "Jugendandacht" cycle which was completed
in 1810. In other words, the imagery and thoughts which the
younger poet at one time felt to be a proper statement of his
relationship with "Poesie" become the point of departure for a
careful study in deception. Nothing could be a more dramatic
and revealing admission as to the exquisite delicacy and recalci-
trant nature of the material. The Eichendorff of 1807-1810 looked
back at an even earlier age, saw how external influences had
misguided him, sought to correct, modify, expand, and refine
his own imagery and was constantly displeased. What he had
attempted is placed on the lips of Rudolf. Friedrich's brother,
who must be understood as portraying a facet of Eichendorff's
own development, suggests that his interest in painting "war im

Grunde nur ein falsches Streben, das Unaussprechliche auszu-sprechen, das Undarstellbare darzustellen. Besonders verspürte ich schon damals dieses Gelüst vor manchen Bildern des grossen Albrecht Dürer und Michelangelo" (II, 274). If the poet suc-cumbs to this aspect of Romantic aesthetics[17] — and here Eichendorff takes such serious issue with Novalis — he will of necessity and even unwittingly define the Infinite in terms of his own finiteness (II, 142). Should the poet give heart and mind to this "Gelüst," he will raise the veil and see him-self. This is the psychological ground of the "Erstarrungsmotiv" which seeks to finalize or give concrete form to the ideal. And thus the Eichendorff of about 1815 exhorts us:

> Doch wolle nie dir halten
> *Der Bilder* Wunder fest,
> Tot wird ihr freies Walten,
> Hältst du es *weltlich fest.*

> (II, 73, italics mine)

The second strophe of "Jugendandacht" 6 speaks of the nightingale. When one sees "vom Baum zu fallen," the mind tends to associate this with the songbird when in fact it refers to the one who has been deceived by "das süsse Herzeleid." From this we deduce that the word "Liebesschlagen" cannot refer to the love song of the nightingale but to the "Sänger." In other words, man's own song of love is responsible for his deception. This reasoning also reveals certain overtones of meaning suggested by the word "Baum." The tree is a place of refuge in our poet's works, and man climbs it in order that he may be nearer to God. Leontin calls the tree "eine wahre Jakobsleiter" (II, 63).[18] In the context of our poem then, to fall dead from the tree is to die to God. This thought is actually continued in the next two strophes which present a confusing array of imagery both as to content and sequence. The reference to "die Laute" is utterly enigmatic unless the poet's works have been consulted as to his own definition of the instrument. Man is the instrument designed to play "die Grundmelodie" in his heart; if man does not sing this song the instrument is "dead"; that is, man does not sing his praises to the Lord. The reader must not be confused by the words "uns beide." The "Taugenichts" says to his violin, "Unser Reich ist nicht von dieser Welt."

The remaining verses of the poem seem to imply that the youth wishes to die because he cannot hope to be rewarded by "die Wünderschöne." But the more often these lines are read the more disturbed one becomes by such words as "hier, endlich, nun," words which cloud a simple and literal interpretation of the death-wish. Furthermore, the reward is a wreath of flowers; but these flowers are his own, a conclusion given us by the word "eignem." We also recall the second poem wherein the youth describes his life as "ein unendlich Schauen in den himmelblauen Grund einer Blume." Seemingly he is to be rewarded by that which has been the object of his desire since his childhood. And here we find another thread in this intricate pattern. The first time that Florio sees the statue of Venus "kam ihm jenes Bild wie eine langgesuchte, nun plötzlich erkannte Geliebte vor, wie eine *Wunderblume,* aus der Frühlingsdämmerung und träumerischen Stille seiner frühesten Jugend heraufgewachsen" (II, 318, italics mine). "Die Wunderblume" is none other than "die Wunderschöne," and both are an image in his heart. And how does the word "eignem" fit in this equation? "Poesie" can give to man only what he has first given to her. We note that Florio's first two songs are called "Liebe in der Fremde," and when Venus appears to him at the dance she sings a continuation of the same song. At this dance she gives him a rose but only after this rose had been identified in another song, "Frau Venus."

> Die Rose seh' ich gehn aus grüner Klause
> Und, wie so buhlerisch die Lüfte fächeln,
> Errötend in die blaue Luft sich dehnen.
>
> (II, 322)

The rose represents Florio's love which has left the green refuge and surges blushingly into the spring breezes (which are called "buhlerisch"). In the tableau the lily and the rose turn toward the woman with the cross. It takes little imagination to realize that Florio's love (rose) turns to the other woman. And as to the reward, the wreath of flowers with which the woman is to crown him, let us look at "Götterdämmerung."

> O rosenbekränztes
> Jünglingsbild,
> Dein Auge, wie glänzt es,
> Die Flammen so mild!
>
> (II, 311)

This is a description of Florio before he encounters **Venus,** before he finds her garden; indeed, if he did not wear the wreath he could not find her temple because it can exist only for those who have left the garden of grace. If man did not first give the flowers to Venus she could not "give" them back to him. The "Taugenichts," in his song "Der Gärtner," admits that there are many flowers in his garden (soul), but he does not dare to give them to the Virgin. "Die müssen alle verbleichen,/Die Liebe nur ohnegleichen/Bleibt ewig im Herzen stehn" (I, 200). Love, the rose, must stay in the heart, "in grüner Klause," but Florio's love is "in der Fremde." The first two lines in "Jugendandacht" 6 repeat this motif in clear and unambiguous terms.

We now are in a position to discuss what the young man really says in the last two strophes of the sixth poem. It would seem that he wishes to die because he cannot be rewarded with the wreath of flowers. But not so! He would die in order that "die Wunderschöne" might crown him with these flowers. The first verse of the sixth poem's third strophe says, "so sag' auch ich." What is the significance of this "so"? It refers to that hypothetical someone who would fall from the tree; that is, who would die to God. And if the youth does this, what are the consequences? I believe this becomes apparent if we read the lines as follows: "Du süsse Laute! lass uns beide sterben,/ . . . *Dass* hier mit eignem, frischem Blumenkranze/Uns endlich krone nun die Wunderschöne." In other words, I suggest that the youth wishes to die so that something else may follow. There can be no other explanation for the singular inclusion of such words as "hier, endlich, nun." Remember that this young man had this vision of the woman in his heart since childhood. He is impatient and would seek the fulfillment of love's desire. Love has gone searching, is no longer content to wait in all humility for the hand that would fashion the new man, but reaches out and makes in its own image. Love enables man to forget for some little time that he is incompletely spiritual, that he is wounded; and when he remembers, if he does, he must learn that wisdom comes only by "the awful grace of God."

Jugendandacht 7

Der Schäfer spricht, wenn er frühmorgens weidet:
"Dort drüben wohnt sie hinter Berg' und Flüssen!"

Doch seine Wunden deckt sie gern mit Küssen,
Wann lauschend Licht am stillen Abend scheidet.

Ob neu der Morgenschmuck die Erde kleidet,
Ob Nachtigallen Nacht und Stern' begrüssen,
Stets fern und nah bleibt m e i n e Lieb' der Süssen,
Die in dem Lenz mich ewig sucht und meidet. —

Doch hör' ich wunderbare Stimmen sprechen:
"Die Perlen, die du treu geweint im Schmerze,
Sie wird sie sorglich all' zusammenbinden,

Mit eigner Kette so dich süss umwinden,
Hinaufziehn dich an Mund und blühend Herze —
Was Himmel schloss, mag nicht der Himmel brechen."

(I, 277)

The rose has left the haven and love has gone in search of
its desire. Now this woman is found "hinter Berg' und Flüssen"
and not in the vault of heaven where she raises the veil so
that love might shine upon the created. The word "Schäfer" has
a pejorative connotation because it suggests the frivolous love
poetry of another age. This childish love which seeks but its
own joys and pleasures is a manifestation of man's wound, his
incomplete spirituality, which the woman would cover with kisses.
And this is done when listening light has departed.[19] I must
quote that part of "Liebe in der Fremde" which Venus sings.

Über die beglänzten Gipfel
Fernher kommt es wie ein Grüssen,
Flüsternd neigen sich die Wipfel,
Als ob sie sich wollten küssen.

Ist er doch so schön und milde![20]
Stimmen gehen durch die Nacht,
Singen heimlich von dem Bilde —
Ach, ich bin so froh verwacht!

Plaudert nicht so laut, ihr Quellen'
Wissen darf es nicht der Morgen'
In der Mondnacht linde Wellen
Senk' ich still mein Glück und Sorgen. —

(I, 41)

Of course, the morning, the light, must not know what love has done to itself. That is why this love leads to the "Venusberg" where it would be "hidden" from the eyes of heaven, and where light could not "listen" to the words of denial. But deception moves apace and soon love sees only in the light of its own darkness. The morning after the pond scene Florio is depicted as quite confused. "Sinnend blieb er oftmals vor der wunderreichen Aussicht in das Land hinab stehen, als wollte er das freudigkräftige Walten da draussen um Auskunft fragen. Aber der Morgen spielte nur einzelne Zauberlichter wie durch die Bäume über ihm in sein träumerisch funkelndes Herz hinein, das noch in anderer Macht stand. Denn drinnen zogen die Sterne noch immerfort ihre magischen Kreise, zwischen denen das wunderschöne Marmorbild mit neuer, unwiderstehlicher Gewalt heraufsah —" (II, 320). The youth is on the point of asking help from "das Walten," which may remind us of the poem: "Den lieben Gott lass ich nur *walten*." In other words, he almost asks God for help; but this comes much later in the story because in his heart there is darkness broken only by the light of the stars which are really flowers.[21] Love sees in the light of its own darkness! It must not be assumed that this paradox has been devised by this writer; Eichendorff means exactly that. The very first song that Friedrich sings is called "Steckbrief" and it speaks of the love in his heart. I quote the poem in its entirety because it says so much that should be repeated.

"Grüss' euch aus Herzensgrund:
Zwei Augen hell und rein,
Zwei Röslein auf dem Mund,
Kleid blank aus Sonnenschein!

Nachtigall klagt und weint,
Wollüstig rauscht der Hain,
Alles die Liebste meint:
Wo weilt sie so allein?

Weil's draussen finster war,
Sah ich viel hellern Schein,
Jetzt ist es licht und klar,
Ich muss im Dunkeln sein.

Sonne nicht steigen mag,
Sieht so verschlafen drein,

Wünschet den ganzen Tag,
Dass wieder Nacht möcht' sein.

Liebe geht durch die Luft,
Holt fern die Liebste ein;
Fort über Berg und Kluft!
Und sie wird doch noch mein!"

(II, 15-16)

This poem actually describes the circumstances of his first kiss with Rosa. We find in these thoughts a variation of Florio's experience and also of the "Jugendandacht" theme. The first strophe with its reference to the "Augen hell und rein," the roses and the white robe made of sunlight, are conventional references to the Queen of Heaven. The rest of the poem, however, reveals the usual shift in emphasis concerning the nature of love. It should be noted that nature speaks in terms of the love in his heart, "wollüstig." Also, the poet uses the heathen "Hain" rather than the Christian "Wald." Everything would surge toward the beloved, who, as we saw in "Jugendandacht" 7, "wohnt hinter Berg' und Flüssen."

The reader who makes a careful study of all the nouns, verbs, and adjectives used in reference to Venus and the Virgin will see in the last two verses of the second strophe in poem seven, furthr confirmation that the Virgin has long been forgotten by the youth. Eichendorff never refers to the Queen of Heaven as "die Süsse." Indeed, it is only with rare exception that the word "süss" has a positive connotation in his works. (By *positive* we mean a conscious and active awareness on the part of man that his love must be directed first to the Creator and then to the created.) Furthermore, the actions of "suchen und meiden" cannot be imputed to the Mother of God. She neither "seeks" nor avoids man, but holds on to him as long as he permits (II, 429) . If we consider the relationship between Florio and Venus, it is clear that he seeks her, then she pursues and avoids him until the young man's mind has no other thought than to find her. This does not happen to the "Taugenichts" as we shall see later. These last two verses in the second strophe of poem seven are disturbingly elusive in meaning in another sense. The words "fern und nah" find a reasonable counterpart in the verbs "suchen und meiden"; but the former refers to his love and the latter to the "die Süsse." This yields what is tantamount to a mathematical equation, which states that the woman's nearness is relative to the movement of one's love. In "Das Marmorbild" we shall trace the fact that the reality of Venus, her very existence, correlates perfectly with the movement of Florio's mind and heart. By this we mean that he cannot even find her garden when his mind is on other things. Thus she is far when morning glorifies the earth, and near when the nightingale sings.

The last two strophes of the poem return to the pearl. The youth cries "pearls," the woman gathers them, fashions a chain of them and draws him to her. He is her prisoner! "Die Zauberin im Walde," we were told, gives him a pearl which becomes a flower. Eichendorff rejects this earlier formulation. The enchantress, poetry, can "give" you nothing that you have not first given her. We were thus instructed by the rose symbolism in "Das Marmorbild." Our poem categorically speaks of "eigner Kette," which repeats the insinuation in the previous sonnet, "mit eignem, frischen Blumenkranz." The wreath is already his, and this woman has nothing to give him. The "Taugenichts" on the other hand is given a wreath. We shall discuss this later. Now the pearl, as we know, is also associated with pain and sorrow. In "Jugendandacht" 1 the youth states that in the presence of the chaste woman, "musst' ich herzlich weinen." Friedrich tells us that the story of Christ caused him to cry "aus Herzensgrunde." These tears of sorrow, of the penitent sinner, are a demonstrable thread in our poet's works. Even the "Taugenichts," and for very good reason, throws himself upon the ground "und weinte bitterlich" (II, 357). These tears are the "pearls" which the youthful poet "brings" to poetry. They are expressions of pious feelings, for which reason the poet calls them "treu." And what of the voices which seem to suggest that his sensations, these lovely pious feelings, are the proper subject of poetry? They are the "Quellen, die Ströme," the movement of poetry in which the youth was immersed. We must consider the spiritual and intellectual climate which defined poetry for the young poet. "Poesie" was a veritable "Wünschelrute" — I am sure that is why he selected this title — which would enable man to find those living waters which would glorify and dignify human existence. The ultimate truths would flow from poetry, and all was to be "poetisch." It is difficult for us, in this age, to feel the overpowering significance inherent in this daring thrust of early German Romanticism. On the other hand, if we would but substitute the word "science," we should be able to understand and even feel the full import of such sweeping generalizations. (One fatted calf has been replaced by another.) In Eichendorff's formative years, Poetry was a lovely woman who was to serve as a Beatrice. Eichendorff's question is a simple one: Would she lead man to Venus or the Virgin? When we recall that works of ancient Christian literature referred to the Virgin Mother as the heavenly Venus, we begin to understand how deception is a cornerstone of Eichendorff's works. The poet always pursues Venus, is drawn to Venus, is filled with earthly or heavenly light and love, sings the song of heaven or earth, the eternal or the transient. The same words can be used to describe both brides. Each is a beloved. "Dichten" is dangerous! That is why "Jugendandacht" 1 contains those confusing lines: "O sel'ge Zeit entflossener Himmelsbläue,/Der ersten Andacht solch inbrünst'ger Liebe, /Die ewig wollte knien vor der Einen!" Which Venus is "die Eine, Deine?"

The first strophe of the seventh sonnet tells us that she is glad to cover his wound with kisses when listening light fades before the quiet night. The purpose of spring, "Jugendandacht" 1, is to open the wound, but this woman does not want him to remember this. She covers it. And this is said of the "Schäfer," a certain kind of poet. Now "Poesie" is no longer "Die heitre Schöne" but has become "Feig und hohl" and would have man forget that Light listens to him. We recall our discussion of the "Sonette" cycle.

> Wie bald läg' unten alles Bange, Trübe,
> *Du* strebtest lauschend, blicktest nicht mehr nieder,
> Und höher winkte stets der Brüder Liebe:
> . . . .
>
> (italics mine)

The young man feels he experiences this. What the child felt and, perhaps I should even say, saw as in a dream or vision, resulted in a seemingly innocent interpenetration of love and devotion or reverence. All that is insinuated by the word "inbrünstig" taints the pearl and is the seed of the "flower." And yet, so strong is the conviction of a chaste love that this seems ordained by heaven. That is why in "Götterdämmerung" Bacchus-Florio can say: "Hinauf, ach hinauf!/Der Himmel ist offen,/ Nimm, Vater, mich auf!"

Jugendandacht 8

Wenn du am Felsenhange standst alleine,
  Unten im Walde Vögel seltsam sangen
  Und Hörner aus der Ferne irrend klangen,[22]
  Als ob die Heimat drüben nach dir weine,

War's niemals da, als rief die Eine, Deine?
  Lock' dich kein Weh, kein brünstiges Verlangen
  Nach andrer Zeit, die lange schon vergangen,
  Auf ewig einzugehn in grüne Scheine?

Gebirge dunkelblau steigt aus der Ferne,
  Und von den Gipfeln führt des Bundes Bogen
  Als Brücke weit in unbekannte Lande.

Geheimnisvoll gehn oben goldne Sterne,
  Uten erbraust viel Land in dunklen Wogen —
  Was zögerst du am unbekannten Rande?

(I, 277-78)

With this poem, the poet again steps outside the structure
of events by discarding the first person narration and addressing
the reader as "du." In effect the poet wishes to say: "Has
this not happened to you?" The subtle deceptiveness of his imagery takes on greater clarity. The nature of the song heard
by this youth is given us by the words "seltsam" and "irrend,"
words which suggest strangeness, error and deception; and yet,
it seems to him as if man's native country, the heavenly kingdom,
were crying for him. It is apparent that this feeling is vitiated
by the "als ob" construction. The song that he heard in the colors
is his own song; the yearning expressed by the woman is his
own desire. These manifestations in the external are projections
of his inner being, his own love. It would be a gross error on our
part if we were to conclude that the reference to birds and
forest has anything to do with nature. There is little in the entire
cycle of poems which really speaks of nature. The reader may recall
our discussion of "Der Knabe" (I, 336) . The youth released the
bird, his love, which then heard the singing of other birds in
the forest. "Das lockt so hell, das lockt so tief/In wundersüssen
Weisen." As I explained, this refers to the song of poetry which
the youth heard. I also added that it was not really the song
of the other birds but the youth's own call which finally induced

it to fly away. It flys to the forest "zum Dichterwald." Let us look at the pertinent strophe.

. . . .

Das Vöglein frisch die Flügel rührt —
Er ruft: Kommst du nicht balde? —
Das hat das Vögelein verführt,
Fort flog's zum grünen Walde —

. . . .

And now turn to the second strophe of "Jugendandacht" 8. Who calls? To be sure, the feeling is that it is "die Eine" before whom he would kneel, but we shall see in the next poem that she turns from him in anger. That is precisely what happens to the "Taugenichts." Everything comes from the heart of our youth, the "flowers," the "pearls," the song in the colors. It is all his. What happens if you raise the veil — of "Das verschleierte Bild zu Sais?" Novalis gives two answers: "Rosenblütchen" and the self. Eichendorff gives but one answer: the self. This second strophe makes it abundantly clear what the youth has chosen. He no longer can say, "In ihrem Blick gereinigt alle Triebe," for he is now filled with a "brünstiges Verlangen," the perfect equivalent of Florio who looks at Venus "mit flammenden Augen." He would enter that time of long ago, "versunken," when "alte Wünsche und Freuden" are set free and man feels released from the prison of Christianity, which is the Law. This time of long ago is described as "grüne Scheine;" it only seems to be filled with hope, the hope that love will find fulfillment. In "Aufgebot" (I, 77), the pilgrim is asked why he is standing all alone ("Im grünen Scheine?/Lockt dich der Wunderlaut/Nicht auch zur fernen Braut?"). Just these few lines would suggest the very essence of the "Jugendandacht" study.

The last two strophes of the eighth sonnet depict the final phase of deception. It seems that in the distance a new land suddenly emerges. The last line of "Der Fromme" says: "Der Garten Gottes steigt aus Morgenflammen." Our youth stands, we are told, "am Felsenhange," and from these heights, "den Gipfeln," a bridge called "des Bundes Bogen" leads to this other land. To begin with, Eichendorff carefully calls this land "unbekannt" while his standard reference to God's kingdom is "die Heimat." Eichendorff uses exactly the same imagery twenty-five years later when Victor in *Dichter und ihre Gesellen* describes the garden of his poetry and calls these bridges "die Blocksberge seiner Phantasie." When we see the word "Bogen" we must think of "Jugendandacht" 2 in which the youth looks into his own heart "wo schlummernd träumen stille Regenbogen." The word "Bund" is found in a two-poem cycle, "An die Entfernte," and the second poem begins with the line: "Als noch Lieb' mit mir im Bunde . . . ." What follows in this poem describes the movement of love in "Jugendandacht." Our youth is a prisoner "Der aller Glorie möchte Lieb' entkleiden." Deep within he feels that his own love is sufficient to fashion the bridge. All that is implied by the word "Glorie" is forgotten. But it is in "der Glorie des Maien"[23] where "die Stille" raises the veil. The youth has raised it himself and now, in the last two strophes above, he has the sensation that he is crossing a high bridge to a new land. Very carefully Eichendorff weaves into this deception the insinuation of an ocean voyage, which is his standard imagery for man's journey to the Eternal. But this then is voided by the last word in the poem which speaks of "Rande" and not "Strande." Man must live this life with all of its trials and temptations, because in conquering these we conquer ourselves. Poetry must not be an escape from life, but a creative penetration and illumination of mankind's deepest yearning, the desire of God. When we see that our youth stands "am unbekannten Rande" we see him on the rim of an abyss, "am Abgrund." Note that the word "unbekannt" describes "das Land," the heaven that is his goal, and the "Rand," the edge of the abyss. Everything is unknown; he is lost to himself and his God. Thus, at the critical moment in Venus' palace, we see that Florio "kam sich auf einmal hier so *fremd und wie aus sich selber verirrt vor*" (II, 338, italics mine) . "My God, where have I been so long?"

Jugendandacht 9

Es wendet zürnend sich von mir die Eine,
  Versenkt die Ferne mit den Wunderlichtern.
  Es stockt der Tanz — ich stehe plötzlich nüchtern,
  Musik lässt treulos mich so ganz alleine.

Da spricht der Abgrund dunkel: Bist nun meine;
  Zieht mich hinab an bleiernen Gewichtern,
  Sieht stumm mich an aus steinernen Gesichtern,
  Das Herz wird selber zum kristallnen Steine.

Dann ist's, als ob es dürstend Schmerzen sauge
Aus lang vergess'ner Zeit Erinnerungen,
Und kann sich rühren nicht, von Frost bezwungen.

Versteinert schweigen muss der Wehmut Welle,
Wie willig auch, schmölz' ihn ein wärmend Auge,
Kristall zerfliessen wollt' als Tränenquelle.

(I, 278)

The Queen of Heaven is angry with this youth. She drops the
veil, and "die Ferne mit den Wunderlichtern — Der Augen Himmel" plunges into darkness. Now he feels that terrible aloneness
and the pain of the wound which had been covered by the kisses of
the other "Jungfrau." The voices he had heard, the songs of
other poets, the song in the "colors," in life, desert him. All
this cannot sustain him and he sinks. The crystal is a symbol
for Raimund's heart, "ein wunderbares, dunkles Reich von Gedanken." The precious jewels in this garden of denial are man's
thoughts; they are like the pearls given to the woman called
poetry; and suddenly they are no longer bright and glittering,
but simply leaden. Man's own thoughts, that "Scharfsinn" illuminated by a rebellious "Begesterüng" (II, 233), lead him away
from God. Raimund had said, "—ach, wie schrecklich ist es, dann
auf einmal wieder nüchtern zu werden" (II, 974). Our youth,
too, is suddenly sober, and now he remembers what he had
forgotten, which is, "O sel'ge Zeit entflossener Himmelsblaue."
This one line, as I said in the beginning of our discussion, did
not fit into the rhyme scheme of "Jugendandacht" 1. This time
is past. "Das Paradiesgärtlein unserer Kindheit" is behind us, and
man can never return to it. One poem, of many, says this rather
nicely. "Der Götter Irrfahrt," written about 1828, describes the
creation of earth, "Die Schöne," who is amazed at her own beauty.
The immortal ones are lured by her beauty and sail to this new
wonder. On the first day, the sun dies (sets).

Die Genossen fasst ein Grauen,
Und sie fahren weit ins Meer,
Nach des Vaters Haus sie schauen,
Doch sie finden's nimmermehr.
Mussten aus den Wogenwüsten
Ihrer Schiffe Schnäbel drehn
Wieder nach des Eilands Küsten,
Ach, das war so falsch und schön!

Und für immer da verschlagen
Blieben sie im fremden Land,
Hörten nachts des Vaters Klagen
Oft noch fern vom Götterstrand. —
Und nun Kindeskinder müssen
Nach der Heimat sehn ins Meer,
Und es kommt im Wind ein Grüssen,
Und sie wissen nicht woher.

(I, 328 f.)

Although few are chosen, Eichendorff insists that man, especially the poet, is called, and human existence is a searching
for an understanding of this call. In the very first poems discussed, it was stated that if man does not know, "within," where
to find the understanding of this call, "Der wandern und fragen
mag/Bis an den jüngsten Tag!" But shortly after this (1807),
a note of fear creeps into his poems. It looms ever larger as the
young poet realizes with increasing anguish that his songs may
not be God's songs, and that his love, whatever the imagined
purity of its intent, is insufficient in and of itself. Thus "Jugendandacht" ends with prayer, "O Herr! du kennst allein den treuen
Willen. . . ." As the young Eichendorff experiences a period of
intense spiritual and intellectual growth from 1807-1810, this fear
assumes a definite structure and is incorporated in many poems
and prose works. Indeed, almost every major character in his
prose works is touched by this fear. We see it first in Raimund
who is led astray by a curious invitation which is mysteriously
intertwined with the sound of the horn, "das Waldhorn."

Reichen, vollen Liebesgruss
Bietet dir der Hörner Schallen
Süsser! komm, *eh sie verhallen!*

(italics mine)

As in the First Garden, deception speaks the truth. The sound
of the horn is part of "spring," the spring of God's grace which
returns love beyond all measure, but Raimund follows the "Waldhornlied" which is heard only in the fall. This is precisely the same
pattern as in "Das Marmorbild" where we know it is summer but
Florio feels that it is spring. Eichendorff criticism shows little
understanding of the seasons in his works. All depends upon
light. During spring man receives more light or grace; during

summer the earth begins to receive less light, but man does not sense this. It is the perfect season for the deception theme because the world is still warm, beautiful and fragrant, but the soul does not realize it is moving toward darkness. Fall, like spring, is a sea of color, but it is the color of fire, of death. (Read "Todeslust," I, 312) The first day of winter is in truth the first undetected return of light. Eichendorff did not weave this into his light symbolism with any consistency. It is instructive, however, to read "Der Winter" (I, 290) and consider the lines, "Wache auf, mein Herze,/Frühling muss es sein!" And thus Raimund, in effect, pursues "fall" because he fears that "spring" will leave him. Florio follows exactly the same pattern in his first song when he sings "Und so muss ich wie im Strom dort die Welle/Ungehört verrauschen an des Frühlings Schwelle" (II, 310). Friedrich, too, is touched by this fear. His first encounter with Rosa leads to a kiss, even before he knows her name. The next morning he is informed that "Die Dame" already had departed. "Jetzt sah draussen alles anders aus, und eine unbeschreibliche Bangigkeit flog durch sein Herz" (II, 14). He has begun to love, and this love concerns a realm uncovered, we are told, by the woman's glances. It is "eine neue Welt von blühender Wunderpracht, uralten Erinnerungen und niegekannten Wünschen . . ." (II, 10). And Rudolf, we know, is filled with a fear so dense and palpable, that he could fashion of it a temple. In "Jugendandacht" 10 we see that there are certain moments in man's life, "feindlich fremde Stunden,/Wo Ängsten aus der Brust hinunterlauschen,/Verworrene Worte mit dem Abgrund tauschen." This abyss, wherever it is encountered in Eichendorff's works, refers to the depths within man. When the poet exchanges words with this abyss, he has become a duologue. He and woman — "Poesie" — are a self-contained entity with no reference to the world of the other. This was touched upon in the "Assonanzenlied": "Was die andern sorgen wollen, Ist mir dunkel." The next strophe states that the speaker's only concern is with "den eignen, trefen Wonnen/Selig Wunder" (II, 133). Faber, the "professional" poet in *Ahnung und Gegenwart*, addresses the same point. He says that

". . . das Haschen der Poesie nach aussen, das geistige Verarbeiten und Bekümmern um das, was eben vorgeht, das Ringen und Abarbeiten an der Zeit, so gross und lobenswert als Gesinnung, ist doch immer unkünstlerisch. Die Poesie mag wohl Wurzel schlagen in demselben Boden der Religion und Nationalität, aber unbekümmert, bloss um ihrer himmlischen Schönheit willen, als Wunderblume zu uns heraufwachsen. Sie will und soll zu nichts brauchbar sein" (II, 297).

Eichendorff, most emphatically, rejects this thesis. A key word is "unbekümmert." The poet must care. It is his responsibility to care. When he does not, then "Poesie"-woman becomes Venus. Her image, as happens to Florio, can become his entire universe because her "face" is really his own. And thus Eichendorff is ever concerned with the movement of his love as revealed in song. He examined his position and analyzed his own poems. His own errors, as well as those which he saw in the literature of his time, become the subject matter of his songs. He remained concerned with the positive and negative thrust of love. Before presenting Eichendorff's discussion of this subject, I should like to offer, without comment, a poem written just one year after the "Jugendandacht" study was completed. All that I have attempted to deduce from Eichendorff's imagery is woven together in this poem. Fear, the kingdom, the rainbow, the bridge, spring, water symbolism, music, woman, death, the depths, pain, the cross, freedom, imprisonment, helplessness, man's nothingness, the child, the wound, the upward movement; all are here. Particular attention, however, is directed to the first four verses of the second strophe; they must be read properly. Only after "holde Frauenschöne" draws man "zum Abgrund süss" does nature sing a certain alluring song which entices man. That considerable body of criticism which sees evil forces or even sin in nature is utterly in error. Eichendorff's nature is incapable of anything which man does not first command. The song which sleeps in all of creation must first be awakened by man who utters the magic word. Our poet categorically says that nature is silent!

Das Gebet

Wen hat nicht einmal Angst befallen,
Wenn Trübnis ihn gefangen hält,
Als müsst' er ewig rastlos wallen
Nach einer wunderbaren Welt?
All' Freunde sind lang fortgezogen,
Der Frühling weint in einem fort,
Eine Brucke ist der Regenbogen
Zum friedlich sichern Heimats-Port.

Hinauszuschlagen in die Töne,
Lockt dich Natur mit wilder Lust,
Zieht Minne, holde Frauenschöne
Zum Abgrund süss die sel'ge Brust;
Den Tod siehst du verhüllet gehen
Durch Lieb' und Leben himmelwärts,
Ein einzig Wunder nur bleibt stehen
Einsam über dem öden Schmerz. —

Du seltner Pilger, lass dich warnen!
Aus ird'scher Lust und Zauberei,
Die freud- und leidvoll dich umgarnen,
Strecke zu Gott die Arme frei!
Nichts mehr musst du hinieden haben,
Himmlisch betrübt, verlassen, arm,
Ein treues Kind, dem Vater klagen
Die ird'sche Lust, den ird'schen Harm.

Es breitet diese einz'ge Stunde
Sich übers ganze Leben still,
Legt blühend sich um deine Wunde,
Die niemals wieder heilen will.
Treu bleibt der Himmel stets dem Treuen,
Zur Erd' das Ird'sche niedergeht,
Zum Himmel über Zaubereien
Geht ewig siegreich das Gebet.

(I, 302f; 1811)

Notes

1. If a poet reveals a penchant for certain words, the possibility exists that these items are "weighted" and are of particular significance to him. The young Eichendorff is constantly preoccupied with "treu, fromm, Jugend, Andacht, Schmerz." I suspect that many literary critics would be surprised to learn that Eichendorff writes to still the pain. What causes him pain? The early poems leave no doubt that his primary concern is the poet's relationship with woman, "Poesie," the Muse. This relationship is the source of pain, and her temple is a prison in which he breathes the "Kerkerluft des Bösen." We shall return to this.

2. I am quite aware of the fact that in a previous discussion ("Der Knabe") I stated that man must guard his love. Eichendorff is responsible for this apparent inconsistency. We should have no difficulty reconciling this. A man's thoughts are directed toward what he loves. Romana, for example, "falls" to the verge of killing Friedrich because he reminds her of what she should be. He has become hateful to her, because he impedes the movement of her own love.

3. Florio plays with the "spielenden Widerschein" of the divine flame. Venus, as we shall show, is the world of the mirror, of the reflection. Now the word *reflection* also suggests a certain thought process. And the word *muse* means an emphasis on dreamy thought, a becoming absorbed in thought. This is precisely what happens to Florio. He becomes absorbed in dreamy thought. But because they are his own reflections, the Muse (Venus) he embraces is the self. His love for her is a love of "Dichten." He sinks into his own depths.

4. Rudolf has no awareness of the fact that man actually dwells in "ein unermessliches Revier," a realm infinitely greater than the "Welt" of which he speaks.

5. Eichendorff, in speaking of his early childhood, describes a lovely woman who "appeared" in the garden. As she approached, everything seemed touched by a lovely light. She only smiled at him then because he was still too young. He calls her "die Muse." The poem "Der Gefangene" speaks of a woman who gave him a kiss. And then:

> Wie prächtig glänzt' die Aue
> Wie Gold der Quell nun floss,
> Und einer süssen Frau
> Lag er im weichen Schoss.

We are then told that the meadow becomes "ein kristallness Schloss," around which flows "ein Strom." He is trapped on an island surrounded by the "stream" of Poesie. Now we know why Florio sings to the maiden "jenseits überm Fluss." Victor, in *Dichter und ihre Gesellen*, speaks of the same island (II, 519).

6. Almost thirty years separate these two poems. In "Der Knabe," the youth speaks of the bird, "ein zartes Vögelein,/Das sass in Lieb gefangen." It was placed behind "bars." In Venus' garden we found birds behind golden bars. The love song of the "Sänger" has been trapped. In "Trauriger Frühling" it has escaped; but now it is lost. Thus fear is always associated with its escape.

7. The subject matter of this book could have been presented from the viewpoint of the word *remember*. In many instances, as deception weaves its lovely pattern, we find the phrase, "Er konnte sich nicht besinnen." Man forgets what he should remember, and remembers what he should forget.

8. In this spring the flower blossoms. The minstrel's love song is a flower. Raimund's "Fraulein" is also a flower, but of stone. The "flower" is dead, but the minstrel gives her life. When the poet says that the "sprossen" (on the vine) will not blossom unless they are touched by "Freudigkeit," one thinks of Christ's words: "I am the vine and you are the branches."

9. When we see that "Münster" are fashioned out of "Felsen," we may recall Rudolf's words that he could build a "Münster" out of his fear. I have discussed the relationship between fear and love. As the latter escapes, man begins to fear. Eichendorff always uses this fear in the same sense that the body "uses" pain. It is a warning. And Eichendorff insists that we remain deaf to what we feel.

10. We fail to dare, because we are afraid. To keep the splendid image in one's heart demands courage and faith. Man must not objectify it. Man, by nature, is idolatrous. The fatted calf, "Poesie," science, are all variations of the same theme. Because man is wounded (as we use the word), man wants to see, touch, possess. He becomes afraid when he cannot know.

11. I find a very interesting connection between this "schauen" and the flower-woman. The etymology of the word *muse* suggests that it once meant to stare, or gape. Combine this with our interpretation of "woman," and we can see that the youth is enthralled by poetry. She is a lovely woman who appeared to him in his early youth and he cannot forget her. She is the flower in his garden.

12. This is correct in the ultimate sense. Eichendorff insists that religion must be man's love, and the creative artist reveals this love in his works. But the artist must use the sensual to convey this, therefore his object is Beauty. The Beauty is heavenly or earthly.

13. Eichendorff is the gentle antagonist of ancient tradition in his own church which has been too much concerned with "proving" its truth and God's existence. This cannot be done. The human creature is to be charmed by love, and then he will use his mind to find reasons for loving. The Church, too frequently, tends to reverse the process. Man must teach by loving, as he was commanded to do. That is the Law.

14. This is not quite correct. This role is played by Rosa who represents an early religious poetry. Friedrich later calls his love for her "Mädchenliebe." In other words, this poetry was but a step in his development. The Eichendorff who wrote *Ahnung und Gegenwart* has not yet found the perfect resolution of the mystery. Friedrich reminds us of the poem about the nun and the knight. He has turned his back upon Rosa. In the final scenes upon the mountain he cannot see her because the sun blinds him. Eichendorff develops the Venus and Virgin problem in the "Marmorbild" and "Taugenichts" stories. And yet, he already has found the proper question: Which woman is hidden in man's poetry?

15. In "Das Marmorbild," the woman who plays the role of "Poesie" is called Bianca. The name was carefully chosen to suggest the purity of whiteness. The burning colors are always associated with the poet's own love. But we must be careful. The last three sentences of the "Marmorbild" novella also speak of a golden fire. But this refers to the morning light which is cool.

16. I use the word *imprisoned* because in the cycle of six sonnets previously discussed, Eichendorff speaks of "befreite Sehnsucht" (I, 68). Desire must not remain trapped in "die Schlingen" mentioned in the "Zaubernetz" poem.

17. Recent scholarship reveals the premature tendency to define Eichendorff's relationship to Romanticism. We had better understand the poet before making judgments as to the nature of his criticism.

18. As Jacob fled to Haran, he had a vision of angels ascending and descending by a mysterious ladder which reached from earth to heaven. And then Yahweh renewed to him the promises made to Abraham and Isaac. Jacob called the place Beth-El and vowed to worship Yahweh if He would accompany him and take him back home safely. Eichendorff insists "kein Dichter gibt einen fertigen Himmel; er stellt nur die Himmelsleiter auf von der schönen Erde. Wer, zu träge und unlustig, nicht den Mut verspürt, die goldenen, losen Sprossen zu besteigen, dem bleibt der geheimnisvolle Buchstabe ewig tot, und er täte besser, zu graben oder zu pflügen, als so mit unnützem Lesen mässig zu gehn" (II, 99). The tree is a "geheimnisvoller Buchstabe" and we must work with the poet to let it take on life (meaning). He will teach us. To climb a tree is to let one's thoughts soar up to God. And the splendor of the forest (Waldesprachten) is the light from above. There is the dream our poet would have us "see." He tells us that he gives us "Bilder" of our native country. If our thoughts soar, as has been commanded, then Yahweh will keep his promise and take us "back home safely." It is the poet's responsibility to sing of this dream for man has much need of it.

19. The fact that light listens is an obvious reference to the Christ: "I am the Light and the Way." The lark greets the light with its song: the poet greets his God with his love. In Eichendorff's works, the theme of greeting is very important. We greet what we know.

20. Trees that wish to kiss each other! This refers to thoughts. The poet "kisses" the woman who is "Poesie" and the kiss burns on his lips (Cf. "Trauriger Winter" [1, 214]). This happens to Friedrich and Florio as well as the poet figure in numerous poems. This kiss is death, the death of a love imprisoned in its own light. That is why in "Götterdämmerung" Lucifer is prepared to kiss Bacchus-Florio. And Venus is his relative.

21. The poet suggests that flowers become stars ("die ewigen Wegweiser"). The songbird sitting on a golden flower lured Raimund back to the woman who was the object of his thoughts. In other words: stars, flowers, song, bird, woman, and thought are all involved in a fluid complex, where one leads to the other. They are all part of the stream of song which wells forth from the poet's breast.

22. The horns in the distance sound "irrend." This is precisely what happened to Raimund. It seems as if "die Heimat" over there

("drüben") were calling to him. The same sense of direction is expressed by Florio when he sings to the maiden "jenseits über'm Fluss." It is over there, "druben." The "Schäfer" in "Jugendandacht (7-1)" said she is "hinter Berg' und Flüssen." Someplace over there! The songbird in the poem "Der Knabe" hears the words "Kommst du nicht balde?" but it flies away, over there. The pattern is always the same. Man misunderstands the movement of his love, his "Sehnsucht." He runs when he should stop and listen. Always the horn is a signal to be up and away. It is confusing ("irrend") only when man does not know where to go. And the youth in "Jugendandacht" has moved in the wrong direction.

23. As always, it is proper and necessary to investigate Eichendorff's use of words. The word "Maien" refers to May which is a contraction for Mary, the Queen. When man "takes away," "entkleiden," the glory from the Queen, all that remains is Venus, the woman with "strahlend reine Glieder." Therefore, it is not without significance that the last scene in "Das Marmorbild" depicts Florio and Bianca wandering "in das blühende Mailand hinunter." (II, 346). Florio and Bianca ("Poesie") now move toward the country of Mary, the Queen of Heaven. And that is precisely what the "Sänger" should do: travel "nach Hause — heimwarts" on the wings of song. And that, as I shall demonstrate, describes the journey undertaken by the "Taugenichts."

IV

Two Forces and a Song

Der Sänger 1

Siehst du die Wälder glühen,
Die Ströme flammend sprühen,
Die Welt in Abendgluten
Wie träumerische Fluten,
Wo blüh'nde Inseln trunken
Sich spiegeln in dem Duft? —
Es weht und rauscht und ruft:
O komm, eh' wir versunken!

Eh' noch die Sonn' versunken:
Gehn durch die goldnen Funken
Still Engel in den Talen,
Das gibt so leuchtend Strahlen
In Blumen rings und Zweigen. —
Wie frommer Widerhall
Weht noch der Glocken Schall,
Wenn längst die Täler schweigen.

Leis wächst durchs dunkle Schweigen
Ein Flüstern rings und Neigen
Wie ein geheimes Singen,
In immer weitern Ringen
Zieht's alle, die da lauschen,
In seine duft'ge Rund',
Wo kühl im stillen Grund
Die Wasserkünste rauschen.

Wie Wald und Strom im Rauschen
Verlockend Worte tauschen!
Was ist's, dass ich ergrause? —

Führt doch aus stillem Hause
Der Hirt die goldne Herde
Und hütet treu und wacht,
So lieblich weht die Nacht,
Lind säuselt kaum die Erde.

(I, 300)

Der Wegelagerer

Es ist ein Land, wo die Philister thronen,
Die Krämer fahren und das Grün verstauben,
Die Liebe selber altklug feilscht mit Hauben —
Herr Gott, wie lang willst du die Brut verschonen!

Es ist ein Wald, der rauscht mit grünen Kronen,
Wo frei die Adler horsten, und die Tauben
Unschuldig girren in den kühlen Lauben,
Die noch kein Fuss betrat — dort will ich wohnen!

Dort will ich nächtlich auf die Krämer lauern
Und kühn zerhaun der armen Schönheit Bande,
Die sie als niedre Magd zu Markte führen.

Hoch soll sie stehn auf grünen Felsenmauern,
Dass mahnend über alle stillen Lande
Die Lüfte nachts ihr Zauberlied verführen.

(I, 106)

Es walten im Leben der Menschen seit dem Südenfalle zwei geheimnisvolle Kräfte, die beständig einander abstossen und in entgegengesetzten Richtungen feindlich auseinandergehen. Man könnte sie die Zentripetal — und die Zentrifugalkraft der Geisterwelt nennen. Jene strebt erhaltend nach Vereinigung mit dem göttlichen Zentrum alles Seins, es ist die Liebe; während die andere verneinend nach den irdischen Abgründen zur Absonderung, zur Zerstörung und zum Hasse hinabführt (IV, 1069).

Es geht, wie durch die physische Welt, so auch durch das Reich der Geister, eine geheimnisvolle Zentripetal — und Zentrifugalkraft, ein beständiger Kampf zwischen himmlischer Ahnung und irdischer Schwere, welcher in dem grossen Ringe, der die Geister wie die Planeten unfasst, je nach den engeren oder weiteren Kreisen, die sie um den ewigen

Mittelpunkt beschreiben, Licht oder Schatten, belebende
Wärme oder erstarrende Kälte, sehr verschieden verteilt.
Aber das, was in dem Sonnensystem als unvermeidliches
Naturgesetz erscheint, ist im Geisterreich ein Akt der Frei-
heit, die Notwendigkeit dort wird hier durch freie Wahl zur
Tugend oder Sünde, je nachdem die natürliche Harmonie
bewahrt oder willkürlich gebrochen wird (IV, 26-27).

These two rather short passages allow the reader to deduce a surprisingly detailed and emminently logical system
of thought which I shall seek to establish as Eichendorff's
"Weltanschauung." The poet sees two forces in the life of man
which are always and forever of opposite sign.[1] Man's existence
is subject to the law of movement; there is neither rest, compromise, nor a harmonious equilibrium. The basic relationship
between these two forces is given by the word "feindlich." Life
is really "ein beständiger Kampf"; indeed, it is terribly dangerous.
I say dangerous because the gift of life enters man in the lists
and commits him to do battle for that which is more splendid and
precious than the material universe — his immortal soul. The
fact that Eichendorff defines the human situation as a constant
struggle between "himmlischer Ahnung und irdischer Schwere"
dictates that the area of conflict is the inner man. As a being
incompletely spiritual, man is the warrior and the field of battle.
Not only his spirit but the flesh and blood suffer the tension
of decision. The very word "Schwere" suggests that inability of
man to rise and transcend himself. The word "Ahnung," on the
other hand, refers to a profound and seemingly intuitive human
awareness of matters both heavenly and eternal. It is only since
the Fall, when original justice was lost to man, that this struggle
has become the substance of his spiritual activity. Clearly Eichendorff reflects the orthodox position which holds that man now
sees darkly as in a looking glass, and this seeing darkly explains
why the movement of forces is called mysterious or secret. Eichendorff uses the solar system as an analogy to convey his understanding of how man may be deceived by what he sees and feels.

We know that the sun is at the center of the solar system
and that the amount of light and heat (energy) received by each
planet is directly proportional to its distance from the sun. A
planet at too great a distance is hostile to life, bitterly cold, bar-
ren, and unproductive. It is also known that the various bodies
exert a force upon each other. The sun, by far the larger mass,

attracts the planets. The force of this attraction, once again, depends upon the distance between the two bodies. On the other hand, and this is most important, all the planets, due to the attraction of the sun, would plunge to a fiery death if they did not possess the ability to counteract its drawing power. Thus, each planet, in order to preserve its individuality and particular uniqueness, repels, as it were, the sun and the other planets. The entire complex is held in a state of equilibrium by forces which attract and repel. It was these considerations which led, quite naturally, to the selection of the key terms, centripetal and centrifugal force. Let us now apply this same pattern of reasoning to the spiritual world. God, of course, is the sun of our spiritual system. As the energy from our sun makes life possible, so divine grace provides the basis for spiritual growth. As the sun draws the planets, so divine love, our centripetal force, draws man to God. It is important to reconize that the logic of the analogy leaves no room for discussion on this salient point, namely, that it is divine love and not human love which draws man to the center of being. — God. The distance between the creature and the creator is an infinity, and no steps which the creature can take can diminish it. To understand the analogy in any other way is to make a mockery of omnipotence and render the creature the peer of his Maker. The adverb "erhaltend" modifying the verb "streben" in the first quotation might suggest this to the careful reader. "Erhaltend," after all, not only implies to save or preserve but also to receive. As man receives this love which always emanates from God, as energy does from the sun, the process of drawing and saving in the spiritual sense is initiated. But God has left man free to choose, and that is precisely why the adverb "verneinend" was used to modify the essential characteristic of centrifugal force. This, too, is clearly suggested by the analogy.

Our solar system enjoys a certain stability because the forces that attract and repel are in a state of equilibrium. Natural life is possible precisely because these forces are in contention. This element of hostility and struggle in the solar system is termed an "unvermeidliches Naturgesetzt" in the second quotation and is also associated with the concept of natural harmony.[2] This is not true in the spiritual solar system. Eichendorff embraces the faith which holds to the belief that man's ultimate destiny, as willed by the Father, is the vision of God for all eternity. If it is the will of divine love that man be drawn to the Father, I cannot accept the suggestion that natural harmony in nature, the equilibrium of attracting and repeling forces, should apply literally to our spiritual solar system. In the latter instance "natürlich Harmonie" must refer to what is in keeping with God's will and thus implies an accepting or a submitting to divine love. Although man is free to choose — it is called "ein Akt der Freiheit" — the poet's terminology suggests man's helplessness.

We are told that man is drawn by God's love which is equated with centripetal force. The other force, which the poet refuses to identify for us, is called centrifugal force. These two terms confront us with a most disturbing consideration. A person subjected to either one of these forces is quite incapable of differentiating between them; the basic sensation is a being drawn. But in which direction? It would seem Eichendorff has in mind a most surprising possibility, namely, that the human being experiences a movement or influence which he actually may confuse with the effect of divine love. Something acts upon man which seems to have the same effect as though God were drawing the individual, as though he were moving or acting in accordance with His will. The analogy of the solar system suggests an answer. The sun draws the planets but they, empowered, as it were, by their own mass, repel the sun. We may say, in a manner of speaking, that the will of one confounds the will of the other. It must follow, then, that the only force capable of rejecting God's will is man. This seems substantiated not only by the terms of the analogy but by the fact that Eichendorff calls the act of choice "Tugend oder Sünde." We must remember that for Eichendorff, sin is to be understood as a movement away from God, as a rebellious confrontation of His will. Christianity, after all, is the new law or covenant, and the very life of the Founder was a manifestation of the Father's will. The Passion itself, with those words spoken in the garden: "Not as I willt, but as Thou willt," reveals the very essence of what it means to be a Christian. From all this we might conclude that the two hostile forces in the universe are God's will and any other will which pursues a direction contrary to the divine intent. But significantly enough, Eichendorff does not speak of God's will but only of His love. If we can reconstruct the poet's reasoning on this point, we shall be in a position to define the mystery of deception.

In the poems thus far presented I have endeavored to show that Eichendorff's imagery reveals the movement of love. The poet tells us: "Eben weil die Liebe nur von Poesie lebt, bildet sie auch das unverwüstliche Grundthema aller Dichtungen, dessen höhere oder gemeinere Auffassung von jeher den wahren Dichter von dem unberufenen unterschieden hat" (IV. 399). "Love is the life of the flower." The flowers are poems. Venus is a "Wunderblume," and life is given her by Florio's love-song. But poetry itself is given another definition. "Alle Poesie ist nur der Ausdruck, gleichsam der seelische Leib der inneren Geschichte der Nation; die innere Geschichte der Nation aber ist ihre Religion; es kann daher die Literatur eines Volkes nur gewürdigt und verstanden werden im Zusammenhange mit dem jedesmaligen religiösen Standpunkt darselben" (IV, 453). We can use this statement like an equation, and say that poetry expresses religion. But if poetry's theme is love, then it should follow that this love expresses the poet's religion. In fact, the very structure of Eichendorff's thought allows us to conclude that religion *is* the poet's love. We seem substantiated in this when we read that Eichendorff is in full accord with Schlegel's opinion that "die Religion Calderons Liebe sei." Of course, when the word *religion* is used in the Eichendorff context, one immediately thinks of Christianity. It would be quite proper to say that Christianity is his love. On the other hand, this entire presentation argues that the poet is deceived by his love. Raimund, we recall, uses precisely these words. Consequently, if one reasons with the equation I have established, I suggest that man is deceived by his religion. If this is a tenable position, then *religion* must have a very broad spectrum of meaning. Eichendorff insists that poetry expresses a nation's religion. His literary histories were written to determine the movement of religion in Germany, or as we could also say, the movement of love. Examining his results we see that he has, indeed, identified a host of religions. Whereas we tend to associate religion with an organized, institutionalized system of beliefs regulating man's relationship with a higher power, Eichendorff combines the word with "Vernunft, Humanität, Natur, Materialismus, Emanzipation des Fleisches" and "ästhetisch." Romana is called "die zu Stein gewordene Religion der Phantasie," and the poet also speaks of a religion called "Antichristentum." And this does not exhaust the possibilities suggested in his works. In other words, he is not concerned with traditional religions, but with beliefs which predominate at a particular time or place, and which have the impact of what we call religion.

I find this perspective far more reasonable and objective then what one usually finds in the books of theologians and professional students of the subject. Eichendorff sensed that the term *religion* had entered a state of flux or rapid change. An older etymology of the word *religion* suggests that it means "to bind" or "to restrain." However, if the word, in practice, has as many definitions as Eichendorff insists, then it will of necessity become a meaningless expression. This is a conviction amply documented in his works. He tells us that man has always been a rebel, a protestor. However, the Reformation, which he insists was inevitable and even necessary, was tragically and destructively irresponsible in one respect: "Sie hat die revolutionäre Emanzipation der Subjektivät zu ihrem Prinzip erhoben" (IV, 453). In his view, the basic thrust of Protestantism tended to "legalize" rebellion. Man's lawful yearning for freedom — from man and his institutions — became a Pandora's box. Great ideas and religions always find implementation first among the few, and then are slowly embraced by the many. Thus, in this instance, the individual state declared its sovereignty.[3] And then, in the course of a few centuries, the individual slowly learned to make the same demands and assertions. However, in such a spiritual and intellectual context, religion is fragmentized into an "infinite pluralism," and it loses its essential function, *to bind*. Thus religion is perverted and tends to separate. Theoretically, and Eichendorff speaks to this point, we create a society in which state opposes state and group opposes group, until finally it is man against man. Each is bound only to himself; each is his own law and lives his own "religion." This is the trend which Eichendorff discerned; it is the basic subject of his works. We need only effect the substitution he makes, namely, equate religion with love, and we have arrived at the principle of deception. Man's own love introduces the movement he calls "Hinabführen," it leads down "zur Absonderung, Zerstörung und zum Hasse."

This power of love, when it is returned first to God, as Friedrich is urged, leaves the world free. But when man's love turns inward and seeks its own will, then we create a society in which God is dead, man is a useless passion, and each is the enemy of the other. Lest the reader assume we have misused Eichendorff's words concerning religion, let us listen to him.

"Habt Ihr einmal, direkt oder indirekt, dem emanzipierten Subjekt die Souveränität zuerkannt; aus welchem Grunde wollt Ihr ihm nun die Befugnis absprechen, dieses Recht jetzt auch gegen den Protestantismus selbst zu kehren und, eine Schranke nach der andern durchbrechend, endlich die ganze, volle, unbedingte subjektive Freiheit bis zum Naturstande des Orang-Utang zu erstreben? Und in der Tat, das Charakteristische und Unterscheidende dieser neuesten Literatur liegt keineswegs in einer Veränderung des Prinzipes, sondern nur in dem Mehr oder Minder seiner praktischen Anwendung, es liegt darin, dass dieselbe, nachdem sie mit der positiven Religion längst fertig geworden, jetzt aus derselben eigenen Machtvollkommenheit auch das Joch der Moral abschüttelt, und, da sie in diesem Fortschritt von gewissen mittelalterlichen Erinnerungen und Einrichtungen ungebührlich belästiget wird, mit gesteigertem Fanatismus und Wegwerfung aller bisherigen Scham und Scheu, dem Christentum Hass und gänzliche Vernichtung offen proklamiert, gleich jenem Wahnwitzigen, der den Tempel der Diana in Brand steckte, in der wüsten Zerstörung des Heiligen eine eitle Unsterblichkeit suchend. Hinter diesen letzten Trümmern einer tausendjährigen Kultur lauert freilich die Anarchie, die Barbarei, und der Kommunismus: der Proletarier hat an der willkommenen Bresche, wie zur Probe, schon die Sturmleitern angelegt. Aber: après nous le déluge! Was geht das den subjektiven Absolutismus an! (IV, 485).

This passage contains what may well be the fundamental perspective from which Eichendorff understands the movement of events in Europe since the sixteenth century. In a monolithic state the individual may be crushed into a faceless monentity. On the other hand, freedom may become a cancer which destroys the organism called society. Eichendorff seems to imply that either extreme is a monstrosity inimical to the well-being of man. In the one extreme of Communism, man or the state has become a god; in the other extreme of anarchy and barbarism, man is a devil, who also has the name of the destroyer. This passage concerns a religion which has become defective and even inoperative. It behooves us, therefore, to wonder why religion has reached this state. To answer that Eichendorff would have us become Roman Catholics may be correct,[4] but it does not explain religion's defect. We could say that religion no longer binds because each of us tends to live a private definition of the word. This is closer to the truth, but is not yet a complete answer. If, as Eichendorff says, love lives on poetry and poetry expresses a nation's religion, then love is defined in terms of religion. Consequently, if religion is defective, then love suffers the same distortion. In Eichendorff's work, religion and the movement of love are really synonymous. The distortion in one is but a reflection of the defect inherent in the other. And the poet does not leave us in doubt as to the source of the error. We look again at Friedrich's remarks concerning poetry and religion.

> "In wem die Religion zum Leben gelangt, wer in allem Tun und Lassen von der Gnade wahrhaft durchdrungen ist, dessen Seele mag sich auch in Liedern ihrer Entzückung und des himmlischen Glanzes erfreuen. Wer aber hochmütig und schlau diese Geheimnisse und einfältigen Wahrheiten als beliebigen Dichtungsstoff zu überschauen glaubt, wer die Religion, die nicht dem Glauben, dem Verstande oder der Poesie allein, sondern allen dreien, dem ganzen Menschen, angehört, bloss mit der Phantasie in ihren einzelnen Schönheiten willkürlich zusammenrafft, der wird ebenso gern an den griechischen Olymp glauben, als an das Christentum, und eins mit dem andern verwechseln und versetzen, bis der ganze Himmel furchtbar öde und leer wird" (II, 141).

We note that religion demands the participation of the whole man. The stress placed upon this allows us to conjecture that a religion which involves only part of man is somehow defective. The wording in the passage concerning "Verstand, Glauben, Poesie, Phantasie" would tend to substantiate this; but his literary histories are even more convincing. He sees reflected in literature, as we have pointed out, a host of religions, all of which are imperfect or incomplete because they disregard so much of man's nature. In effect, man imprisons the magnificent whole which he could be in a small facet of his potential. Eichendorff seems to suggest that the parts of man must be in harmony. What the young poet argues is repeated, years later, in the literary histories. He tells us that poetry is

> . . . die eigentliche Lebensluft, in der wir alle, gleichviel ob bewusst oder unbewusst, mehr oder minder gesund und

kräftig atmen; unsichtbar, aber alldurchdringend, nicht selbst das Licht, aber das Medium des Lichts, wie die Luft, die
uns die Sterne spiegelt und den Boden lockert und wärmt,
das die Blumen und Wälder sehnsüchtig daraus zum Himmel
wachsen;[5] und gäbe es Menschen, die gar keine Poesie in
sich, oder ihre Poesie an die Altklugheit der Welt ausge-
tauscht hätten, so wären dies eben nur kranke, defekte Leute.
Wenn nun aber die Religion nicht einseitig diese und jene
Anlage, sondern den ganzen Menschen, also auch Phantasie
und Gefühl, deren Ausdruck eben die Poesie, gleichmässig
in Anspruch nimmt, so ist gar nicht abzusehen, warum der
Mensch gerade in seinem Innersten auf jene mächtige
Schwinge verzichten, aus dem wunderbaren Instrument, über
das der Finger Gottes gleitet, eine Saite herausnehmen und
so die ursprünglich vorgesehene Harmonie willkürlich zer-
stören soll (IV, 814).

It is imperative that due emphasis be given the phrase "gleichmässig in Anspruch nimmt." According to his view it is clearly
improper that a particular facet ("Anlage") of the whole man
should be unduly emphasized. He gives us the "Strassburger
Ganz" (IV, 472) as an example of this disease. The insinuation
of the word "gleichmässig" is repeated by the word "Harmonie."
If all of man's powers were equally employed, the result would be
a harmony, which was the original intent (of God). The passage
instructs us that "Poesie," the expression of "Gefühl und Phantasie," is only one string on the instrument which is man. In other
words, man needs "Gefühl und Phantasie (Poesie)," and its lack
would make man defective. On the other hand, "Poesie" must not
become man's *all*, because it is not primarily the manifestation
of another important facet of man, "Verstand." The significance
of this will escape us unless we recall Eichendorff's conviction
that love thrives on "Poesie" which, in turn, is the expression of
a nation's religion. Injecting these factors into our basic equation
we see that love-religion-poetry becomes defective when not
checked by reason. In the discussion of Florio and the "Taugenichts" I shall show that the love of the former is grounded in
feeling and phantasy, while the latter examines his doing and
his feelings. The "Taugenichts" analyses his experiences and
Florio cannot bring himself to do this. He feels fear but does
not ask why. The "Taugenichts" is a delightfully harmonious personality by Eichendorff's definition, while Florio is actually de-

scribed as being sick. If we would understand Eichendorff, we must achieve clarity on this point. He thinks of poetry as a vessel devised by God. But man may misuse his talents.

> "Indem nämlich die Poesie, ihrer Natur nach, zwei Grund-kräfte der menschlichen Seele, welche die Religion nur als organische Teile eines grössern Ganzen schirmend und ver-mittelnd umfasst, die Phantasie und das Gefühl, vorzugsweise herauszubilden strebt, so liegt hier die Versuchung und die Gefahr eben darin, dass sie im Verlauf der Zeiten und Erfolge, ihrer ursprünglichen Heimat vergessend, jene beiden Kräfte selbständig aus aller Gemeinschaft mit dem Komplex der göttlichen Geheimnisse, ja als eine Religion der sub-jetiven Eigenmacht geradezu in Opposition gegen jenen hö-hern Organismus zu setzen unternimmt, und somit, gleich den gefallenen Engeln, jenseit dem Hass, der Hoffart und all' der barbarischen Verwirrung verfallen muss, in welcher wir sie gegenwärtig befangen sehen (IV, 815).

Eichendorff sees an intimate relationship, even interdependence, between love, religion, and "Poesie (Dichtkunst)." And precisely because of this he speaks of "Versuchung und Gefahr." This is the point where "hinabführen" (used in reference to centrifugal force) becomes operative. It leads to a "Religion der subjektiven Eigen-macht" which the poet also calls "Poesie des Hasses." But, and I stress this most emphatically, the poet, or man, never begins with rejection or denial of God's law (religion). This follows gradually and imperceptibly. That is why what began as "Jugend-andacht" terminates in "der Kerkerluft des Bösen." We shall see the same movement in Florio's case. He is good and pious but, because his love is "in der Fremde," he consorts with evil. Al-though Eichendorff, in this context, speaks of poetry and the poet, I do not hesitate to generalize and apply the same principle to all human behavior. Man's search for the "good" is blind, ruthless, savage, and even perverted. This tragedy of Chris-tianity is explained for us in a poem written in 1819.

Memento

Solange Recht regiert und schöne Sitte,
Du schlicht und gläubig gehst in sicher Mitte,
Da trittst du siegreich zwischen Molch und Drachen,
Und wo du ruhst, da wird ein Engel wachen.

Doch wenn die Kräft', die wir "U n s   s e l b e r" nennen,
Die wir mit Schaudern raten und nicht kennen,
Gebundne Bestien, wie geklemmt in Mauern,
Die nach der alten Freiheit dunkel lauern —
Wenn die rebellisch sich von dir lossagen,
Gewohnheit, Glauben, Sitt' und Recht zerschlagen,
Und stürmend sich zum Elemente wenden:
Musst Gott du werden oder teuflisch enden.

(I, 75-76)

If we look at the poem and ask what does man do, we reach
the conclusion that man either walks with God or by himself.
When he walks alone he tends to gravitate toward two extremes
which are essentially the same, that is, a denial of God. The other
possibility is called "gläubig gehen," which must be understood
as a movement toward the Father. All human existence is subject to this tension, this light and darkness, a spiritual life and
death struggle between a positive and a negative movement.
When our poet insists that there is an element in man, "gebundne
Bestien," which rebels and compels a movement or course of action, he only paraphrases the Apostle's words: "Now if I do
that which I will not, it is no more *I* that do it, but sin that
dwelleth in me" (Rom. 7:20, italics mine). Who is this *I*, this inward man? Our poet presents us with the same problem when
he remarks, in speaking of the rebellious "uns selber," "Wenn die
rebellisch sich von dir lossagen." Who is this "dir"? Clearly, it
must be that facet of the human being which is not involved in
rebellion and which our poet defines as "gläubig gehen," something that neither Rudolf nor Romana can accomplish because
they do not believe in God. The counterpart to the self that rebels is the "dir" in the poem "Memento" and is defined for us
in the first novel. We find Leontin and Friedrich perched in
the crown of a tree and observing the dancers. I quote the conversation which takes place.

"Es ist doch ein sonderbares Gefühl," erwiderte Friedrich
nach einer Weile, "so draussen aus der weiten, stillen Einsamkeit auf einmal in die bunte Lust der Menschen hinein-
zusehen, ohne ihren inneren Zusammenhang zu kennen; wie
sie sich, *gleich Marionetten,* voreinander verneigen und beugen,
lachen und die Lippen bewegen, ohne dass wir hören, was
sie sprechen." "O, ich könnte mir", sagte Leontin, "kein

schauerlicheres und lächerlicheres Schauspiel zugleich wünschen, als eine Bande Musikanten, die recht eifrig und in den
schwierigsten Passagen spielten, und einen Saal voll Tan-
zenden dazu, ohne dass ich einen Laut von der Musik ver-
nähme." — "Und hast du dieses Schauspiel nicht im Grunde
täglich?" entgegnete Friedrich. "Gestikulieren, *quälen und
mühen* sich nicht überhaupt alle Menschen ab, *die eigntüm-
liche Grundmelodie äusserlich zu gestalten, die jedem in
tiefster Seele mitgegeben ist,* und die der eine mehr, der
andere weniger und keiner ganz auszudrücken vermag, wie
sie ihm *vorschwebt?* Wie weniges verstehen wir von den
Taten, ja selbst von den Worten eines Menschen!" — "Ja,
wenn sie erst Musik im Leibe hätten!" fiel ihm Leontin lachend
ins Wort. "Aber die meisten fingern wirklich ganz ernsthaft
auf *Hölzchen ohne Saiten,* weil es einmal so hergebracht ist
und das vorliegende Blatt heruntergespielt werden muss; aber
das, was das ganze Hantieren eigentlich vorstellen soll, die
Musik selbst und *Bedeutung des Lebens,* haben *die närrisch
gewordenen Musikanten darüber vergessen und verloren"* (II,
64, italics mine) .

Human beings, dancers, executing gyrations like marionettes governed by forces outside of them, and musicians involved in the
movements of play and yet producing not a sound — such is the
description which is really an indictment, for this is a description
of the dance of life. What is the nature of their dance and who
is the fiddler, "der Spielmann," of whom Eichendorff speaks in
prose and poetry? Is the Christian not to dance Christ and does
not Christ also play the dance? The second half of the conversation instructs us as to the source of this music. Each is given an
"eigentümliche Grundmelodie," a highly individualized and utterly unique song which each is to play. We note that the verb is
"mitgegeben," a veritable *along with,* and this allows us to conclude that it is the complement to the "u n s   s e l b e r" defined in
the poem "Memento," while the word "dir" must be the equivalent
of the "eigentümliche Grundmelodie." In other words, the basic
melody placed in the depths of man's soul is the spiritual mode
of the human being which is to deal with the rebellious will,
the law of a love, which always seeks its ancient freedom.
Friedrich, as we have seen, reminds Romana "[sie] soll . . .
die wilden Elemente . . . *mit göttlichem Sinne besprechen* und
zu einem schönen, lichten (the light symbol) Leben die Ehre,

Tugend und Gottseligkeit in Eintracht *verbinden und formieren.*" The human being ("das Wundertier," as our poet calls him) is to invoke divine magic, and labors to transfigure this "uns selber, die wilden Elemente." These words of divine power are nothing other than "die Grundmelodie." Near the end of "Das Marmorbild" Fortunato explains to Florio the type of song which had induced the youth to call for divine help. "Ich sang ein altes *frommes Lied,* eines von jenen ursprünglichen Liedern, die, wie Erinnerungen und Nachklänge aus einer *andern heimatlichen Welt,* durch das Paradiesgärtlein unsrer Kindheit ziehen und ein rechtes Wahrzeichen sind, an dem sich *alle Poetischen später* in dem älter gewordenen Leben immer wieder *erkennen.* Glaubt mir, ein redlicher Dichter kann viel wagen, denn die Kunst, die ohne Stolz und Frevel, bespricht und bändigt die wilden Erdengeister, die aus der Tiefe nach uns langen" (II, 344, italics mine). This song from another world, man's native country, is the song described by Faber, "eine grosse, himmlische Melodie, wie von einem unbekannten Strome, der durch die Welt zieht." This hosanna, the spiritual song of love and adoration, has the power to invite God's transformational grace which reconstitutes the rebellious spirit of man, "die wilden Erdengeister."

Let us look again at the passage which discusses "die Grundmelodie." Leontin observes that most people play instruments which do not have strings, and yet they play from force of habit. But note, they do not play the song given them in the depths of their souls, but take their music from "das vorliegende Blatt." In other words, they do not play the song of love and adoration, but some other song. In effect, people have become insane musicians who play defective instruments and produce what is not really music. The seriousness of the charge can be deduced from the assertion that they have lost all awareness of the significance of their actions and the meaning of life itself. Man has forgotten why he is alive. Can there be an explanation as to why man is alive other than that man is to love his God and have no strange gods before Him? Friedrich gives his love back to God and the Father magnifies him. Romana, Rudolf, and Renald are consumed by the fire of their own love. Appropriately enough, the last three persons mentioned above do not sing a song of love. Eichendorff explains this to us in a conversation between Romana and Rosa. At one point in the conversation, Romana recalls that Leontin had once described her as "eine Flöte, in der viel himmlischer Klang ist, aber das frische Holz habe sich geworfen, habe einen genialischen Sprung, und so tauge doch am Ende das ganze Instrument nichts" (II, 125). The above insinuation as well as the suggestion in the passage discussing "die Grundmelodie" is clear and unambiguous: Man is the instrument and he is to sing a song. When he touches "die goldnen Saiten" he sings a song of praise to the Creator; but, when the instrument is defective or not used, then the song of love concerns only the self and God is forgotten. As the "Taugenichts" prepares to go in search of "die viel schöne gnädige Frau," he evaluates his state of affairs. "Das Gärtchen war geplündert und wüst, im Zimmer drin lag noch das grosse Rechnungsbuch aufgeschlagen, *meine Geige, die ich schone fast ganz vergessen hatte,* hing verstaubt an der Wand. *Ein Morgenstrahl* aber aus dem gegenüberliegenden Fenster *fuhr* gerade blitzend *über die Saiten. Das gab einen rechten Klang in meinem Herzen.* Ja, sagt' ich, komm nur her, du getreues Instrument! Unser Reich ist nicht von dieser Welt! —" (II, 368, italics mine). "Das Gärtchen — das Rechnungsbuch — die Geige," all words of vital significance! The garden is another symbol for man's spiritual disposition, but this garden has been laid waste because our foolish young hero has neglected to sing the love song. The instrument is dusty from lack of use. (We shall see later just what song this wanderer has been singing.) At this point the genius of our poet fairly sparkles; a beam of light passes through the window, touches the strings of the instrument, and the heart of the "Taugenichts" seems to jump with joy. The light produces a note, a song, in his heart! In other words, grace, the movement of divine love, touches the soul and the human creature responds. (The song is "in" this light, and in "Jugendandacht" the song is "in" the colors. The difference is fundamental.) That is why the "Taugenichts" can tell the instrument their kingdom is not of this world. As I have said several times before, Eichendorff's human being is a stranger in this world who wanders in search of the native country which he dimly recollects deep within him. He is constantly confused and deceived, thinking he has found it. But wandering, "das Reisen," does not mean that man must travel from point A to B; the conventional "das romantische Wandern" has nothing to do with the movement in Eichendorff's world. "Das Reisen" means a search for God's world which must be formed within.

Let me paraphrase some of the passages which we have discussed. "If you love Me, give yourself to Me utterly and completely. I shall let you be a sun to the world bringing My love and light to warm the hearts of the wanderers lost in darkness. Become My instrument and *I* shall play your heart string and produce a lovely song that will entice the wanderer, lure him to the waters that will quench his thirst and fill him with home-sickness. Wear My armor and I shall make you invincible, enabling you to challenge the Prince who would devour My sheep, lay waste the beauty of My garden, and drive men to the madness of fear, hatred and death. Sing My song, dance My dance, and *I* shall give you wings, so that you can fly to the sun (Father) and not fear the flame for My love is cool. Between Me and thee is but a veil of beauty to remind you of My beauty. Do not be deceived or tempted by the veil's glory for the Prince hides in its folds. To *the woman* I have given power to raise the veil so that the light may be with you always. Be My prisoner, dance My dance, sing My song!" This is the song that Eichendorff would sing. It is the song of Christ which can be reduced to the simple and incomprehensible statement, "Thy will be done." This is the problem presented in "Memento": whose will is to be done, which love will become flesh and blood? Let us look at a poem written in 1814, one year before *Ahnung und Gegenwart* was published.

Treue

Frisch auf, mein Herz! Wie heiss auch das Gedränge,
Bewahr' ich doch mir kühl und frei die Brust!
Schickt Wald und Flur doch noch die alten Klänge,
Erschütternd mich mit wunderbarer Lust.
Und ob die Woge feindlich mit mir ränge:
So frömmer nur sing' ich aus treuer Brust;
Da bleicht das Wetter, Himmelblau scheint helle,
Das Meer wird still und zum Delphin die Welle.

"Was wollt ihr doch mit eurem Liederspasse!
Des Würd'gern beut die grosse Zeit so viel!"
So schallt's hoffärtig nun auf jeder Gasse,
Und jeder steckt sich dreist sein glänzend Ziel.
Die Lieder, die ich stammelnd hören lasse,
Ew'ger Gefühle schwaches Widerspiel, —

Sie sind es wahrlich auch nicht, was ich meine,
Denn ewig unerreichbar ist das Eine.

Doch lieben oft, der Sehnsucht Glut zu mildern,
Gefangne wohl, das ferne Vaterland
An ihres *Kerkers Mauern* abzuschildern.
Ein Himmelsstrahl fällt schweifend auf die Wand,
Da *rührt's lebendig* sich in allen *Bildern* —
Dem Auge scheint's ein lieblich bunter Tand —
Doch *wer der lichten Heimat recht zu eigen,*
Dem wird der Bilder ernster Geist sich zeigen.

(I, 94, italics mine)

The poem says: "Why do you sing? Our age offers so much that needs to be done, trials, challenges, problems, all so much more worthy of your energy and time!" But the question is arrogant and presumptuous. Strange! Is there really something more important than the pressing problems of today? "Jeder," everyman, takes issue with the problem as he sees it, and labors to achieve the goal. "Glänzend!" The insinuation of light in conjunction with the word *goal* reminds us of "Mahnung" (1839): "Die Sterne, die durch alle Zeiten tagen,/Ihr wolltet sie mit frieher Hand zerschlagen/Und jeder leuchten mit dem eignen Lichte." There can be no doubt that the thoughts are the same. Because this is the voice of arrogance and pride, it follows that the humble man has another purpose, a different goal, which is the object of his singing. But the song is an awkward stammering which, in truth, is not what the poet means. The one thing, "das Eine," which is the purpose of the song, the goal of his doing, is simply and eternally unattainable. Indeed, that which is made, the song, is but a pale reflection of the eternal feeling which engenders it. This is a confusing and even terrifying statement. The poet has the courage to defy his time, do what others scorn, and then must confess he cannot do that for which he embraces aloneness and mockery. "Ew'ger Gefühle" . . . this we have seen before. It is the same "ewiges Gefühl . . . das uns in den Mittelpunkt alles Lebens versenkt, wo alle die Farbenstrahlen, gleich Radien, ausgehen und sich an der wechselnden Oberfläche zu dem schmerzlich-schönen Spiele der Erscheinung gestaltet" (II, 75). This "Mittelpunkt alles Lebens" is also "der Zentrum alles Seins," which is God. Surely we can no longer misunderstand or debate this point. And what feeling is it that places man into this flaming heart? Once again: Friedrich is told by Christ, "If you love me then immerse yourself in me; be my prisoner." Therefore the poet's singing is praise and adoration of his God — "Es reisen die Gedanken/Zur Heimat ewig fort." The mind and the heart are drawn, in love, to the Father and the poet's song is an externalization of this movement. We have defined "das Eine" but are still responsible for the reason the poet's lovely song should be only "[ein] schwaches Widerspiel." The next strophe offers an explanation.

Despite the fact that his high endeavor is utterly impossible, the poet persists: He paints pictures of his native country upon the prison walls. These are the "Bilder" he wants us to see. But seeing is not enough, because to the eye alone it is but "ein lieblich bunter Tand." If a heavenly light falls upon these pictures, the same light that strikes the strings of the violin which belongs to our "Taugenichts," then these images take on life. (It was Florio's light-love-song which gave Venus life.) Whoever is a part of "der lichten Heimat," whoever seeks to "see" in terms of God's love for man, will understand what these "Bilder" seek to convey. The light or love by which one sees is the crux of the matter. Almost without exception, everything in our poet's emblematic language is prefixed by a positive or negative sign. As the poet insists, nature, the thing, is important not for what it is but what it means. Eichendorff's works are filled with "Bilder" or veritable paintings which conceal more than they reveal at first glance. The poet would have us understand that what he gives us is almost the opposite of the real intent. That is not difficult to understand. It is written that a kingdom is prepared for man and its beauty exceeds what he can imagine; but still he would show us "das ferne Vaterland." Man's yearning, Eichendorff insists, must express itself in doing, and so he "paints" his heart's desire, "draws pictures" of a loveliness which he cannot see. If he did see it, it would not be "das ferne Vaterland." In the cycle of poems called "Der Pilger," and in the last two strophes of the sixth poem we hear God speaking to the pilgrim.

> "Meine Lieder sind nicht deine Lieder,
> Leg ab den falschen Schmuck der Zeit,
> Und nimm das Kreuz, dann komme wieder
> In deines Herzens Einsamkeit."

Und alle Bilder ferne treten,
Und tief noch rauschet kaum die Rund' —
Wie geht ein wunderbares Beten
Mir leuchtend durch der Seele Grund!

(I, 298 f.)

The poet is a "Sänger" and he sings "Bilder." But just as his "Bilder" are "ein schwaches Widerspiel," so his songs are not God's songs. Much of Eichendorff's poetry and prose, I would insist, is a form of prayer. But there are levels to that relationship between God and man which are concealed by the general term *prayer*. Poetic creativity, "Dichten," no matter how dedicated the mind, may be a barrier to that unqualified, total immersion in divine love which is the labor of the contemplative. That is why Friedrich the poet must become a priest. When the heart has been emptied and there is just the yearning heart, then the whole man is prepared, as the younger Eichendorff formulated it, "den Himmel in sich aufzunehmen." All images are removed, and the sounds of earthly things, as though they were far below, are hardly perceptible. At such moments, prayer, like a wonderful light, illuminates the very depths of the soul. This is that prayer of the contemplative, the soul of mystical bent, that has learned to discipline mind and body so that the light will have its way. This is achieved only when man does not have his own thoughts, when he does not sing his own song. Because whatever is his cannot be from God; it is only "ein schwaches Widerspiel." The word "schwach" is most interesting. It is as though the best that man can achieve is a weakened opposition to God's will, as though it were not intended but it is still a fact. One immediately thinks of St. Paul's words: "For to will, is present with me; but to accomplish that which is good, I find not. For the good which I will, I do not; but the evil which I will not, that I do" (Rom. 7, 5-19). And Eichendorff wrote in 1809:

Gott, inbrünstig möcht' ich beten,
Doch der Erde Bilder treten,
Immer zwischen dich und mich,
Und die Seele muss mit Grauen
Wie in einen Abgrund schauen,
Strenger Gott, ich fürchte dich!

Ach, so brich auch meine Ketten!

(I, 295)

The images between God and man, the song which the creature sings, the chains that bind the human being, all say the same thing. The "Taugenichts," who undergoes the same temptations as Florio, expresses this infirmity in seemingly humorous fashion. After being informed that he now has a position, he remarks, "mir war wie einem Vogel, dem die Flügel begossen worden sind, — So war ich denn, Gott sei Dank, im Brote, . . ." (II, 352). Man was made to "fly," but he cripples his own wings; he was made to love his God but his wounded nature is fettered by what he sees, feels, touches; he wants to be free but is afraid of losing himself; rarely does he learn that only the willing, loving slave is truly free. Our poet was given a splendid talent, but because he also loved his God he insists that the gift must be placed in the service of the Lord. This means that he could not speak freely of himself but must sing darkly of his God. He does not want to stand between us and the vision which we are to "see." All of Eichendorff's utterances concerning "Dichter, Dichten und Dichtung" substantiate this point. We must work and cooperate with him, seek to do his will, and then his "Bilder" will take on deeper significance, indeed, only then will they communicate. Many of his "paintings" by his own admission are incomplete; they point to or suggest their true intent. Because of this we must not prematurely identify them. They are part of a movement, and if we "arrest" them then their secret meaning is voided. Eichendorff's creativity is governed by this law; hence his stories always have an open ending. This, of course, is Romantic doctrine. For our poet, however, it is a spiritual law. It is not difficult to find a poem which discusses this problem. "Wehmut" is a cycle of three poems of which the first and third are included in *Ahnung und Gegenwart* (II, 177, 90-91), and the second was printed in the collection of 1837. The third poem speaks of two young counts who are in love and find no peace.

Wir grüssen Land und Sterne
Mit wunderbarem Klang
Und wer uns spürt von ferne,
Dem wird so wohl und bang.

Wir haben wohl hienieden
Kein Haus an keinem Ort,
Es reisen die Gedanken
Zur Heimat ewig fort.

Wie eines Stromes Dringen
Geht unser Lebenslauf,
Gesanges Macht und Ringen
Tut helle Augen auf.

Und Ufer, Wolkenflügel,
Die Liebe hoch und mild —
Es wird in diesem Spiegel
Die ganze Welt zum Bild.

Dich rührt die frische Helle,
Das Rauschen heimlich kühl,
Das lockt dich zu der Welle,
Weil's draussen leer und schwül.

Doch wolle nie dir halten
Der Bilder Wunder fest,
Tot wird ihr freies Walten,
Hältst du es weltlich fest.

Kein Bett darf er hier finden.
Wohl in den Tälern schön
Siehst du sein Gold sich winden,
Dann plötzlich meerwärts drehn.

(I, 72 f. italics mine)

The second and last strophes above provide a frame for the essential idea: life is constant movement. But this movement is not restricted to the usual insinuation of physical activity; it refers also to mental or intellectual activity. Man's thoughts must always travel "Zur Heimat"; that is, he must keep his mind on life's goal, a confrontation with God. This movement through time is thought of as the pressing forward of a stream, which, in the last strophe, is depicted as winding through the valley of existence and then turning suddenly towards eternity ("Meerwärts"). We also note the this stream is really to be understood as a song. In the first strophe, the song sung by the count is a greeting of the entire universe, an understanding suggested by the phrase "Land und Sterne," which draw the eyes from the earth to the depths of space. This song must be equated with "die Gedanken" which travel toward heaven. The last two verses of strophe three above introduce us to our essential concern, "das Bild." This song has a purpose, to open "helle Augen," and this is accomplished by the idea in the third verse, namely, "Gesanges Macht und Ringen." Not only does this song have a power, but it is accorded a certain dynamic quality because it involves struggle; we are left with the impression that "das Lied ringt," but for what? Yes, to be sure, the song struggles to open or keep open "helle Augen." And what does this mean? Poem one of "Jugendandacht" informed us that the Virgin humbly raises the veil so that "offen bliebe/Der Augen Himmel, in das Land zu scheinen." If we understand our poet correctly then the song "[Gedanken, die] zur Heimat ewig fort [reisen]" is, in one sense, a struggle on man's part to keep heaven open. In other words, and this is grounded in Eichendorff's Catholic faith, man must participate in the work of salvation even though faith and grace are not of man's doing but a gift. Man is both responsible and helpless. And the power of this song? When Fortunato sings "ein altes frommes Lied," the reality resurrected by Florio reverts to weeds and ruins after he calls for help. That is to say, not just the song but man's humble participation in its movement are necessary prerequisites for the manifestation of its power. The song transfigures the world, but only if man wills and sings it with all his heart. And even the ability to sing this song is a gift from heaven. The poem "An die Dichter" tells us categorically that the word is given to him, the poet, from on high. And the poet is commanded:

> Da soll er singen frei auf Erden,
> In Lust und Not auf Gott vertraun,
> Dass aller Herzen freier werden,
> Eratmend in die Klänge schaun.
>
> (I, 111)

"Eratmend in die Klänge schauen." In the fifth strophe of "Wehmut" the poet addresses the reader or listener and informs him that "die frische Helle" and "das kühle Rauschen" lure him to the wave. This wave is part of the stream, "eines Stromes Dringen," which is the "Lebenslauf" of the two counts in the poem. It is their way of life, their song, just as it is the poet's song, that makes all hearts breathe freer and lures them to the stream. This is what happens to Florio when he hears the old pious song. The words "Klänge, Welle, Lied, Strom" must be viewed as being essentially of the same order of significance and meaning. Faber's heavenly melody, the stream, unknown to many, attracts our words, which are a song, and "sie [wollen] mitziehen." Perhaps the reader will recall our discussion of "Trost" (I, 137), which speaks of "das Bächlein" from the cool heights which the great stream feels in its "Glieder." The great stream admits that "Die Felsenluft [which is the little rivulet], so kühl und hell,/Lockt zu mir alle Brüder." That is precisely what we are told in the fifth strophe of our poem. The fresh brightness, the mysterious coolness of this stream, which is a song, lures the listener. But we are also warned. This stream really consists of "Bilder" and we must not seek to hold on to "Der Bilder Wunder." If one imprisons, "festhalten," these images then they "die"; that is, they are defined in terms of ourself. Now the very first lines tell us why this is of paramount significance: "Es waren zwei junge Grafen/Verliebt bis in den Tod. . . ." Once again love and death are brought together. This "Lebenslauf, Stromes Dringen, Gesanges Macht," is a song of love. If that love should center upon any "Bild" then the thoughts no longer travel "Zur Heimat ewig fort." If love tarries along the way then it has forgotten its God, it pursues its own will, and soon it travels the path which leads down "zur Absonderung und Hasse." That is what Eichendorff keeps saying again and again. We are like physicians who worry about and endlessly treat the fever, and are too blind and proud to investigate the cause. That is why our poet wrote. In his love song man can breathe more freely; he willed to be the prisoner of love so that the loveless world where it is "leer und schwül" would be introduced to the warmth of the cool light, hear the night song of the trees (his thoughts), and see the face of the woman who was in God's mind before chaos become cosmos. Eichendorff is the rarest of poets in our heathen civilization. He has given us a most precious mirror. What does our poem say about the "Spiegel"?

Looking at the sequence of thoughts in strophes four and five, we see that the song effects an opening of the eyes. Once this is accomplished something else happens. "Und Ufer, Wolkenflügel, /Die Liebe hoch and mild —/Es wird in diesem Spiegel/Die ganze Welt zum Bild." There seems to be no reasonable and acceptable reference for the mirror other than the stream. Rudolf is hard like a rock; he will not let the light touch him so that a spring will burst forth, becoming a light-filled stream of song which should contain "Bilder" of man's eternal home. Now we, the readers, are to be touched by "die frische Helle" and "Das Rauschen heimlich kühl"; this, so it is suggested, is even more important than "die Bilder" themselves. To say it in another way, our poet would have us become engrossed in the mystery which he cannot show us rather than the concrete images which the poet must employ if he is to create. He deliberately wants us to forget him and his faltering efforts and:

> So schauet denn das buntbewegte Leben
> Ringsum von meines Gartens heitrer Zinn',
> Dass hoch die Bilder, die noch dämmernd schweben —
> Wo Morgenglanz geblendet meinen Sinn —
> An eurem Blick erwachsen und sich heben.
> Verwüstend rauscht die Zeit darüber hin;
> In euren treuen Herzen neu geboren,
> Sind sie im wilden Strome unverloren.
>
> (I, 179)

His song, the stream of love, contains "die Bilder" which should take on new life within us — how closely this resembles the Florio-Venus story — and bring us to the morning light which is the grace of God. But the poet himself tells us, warns us, that his song is but a mirror. Why? In the discussion of the "den literarischen Abend" which Friedrich experiences I singled out the man and woman who heard only their own song, and the man who looked into the mirror because the other did not really exist for him. When Venus first comes to life for Florio, she is depicted as having just emerged from the waters: "und betrachte nun, selber verzaubert, *das Bild der eigenen Schönheit*" (II, 318, italics mine). The last scene in the castle portrays her as constantly looking into a mirror. And finally, just before the power of evil is broken, Florio notices that the numerous paintings on the wall "sahen auf einmal aus wie er und lachten ihn hämisch an" (II, 339). Eichendorff tells us that when man looks into the created he will always and everywhere find only himself, a reflection of his mind, his love, his desires. And indeed man is filled with an overwhelming, restless passion for a completeness, for an answer to a pressing question which he cannot answer, and so he despoils and loves and searches the universe for that which might still the hunger. But always the created deceives him because it has no answer. For this reason the poet tells us that creation (and his

"Bilder" are a part of *being* which surrounds man) must be seen in the light of the stream which is a song of love. All that is must be touched by that other light (II, 75) which reveals the true uniqueness and dignity of creation. Take it out of this light and it dies to God; it is no longer free. It becomes imprisoned in man's own light and in the city of Lucca there is darkness. And in this process man, too, is bound and becomes a prisoner. He becomes a prisoner of the created to the extent that he is imprisoned within the self. The poem "Durch," written about 1821, touches upon this matter.

> Lass dich die Welt nicht fangen,
> Brich durch, mein freudig Herz,
> Ein ernsteres Verlangen
> Erheb' dich himmelwärts!
>
> Greif in die goldnen Saiten,
> Da spürst du, dass du frei,
> Es hellen sich die Zeiten,
> Aurora scheinet neu.
>
> Es mag, will alles brechen,
> Die gotterfüllte Brust
> Mit Tönen wohl besprechen
> Der Menschen Streit und Lust.
>
> Und eine Welt von Bildern
> Baut sich da auf so still,
> Wenn draussen dumpf verwildern
> Die alte Schönheit will.
>
> (I, 74-75)

Man escapes by an act of the will. He must strive quite deliberately to break through the veil. The imagery in "Wehmüt" 2 is repeated here: man must be driven by a more serious and profound desire, a desire which can find no satisfaction in the created alone. And, in Eichendorff's mind, man's historical existence is evidence of this truth. Only when man plays the heart strings and sings his song of love to God does he feel his freedom. Then Aurora, the dawn light of man's intended magnificence, shines upon him and within his heart a new world of images takes form. A comparison of the last strophe above with Friedrich's discussion of creativity (II, 75) reveals that the thoughts are perfectly similar. Furthermore, we note that the word "draussen" is used in exactly the same sense as it was employed in the earlier poem "Wehmut." "Draussen" is the world of man's doing, the world which would trap man (see poem "Rettung") and make of him a prisoner. It is a world that calls to him as a beautiful woman might whisper the poet's name, but only to impose its will, to exploit the soul and rob it of its heavenly beauty; it is a world that is "leer und schwül" and subject to "ein dumpf verwildern." The garden is going to seed, the song of love is being perverted. For the men of this world are shrewd; recognizing that man's love is really a marvelous source of energy for doing the world's business and not God's, they offer the soul an activity which never satisfies until the human creature has all but forgotten why he exists. "Wohl ist der Weltmarkt grosser Städte eine rechte Schule des Ernstes für bessere, beschauliche Gemüter, als der *getreueste Spiegel* ihrer Zeit. Da haben sie den *alten, gewaltigen Strom in ihre Maschinen und Räder aufgefangen,* dass er nur immer schneller und schneller fliesse, bis er gar abfliesst, da breitet denn das arme Fabrikenleben in dem ausgetrockneten Bette seine *hochmütigen Teppiche* aus, deren inwendige Kehrseite *ekle, kahle, farblose Fäden* sind, verschämt hängen dazwischen wenige Bilder in uralter Schönheit verstaubt, die niemand betrachtet, das Gemeinste und das Grösste, heftig aneinander geworfen, wird hier zu Wort und Schlag, die Schwäche wird dreist durch den Haufen, das Hohe ficht allein" (II, 164, italics mine). We recall that Venus says to Florio that he should accept "die Blumen des Lebens fröhlich, wie sie der Augenblick gibt, und forscht nicht nach den Wurzeln im Grund, denn unten ist es freudlos und still!" The imagery is the same. One can almost see the flowers woven into the design of this rug — flowers that are "hochmütig" because they represent man's pleasures, joys, desire, and a love which would forget God. This stream is best understood as that general movement of an earlier civilization, perhaps the twelfth to the fifteenth century, when all thought and action was seen, ideally, as a movement toward God. This stream has now gone dry. Civilization is no longer a painfully dark yet beautiful endeavor to do God's will but a terribly ruthless and violent endeavor to assert man's own will. With his imagery of the stream our poet actually describes his understanding of events during the last several centuries. What he saw as a movement toward God has been subverted and directed as a movement toward the created. Man, with supreme arrogance, has decreed that the created is sufficient for him, that he is sufficient unto himself, and God has no voice in his affairs. Man can "save" himself. The ideal of unity under God has been voided and reduced to a pluralism under man. There is no law but man's law, no light but man's light. And Eichendorff, a most angry poet, warns us.

Mahung

Genug gemeistert nun die Weltgeschichte!
   Die Sterne, die durch alle Zeiten tagen,
   Ihr wolltet sie mit frecher Hand zerschlagen
   Und jeder leuchten mit dem eignen Lichte.

Doch unaufhaltsam rucken die Gewichte,
   Von selbst die Glocken von den Türmen schlagen,
   Der alte Zeiger, ohne euch zu fragen,
   Weist flammend auf die Stunde der Gerichte.

O stille Schauer, wunderbares Schweigen,
   Wenn heimlich flüsternd sich die Wälder neigen,
   Die Täler alle geisterbleich versanken,

Und in Gewittern von den Bergesspitzen
   Der Herr die Weltgeschichte schreibt mit Blitzen —
   Denn seine sind nicht euere Gedanken.

(I, 313, italics mine)

This poem was written about 1839, but the imagery and profound conviction of its truth surely were etched in the mind and heart of the young man. At least twenty-seven years earlier, Eichendorff placed the following observation upon the lips of Leontin.

"Den Rhein seh' ich kommen, zu dem alle Flüsse des Landes flüchten, langsam und dunkelgrün, Schiffe rudern eilig ans Ufer, eines seh' ich mit Gott geradaüs fahren; fahre, herrlicher Strom! Wie Gottes Flügel rauschen, und die Wälder sich neigen, und die Welt still wird, wenn der Herr mit ihr spricht! Wo ist dein Witz, deine Pracht, deine Genialität? Warum wird unten auf den Flächen alles eins und unkenntlich wie ein Meer, und nur die Burgen stehen einzeln und unterschieden zwischen den wehenden Glockenklängen und schweifenden Blitzen? Du könntest mich wahnwitzig machen unten, erschreckliches Bild meiner Zeit, wo das zertrümmerte Alte in einsamer Höhe steht, wo nur das Einzelne gilt und sich, schroff und scharf im Sonnenlichte abgezeichnet, hervorhebt, während das Ganze in farblosen Massen gestaltlos liegt, wie ein ungeheurer, grauer Vorhang, an dem unsere Gedanken, gleich Riesenschatten aus einer andern Welt, sich abarbeiten" (II, 182).

Eichendorff always thinks of life as movement, generally conveyed by the emblematic terms *water, song, light,* and *color.* These four terms are actually interchangeable; that is, color becomes song, light becomes song, water becomes song. And the equation is reversible. There is in this structure an adumbration of the ancient Greek notion that creation consists of fire, water, air, and earth. All these, as Eichendorff uses them, are one! In the discussion of creativity (II, 75), the poet speaks of the focal point of life from which the colorful radii emerge and form the phenomenon ("Erscheinung") on the surface ("die Oberfläche"). The word "Erscheinung" is in the singular. Despite the diversity all things are one. We detect the same pattern in his emblematic words. Our poet's imagery argues that life depends upon light which, in turn, manifests itself in colors. Consequently, a world that is like a gray rug, or a world where the "stream" has dried up leaving a rug whose threads are "kahl und farblos," is a world without light and love. It is a world curiously flat, without heights, having no Mount of God that man would climb. It is like the great deep over which the spirit of the Lord hovers — "Gottes Flügel rauschen." All is monotonous and unrecognizable because the Lord does not turn His countenance to it. (That is why Florio's song at the end of his "Marmorbild" experience must contain the plea: "O Vater du *erkennst* mich doch!") Only the "Burgen" stand alone above the deep. Eichendorff deliberately uses this word rather than "Schloss" to suggest that man must be a fortress, a rock which defies the waves of the deep that do not know God. These "Burgen," which are really human beings, are outlined and defined in a reality that is separate from "das Meer" by the action of the light and the song; for thus would we interpret the words "Glockenklänge und Blitze." And then, in case the reader did not understand his nature imagery, Eichendorff redescribes the same scene. "Burgen" are replaced by "das Einzelne," lightning is rendered by sunlight, and "das Meer" is a formless, colorless mass — "Das Ganze in farblosen Massen gestaltlos liegt." And finally, so that the symbolism cannot be misunderstood, the poet calls all this "ein ungeheurer, grauer Vorhang."

In the poem "Wunder über Wunder," Eichendorff tells us there are two worlds or realities: That which man can comprehend, and the reality, "das Revier," a veritable infinity which is beyond his grasp. And man, according to Eichendorff, belongs and is in that realm which he cannot comprehend. And what of the reality which man does seem to understand — what is its meaning? We are told it is nothing, just "Plunder." Reasoning with Eichendorff's imagery, it seems that man confronts the veil, "die Oberfläche," the phenomena that he can see, and makes of it that which conforms to his mind. In doing this, the veil with its "schmerzlich-schönen Spiele der Erscheinung" becomes a rug whose substance is ugliness, or a gray curtain "an dem unsere Gedanken, gleich *Riesenschatten aus einer anderen Welt,* sich abarbeiten" (italics mine). Note the comparison: God's thought creates "die Erscheinung," and man's thought engenders shadows. Why? Because the reality which he has made has nothing to do with "das Revier" in which he actually does exist. That is why his thoughts, as the "play" upon the curtain, come from another world. Man is always a stranger to what he has done. But, like the prisoners in Plato's parable, he insists the shadows are real. And thus, the spirit in the poem "Der Geist" looks at his universe and sees it as "das wesenlose Meer." Then, when the morning sun looks at him, "Da versinkt das Bild mit Schauern/Einsam in sich selbst zurück." Eichendorff always portrays human beings who achieve varying degrees of insight as to helplessness, loneliness, and painful otherness in a world fashioned by man in his own name and for himself. The city, for our poet, is a grave and its buildings are tombstones.

If we have understood our poet correctly, man's capacity to love and be loved is the particular uniqueness which best enables us to understand the significance of those words: "Let us make him in our image." All other human powers are energized by love. Look wherever you will in Eichendorff's entire works and you will find nothing that degrades the movement of love, unless it be found on the lips of such as Leontin and Rudolf, who have defiled the most precious jewel of man's human nature. This love, if properly used, must be dedicated to the will of the Father, and then the individual becomes like a sun which brings light and warmth and truth to the created. This is "lebendig eindringen"; it is achieved, with God's help, by an upward penetration of the veil, "die Oberfläche," and a union with the light, "der Mittelpunkt alles Lebens," who is its author. But the creature is free, and the power of love may be placed at the disposal of human will. Then "die Oberfläche" which contains "die Erscheinung" is the substance of man's reality, which then loses original beauty and becomes a rug or grey curtain. This is then a veritable nothingness, "ein wesenloses Meer." All this compares very favorably with the discussion presented on the last few pages of Plato's *Republic*, Book V. We have in mind the realm of ideas, absolute and unchangeable, or complete non-being or nothingness. The pages of Eichendorff's works are filled with "dem schmerzlich-schönen Spiel der Erscheinung" to which man gives his love and sings his song which burns with the splendor of his yearning. Man wanders about in this world of sounds and light, tones and colors (words also used by Plato), and is sure that the ultimate answer to the mystery can be found in his understanding of creation. But these are just images, "Bilder," of what utterly transcends them. Man must not "hold on to them" with his love because then they die and man is left with himself. Then he will remain forever blind to the hidden beauty of the world.

These thoughts are a proper introduction to the "Marmorbild" story. Florio is "der Blöde" who is blind to reality and lives a dream. Seeing, he does not see, and hearing, he does not hear. His own love song has become a Beatrice who would lead him to the Father. She is the woman "in" the flowers which grow in the garden of his creativity.

Notes

1. The words "of opposite sign" are intended to convey the notion of *reflection*. This one term includes all the variables which concern our book. The forces seem to be so similar that man is deceived. One is the reverse of the other. That is why the poet can use the word "vernienend." One is the world of substance and reality, the other of illusion. Whatever picture ("Bild") man sees is always a faint approximation; the truth is seen darkly as in a mirror. Eichendorff's thoughts, his use of imagery, always return to this point.

2. In principle, and through grace, man is endowed with the potential to approach this harmony. But Eichendorff insists that the human creature remains wounded because he places his faith and hope in the image. Indeed, he venerates himself.

3. We could, and should, go back even further. As late as the Roman period, a man declared himself a god; he was, indeed, sovereign. Much later a French king said "I am the state." I wonder what Hitler and Stalin thought. The "man in the street" learns from his "leaders." They are the teachers and establish values. Thus it was written: "Go ye out and teach ye all nations." Not what we say, but what we do, is burned into the heart of the other.

4. Let me add that in the "Taugenichts" novella he offers a stinging criticism of the Roman church and the clergy. They have been asleep in God's vineyard.

5. I reject the notion that Eichendorff speaks of flowers and trees. He is concerned with poems and thoughts. Man is the garden, the soil ("Boden") which receives the seed and is warmed by the light so necessary for growth.

V

Marmorbild

Anklänge

3

Wenn die Klänge nahn und fliehen
In den Wogen süsser Lust,
Ach! nach tiefern Melodien
Sehnt sich einsam oft die Brust.

Wenn auf Bergen blüht die Frühe,
Wieder buntbewegt die Strassen,
Freut sich alles, wie es glühe,
Himmelwärts die Erde blühe:
Einer doch muss tief erblassen,
Goldne Träume, Sternenlust
Wollten ewig ihn nicht lassen —
Sehnt sich einsam oft die Brust.

Und aus solcher Schmerzen Schwellen,
Was so lange dürstend rang,
Will ans Licht nun rastlos quellen,
Stürzend mit den Wasserfällen,
Himmelstäubend, jubelnd, bang,
Nach der Ferne sanft zu ziehen,
Wo so himmlisch Rufen sang,
Ach! nach tiefern Melodien

Blüten licht nun Blüten drängen,
Dass er möcht' vor Glanz erblinden;
In den dunklen Zaubergängen,
Von den eigenen Gesängen

Hold gelockt, kann er nicht finden
Aus dem Labyrinth der Brust.
Alles, alles will's verkünden
In den Wogen süsser Lust,

Doch durch dieses Rauschen wieder
Hört er heimlich Stimmen ziehen,
Wie ein Fall verlorner Lieder
Und er schaut betroffen nieder:
"Wenn die Klänge nahn und fliehen
In den Wogen süsser Lust,
Ach! nach tiefern Melodien
Sehnt sich einsam oft die Brust!"

4

Ewig's Träumen von den Fernen!
Endlich ist das Herz erwacht
Unter Blumen, Klang und Sternen
In der dunkelgrünen Nacht.

Schlummernd unter blauen Wellen
Ruht der Knabe unbewusst,
Engel ziehen durch die Brust;
Oben hört er in den Wellen
Ein unendlich Wort zerrinnen,
Und das Herze weint und lacht,
Doch er kann sich nicht besinnen
In der dunkelgrünen Nacht.

Frühling will das Blau befreien,
Aus der Grüne, aus dem Schein
Ruft es lockend: Ewig dein —
Aus der Minne Zaubereien
Muss er sehnen sich nach Fernen,
Denkend alter Wunderpracht,
Unter Blumen, Klang und Sternen
In der dunkelgrünen Nacht.

Heil'ger Kampf nach langem Säumen,
Wenn süsschauernd an das Licht
Lieb' in dunkle Klagen bricht!
Aus der Schmerzen Sturz und Schäumen
Steigt Geliebte, Himmel, Fernen —
Endlich ist das Herz erwacht

Unter Blumen, Klang und Sternen
In der dunkelgrünen Nacht.

Und der Streit muss sich versöhnen,
Und die Wonne und den Schmerz
Muss er ewig himmelwärts
Schlagen nun in vollen Tönen:
Ewig's Träumen von den Fernen!
Endlich ist das Herz erwacht
Unter Blumen, Klang und Sternen
In der dunkelgrünen Nacht.

(I, 59-60)

Es war ein schöner Sommerabend, als Florio, ein junger Edelmann, langsam auf die Tore von Lucca zuritt, sich erfreuend an dem feinen Dufte, der über der wunderschönen Landschaft und den Türmen und Dächern der Stadt vor ihm zitterte, sowie an den bunten Zügen zierlicher Damen und Herren, welche sich zu beiden Seiten der Strasse unter den
hohen Kastanienalleen fröhlich schwärmend ergingen (II,
307).

The casual reader, and too many of us have been casual readers, will see in this paragraph a delightfully vague romanticism;
it will convey nothing more than "Stimmung." As has been pointed
out, the season may be summer, but the story is based upon
spring. The city is called Lucca but Florio enters darkness, the
darkness of the very same "Heide" which the "Taugenichts" crosses. The entire scene of landscape and city are immersed in a
delicate fragrance. With this the poet insinuates the flower symbolism and the realm of Venus belonging to "einer langen versunkenen Welt." The movement imputed to the people is also
suggestive. "Sich schwärmend ergehen" connotes Romana's "Und
ich mag mich nicht bewahren." We are told that this fragrance
"zitterte" above the scene. This describes rather accurately the
movement of air in a mirage. Eichendorff knew Latin, and the
root of the word *mirage* suggests the idea of mirror, reflection,
inversion, and even the action of wondering. And our story is
about a wonderful flower, a love that is a mirror in which the
self experiences inversion. I suspect the verb "zittern" was
carefully selected to prepare the mind of the reader for the images
which are to follow.

The first person Florio encounters is a certain Fortunato whose essential characteristics are given by the words "frisch, keck und fröhlich," the very opposite of the mysterious Donati who will appear later. These words are often used to describe the morning, while Donati is a creature of the night. Fortunato asks him what business takes him to Lucca and the youth answers somewhat shyly "ich habe gar keine Geschäfte." This is an error! The man who does not have a specific purpose in life or who does not know where he is going has already lost his way. The fact that Fortunato deduces from his answer that he must be a poet is a direct criticism of then-contemporary poet and his poetry. Eichendorff's poet must be about his Father's business. Florio blushes maidenlike at being called a poet and denies it. This is to his credit; it shows his basic humility. He admits earlier efforts "in der fröhlichen Sangeskunst" but became discouraged upon reading the old masters[1] and compares himself to "ein schwaches, vom Winde verwehtes Lerchenstimmlein unter dem unermesslichen Himmelsdom." Now the lark is the morning bird, the first to greet the dawn and sing the praises of the Lord; but "vom Winde verweht" suggests it has lost its way. This is the same pattern that we saw in Eichendorff's early poetry which led to the study "Jugendandacht." Fortunato responds that each praises God in his own way "und alle Stimmen zusammen machen den Frühling." The first time that spring is mentioned it is associated with poetry, the song, and praising the Lord. Let us not forget this. As he says this, Fortunato's eyes rest with obvious approval upon this beautiful youth "der so *unschuldig* in die dämmernde Welt vor sich hinaussah" (italics mine). The young man seems to feel the kindliness of the other and speaks more boldly. He admits that he has elected to travel and feels as though released from a prison (308) and "alle alten Wünsche und Freuden sind nun *auf einmal* in Freiheit gesetzt. Auf dem Lande in der Stille aufewachsen, wie lange habe ich da die fernen blauen Berge sehnsüchtig betrachtet, wenn der *Frühling* wie ein zauberischer *Spielmann* durch unsern Garten ging und von der wunderschönen Ferne verlockend sang und *von grosser, unermesslicher Lust*" (italics mine). Fortunato seems seriously disturbed by these words and warns him of a certain marvelous minstrel whose tones lure youth into a magic mountain from which none return. His final words are: "Hütet Euch!" I have said that the lack of a particular purpose or goal was an error;

deciding to travel is another. This decision had to be made in the past, because the opening scene of the story finds him traveling. Fortunato recognizes what has happened. We need but compare Florio's words with Romana's childhood experience and her mother's warning not to leave the garden. In other words, the temptation to walk without God, which is a negative "wandern," begins early in the life of the human being. The human aspiration to grow and exceed one's own dimension is a veritable song which fills the soul with "grosser, unermesslicher Lust." Eichendorff does not deny this absolutely essential thrust of human nature; the point is, just how does man become "grösser"? Only love magnifies the creature or the created, and the problem is determining which love man lives. Fortunato warns the youth of that siren song by which man, or what he loves, becomes an end in itself. But Florio does not understand that the reference to a "Zauberberg" is a metaphorical allusion to the finite self in which man becomes the prisoner of his own thoughts and desires.

The two men ride past the city gates and come to a lovely meadow ". . . auf dem sich ein fröhlich schallendes Reich von Musik, bunten Zelten, Reitern und Spazierengehenden in den letzten Abendgluten schimmernd hin und her bewegte." The word "Reich" seems carefully selected because this is indeed a new world for Florio, a world whose movement and light echoes the verb "zittern" which we saw in the first paragraph. Very deftly and discreetly our poet paints for us a graphic definition of the word "Erscheinung." Everything is associated with light; "schimmern, zitternder Duft, glänzen, Abendgluten, glänzende Bogen, glänzende Wiesen." All this describes the veil of light and color which hides "einer Jungfrau strahlend reine Glieder." It is a world filled with music provided by hidden orchestras. Everything is movement; the decorative hats of the ladies are called "ein Blumenbeet, das sich im Winde wiegte." The game played by the young maidens continues the suggestion of soft and gentle movement, like a graceful dance that beguiles the eyes. Even the ball with which they play is called a butterfly, a creature that floats lightly and aimlessly on the breezes and which is a symbol of life, death, and resurrection. Florio watches the game and is attracted by one maiden in particular (309). She has a colorful wreath of flowers in her hair "und war recht wie ein fröhliches Bild des Frühlings anzuschauen." Bianca, white light, is like an image of spring, and Fortunato had said "alle Stimmen zusammen machen den Frühling." Is Bianca an image of that spring?[2]

Florio watches the game played by the young maidens and then follows the throng. "Der grössere, funkelnde Strom von Wagen und Reitern, der sich in der Hauptallee langsam und prächtig fortbewegte, wendete indes auch Florio von jenem reizenden Spiele wieder ab, und er schweifte wohl eine Stunde lang allein zwischen den ewig wechselnden Bildern umher" (309). The description of this movement, the stream, with its insinuation of light, reminds us of Romana's song "Frische Fahrt" with the lines: "Auf dem Strome will ich fahren,/Von dem Glanze selig blind." To appreciate what is happening we must recall the first two verses of "Jugendandacht" 5: "Wenn Lenzesstrahlen golden niederinnen, /Sieht man die Scharen losgebunden ziehen." The first three pages of the novella delicately insinuate the watery realm of Venus. As we can see in the passage above, Florio is alone among eternally changing "Bilder," and we have reason to ask ourselves if all this is, indeed, real. At this point Florio comes upon Fortunato surrounded by people listening to his songs. Only some of them seem to respond to what he is singing. Considering the nature of his song, which we shall discuss later, it is significant that most of the listeners do not answer. Among the bystanders is Bianca, "die in stiller Freudigkeit mit weiten, offenen Augen in die Klänge vor sich hinaussah." The way Eichendorff says this, and it must not be understood as vague and romantic rhetoric, it seems as if the song were a reality that one sees, a reality which seems to captivate the maiden and fill her with an inner joy. The song has a similar effect upon Florio, for he could have listened all night long "so ermutigend flogen ihn diese Töne an." This is the song that seems to be a reality, fills one with a quiet joy and gives courage to the heart; we must keep in mind that there is another singer and another song which lures youth into a magic mountain. As Fortunato finishes he sees Florio and, as if he were the only listener, comes directly toward him, grasps "den Blöden" and leads him "wie einen lieblichen Gefangenen" into a nearby tent. "Der Blöde," with its gentle insinuation of being blind, reminds us of "Jugendandacht" 3:1 and Romana's words, " von dem Glanze selig blind." He is called a prisoner, a lovely prisoner, and we recall Florio's own words which describe him as one who has been released from a prison. Deftly and unobtrusively Eichendorff weaves the threads: to be free or a slave, to sing a certain song, to be a certain spring. As Florio enters the tent everyone greets him "wie alte Bekannte," and young, beautiful eyes rest with pleasure "auf der jungen, blühenden Gestalt." Florio, indeed, is filled with spring! The fact that everyone seems to know him is not unrelated to the question of reality.

The very same atmosphere that surrounds the city of Lucca also reigns in the tent. The glasses are "hellgeschliffen," the table cloth is "blendendweiss," the scent of flowers fills the air, and the faces of beautiful maidens are visible among the bouquets of flowers just as though they were part of "ein Blumenbeet." The evening lights play golden upon the meadow and the small stream in front of the tent is mirror-smooth. This could easily be a painting, "ein Bild." At this juncture the men improvise a song to their beloved. "Der leichte Gesang, der nur gaukelnd wie ein Frühlingswind die Oberfläche des Lebens berührte, ohne es in sich selbst zu versenken, bewegte fröhlich den Kranz heiterer Bilder um die Tafel." This scene, this city, these people — are they real? The final scenes of the "Marmorbild" experience depict the young hero in conversation with Venus and he describes his early childhood. "Damals . . . wenn ich so an schwülen Nachmittagen in dem einsamen Lusthause unseres Gartens vor den alten Bildern stand und die wunderlichen Türme der Städte, die Brücken und Alleen betrachtete, wie da prächtige Karossen fuhren und stattliche Kavaliere einherritten, die Damen in den Wagen begrüssend — da dachte ich nicht, dass das alles einmal lebendig werden würde um mich herum" (II, 337). Pictures that seem to come alive! Perhaps our poet is trying to tell us that the movement of events is really a dream, that is to say, a dream has become Florio's reality. The light and airy song of love which each man sings is called "gaukelnd"; it only touches the surface of life, not life itself. And Friedrich has told us of "jenes ewige Gefühl" which immerses man "in den Mittelpunkt alles Lebens . . . wo alle die Farbenstrahlen, gleich Radien, ausgehn und sich an der wechselnden Oberfläche zu dem schmerzlich-schönen Spiele der Erscheinung gestalten" (II, 75). The intellectual content of these two passages is similar. The song of love which Florio sings touches only the painfully beautiful "Erscheining" but not "den Mittelpunkt alles Lebens." Let us listen to the first song that he sings, "Liebe in der Fremde."

> "Jeder nennet froh die Seine,
> Ich nur stehe hier alleine,
> Denn was früge wohl die Eine,

> Wen der Fremdling eben meine?
> Und so muss ich wie im Strome dort die Welle
> Ungehört verrauschen an des Frühlings Schwelle".
>
> (II, 310)

Just who is the one, "die Eine," whom the youth means? That, of course, is the mystery. The last two verses of Florio's song express his fear that he will not be heard, that like the wave in the stream, he will surge to the very threshold of spring and then die away. Spring, that is a praising of God, the image of a maiden, "ein zauberischer Spielmann," the song that touches just the surface of life, or the gentle waves that beat against the heart "Dass des verlornen Himmels es gedächte"; all these possible definitions of spring are related to the question in the song: "die Eine/Wen der Fremdling eben meine." When we have identified her we can define spring.

Florio's efforts are rewarded with a kiss from the maiden wearing the wreath of flowers. Each has now selected his favorite, "Nur Fortunato allein gehörte allen oder keiner an und erschien fast einsam in dieser anmutigen Verwirrung." In many poems which concern a certain enchantress, we are told that she wants a particular person and would have no other. Each poet has his own "Venus." Fortunato is associated with that love which belongs to all and not that movement which leads to the utter isolation of the individual. The song which he now sings is both summary and commentary upon what has transpired. His contribution is called "Götterdämmerung."

> "Was klingt mir so heiter
> Durch Busen und Sinn?
> Zu Wolken und weiter —
> Wo trägt es mich hin?
>
> Wie auf Bergen hoch bin ich
> So einsam gestellt
> Und grüsse herzinnig,
> Was schön auf der Welt.
>
> (II, 311)

The heart and mind of this man are filled with a song that carries him high above the created, from which vantage point he greets whatever is beautiful. As the prose passage suggests, he is alone and does not really belong to any given individual. This reference to song and movement may remind us of Faber's words that the soul hears in the distance, "eine grosse, himmlische Melodie, wie von einem unbekannten Strome, der durch die Welt zieht," a stream which man would like to join (II, 296). But Eichendorff's imagery has instructed us concerning the existence of another stream in which the heart and mind of man see splendor and loveliness which man would embrace. One stream is invisible and all the faith and love of man are needed if he is to entrust himself to its "waters." Fortunato is a part of this heavenly melody and his greeting is an invitation to join him.

> Ja, Bacchus, dich seh 'ich,
> Wie göttlich bist du!
> Dein Glühen versteh' ich,
> Die träumende Ruh'.
>
> O rosenbekränztes
> Jünglingsbild,
> Dein Auge, wie glänzt es,
> Die Flammen so mild!
>
> Ist's Liebe, ist's Andacht,
> Was so dich beglückt?
> Rings Frühling dich anlacht,
> Du sinnest entzückt. —
>
> (II, 311 f.)

The above strophes address Bacchus, "ein Jünglingsbild, und du," all of which refer to Florio. He is, indeed, the very image of youth crowned with roses, the symbol of love; he is Bacchus because we have just seen his involvement in wine, woman, and song which Eichendorff calls "diese anmutige Verwirrung." He is the "du" in the last strophe above. Listen to how the poet describes him just before Florio sings his song. "Florio war recht innerlichst vergnügt, alle blöde Bangigkeit war von seiner Seele genommen, und er sah fast träumerisch still vor fröhlichen Gedanken zwischen den Lichtern und Blumen in die wunderschöne langsam in die Abendgluten versinkende Landschaft vor sich hinaus" (310). Looking at the first two strophes above we see that "die träumende Ruh' " is his "Glühen" which, in turn, is equated with the gentle flame that seems to blaze in his eyes. This gentle light is the movement of Florio's love which learns to look at Venus "mit flammenden Augen." And Friedrich, at the beginning of his spiritual development, asserts: "Aus dir selber muss doch die Sonne das Bild bescheinen, um es zu beleben" (II, 35). There can be no question that the flame is man's love, but this love is also "die träumende Ruh'." This suggests an inversion or retreat within the self where all is seen and understood in terms of one's own light. We saw (in II, 41) that man's being in the world must be illuminated by the light of grace if he is to see the true value and dignity of what surrounds him. Human love, in and of itself, tends to exclude because it selects. Thus the last strophe above asks that significant question which is the cornerstone of the novella: "Ist's Liebe, ist's Andacht,/Was so dich beglückt?" But this question, if it is to be answered properly, must be understood in terms of Florio's own question, that is: "Denn was früge wohl die Eine,/Wen der Fremdling eben meine?" It may be apparent that one half of the equation could be defined as love and Venus and the other half as reverence or devotion and the Virgin. But what if they are confused? What if "Liebe" and "Andacht" were finely woven together in Florio's heart and he found it impossible to distinuish between them? Then he would follow the same deception which caused the speaker in "Jugendandacht" to cry out: "O Herr! du kennst allein den treuen Willen, /Befrei ihn von der Kerkerluft des Bösen." This "Kerker" is the "Zauberberg" of which Fortunato speaks; it is the prison which man enters when he is governed by "[sein] Glühen . . . Die träumende Ruh'." And thus "Götterdämmerung" continues:

> Frau Venus, du frohe,
> So klingend und weich,
> In Morgenrots Lohe
> Erblick' ich dein Reich.
>
> Auf sonnigen Hügeln
> Wie ein Zauberring. —
> Zart' Bübchen mit Flügeln
> Bedienen dich flink,
>
> Durchsäuseln die Räume
> Und laden, was fein,
> Als goldene Träume
> Zur Königin ein.

In the poem "Die Werber" we are told that the Prince of De-
ceivers disguises himself as Cupid and introduces man to Venus,
"Die schönste Frau,/Die macht erst all' verwirrt." The second
strophe above employs the same imagery. Cupid searches and
invites "was fein,/Als goldene Träume/Zur Königin ein." The
words "Glühen" and "träumende Ruh' " are condensed to "goldene
Träume." These golden dreams are part of man and through
them he is enticed to appear before the queen whose realm is
a magic circle upon sunny heights. We have had occasion to discuss Eichendorff's use of the circle motif; it also applies to love.
When Friedrich first falls in love he visits Rosa almost daily.
"Drüben in ihrem schönen Garten hatte die Liebe ihr *tausend-
farbiges* Zelt aufgeschlagen, ihre wunderreichen Fernen ausge-
spannt, ihre *Regenbogen und goldenen Brücken* durch die blaue
Luft geschwungen, und rings die Berge und Wälder wie einen
Zauberkreis um ihr *morgenrotes Reich* gezogen" (II, 35, italics
mine). We have seen all of this imagery in numerous poems. The
power of human love is such that it creates its own world; but its
magic is limited, and, as Friedrich says, it closes man's eyes to
God's "weite Welt." We observe that love's realm is described by
the adjective "morgenrot," and Fortunato, in speaking of Venus,
states, "In Morgenrots Lohe/Erblick ich dein Reich." Whatever
is associated with morning always has a positive connotation in
Eichendorff's works. Morning is new light from the East, the Orient, which is an ancient term for the Messiah. Morning is rebirth,
dedication, transfiguration; it is the tongues of cool light that
symbolize love; but only the fire, the flame, is in Florio. The remarkable subtlety of our poet's carefully structured imagery can
be seen in the light theme. Venus' realm exists in the flame
("Lohe") of the dawn; at the end of the self-deception Florio
turns to the Lord and the light which bursts into his heart "mit
seiner strengen Kühle." Man's love is a flame which, if not carefully guarded in the name of the Father moves to render golden
and then, if thwarted, will destroy what it touches. Spiritually
speaking, man is Midas: what his love touches turns to stone.
Man's love does not give life but takes it. The reader may feel
that I have contradicted myself, but this is not so. Human love
is a paradox and thus our poet would have it understood. Rudolf
takes life from all that he touches; like Raimund he kills his
"Doppelgänger," the self, who is his "Herzensbruder" and whom he
hates with a consuming passion. In the end there stretches before

him "ein wesenloses Meer." All is dead. Florio is the opposite
extreme. With his love he creates. He brings back to life that
which had died; Venus, arrested in her dance by the light reflected from the second Eve, feels life in her limbs and would dance
with her lover the dance of death.[3] Love is the movement of
a power which would create and destroy. That is why the poem
"Memento" tells us that if man does not walk with God he must
either become like God, the Creator, or end like Lucifer, the destroyer. The problem-mystery of love creates the garden in which
Venus sings her song; it is the spring in which she grows like a
flower and it is that commitment of mind and heart which rebuilds her temple. Thus love is power and potential which enables
man to move from God and toward an order of reality which
derives its self sufficiency from man, or it may move the human
being to say with the "Taugenichts": "Den lieben Gott lass ich
nur walten." It is impossible for even the most faithful of Eichendorff's characters to reduce this problem to a simple either-or
choice. The very title of the poem, "Twilight of the Gods," suggests that nebulous dimension where the light of God's love and
the darkness of man's love are in contention.

> Und Ritter und Frauen
> Im grünen Revier
> Durchschwärmen die Auen,
> Wie Blumen zur Zier.
>
> Und jeglicher hegt sich
> Sein Liebchen im Arm,
> So wirrt und bewegt sich
> Der selige Schwarm." —

(II, 312)

These two strophes are a faithful rendition of the scene first
encountered by Florio. The fact that these people are called flowers is a deliberate reminder that the reality of what Florio is
experiencing embraces the illusory and dreamlike. We must recall his words to Venus that while lying in the garden "Die Gräser
und Blumen schwankten leise hin und her [and were the opening scenes not described with the same strange, hypnotic "hin
und her" movement?] über mir, als wollten sie seltsame Träume
weben."[4] The dream is coming to life and Fortunato warns the
gentle youth. Thus far "der Sänger" has described the events

leading up to the time that he sings his songs. He has explained for us what he saw in Florio's heart and which led him to remark, "Hütet Euch!" This is approximately one-fourth of the entire poem. Fortunato now changes "Weise und Ton" and the next ten strophes explain how love seduces the young man's soul.

> "Die Klänge verrinnen,
> Es bleichet das Grün,
> Die Frauen stehn sinnend,
> Die Ritter schaun kühn.
>
> Und himmlisches Sehnen
> Geht singend durchs Blau,
> Da schimmert von Tränen
> Rings Garten und Au. —

(II, 312)

Something, like a frigid breeze breathing a cold and nameless hostility, has descended upon the warm meadow and the gay company. The sounds of nature, its song of joy and praise, becomes a whisper and dies away. The very green pales as though in fright. The women become silent and thoughtful and the men strike a defiant pose. In nature, be it in the depths of the ocean or the jungle, whenever the great beast prowls to seek his fill, the "little ones" are aware of death and fall silent. The intruder is abroad and someone will die! Here, because our subject is spiritual and not physical, there is an overpowering yearning that the hand on high may stay the violence of evil that despoils, and nature has only tears to express its agony. All this is in preparation of him who is to come. Our poet has labored, and very successfully, to create an atmosphere. It is imperative that we note the startling contradiction between the frightening overture and the imagery used to describe the new arrival.

> Und mitten im Feste
> Erblick' ich, wie *mild!*
> Den stillsten der Gäste.
> *Woher, einsam Bild?*
>
> Mit blühendem *Mohne,*
> Der *träumerisch glänzt,*
> Und Lilienkrone
> Erscheint er bekränzt.

Sein Mund schwillt zum Küssen
So lieblich und bleich,
Als brächt' er ein Grüssen
Aus himmlischem Reich.

(II, 313, italics mine)

This nameless and uninvited guest is called "mild." Why did Eichendorff prepare us for a something both dangerous and frightening and then confound us with gentleness? Because it is absolutely necessary! If Florio is to be lured into "einen Zauberberg," as Fortunato warns him, would he go willingly with someone who is not "mild"? Consider the word that Eichendorff used to describe those susceptible to such a deception; only one who is "fein" would be tempted by the invitation. The significant mystery in the first strophe above concerns the origin of this guest. Where, indeed, does he come from? We are reminded of a conversation between Friedrich and Maria, a Magdalena figure in *Ahnung und Gegenwart.* Friedrich's words are most appropriate in the present context. "Wie der schwarze Ritter heute auf dem Balle, tritt überall ein freier, wilder *Gast ungeladen in das Fest.* Er ist so lustig aufgeschmückt und ein rüstiger Tänzer, aber seine Augen sind leer und hohl und seine Hände totenkalt, und du musst sterben, wenn er dich in die Arme nimmt, denn dein Buhle ist der Teufel" (II, 117, italics mine). Maria abandons herself to a life of revelry; Florio's nature is different, and to each the Seducer appears in appropriate guise; to the one as a dancer, to the other, as we shall see, as an envoy from heaven.

The second strophe above uses the flower symbolism to convey contradiction and deception. The stranger wears a wreath containing poppies and lilies. One speaks of chastity and purity, an immaculate heart, the other introduces what we may well refer to as the flaw in Florio. The poppy represents the dream, the lovely world of vision and phantasy nourished by flesh and blood and uncontrolled by a system of values grounded in man's relationship with or love for his God. This poppy is the perfect symbol for a movement of the heart which Florio describes when he says at the very beginning of the story — "alle alten Wünsche und Freuden sind nun auf einmal in Freiheit gesetzt" (II, 308). These desires and joys are set free and appear again as a wreath crowning the brow of the Tempter who always appeals to man in perfect accordance with the individual's desires and his will.

That, of course, is why the poet speaks of the poppy "Der träumerisch glänzt." This unusual structure expresses with wonderful
economy the very essence of what I have been trying to convey:
what man sees in his own light ("glänzen") is but a *dream* of
reality; it is not God's world. We recall that Fortunato refers to
Florio with the words "Dein Glühen und die Flamme." "Träumerisch glänzen" also paraphrases what our poet conveyed in the
eighth strophe, in which he speaks of cupid inviting "was fein,
/als goldene Träume/Zur Königin ein." These two expressions,
so similar in nature, suggest that Florio's personal light is the
determining factor in both quarters of the poem; in other words,
we are concerned with love and Venus and not the Virgin and
reverence. In fact, the poppy and the lily were chosen with metic-
ulous care to express the spiritual reality conveyed by the words
"Liebe und Andacht." So, keeping in mind the person of Florio,
we must understand that the Tempter comes and offers "Liebe"
in the guise of "Andacht."[5] This resolves any contradiction inherent in the symbolism of the flowers and introduces the last
strophe above. All the imagery in these verses is calculated to
express a mode of being, a relationship, from which Florio thinks
or feels that he draws his inspiration. What would seem to be
the kiss of peace is the caress of Judas, for the tempter, indeed, betrays man to himself. The subjunctive "Als brächt" is a
clear insinuation of the contrary-to-fact nature of what the kiss
would wish to convey — a greeting from heaven. It is this notion that events are precisely the opposite of what they appear
to be which brings the remainder of the poem into proper perspective. The next three strophes come to grips with the problem
of light.

> Eine Fackel wohl trägt er,
> Die wunderbar prangt.
> "Wo ist einer", frägt er,
> "Den heimwärts verlangt?"
>
> Und manchmal da drehet
> Die Fackel er um —
> Tiefschauend vergehet
> Die Welt und wird stumm.
>
> Und *was hier versunken*
> *Als Blumen zum Spiel,*

Siehst *oben* du funkeln
Als *Sterne* nun *kühl.*

(II, 313, italics mine) .

What I would like to say about the above lines must be pre-
ceded by a brief excursion into the meaning of the name *Venus;*
I would offer nothing more than a simple listing of information
available in many books, an encyclopedia, or even a good diction-
ary. In the Roman religion Venus was the goddess of bloom and
beauty, the protectress of gardens. We all know how often the
poet speaks of "Blühen," the flower, the reference to spring
and the discussions of various gardens. Their total number is in
the hundreds and their summation exercises an overpowering effect upon the reader who seeks to determine its significance.
Venus is also associated with sexual intercourse, and Eichendorff
reveals his awareness of how human love may seek its object
on the broad spectrum of Sexus-Eros-Agape. In the ancient and
memorable science of alchemy, copper was used in the making
of mirrors and the astronomical symbol for Venus is, even today,
a mirror. Venus, of course, is a planet that shines with such
brightness that under certain conditions it can be seen in the
daytime, provided one knows where to look. As the well-known
evening star, the ancients called this planet Hesperus; however,
when seen in the morning it was called Lucifer. Lucifer, the
brightest star in the heavens (the name means light-bearer),
was named for the proud and defiant being who refused, at the
command of the Father, to venerate disgusting matter. Venus-
Lucifer-the Seducer; one and the same? Donati, whom we shall
present as the personification of the Evil One says of the marble
statue that Florio calls into life: "Die Dame ist *eine Verwandte
von mir,* reich und gewaltig, ihr Besitztum ist weit im Lande
verbreitet" (II, 323, italics mine). And finally, the planet Venus
whose atmosphere abounds in clouds is represented in astronomy
with a very interesting symbol, namely, ♀. Many Christians, including non-Catholics, are familiar with paintings and statues of
the Virgin holding the Christ Child in her arms. The Child has
its hand extended and in its palm is the following symbolic arti-
fact, ♂. This represents the earth and the cross that has con-
quered death. Surely it is unnecessary to point out that these two
symbols are the exact reverse of each other. The two component
parts, earth and cross, are retained but everything is of reverse

order, everything is, as it were, upside down! And how perfectly this conforms to the theory of two forces, centrifugal and centripetal! All movement seems the same, yet it is of opposite sign. And then love posing as reverence, Venus present as the Virgin, the goddess who would be queen! We should add that everything said above concerning the name Venus is incorporated in the novella. Eichendorff did not neglect one item. It seems unthinkable that this could be due to chance. Eichendorff, it is my absolute conviction, exploited the remarkable parallelism and subtle difference between Venus and Mary. Indeed, Venus Genetrix even came to be regarded as the mother of the Roman people, especially of the Julian family, which claimed descent from Aeneas. And what Catholic child has not been taught to look at Mary as his heavenly mother? Let us return to our poem and apply some of the above material.

What this uninvited guest does tells us who he is. Christ *is* the Light, but this being *carries* light in the form of a torch. Lucifer, the light-bearer, the being who carries this torch, asks if anyone is anxious to *go home,* an expression used by Novalis to imply man's yearning for heaven. Satan asks if anyone desires heaven! And why not? It is written: "False apostles are deceitful workmen transforming themselves into the apostles of Christ." And no wonder: "for Satan himself transformeth himself into an angel of light!" (2 Cor.: 13-14). What happens when he inverts the torch? The pretense of the lily is discarded and only the phantasy induced by the poppy, the dream, remains. "Tiefschauend vergehet/Die Welt und wird stumm." The world seems to disappear and only the depths, the abyss to which Lucifer was given the key, remain visible. In this world there is silence because the Alleluia, the world singing the praises of the Creator, is not heard in darkness where true love and reverence are anathema. But, of course, Florio does not see this yet. This brings us to the all-important eighteenth strophe. With consummate care and conciseness our poet suggests to us the principle of inversion which flows with absolute necessity from the original question: "Ist's Liebe, ist's Andacht/Was so dich beglückt?" The flower — and I shall return to this point several times in the course of subsequent discussions — is the symbol for a poetry grounded in man's flesh and blood, his earthly desires. Romana's poem, as I have suggested, describes not only Romana but a certain movement of poetic creativity which Eichendorff saw within himself. The last few verses of this long poem (II, 135 ff.) belong in this context. The word "sie" refers to poets.

> Und sie müssen töricht tanzen,
> Manche mit der Kron' geschmücket
> Und im purpurnen Talare
> Feierlich den reigen führen.
> Andre schweben lispelnd lose,
> Andre müssen männlich lärmen,
> Rittern reissen aus die Rosse
> Und die schreien gar erbärmlich.
> Bis sie endlich alle müde
> Wieder kommen zu Verstande,
> Mit der ganzen Welt in Frieden,
> Legen ab die Maskerade.
> 'Jäger sind wir nicht, noch Ritter',
> Hört man sie von fern noch summen,
> 'Spiel nur war das — wir sind Dichter!' —
> So vertost der ganze Plunder,
> Nüchtern liegt die Welt wie ehe,
> Und die Zaub'rin bei dem Alten
> Spielt die vor'gen Spiele wieder
> Einsam wohl noch lange Jahre. —"
>
> (II, 140)

All this is just a game; we are poets! In a reality separated from God and illuminated by the fire of self love, this poetry transforms flowers into stars. Once again our poet is the critic, not only of Romanticism but of his own earliest endeavors in poetry. This self analysis may be traced in several poems, but especially in "Jugendandacht." That is why "Jugendandacht" 6:2 asks: "Wen nicht das süsse Herzeleid verführen,/Im Liebesschlagen tot vom Baum zu fallen?" The Christ said: "I am the vine," and if man falls from the tree, he dies. In the poem "An die Freunde" the first strophe ends as follows: "Und was sich spielend wob als ird'sche Blume,/Wölbt still den Kelch zum e r n s t e n Heiligtum." Now Eichendorff means this in a positive sense, not as I am using it, to suggest deception. I cite these lines because the earthly flower *is* the poet's poem. If the poet feels and begins to think that his song contains the truth and his thoughts are the truth and his love is sufficient, then what he has made becomes "stars," the guide to heaven. If man insists upon doing what it is not given him to do he becomes guilty of that first sin in the created universe, *superbia;* he falls upward. And this is precisely what the last two strophes seek to express.

> O Jüngling vom Himmel,
> Wie bist du so schön!
> Ich lass' das Gewimmel,
> Mit dir will ich gehn!
>
> Was will ich noch hoffen?
> Hinauf, ach hinauf!
> Der Himmel ist offen,
> Nimm, Vater, mich auf!"

The youth from heaven is he who seemingly brings a greeting from the Father's house; he is the guest who is called an "einsam Bild." We must not be disturbed by the adjective "schön." Lucifer, the most brilliant angel in the heavens, was indeed beautiful; so much so that, if we may be allowed the thought, he fell in love with his own beauty and now labors to distort man in *his* own image. Who is the person who speaks in the last few lines? We really have no choice in the matter. The song is sung by Fortunato and concerns Florio. Lucifer, in strophe sixteen, was the last person to speak. Only Florio-Bacchus can reply. His response indicates that his heart yearns for the Father. But the Mediatrix, as we learn from the entire poem, is Venus, that is, the symbol of a heathen love. Therein lies the flaw, the error of a love which almost costs the young hero his life. One cannot move toward the Father when one's heart is filled with "ancient joys and desires." The entire novella revolves about this spiritual problem. The youth thinks to move toward the Father, and the heart embraces Venus and makes of her the beloved that would lead Florio "nach Hause." He says heaven is open, but the preceeding strophes and the entire story will reveal that his movement is toward the abyss, "ein Versinken." The "Zauberberg" of which Fortunato warns him is not the heaven that the youth imagines but the grave of Venus, the tomb of a pagan love. Look again very carefully at the last two strophes and remember that this is a youth speaking. What we see is a rejection of life and a desire to die.[6] For this man there is nothing left but death — "Was will ich noch hoffen?"

From the first half of "Götterdämmerung" I have drawn an outline of what has happened and what will take place up to that
moment when summer returns, and Florio has said "aus tiefstem
Grund der Seele: "Herr Gott, lass mich nicht verlorengehen in der
Welt!" From that moment on, Lucifer is vanquished, Venus is
dead, and Florio is resurrected from the tomb of his own making.
He will move painfully from darkness to sunlight until he can
sing "mit heller Stimme: Hier bin ich Herr! Gegrüsst das Licht."

It is part of Eichendorff's technique that the ideas in a song
merge with the movement of events in the story proper. As
Fortunato stops singing we are told, "draussen waren nun die
Klänge verronnen und die Musik, das Gewimmel und alle die
gaukelnde Zauberei nach und nach verhallend untergegangen vor
dem unermesslichen Sternenhimmel und dem gewaltigen Nachtgesange der Ströme und Wälder." The lovely world which Florio
had come upon is called "eine gaukelnde Zauberei," a phrase
which suggests rather emphatically the spurious nature of its
reality. This beautiful finiteness is contrasted with the immensity
of the heavenly dome, and the sweet love songs are replaced
by the power and majesty of nature's song. And now, suddenly,
a richly attired stranger appears. "Sein Blick aus tiefen Augenhöhlen war irre flammend, das Gesicht schön, aber blass und wüst.
Alle dachten bei seinem plötzlichen Erscheinen unwillkürlich
schaudernd an den stillen Gast in Fortunatos Liede" (II, 314).
Eichendorff *tells* us that this stranger is "Der Jüngling vom Himmel," the torch-bearer who brings a greeting from home. This
man greets Florio as "einen früheren Bekannten in Lucca."
Florio has admitted having seen pictures of Lucca and of the
very scenes which he now experiences. The dreams in the garden,
dreams of many years ago, have become flesh and blood. And
the stranger was there then; he was the "Spielmann"; he even
describes Florio's garden and the secret places he had loved so
well. He walks to the buffet "und schlürfte hastig dunkelroten
Wein mit den bleichen Lippen in langen Zügen hinunter." He
is called beautiful, as in the poem, but also pale and "wüst"
with its insinuation of wild and evil. His eyes are hollow and
emit a wierd flame and the entire company is vaguely uneasy in
his presence. Even Bianca, like Margareta in the presence of
Mephistopheles, is filled "mit heimlicher Furcht." And despite
this abundant evidence that this creature who "steps out of the
poem" and into Florio's life must be identified as Lucifer, there

are casual Eichendorff readers who insist that the figure in the poem is Christ or Thanatos.

The appearance of this unwelcome stranger puts an end to the gaiety, and everyone prepares to leave "und bald war die ganze schimmernde Erscheinung in die Nacht verschwunden" (315). Once again the word "Erscheinung" suggests that all this is somehow unreal. The last three people to leave are Florio, Fortunato, and the stranger, and we are told that "Florio, noch im Nachklange der Lust, ritt still wie ein träumendes Mädchen zwischen beiden." Florio dreams and is immersed in the melody of his own joy; he does not see the reality that begs to be understood. As they approach the city, Donati (the stranger) finds that his horse will not enter the gate. "Ein funkelnder Zornesblitz fuhr, fast verzerrend, über das Gesicht des Reiters und ein wilder, nur halb ausgesprochener Fluch aus den zuckenden Lippen, worüber Florio nicht wenig erstaunte, da ihm solches Wesen zu der sonstigen feinen und besonnenen Anständigkeit des Ritters ganz und gar nicht zu passen schien." The young hero observes this contradiction, the flickering flame of rage barely concealed by the veneer of politeness, but he does not think about it. Lucifer is the personification of what Eichendorff calls "der eiserne Wille"; he forces obedience and enslaves while God woos with love and leaves man free. Florio even defends this creature when Fortunato, who can hardly tolerate the presence of the man, calls him "einer von den falben, ungestalten Nacht-schmetterlingen, die, wie aus einem phantastischen Traume ent-flogen, durch die Dämmerung schwirren und mit ihrem langen Katzenbarte und grässlich grossen Augen ordentlich ein Gesicht haben wollen." Almost instinctively one thinks of a vampire, the spiritual vampire, who feeds upon the souls of men.

When the young man reaches his room he throws himself upon his bed without even bothering to undress. "In seiner von den Bildern des Tages aufgeregten Seele wogte und hallte (the insinuation of the water and song theme) es noch immer fort."[7] Gradually all sounds subside "bis endlich Haus, Stadt und Feld in tiefe Stille versank." And now we are told: ". . . da war es ihm, als führe er mit schwanenweissen Segeln einsam auf einem mondbeglänzten Meer. Leise schlugen die Wellen an das Schiff, Sirenen tauchten aus dem Wasser, die alle aussahen wie das schöne Mädchen mit dem Blumenkranze vom vorigen Abend. Sie sang so wunderbar, traurig und ohne Ende, als müsse er vor

Wehmut untergehn. Das Schiff neigte sich unmerklich und sank langsam immer tiefer und tiefer. — Da wachte er erschrocken auf" (316). The imagery is provocatively suggestive.[8] The ship is Eichendorff's standard symbol for man's life as he lives it. Florio sails all alone upon a vast, moon-drenched ocean and the sirens all look like Bianca who is the image of spring. Her lovely, sad song seems to draw him down; the movement of the ship, his life, is not abrupt but imperceptible. Slowly he sails deeper and deeper into Venus' "versunkene Welt." The last sentence is separated from the rest of the paragraph by a dash. What fear rouses him and when does he awaken? The question is not irrelevant because we were not told that he fell asleep. Eichendorff is a careful and most conscious artist, and we cannot dismiss this as a simple oversight. I have quoted Friedrich's dream of the Christ Child; let us look at the lines which introduce this passage. "Ihm träumte einmal, als er in der Nacht einst so über seinen alten Büchern eingeschlummert, als weckte ihn ein glänzendes Kind aus langen lieblichen Träumen" (165). Within a dream he awakens from a dream; this suggests that Friedrich, while awake, had been living a dream. The word *dream* in this context must be understood as a mode of life which is not God-oriented. I apply this interpretation to the "Marmorbild" discussion and conclude that Florio does not truly awaken until summer returns, which does not occur until page 340. To be sure, in the immediate context of the story Florio seems to awaken; he jumps up from his bed and looks out upon a beautiful moon-filled night. "Auch da draussen war es überall in den Bäumen und Strömen noch wie ein Verhallen und Nachhallen der vergangenen Lust, als sänge die ganze Gegend leise, gleich den Sirenen, die er im Schlummer gehört." The reference is abundantly clear; nature now sings the song of his dream. What has happened to that other song, "dem gewaltigen Nachtgesange der Ströme und Wälder?" But of course, nature must sing the song that is in man's heart, and reality must be defined in terms of Florio's "Wünsche und Freuden, die nun auf einmal in Freiheit gesetzt," that is to say, in terms of his dreams. That other song will not be heard again until Fortunato sings it and reminds Florio to ask for help!

Our hero, we are told, cannot resist the temptation. He takes "die Gitarre" left him by Fortunato and wanders out into the intoxicating loveliness of the night, where "viele weissglänzende

Schlösser, hin und wieder zerstreut, ruhten wie eingeschlafene
Schwäne unten in dem Meer von Stille" (317). These lines must
be compared with Florio's dream-vision. We find the same reference to "die versunkene Welt" of Venus, the same use of the
swan symbolism; in other words, more and more he begins to
see reality in terms of the dream. This is the psychological orientation from which we must understand the song he now sings,
"Liebe in der Fremde."

> "Wie kühl schweift sich's bei nächt'ger Stunde,
> Die Zither treulich in der Hand![9]
> Vom Hügel grüss' ich in die Runde
> Den Himmel und das stille Land.
>
> Wie ist das alles so verwandelt,
> Wo ich so fröhlich war, im Tal.
> Im Wald wie still, der Mond nur wandelt
> Nun durch den hohen Buchensaal.
>
> Der Winzer Jauchzen ist verklungen
> Und all der bunte Lebenslauf,
> Die Ströme nur, im Tal geschlungen,
> Sie blicken manchmal silbern auf.
>
> Und Nachtigallen wie aus Träumen
> Erwachen oft mit süssem Schall,
> Erinnernd rührt sich in den Bäumen
> Ein heimlich Flüstern überall.
>
> Die Freude kann nicht gleich verklingen,
> Und von des Tages Glanz und Lust
> Ist so auch mir ein heimlich Singen
> Geblieben in der tiefsten Brust.
>
> Und fröhlich greif' ich in die Saiten;
> O Mädchen, jenseits überm Fluss,
> Du lauschest wohl und hörst's von weiten
> Und kennst den Sänger an dem Gruss!"

(II, 317)

Fortunato's song, he tells us, thrusts him high above the firmament: "Zu Wolken und weiter — . . . wie auf Bergenhoch bin
ich." Florio stands "auf einem Hügel." The difference in elevation corresponds perfectly with the nature of the song each sings.

The speaker in the poem "Der Geist," we are told, "tritt auf die Zinne,/Und noch stiller wird's umher." Donati's home, it is said, "lag auf einem der höchsten Plätze mit der Aussicht über die Stadt und die ganze umliegende Gegend" (II, 340). And Friedrich tells Romana: "Sie wohnen hier so schwindlich hoch . . . dass Sie die ganze Welt mit Füssen treten" (II, 157). And finally, we must not forget that the realm of Venus is "auf sonnigen Hügeln,/Wie ein *Zauberring*," the same word which describes the particular vantage point from which Florio greets "die Runde." Human love transfigures and elevates, but only to a certain degree. In each of the above instances a particular character reaches a certain height to which the imagery ascribes a specific limitation. Leontin, in speaking of the female characters he finds in literature, describes them as "ein verliebtes Ding, das die Liebe mit ihrem *bisschen brennbaren Stoffe* eine Weile *in die Lüfte treibt,* um desto jämmerlicher, wie ein ausgeblassener Dudelsack, wieder zur Erde zu fallen" (II, 40 italics mine). Florio, too, is filled with "ein Glühen, eine milde Flamme," and the poem above tells us he has left the valley and is now on a "Hügel," that is, "in die Höhe." But, as is always true in our poet's works, this human love and its power to elevate results in isolation. As man closes his heart to God the world first becomes silent, as we saw in the poem "Der Geist" and in "Götterdämmerung," then in accordance with the principle of obedience, it begins to sing the song in man's heart. This development can be traced in "Liebe in der Fremde." We note in strophe four: *"Einnernd rührt sich* in den Bäumen/Ein heimlich Flüstern überall." The words in italics can be understood only in conjunction with the demonstrated fact that the entire novella structures a reality, a movement of love first experienced in childhood. And again we see that nature must sing that song to which man has committed his love.[10] This song is a greeting and the woman who listens understands the call. Florio, as yet, is not sure who "Die Eine" is, but we are; she is beyond the garden of grace, outside the prison that Florio left, on the other side of the river.[11] She is Venus.

Little Bianca, the image of spring, the maiden who in his dream-vision seemed to be singing such a lovely song, is not the real object of his love. "Die Musik bei den Zelten, der Traum auf seinem Zimmer und sein die Klänge und den Traum und die zierliche Erscheinung des Mädchens nachträumendes Herz hatten ihr Bild unmerklich und wundersam verwandelt in ein viel schöneres, grösseres und herrlicheres, wie er es noch nirgends gesehen." Florio's dreaming heart takes the essential components of his experiences and weaves them into a lovely pattern, "seltsame Träume," which have their roots in earlier years. What now follows is introduced by a very important phrase: "So in Gedanken schritt er fort." If Florio's mind were not directed toward the maiden on the other side of the river, he could not find her. And now his "Gedanken" are about to become flesh.

Der Mond, der eben über die Wipfel trat, beleuchtete scharf ein marmornes Venusbild, das dort dicht am Ufer auf einem Stein stand, als wäre die Göttin soeben erst aus den Wellen aufgetaucht und betrachte nun, selber verzaubert, das Bild der eigenen Schönheit, das der trunkene Wasserspiegel zwischen den leise aus dem Grunde aufblühenden Sternen widerstrahlte. Einige Schwäne beschrieben still ihre einförmigen Kreise um das Bild, ein leises Rauschen ging durch die Bäume ringsumher. Florio stand wie eingewurzelt im Schauen, denn ihm kam jenes Bild wie eine langgesuchte nun plötzlich erkannte Geliebte vor, wie eine Wunderblume, aus der Frühlingsdämmerung und träumerischen Stille seiner frühesten Jugend heraufgewachsen. Je länger er hinsah, je mehr schien es ihm, als schlüge es die seelenvollen Augen langsam auf, als wollten sich die Lippen bewegen zum Grusse, als blühe Leben wie ein lieblicher Gesang erwärmend durch die schönen Glieder herauf. Er hielt die Augen lange geschlossen vor Blendung, Wehmut und Entzücken. — (318).

The statue seems to have just emerged from the waves, and Florio in his song compares himself to a wave in the stream. This imagery suggests what the next paragraph confirms, namely, that she is a "projection" grounded in his very being and rooted, like a flower, in the dreams of his earliest years. The insinuation of narcissism is quite necessary because Florio's love is really a preoccupation with self and does not concern the other. The pond is an enchanted mirror, which is the same as "das mondbeglänzte Meer" in which he saw the sirens. But mirror, pond, and ocean are really metaphoric references to the soul. I have already commented upon the lines which introduce Florio's first dream-vision: "In seiner von den Bildern des Tages *aufgeregten Seele wogte* und hallte und sang es noch immer fort." Now compare this with the discussion of creativity as it applies to Friedrich. "Seine Seele befand sich in einer kräftigen Ruhe, in welcher allein sie imstande ist, *gleich dem umbewegten Spiegel eines Sees, den Himmel in sich aufzunehmen*" (II, 74, italics mine). The imagery is deceptively similar, as Eichendorff intended, but in one instance the soul is called "aufgeregt" and in the other it finds itself in "einer kräftigen Rühe." This difference is absolutely crucial and it is best understood by the words "den Himmel in sich aufzunehmen" and "aus den Wellen aufgetaucht." Here we have a perfect example of that difference in direction or orientation which is the substance of this discussion of Eichendorff; does heaven come from above or below? This is the very same movement of love that we saw in "Jugendandacht." As we were told in "Morgenlied," "Zur Erde geht was feucht und schwer,/Was klar, zu ihr (die Sonne) hinauf." Venus, the love poetry which she represents, comes from the waters, the deep that is man and which must be formed by God. Friedrich gives himself to the sun and the world is free; Florio orders and forms in the name of his own love and the created must sing his song. And yet, because he desires good and not evil, "Die Eine" to whom he sings his love song is presented with all the symbolism usually associated with the Queen of Heaven. We observe that the image of the statue is outlined in stars and represents a conventional portrayal of the Virgin. These stars, however, are only a reflection in the pond; with such a simple device Eichendorff reiterates the principle of inversion presented in strophe thirteen of "Götterdämmerung": "Und was hier versunken/Als Blumen zum Spiel,/Siehst oben du funkeln /Als Sterne nun kühl." Of course, "oben" is really "unten," in the depths of the pond, or Florio's soul. These flowers that have become stars are our poet's standard symbol for man's "alte Wünsche und Freuden" with which the poet must not concern himself. The flower symbolism extends into the next paragraph. We are told that Venus is like a wonderful flower whose roots are found in the "Frühlingsdämmerung," the first movement of love, experienced by Florio in his earliest years. It is those first dreams, the initial awakening of love which gave the flower substance and nourishment for growth. We now see that Florio's love song courses like blood through the limbs of the statue and its lips part to return the greeting. And one further delicate touch. The last paragraph of the above passage tells us **Florio** "stand wie eingewurzelt im Schauen." The last sentence says "Er hielt die Augen lange geschlossen vor Blendung, Wehmut und Entzucken." Now when did he close his eyes? Does he not see with his eyes closed? Is this not the same order of significance as a previous question: When did he fall asleep? Once again, our poet is much too careful a craftsman to commit such inconsistencies. The statue, we are told, "betrachtete nun, selber verzaubert, das Bild der eigenen Schonheit." We look again at "Jugendandacht" 2:1 : "Wie in einer Blume himmelblauen /Grund, wo schlummernd träumen stille Regenbogen,/Ist mein Leben ein unendlich Schauen,/Klar durchs ganze Herz Ein süsses Bild gezogen." The imagery is the same. The goddess that Florio sees is in his heart. Love looks at itself, sees that it is beautiful and falls in love with its own image. But this love is not the seeking of the other's will, but of one's own will; this love is grounded in man's joys and desires for which Venus is a symbol, while the Queen of Heaven represents that love which was moved to say: "Let it be done unto me according to Thy Word." These words are sung and lived by the "Taugenichts"; it is the eternal song that lies dormant "in allen Dingen," but Florio does not know the true magic word — until the end of the story.

As Florio opens his eyes a hostile element has invaded the scene. The pond is no longer smooth but ruffled; the statue, "fürchterlich weiss und regungslos, sah ihn fast schreckhaft mit den steinernen Augenhöhlen aus der grenzenlosen Stille an." The youth retreats in fright and, at some distance from the pond, even the rustling of the trees seems to be "ein verständiges, vernehmliches Geflüster" and the very shadows would reach out and seize him. Now that his love is "in der Fremde" nature seems fearful because he is afraid.[12] Our young hero runs home and falls asleep "unter den seltsamsten Träumen." Early the next day, Fortunato, seemingly without cause or introduction, gives the following lecture. "Der Morgen . . . ist ein recht kerngesunder wildschöner Gesell, wie er so von den höchsten Bergen in die schlafende Welt hinunter jauchzt und von den Blumen und Bäumen die Tränen schüttelt und wogt und lärmt und singt. Der macht eben nicht sonderlich viel aus den sanften Empfindungen, sondern greift kühl an alle Glieder und lacht einem ins lange Gesicht, wenn man so presshaft und noch ganz wie in Mond-

schein getaucht vor ihn hinaustritt." Morning is light, is a person, is divine grace; the morning is joyous but not gentle; it grasps firmly and is "kerngesund." Florio, on the other hand, shows signs of an approaching illness; we are told "er sah blässer als gewöhnlich . . . aus." As Venus becomes more and more alive, as the evening star becomes his morning star, Florio moves ever further from life and reality, even to the point of wishing to die. And this, as we have discussed, was foretold in the poem "Götterdämmerung."

Fortunato continues to chide the youth and imputes to him the following remarks: "O schöne, holde Seele, o Mondschein, du Blütenstaub zärtlicher Herzen und so weiter, ob das nicht recht zum Lachen wäre! Und doch wette ich, habt Ihr diese Nacht dergleichen oft gesagt und gewiss ordentlich ernshaft dabei ausgesehen. —" With these words, our poet, as a critic, mocks the Romanticism that he sees in his generation, a generation that treats seriously what he terms nonsense. Florio in large measure represents this age and he defends himself. ". . . Ich lasse mich von Euch nicht irremachen, es gibt noch sanfte und *hohe Empfindungen,* die wohl schamhaft sind, aber sich nicht zu schämen brauchen, und ein stilles Glück, das sich vor dem lauten Tage verschliesst und nur dem Sternenhimmel den *heiligen Kelch* öffnet wie eine *Blume,* in der ein *Engel* wohnt" (italics mine). The morning, God's grace, has no interest in this world which belongs to the darkness. Again the imagery must be compared with "Jugendandacht." His happiness is a flower which closes itself to the light of day and opens only for the night. And in this flower there is an angel. Just as Lucifer is called "der Jüngling vom Himmel," so Venus is described as an angel. And this must be so! Florio is gentle and pious and love is indeed precious and beautiful; he could not be deceived by that which is evil and ugly. In keeping with this, Fortunato tells him: "Nun wahrhaftig, Ihr seid *recht ordentlich verliebt!*" (italics mine). After a short pause he goes on to say that there are too many ". . . sanfte, gute, besonders verliebte junge Leute, die ordentlich versessen sind auf Unglücklichsein. Lasst das, die Melancholie, den Mondschein und alle den Plunder; und geht's auch manchmal wirklich schlimm, nur frisch heraus in Gottes freien Morgen und da draussen sich recht abgeschüttelt, im Gebet aus Herzensgrund — und es müsste wahrlich mit dem Bösen zugehen, wenn Ihr nicht so recht durch und durch fröhlich

und stark werdet!" What Florio feels and experiences is nothing but "Plunder," it is worthless; moreover, his love opens the door to evil. Prayer makes one strong and Florio is weak, "ein träumendes Mädchen." Fortunato, on the other hand, is "selber so bunt und freudig anzuschauen, wie der Morgen vor ihm"; in other words, he is part of that morning which I have described.

These words leave Florio "seltsam verstört und verwirrt," much like a "Nachtwandler, der plötzlich bei seinem Namen gerufen wird." To be sure, our young hero is a man walking in his sleep, and that is precisely what Eichendorff's imagery suggests to the careful reader. But what is it that makes this youth feel as though he had been called by name? The context leaves no doubt that Fortunato's words were a calling to the youth. Then what is Florio's name? Obviously his name is *to be a Christian!* He is to love his God first, to pray and ask for help. This *defines* a Christian. Eventually he will do this; indeed, he looks into the beautiful morning before him "als wollte er das freudigkräftige Walten da draussen um Auskunft fragen." But it is of no avail. Nature cannot speak to man of God unless God is already in man's heart. And our poet is most careful to suggest this. "Aber der Morgen spielte nur einzelne Zauberlichter wie durch die Bäume über ihm in sein träumerisch funkelndes Herz hinein, das noch in anderer Macht stand. Denn drinnen zogen die Sterne noch immerfort ihre magischen Kreise, zwischen denen das wunderschöne Marmorbild mit neuer, unwiderstehlicher Gewalt heraufsah. —" The morning light, God's grace, cannot touch the youth yet because he has committed his heart to other pursuits. The imagery of the stars and the woman are exactly the same as in the initial pond scene, for this pond, metaphorically, is the soul in which this loveliness has its origin. And so he decides to find the pond again. But, to his consternation, all seems changed. People are working, children play and "der Mond stand fern und verblasst am klaren Himmel, unzählige Vögel sangen lustig im Walde durcheinander. Er konnte gar nicht begreifen, wie ihn damals hier so seltsame Furcht überfallen konnte" (321). Yes, that is the point! How could nature make man afraid unless man had death in his heart?[12] The moon has no light of its own; it can only reflect the sun's brightness. When the sun shines, the moon is distant and pale. And we have been told that Florio is pale in the morning light. In the light of God's love man need feel no fear, but in the darkness of his own love man should be fearful. The moment that Florio begins to wonder and reflect, the moment that his mind entertains doubt about what he had seen the night before, it follows "dass er *in Gedanken* den *rechten Weg* verfehlt."[13] This awareness of having lost his way brings to mind what he had been searching for. Now he seeks consciously, diligently, and persistently, and soon the healthy activity of the world sinks into quietness, the birds stop singing, the freshness and newness of the morning is dissipated, and "der Kreis der Hügel wurde nach und nach immer stiller, die Strahlen der Mittagssonne schillerten sengend über der ganzen Gegend draussen, die wie unter einem Schleier von Schwüle zu schlummern und zu träumen schien." We recall "Götterdämmerung" 6:7 which speaks of Venus and her kingdom: "In Morgenrots Lohe/Erblick ich dein Reich . . . Auf sonnigen Hügeln/Wie ein Zauberring. —" Florio now approaches the "Zauberring," "den Kreis der Hügel"; indeed, the word "draussen" suggests that he is inside the magic circle, that is, the "Zauberberg" of which he had been warned by Fortunato. And this veil! We were told in "Jugendandacht" 3, "Sie schlummert drunten fort seit Ewigkeiten."[14]

The strength of the morning, the time of God's grace, has been dispelled and rejected because the youth persists in his search for the pond and the statue. He now enters the sixth hour, frequently used by our poet as a time of danger to man's soul. The word "schillern" reiterates the suggestion of the verb "zittern" which we have discussed; the mirage is about to appear. Everything seems to be asleep and dreaming. "Da kam er unerwartet an ein Tor von Eisengittern, zwischen dessen zierlich vergoldeten Stäben hindurch man in einen weiten, prächtigen Lustgarten hineinsehen konnte." Note that the iron gates are merely covered with gold and thus conceal the base metal which is their essential composition. The tired youth is welcomed by "Ein Strom von Kühle und Duft" and Florio enters the forbidden garden. "Hohe Buchenhallen empfingen ihn da mit ihren feierlichen Schatten, zwischen denen goldene Vögel wie abgewehte Blüten hin und wieder flatterten, während grosse, seltsame Blumen, wie sie Florio niemals gesehen, traumhaft mit ihren gelben und roten Glocken in dem leisen Winde hin und her schwankten" (321). Florio has found the garden filled with the gold or light of his love and the burning flowers of a splendid poetry; but the castle is still some distance away and shimmers like a vision of enchantment into the relatively cool darkness of the forest. And now this uninhabited garden which seems to be dreaming of a past life suddenly echoes with the sound of a lute (322). He pursues the notes and comes upon the living counterpart of the statue, whose lips seemed to part in greeting the night before. Before listening to her song, let us see what she looks like. "Sie trug eine prächtige, mit goldnem Bildwerk gezierte Laute im Arme, auf der sie, wie in tiefe Gedanken versunken, einzelne Akkorde griff. Ihr langes, goldenes Haar fiel in reichen Locken über die fast blossen, blendendweissen Achseln bis auf den Rücken hinab; die langen, weiten Ärmel, wie von Blütenschnee gewoben, wurden von zierlichen, goldenen Spangen gehalten; den schönen Leib umschloss ein himmelblaues Gewand, ringsum an den Enden mit buntglühenden, wunderbar ineinander verschlungenen Blumen gestickt" (II, 322). The sleeves of her gown seem to be woven of snow-white flower petals and the gown proper is decorated with the same burning flowers that grow in the garden. This imagery, the garlands of flowers, we have seen in "Jugendandacht" 6 and 7 as well as in the tableau. This woman of indescribable beauty is clothed, as it were, in Florio's dream and desires, *his* flowers, "die irdischen Blumen." Now let us look at another gown.

Mariä Sehnsucht

Es ging Maria in den Morgen hinein,
Tat die Erd' einen lichten Liebesschein,
Und über die fröhlichen, grünen Höh'n
Sah sie den bläulichen Himmel stehn.
"Ach, hätt' ich ein Brautkleid von Himmelsschein,
Zwei goldene Flüglein — wie flög' ich hinein!" —

Es ging Maria in stiller Nacht,
Die Erde schlief, der Himmel wacht',
Und durchs Herze, wie sie ging und sann und dacht',
Zogen die Sterne mit goldener Pracht.
"Ach, hätt' ich das Brautkleid von Himmelsschein,
Und goldene Sterne gewoben drein!"

Es ging Maria im Garten allein,
Da sangen so lockend bunt' Vögelein,
Und Rosen sah sie im Grünen stehn,
Viel' rote und weisse so wunderschön.

"Ach hätt' ich ein Knäblein, so weiss und rot,
Wie wollt' ich's lieb haben bis in den Tod!"

Nun ist wohl das Brautkleid gewoben gar,
Und goldene Sterne im dunkelen Haar,
Und im Arme die Jungfrau das Knäblein hält,
Hoch über der dunkelerbrausenden Welt,
Und vom Kindlein gehet ein Glänzen aus,
Das ruft uns nur ewig: Nach Haus, nach Haus!

                                        (I, 273-274; 1808)

One white gown is made of man's dreams; the other is fashioned from the eternal light. The light or love which emanates
from this Child calls man up and home; man's own light and
love draws him down into the darkness of the self — if it is
not first given back to the Child. But there is more. The gown
is white and blue; now add to this that the vision, as we have
seen, is also surrounded by a halo of stars, and we have a conventional rendering of the Virgin Mary. This should not surprise us. It is not as though this novella offered us the sequence
of events leading to a decision — that was made before the
story begins; what we see is a confusion due to Florio's inability
to distinguish between "Liebe und Andacht." Remember that
Florio is a poet, and the kind of song that he sings identifies
the woman in his heart. And now the song "Frau Venus."

Was weckst du, Frühling, mich von neuem wieder?
Dass all' die alten Wünsche auferstehen,
Geht übers Land ein wunderbares Wehen;
Das schauert mir so lieblich durch die Glieder.

Die schöne Mutter grüssen tausend Lieder,
Die, wieder jung, im Brautkranz süss zu sehen;
Der Wald will sprechen, rauschend Ströme gehen,
Najaden tauchen singend auf und nieder.

Die Rose seh' ich gehn aus grüner Klause
Und, wie so buhlerisch die Lüfte fächeln,
Errötend in die laue Flut sich dehnen.

So mich auch ruft ihr aus dem stillen Hause —
Und schmerzlich nun muss ich im Frühling lächeln,
Versinkend zwischen Duft und Klang vor Sehnen.

                                        (II, 322)

Spring awakens Venus. Previous discussions have made it clear that Florio is responsible for this season of rebirth. After all, we know that it is really summer, that the woman has been described to us as "eine Wunderblume, aus der Frühlingsdämmerung und träumerischen Stille seiner [Florio's] frühesten Jugend heraufgewachsen" and that his song is a call to a maiden on the other side of a stream. And what is the effect of this call? Venus says, "*Das* schauert mir so lieblich durch die Glieder." Now when Florio first saw the statue it seemed to him "*als blühe Leben* wie ein lieblicher *Gesang* erwärmend durch die schönen *Glieder* herauf." There can be no doubt that the youth's song, called "Liebe in der Fremde," is her life blood, so to speak. The demonstrative "das" of this verse refers to the previous lines. In other words, his love song is responsible for "das Wehen" — that mysterious movement, so much like birth pangs, which causes the ancient desires to be reborn. This insinuation of emerging life and a new reality is continued in the second strophe. Earth wears the raiment of spring, although it is summer. Mermaids emerge from the waters: the same figures that Florio saw in his dream-vision. The forest wishes to speak, and in Florio's song we are told: "Erinnernd rührt sich in den Bäumen /Ein heimlich Flüstern überall." In short, Venus sings only of what Florio feels and experiences in his heart. She gives him back his own world of "Phantasie und Gefühl." The imagery of the third strophe makes this even clearer. To give someone a rose is to say "I love you." Love has left its secret hiding place, "die grüne Klause," just as Florio has left the prison and released the ancient joys and desires. The breezes move almost seductively and the verb "fächeln" reiterates with astounding nicety the insinuation of a gentle undulation, a languid to and fro which we saw in the opening scenes. Eichendorff places great emphasis upon this kind of movement; it is seen in such details as "die buntgefiederten Bälle" with which the girls play in the opening scenes. If one imagines their movement in flight, the resulting picture is nicely described by the scene in Venus' garden where "goldene Vögel wie abgewehte Blüten hin und wieder *flatterten*." Even the same verb is employed. The same principle of movement is now imputed to the rose which blushingly extends itself "in die blaue Luft." We may think of Florio's own words to Fortunato which describe his dreams in the garden: "wie lange habe ich da die fernen *blauen* Berge sehnsüchtig betrachtet." Add to this metaphor that Florio has left a prison, and we must conclude that Florio is the rose; or, to be more precise, his love has left "die Klause." (We shall see the same problem in "Der Tauge-nichts.")

The first verse of the last strophe informs us that Venus is called "aus dem stillen Hause," that is, the grave. We must ask ourselves how Florio effects communication. The first word in this same line, "so," suggests a comparison. The second and third strophes speak, respectively, of the song and the rose; they are, so to speak, the signs of spring. And she tells us that spring awakens her again. We also know that Florio is responsible for this spring and that his song, "Liebe in der Fremde," courses like blood through the limbs of the statue. As a consequence, the word "ihr" can refer only to the young man's joys and desires which were mentioned at the beginning of the novella and again in the first strophe of our poem above. He calls her from the grave and gives her life. Venus *must* obey. Contrary to the standard interpretation of her function in this novella, she has no power over Florio, other than what he gives her. Some readers have failed to understand that Venus, in a certain sense, is the image of the poet's love song. The last two verses of Florio's first song read as follows: "Und so muss ich wie im Strome dort die Welle/Ungehört verrauschen an des Frühlings Schwelle." Now look at the last two verses of Venus' song. She echos his very words. Like the speaker in the "Assonanzlied" his song flows "in die Ferne," is heard by "her," and flows back bringing "Kunde" of his own love. In other words, *Venus is the walking image of the love expressed in Florio's song, his poetry.* Poetry is a woman to whom the poet gives of his love, and she may wear one of two faces. If the poet's song concerns "ird'sche Lust und Schmerzen" then the Venus-type image appears. If the poet sings his love song to the Creator then poetry wears the face of the Queen of Heaven. The careful reader can always distinguish between them; Venus leads man down, the Queen always draws man up.

The same last two lines of Venus' song reveal another facet to which we must devote our attention. In 1837 Eichendorff published the poem "Dichterglück" (I, 98). I need but the first strophe for my purpose.

> O Welt, bin dein Kind nicht vom Hause,
> Du hast mir nichts geschenkt,

So hab' ich denn frisch meine Klause
In Morgenrot mir versenkt.

I submit that we saw this "Klause" in Venus' song: it can refer only to the poet himself. He has given himself to the "Morgenrot." This word, in turn, should remind us of the child outlined in the sun who told Friedrich "Gehe mit mir unter." In both instances we are confronted with the action of "versenken." Venus, however, speaks of "versinken," a movement which seems the same yet is delicately and significantly different. "Versenken" insinuates Eichendorff's "sich bewahren," while "versinken" seems to connote a helpless sinking beyond the control of the individual. Its essential characteristic is a certain impuissance so nicely rendered by the assertion that Florio is a "träumendes Mädchen" and feels like "ein vom Winde verwehtes Lerchenstimmlein." As we have suggested, that is precisely the point of Fortunato's objection. It is repeated in "Götterdämmerung" when he speaks of Venus as "klingend und weich." In other words, Venus and Florio are described with the same words; indeed, they are one. In her song, "Frau Venus" speaks of being called back from the grave; but her very existence, as the last two verses clearly state, is a "versinken[d] zwischen Duft und Klang vor Sehnen." But that describes Florio. He is the one filled with yearning and immersed in the shimmering fragrance; he spins helplessly upon the ocean-pond and sinks. His entire existence is a sinking which he misinterprets as a rising. Venus is the image of his song, and Bianca, that other "Bild des Frühlings," has been perverted.

When the song is finished and Venus has disappeared in the distance, Florio stands in "blühende Träume versunken, es war ihm, als hätte er die schöne Lautenspielerin schon lange gekannt und nur in der Zerstreuung des Lebens wieder vergessen und verloren, als ginge sie nun vor Wehmut zwischen dem Quellenrauschen unter und riefe ihn unaufhörlich, ihr zu folgen. —" (323). The imagery is now familiar. The dreams are "blühend" to suggest his spring, the woman he has seen before in the garden of his youth; and she urges him to follow her into the depths, as in the dream-vision which depicts his boat as sinking. And the "Quellen" — is that not the stream of poetry into which she, "Poesie," lures him? The youth presses forward into the garden and comes upon the sleeping Donati. "Aber seine Mienen schienen im Schlafe sonderbar verändert, er sah fast wie ein Toter aus." He sleeps among the ruins, the grave, as it were, of a bygone age and, keeping in mind Fortunato's description of this "Nachtschmetterling," one is again reminded of a vampire, a spiritual vampire,[15] who hungers for the souls of men. Florio awakens him and Donati's "erster Blick war so fremd, stier und wild, dass sich Florio ordentlich vor ihm entsetzte." The youth is afraid, but not enough. Donati, "wie es schien," is surprised to see him. Eichendorff carefully tells us that this surprise is feigned and that Donati did not have to ask, "wie seid Ihr in diesen Garten gekommen?" In the garden of love the Tempter lies in wait for man and seduces him with the truth! Donati tells him that Venus is a relative of his who can be found almost anywhere "auch in der Stadt Lucca ist sie zuweilen." But he does conceal the most important fact. Florio asks what the beautiful singer's name is, and he avoids the question. This is more significant than one might think. In *Ahnung und Gegenwart* Leontin encounters a student who is pathetically in love with a young actress. He tells him: "Lass doch die Jugend fahren! . . jeder Schiffmann hat seine Sterne und das Alter treibt uns zeitig genug auf den Sand. Du brichst dem tollen Nachtwandler doch den Hals, wenn du ihn bei seinem prosaischen, bürgerlichen Namen rufst. Aber härter müssen Sie sein," sagte er zu dem Studenten, "denn die Welt ist hart und drückt Sie sonst zuschanden' " (II, 151). The "Nachtwandler," the person who sleeps in the ruins of the past during the daytime, and the creature called a "Nachtschmetterling" by Fortunato are all one and the same. To call by name is to identify, that is to say, understand the Tempter's wiles and half the battle is won. If Venus were called Venus, Florio would examine his love and, as the young man in "Jugendandacht," realize that his feeling has nothing to do with "Andacht." As we shall see, the "Taugenichts" does not fail to examine his love!

Donati's words convince the youth that he had seen this beautiful woman "in früher Jugend" but cannot recall where. He asks when he might see her and is told perhaps tomorrow. The youth is overjoyed. "Das schöne Marmorbild war ja lebend geworden und von seinem Steine in den Frühling hinuntergestiegen, der stille Weiher plötzlich verwandelt zur unermesslichen Landschaft, die Sterne darin zu Blumen und der ganze Frühling ein Bild der Schönen —" (324). And the poet explains his own imagery. The pond, his own soul, is the deep in which he is immersed and the landscape can have nothing to do with nature, but must be understood in terms of Florio's love. He gave her life and now his life depends upon her. Eternal spring, divine love, has been replaced by a woman, poetry. And the stars! We recall that the statue looked at itself in the pond and its reflection was surrounded by stars, the reflection of real stars. These stars, so consistently used by Eichendorff as symbols for the eternal, have become flowers; they are "Blumen zum Spiele." In other words, Florio, the would-be artist, plays with things eternal. But this is not done with evil intent; he is deceived!

The next morning is Sunday, and we are told that Florio "hat seine *Traumblüten abgeschüttelt* (325, italics mine). This is not a coincidence; on Sunday he thinks again of God rather than his dreams of spring. And he proves it. Quite unexpectedly Donati appears and the youth's first thought is of "die schöne Frau." He asks if he could see her and is told no, for it is Sunday. Donati then asks if he would like to go hunting and Florio answers in amazement, "heute am heiligen Tage?" The ridicule which follows this remark evokes the following response from Florio: " 'Ich weiss nicht, wie Ihr das meint,' sagte Florio, 'und Ihr mögt immer über mich lachen, aber ich könnte heute nicht jagen. Wie da draussen alle Arbeit rastet und Wälder und Felder so geschmückt aussehen zu Gottes Ehre, als zögen Engel durch das Himmelblau über sie hinweg — so still, so feierlich und gnadenreich ist diese Zeit!' " (325). As this is said Donati is standing by the window and Florio seems to note "dass er heimlich schauerte, wie er so in die Sonntagsstille der Felder hinaussah." At the sound of the church bells which surges like a prayer through the clear air, Donati seems frightened, reaches for his hat (326), urges Florio — almost fearfully — to accompany him and, being refused, rushes out of the house. Can there be any question that this man who is so violently fearful of all that speaks of God is the Seducer? In case there could be any further doubt, we are told: "Florio wurde recht *heimatlich* zumute, als darauf der frische, klare Sänger Fortunato, wie ein *Bote des Friedens,* zu ihm ins Zimmer trat" (italics mine). The word "heimatlich" can refer only to "nach Hause" from which heavenly realm he is a messenger of peace. Remember that this is Sunday and that Florio has shaken off his "Traumblüten." To see how the principle of inversion is implemented we need but recall that the poem "Götterdämmerung" speaks of the Evil One as the "Jüngling vom Himmel" who brings "ein Grüssen/Aus himmlischem Reich!"

Fortunato has come with an invitation to visit "eine alte Bekannte." He has in mind Bianca, the woman of white light, but Florio of course thinks of "die schöne Sängerin." He goes to church but cannot pray, "er war zu fröhlich zerstreut." All that day and even the next he searches for the beloved, but without avail. That evening Fortunato calls for him and young Florio, filled with joy and anticipation, rides with him to their engagement. "Eine fröhliche Tanzmusik scholl ihnen dort entgegen, eine grosse Gesellschaft bewegte sich bunt und zierlich durcheinander im Glanze unzähliger Lichter, die gleich Sternenkreisen in kristallenen Leuchtern über dem lustigen Schwarme schwebten." (327) And Florio, we are told, "stand . . . still geblendet, selber wie ein anmutiges Bild, zwischen den schönen schweifenden Bildern." Once again, Eichendorff sees fit to use the same disturbing imagery which we saw at the beginning of the novella. In fact, if we reflect and seek to define the basic impression generated by these passages, I would say that it is light and color to which our Eichendorff imparts a subtle sense of movement. One immediately thinks of ". . . dieser *Farben heimlich* Spreiten/Deckt einer Jungfrau strahlend reine Glieder," and "Mir ist in solchen *linden blauen* Tagen,/Als müssten alle Farben auferstehen,/Aus blauer Fern' *sie* endlich zu mir gehen." And indeed, at this moment in our story, a maiden dressed in a Greek costume comes up to him, "verneigte sich flüchtig, überreichte ihm eine Rose und war schnell wieder in dem Schwarme verloren." She does seem to emerge from the colors. And this rose! Venus, we know, saw a rose thrusting itself "Aus grüner Klause." Surely Eichendorff asks us to understand that this is love which has left a prison, which has been left unguarded, and which Venus now offers him, But there is something else in this equation. We are told that Florio is like a "Bild," an image among images. That is to say, Florio is becoming like Venus, "ein Bild."

The youth is vexed with himself for having accompanied Fortunato "so leichtsinnig auf dieses Meer von Lust." And then the dance music effects a remarkable change. "Wohl kommt die Tanzmusik, wenn sie auch nicht unser Innerstes erschüttert und umkehrt, recht wie ein Frühling leise und gewaltig über uns, die Tone tasten zauberisch wie die ersten Sommerblicke nach der Tiefe und wecken alle die Lieder, die unten gebunden schliefen, und Quellen und Blumen und uralte Erinnerungen und das ganze eingefrorene, schwere, stockende Leben wird ein leichter, klarer Strom, auf dem das Herz mit rauschenden Wimpeln den lange aufgegebenen Wünschen fröhlich wieder zufährt" (327). When our poet compares the effect of dance music with that of spring, then we know that he is talking about the movement of love, but a love whose essential thurst is into the depths, the self, and not toward the heights or God. The metaphors and emblems describe the world of Venus; the song of love that was "asleep" until Florio called, the earthly desires that had been given up but were released from the prison, the heart that is like a ship under full sail — but we remember that the dream-vision depicts the ship thrusting its bow ever deeper into the old memories which now become reality. We must refer to the first few pages where Florio, along with the others, sings a toast to his "Liebchen." And this love song is compared to a "gaukelnder Frühlingswind" which only touches "die Oberfläche des Lebens . . . *ohne es in sich selbst zu versenken.*" I have had occasion to point out that this "Oberfläche" is the realm of colors (II ,75) but not "der Mittelpunkt alles Lebens." The effect of dance music is such that Florio feels "als müssten sich alle Rätsel, die so schwül auf ihm lasteten, lösen" (328). He now searches for the Greek maiden, finds her, and asks her to dance. "Sie verneigte sich freundlich, aber ihre bewegliche Lebhaftigkeit schien wie gebrochen, als er ihre Hand berührte und festhielt. Sie folgte ihm still und mit gesenktem Köpfchen, man wusste nicht, ob schelmisch oder traurig." This is the opening scene of a rather confusing sequence of events. The fleeting impression one gathers from such a description is that of a modest, shy, and demure maiden. And we are left asking ourselves, why this insinuation? As the music begins, the youth finds it impossible to take his eyes "von der reizenden Gauklerin, die ihn gleich den Zauber-gestalten auf den alten fabelhaften Schildereien umschwebte." Now this is almost a contradiction. A sweet and gentle shyness is suddenly called "eine reizende Gauklerin." And there is some-thing else; Eichendorff employs his usual technique of being provocatively suggestive. It is as though Florio were surrounded by figures which are part of certain decorations called "alt und fabelhaft." To see this in proper perspective we turn quickly to the final scenes in Venus' castle which describe the interior decorations. "Die übrigen Wände füllten köstliche Tapeten mit in Seide gewirkten lebensgrossen Historien von ausnehmender Frische. Mit Verwunderung glaubte Florio, in allen den Damen, die er in diesen letzteren Schildereien erblickte, die schöne Herrin des Hauses deutlich wiederzuerkennen" (337). Everywhere he sees Venus! And we know that for Florio "der ganze Frühling" had become "ein Bild der Schönen." The insinuation, I believe, is quite clear: the maiden with whom he dances is one person and what he sees is someone else. After all, this is but an extension of Florio's own thoughts, namely, that he did not have Bianca in mind, but someone "viel schöner, grösser und herrlicher." The young maiden is but a point of departure. As the dance ends his partner whispers, "Du kennst mich." Again, the same ambiguity; who speaks here? He knows Bianca, but he also knows the woman of his daydreams, dreamt in the garden many years ago. I suggest that the reference to humility and shyness dictates that he dances with Bianca, but because his mind is on someone else, Bianca, *as a person,* is not there for him. The next lines seem to bear this out.

As the music stops and the dance is over, "da glaubte Florio seine schöne Tänzerin am anderen Ende des Saales noch einmal wiederzusehen. Es war dieselbe Tracht, dieselben Farben des Gewandes, derselbe Haarschmuck. Das schöne Bild schien unverwandt auf ihn herzusehen und stand fortwährend still im Schwarme der nun überall zerstreuten Tänzer, wie ein heiteres Gestirn zwischen dem leichten, fliegenden Gewölk bald untergeht, bald lieblich wieder erscheint." Eichendorff is careful to point out that this double looks just like the maiden with whom he is dancing, especially such details as color and hair style. Eichendorff's "unverwandte Ansehen" is always associated with evil, and this alone would serve to identify Venus; we do, however, have further evidence. The fact that she is compared to a star is a clear reference to Venus, the evening star, and veiled reference to Lucifer, the morning star who is her relative; but the full depth of the imagery is not apparent unless we recall that Christ, too, is called the morning star. And finally, we must remember that the flower has become a star. The imagery which describes the people as clouds among which this star is found suggests that reality is rapidly fading from the awareness of our youth. To say it another way, the movement of his love does not *unite* him with all that is, but *isolates and even alienates* the human being from the other and then the self. The alternating appearance and disappearance of this star is like the to-and-fro movement which we have pointed out; Eichendorff now uses it again to show that even the people are becoming more and more unreal for Florio. "Die hin und her schweifenden *Masken* mit ihren veränderten, grellen Stimmen und wunderbarem Aufzuge nahmen sich hier in der ungewissen Beleuchtung noch viel seltsamer und fast *gespenstisch* aus" (italics mine). We may recall Fortunato's poem which describes nature as the Evil One appears: "Die Klänge verinnen/Es *bleichet* das Grün." As I have said, reality fades or pales for this youth.

We are told that Florio now follows a path which takes him away from the others; and then he hears a song (329).

> "Über die beglänzten Gipfel,
> Fernher kommt es wie ein Grüssen,
> Flüsternd neigen sich die Wipfel,
> Als ob sie sich wollten küssen.
>
> Ist er doch so schön und milde!
> Stimmen gehen durch die Nacht,
> Singen heimlich von dem Bilde —
> Ach, ich bin so froh erwacht!
>
> Plaudert nicht so laut, ihr Quellen!
> Wissen darf es nicht der Morgen,
> In der Mondnacht linde Wellen
> Senk' ich stille Glück und Sorgen."

He comes upon a Greek maiden who is seated like "eine schöne Najade" by a fountain. Thoughtfully she plays with a rose "in dem *schimmerden* Wasserspiegel" as the moonlight plays upon "den blendendweissen Nacken." The song which the youth hears is called "Liebe in der Fremde," Florio's own song. It seems unnecessary to comment upon imagery which surely is most familiar now. Florio is called "schön und mild," the very same words that are used to describe Donati, the Seducer. Florio is called "ein Bild," and so is Lucifer. It is Florio's joys and desires, his love song, which fill and enchant the night, and it is spring, "ein zauberischer Spielmann," which sings "verlockend von grosser, unermesslicher Lust." The second strophe above could describe either Florio or Donati, a fact which must be more than a coincidence. Eichendorff says: "Den lieben Gott *lass in dir walten,*/Aus frischer Brust nur *treulich* sing!/Was *wahr in dir* wird sich gestalten." This is the new man, the Word becoming Flesh in man. But there is another word, and it is called *denial.* In other words, man becomes like one or the other! Donati says Venus is his relative and Venus is but the flower (poem) that grows in Florio's heart. Her life is his love song, and his love is a being imprisoned in the self. His soul is his own infinity, the *deep* in which he dwells and which does not know God's love. That is why the morning must not know of this love, for the morning is "ein recht kerngesunder wildschöner Gesell" who chides and mocks the lameness of the soul that would delight in the tenderness of its own embrace rather than live and suffer the loving but harsh hands of the artist who would fashion man anew. And thus our youth sinks into "Phantasie und Gefühl" and neglects the faculty of reason which would enable him to hear the warning that Fortunato *is.*

Although we know that Venus sings this song, the sequence of events confronts us with a problem. Who is the "Griechin" by the fountain? We may remember that in the dream-vision (316) the sirens emerging from the waters looked like Bianca, and the Greek maiden in our passage above is called a water nymph, a term which could also define Venus. She has a "Larve" which Venus wears as she gives him a rose (327). On the other hand, when she hears Florio approach, she runs back to the others like "ein aufgescheuchtes Reh." The deer is one of Eichendorff's favorite and loveliest symbols. The readers familiar with this type of imagery may know that deer drinking from a pond is an ancient symbol for the faithful and the Church. This alone should cause us to hesitate before deciding that "die Greichin" is Venus. Furthermore, this maiden toys with a rose while Venus has given hers to Florio. But, she is called "ein Bildchen" and that would seem to indicate Venus. To be sure, Bianca is also called "ein Bild des Frühlings." I am deliberately presenting various possibilities to demonstrate the ease with which a critic can misjudge. It is possible to organize evidence which would support either conclusion. And yet, our poet gave it to us deliberately and with reasoned intent because it reflects so precisely the twilight atmosphere in Florio's soul. Which will prevail, "Liebe" or "Andacht"? Bianca and Venus, and what they represent, are so confused that he cannot tell them apart! We shall see, very shortly, how Eichendorff aids us in making an identification.

When the Greek maiden runs away, Florio returns and joins the crowd of "Spazierengehenden." We are told that "Manch zierliches Liebeswort schallte da leise durch die laue Luft, der Mondschein hatte mit seinen unsichtbaren Fäden alle die Bilder wie in ein goldnes Liebesnetz verstrickt, in das *nur die Masken* mit ihren ungeselligen Parodien manche komische Lücke gerissen" (italics mine). Much of this imagery is most provocative, but let us first concentrate on the surprising yet obvious intent to distinguish between "Bilder und Masken." I have already declared my understanding that Florio, from the very beginning, is involved in a universe that is a compositum of the real and the unreal. Everything that is "Bild" is illusory, but those who wear masks are somehow different. As Fortunato and Florio begin to mingle with this festive group, we are told that some were dancing, "andere ergözten sich in lebhaftem Gespräch, viele waren maskiert und gaben unwillkürlich durch ihre wunderliche Erscheinung dem anmutigen Spiele oft plötzlich eine tiefe, fast schauerliche Bedeutung" (327). It is clearly stated that many were masked, but not all. And it is the masked ones who give a profound and even disturbing note of significance to this "Spiel." When he searches for the maiden who had given him the rose he comes upon another "Griechin" who is engaged "in einem lebhaften Gespräch mit andern Masken" (328); the wording, "mit anderen Masken," instructs us that she, too, wears a mask. And finally, Fortunato had changed costumes several times that evening "und trieb fortwährend seltsam wechselnd sinnreichen Spuk, immer neu und unerkannt und oft sich selber überraschend durch die Kühnheit und tiefe Bedeutsamkeit seines Spieles, so dass er manchmal plötzlich still wurde vor Wehmut, wenn die andern sich halb totlachen wollten" (329). If we reflect upon Eichendorff's use of the word "Masken" it seems that they are not only different but seem designed to destroy "das goldne Liebesnetz" in which "die Bilder" are entangled. This is particularly true of Fortunato, who was described at the beginning of the story as "einsam, ausgelassen lustig, übermütig," and who belongs to all of them or none. In other words, I would say this man is there to destroy illusion and to teach.

All this might be construed as an effort on my part to "reach" for significance which is questionable and even untenable. But there is one further fact. Eichendorff refers to these people as

"Masken" or "Bilder," but only one "person," the Venus-Bianca figure, wears a "Larve." From the description (327) we would call this a domino or half mask. Three times Eichendorff carefully associates her with the wearing of a "Larve." This insistence and the fact that she is the only one underwrites a significance which must be defined. It seems suggested that "Masken" refers to those who are free, not entangled in the game of love, not involved in the illusion. We observe with interest that the Latin *persona,* from which English and German derive their word *person,* actually means *mask*. I dare to suggest that Eichendorff would have us understand "Masken" as meaning *real* persons. Before the reader becomes outraged at this bit of "Volksetymologie," let us look at "Larve." These two words "Maske und Larve," despite certain regional preferences, were used interchangeably in Eichendorff's time, and both meant a mask. But "Larve" has a most interesting spectrum of meaning. This word, as a complex structure, contains the idea of evil spirit or apparition, a wanton woman, a stage in the development of the chrysalis, the gold-colored pupa of the butterfly which at a point in its development is referred to as the nymph. It is remarkable how all this is woven into our story. (The reader should recall the analysis of Venus and how the total meaning of the name fits this story). Venus is, and is called "eine Erscheinung." She is a relative of Donati's who is referred to as "ein Nachtschmetterling" and the final scenes in her castle present her as a wanton woman who seeks to seduce Florio. She is called "eine Najade," that is, a water nymph. I know that the literary "scientist" cannot weigh and measure as his colleague in the physical sciences, but it seems to me this evidence is indeed, weighing and measuring; all this cannot be coincidence. This affair to which Fortunato has taken our young hero takes place, by actual word count, in the precise geometric center of the story. That is to say, deception is partially completed. In fact there are three such festive affairs, at the beginning, middle, and end of the story, and each reveals a stage in the development of deception. I use the word *stage* because it brings us back to the larva and the concept of development, of "entpuppen." Venus is the chrysalis, the gold-colored pupa, from which the butterfly, Donati-Lucifer, develops. Remember, he calls her his relative, "eine Verwandte von mir." At this stage of deception, the middle festive affair in our story, Venus is halfway between "Bild" and "Maske," between the statue and a flesh and blood being. We are told "Eine Larve verbarg *ihr halbes Gesicht* und liess die *untere Hälfte* nur desto rosiger [a rose] und reizender sehen" (327). It is of the utmost importance that we realize why the upper half of her face, the eyes, are concealed. The eyes are the window of the soul, and Venus is dead. She has not yet taken sufficient life from Florio to appear alive; this complete unveiling will occur in the final scenes. We may say that the golden pupa should be equated with Florio's "goldene Träume" which is the spiritual matrix for the flower that is Venus, and its seeds are sown in early youth when the flesh first becomes aware of that magnificent leaven within the breast which we call love.

Up to this moment Florio has seen the Greek maiden three times and she has always eluded him. There is a purpose in this and it becomes clear as he now comes upon "mehreren Masken . . . unter denen er unerwartet die Griechin wieder erblickte. Die Masken sprachen viel und seltsam durcheinander, die eine Stimme schien ihm bekannt, doch konnte er sich nicht deutlich besinnen." This is the repetition of a scene already described. The first time that he sees "die niedliche Griechin," Bianca, he found her "in einem lebhaften *Gespräch mit anderen Masken.*" It is now suggested that Venus is found among "mehreren Masken." But there is something disturbing about these particular "Masken." The group to which Bianca belongs is involved in a conversation called "lebhaft," while the above "Masken sprachen viel und seltsam durcheindander." The conversation of these "Masken" is a strange confusion, a bedlam of sound which lacks harmony and even seems devisive ("durcheinander"). This duality, this negative and positive aspect of the term "Masken," is essential because it conforms to Eichendorff's general understanding of the spiritual universe in which man dwells. In "Das Marmorbild" the truth, a positive spirituality, is masked and the unreal "das Bild," has become visible. But the image must wear a "Larve," must seem to be part of the hidden truth, because the victim is not yet wholly deceived. Remember the first time that he sees her by the pond? Florio's very soul is in his eyes, but when the dream-vision fades, the statue looks at him "fast schreckhaft mit den steinernen Augenhöhlen," and "ein nie gefühltes Grausen überfiel da den Jüngling" (II, 318). In a moment now, in the center of the story, we shall see this again. Only at the end, in her castle, can he look at death and desire to possess her loveliness. Deception moves slowly so the victim will not be unduly frightened. Florio must not reason about what he sees; he must be left within himself, within the world created by "Phantasie und Gefühl." As a matter of fact, Florio himself gradually *becomes* "ein anmutiges Bild" (327).

Soon after joining this particular group of "Masken," everyone leaves — this happens again in the final scenes for which this is but a prelude — and he finds himself alone with the maiden. "Die Larve war fort, aber ein kurzer, blütenweisser Schleier, mit allerlei wunderlichen, goldgestickten Figuren verziert, verdeckte das Gesichtchen." (330). The mask is gone and the face will soon be unveiled. At this point Florio is almost ready to come face to face with the vision in his heart, which means that he is moving ever further from the truth that is masked. And this is another fundamental therorem in our poet's spiritual geometry: What man sees will always deceive him when he seeks to give definite and visible form to the thrust of his spiritual yearning. That is why our poet wrote:

> Doch wolle nie dir halten
> Der Bilder Wunder fest,
> Tot wird ihr freies Walten,
> Hältst du es weltlich fest.
>
> (I, 73)

This fits our Florio's "Marmorbild" experience; he is a pious youth whose yearning has led him into the error of "weltlich festhalten." The poet, and Florio is one, can never find the truth in "Poesie"; should he persist, then she will possess him. But because she "exists" within him, he is lost in the depths of his own being. As flesh and blood seek to possess and reveal the vision, its spiritual quality is destroyed and the poet gives form to his own love. He does not rise to the heights but sinks to the depths. And these depths seem gilded with all the beauty of the heights. Venus tells him that he has been listening to her song, and these first words that he hears her utter seem to penetrate his very soul: "es war, als rührte sie erinnernd an alles Liebe, Schöne und Fröhliche, was er im Leben erfahren." At that moment voices approach and she "ging rasch tiefer in die Nacht hinein. Sie schien es gern zu sehen, dass Florio ihr folgte." The action of "folgen" has been the purpose of Venus' appearance and disappearance. She lures him away from reality; that is to say, Florio's own love isolates him. He now asks Venus to reveal her name, "damit ihre liebliche *Erscheinung* unter den tausend verwirrenden Bildern des Tages ihm nicht wieder verloren ginge" (italics mine). But she refuses, because to utter her name would be to reveal her identity; instead, she answers dreamily, "Lasst das, . . . nehmt die Blumen des Lebens fröhlich, wie sie der Augenblick gibt, und forscht nicht nach den Wurzeln im Grunde, denn unten ist es freudlos und still." These words are a remarkable summary of the spiritual problem. The flowers are earthly joys and desires which Florio released at the beginning of the story. We recall the rose, Florio's love, which escaped "aus grüner Klause," the same rose which Venus gave him. He is to enjoy this love, these desires, and not seek to determine an origin. The image warns him, but Florio does not really listen nor understand. In his heart are the words, "Der Himmel ist offen,/Nimm, Vater, mich auf!" His mind cannot adjust to the reference to "unten . . . freudlos und still." And once again, illusion speaks the truth and the youth does not think.

As he stands there and sees how the moonlight plays upon the figure of the maiden, it seems to him "als sei sie nun grösser, schlanker und edler als vorhin beim Tanze und am Springbrunnen" (331). Now we know the identity of his dancing partner and the maiden by the fountain; it was Bianca. We recall Florio's own admission (317-18) that he was no longer thinking of Bianca but dreaming of a someone "viel schöner grösser und herrlicher." The modifying adjectives leave no doubt as to the identity of the woman before him. In the paragraph after the poem (329), I find one item which instructs us that this girl could not be Venus. Immediately after the dash, a "Gedankenstrich" — this should always alert the reader, because our poet uses it to stress the significance of what follows — we are told that "das schöne Bildchen" ran away. The diminutive form of "das Bild" dictates that this person cannot be Venus who is consistently portrayed as being more than mortal, as a being who transcends anything ever seen before by Florio. Now that Florio has been lured away from the others and stands alone with Venus, Eichendorff invokes the circle imagery to continue the theme of isolation. "Draussen ruhte der weite Kreis der Gegend still und feierlich im prächtigen Mondschein. Auf einer Wiese, die vor ihnen lag, bemerkte Florio mehrere Pferde und Menschen, in dem Dämmerlichte halbkenntlich durcheinander wirrend" (II, 331). The last four words above are an effective description of what transpires in the youth's heart; twilight, confusion, partial recognition, but, and I repeat a significant phrase: "Er konnte sich nicht besinnen." Now the time is ripe for Venus to extend a personal invitation. She hopes to see him soon and adds that their friend, Donati, will lead him to her. With these words she brushes back her veil and Florio recognizes the songstress first seen at high noon in the garden; but the face that he now sees reminds him of the statue by the pond. So Eichendorff traces the metamorphosis for us. As this woman leaves we are offered an important description. "Wie festgebannt von Staunen, Freude und einem heimlichen Grauen, das ihn innerlichst überschlich, blieb er stehen, bis Pferde, Reiter und die ganze seltsame Erscheinung in die Nacht verschwunden war." The same hypnotic gazing which occurred at the pond scene is repeated here. Also, Florio once more knows fear, but again he fails to reflect upon its nature. Then we are told: "Ein Rufen aus dem Garten weckte ihn endlich aus seinen Träumen." This prefigures events in the final scene, where a pious song becomes instrumental in destroying the evil enchantment. Our Eichendorff even has Fortunato sing a song in the present context which tells us what has happened and what will take place in the future.

> "Still in Luft
> Es gebart,
> Aus dem Duft
> Hebt sich's zart,
> Liebchen ruft,
> Liebster schweift
> Durch die Luft;
> Sternwärts greift,
>
> Seufzt und ruft,
> Herz wird bang,
> Matt wird Duft,
> Zeit wird lang —
> Mondscheinduft,
> Luft in Luft
> Bleibt Liebe und Liebste, wie sie gewesen!"

(II, 331-32)

This poem is a magnificently condensed program of events. The first two lines echo that impression of a subtle movement and becoming which was seen in the first paragraph in the story. It reflects an understanding of "das Wehen"; a something is being born, or coming into being. This *something* is in the very air — again the first paragraph — it is the substance of Florio's "Gefühl und Phantasie" which induce him to reach for the stars which are but flowers. The last line informs us that he will return to Bianca. At this moment, however, he is caught in that phase of deception characterized by the words, "Zeit wird lang." Fortunato asks, "Wo seid ihr denn so lange *herumgeschwebt?*" (italics mine). And the youth answers: "Lange?" The novella begins with Florio's admission that he has elected to travel. When he realizes that he has not gone anywhere but only remained with his dream world then time will again become meaningful. For time, in Eichendorff's works, knows the same contraction or isolation and expansion or universality which the individual experiences. In the world of illusion and phantasy time is lost and meaningless. That is why Eichendorff, in most of his prose works, has the individual return to an initial point of departure; his movement is *circular*. Then the ascent can be begun. And now time is expanded and meaningful; man is in a dimension that is infinite.

Florio is now introduced to Pietro's niece, Bianca, the maiden he had kissed on that first day. But a change has taken place. "Der fröhliche Blumenkranz fehlte heute in den Haaren, ohne Band, ohne Schmuck wallten die schönen Locken um das Köpf-chen und den zierlichen Hals" (332). In case the reader has questioned my interpretation of the poet's alternation between reality and illusion, Bianca and Venus, I point out that the maiden who gave Florio a rose had her hair braided "in künstliche Kränze." And the maiden with whom he danced was a shy and demure person. We are now told of Bianca: "Sie schien ganz verschüchtert, als er sich ihr näherte, und wagte es kaum, zu ihm aufzublicken." She also tells him, "Ihr habt mich öfter gesehen, sagte sie leise, und er glaubte dieses Flüstern wieder-zuerkennen. —" The words "dieses Flüstern" assure us that Bi-anca had danced with Florio because the maiden had whispered "Du kennst mich!" All this uncertainty, as indicated in our dis-cussion of "Masken," "die Larve" and the "Doppelgängermotiv" is part of a designed structure which reveals how the illusory and the real are confused in Florio's heart. That is why this takes place in the center of the story and why Florio sees both Venus and Bianca at the *same time*. Florio now seems to see this very confusion in nature but he does not understand. He leaves Bianca and rides home to his room. "Das Fenster in seinem Zimmer stand offen, er blickte flüchtig noch einmal hinaus. Die Gegend draussen lag unkenntlich und still wie eine wunderbar *verschränkte* Hieroglyphe im zauberischen Mondschein. Er schloss das Fenster fast erschrocken und warf sich auf sein Ruhebett hin, wo er wie ein Fieberkranker in die wunderlichsten Träume versank" (333). Eichendorff frequently speaks of the message or word which nature would like to communicate to man; but now, in the enchanted moonlight, all is confused. And this is so because of the turmoil in his own breast. We may recall Fortunato's words as they apply to Florio, "Dein Glühen" and "die Flammen so mild" (311); the flame, his love, is now a fever which threatens to consume him. Bianca had thought that Florio might be in love with her, but it seems that everything "war [eine] Lüge, er war ja so zerstreut, so kalt und fremde! —" Cold, and yet the fire of a fever! Events now move rapidly toward "das stille Haus" where the poet's dream will embrace young Florio.

Several days have passed since Florio's experience at the dance. The degree to which deception has mastered his heart is indicated by the fact that he now visits Donati at his "Landhaus vor der Stadt," (334) the same country estate which later turns into a peasant's humble cottage. This means the estate is an illusion and Florio is already isolated from all reality and has accepted it! A servant plays the guitar; the windows are wide open and filled with flowers whose fragrance permeates the air. "Draussen lag die Stadt im farbigen Duft zwischen den Gärten und Weinbergen, von denen ein fröhliches Schallen durch die Fenster heraufkam. Florio war innerlichst vergnügt, denn er gedachte im stillen immerfort der schönen Frau." Again this is the same atmosphere already suggested by the first paragraph of the novella. And out of this "farbigen Duft" — we recall "Jugendandacht" — the beautiful maiden suddenly appears. Donati, of course, points her out, and Florio sees her riding upon a white horse, "Ein Falke, mit einer goldnen Schnur an ihrem Gürtel befestigt, sass auf ihrer Hand, ein Edelstein an ihrer Brust warf in der Abendsonne lange, grünlichgoldne Scheine über die

Wiese hin. Sie nickte freundlich zu ihm herauf." The falcon, Raimund's-Florio's escaped thoughts, are held prisoner! The jewel which she wears, with its green-golden shimmer, offers an interesting identification. We recall the original appearance and descriptions of Donati, "ein hoher, schlanker Ritter in reichem Geschmeide, das grünlichgoldene Scheine zwischen die im Walde flackernden Lichter warf" (314). And to complete the progression of this imagery, as the illusion is destroyed and the flowers become weeds and the walls of the castle turn into ruins, "Eine Schlange fuhr zischend daraus hervor und stürzte mit dem grünlichgoldnen Schweife sich ringelnd in den Abgrund hinunter" (338). Donati tells him the lady is rarely at home — it seems she is always hunting — and today would be an acceptable time to pay her a visit. Upon hearing this, Florio "fuhr . . . freudig aus dem traümerischen Schauen, in das er versunken stand, er hätte dem Ritter um den Hals fallen mögen." Surely these essential characteristics of Florio's spiritual disposition, "versunken und Schauen," have been stressed sufficiently to clarify their importance. Eichendorff has paraphrased for us "Jugendandacht" 2:1 written some ten years earlier. And what Florio is about to experience is given to us in the next strophe of the same poem, the last line of which reads: "Ach wann lohnst du endlich auch mein treues Lieben!" We shall now examine love's reward.

It is a very short ride to the castle, and Florio is amazed (335) that he had been unable to find the garden. The castle is made of marble "und seltsam, fast wie ein *heidnischer Temple*" (italics mine). As we know, "die . . . hochaufstrebenden Säulen" of this heathen temple are called "jugendliche Gedanken," and the various decorations portrays scenes "aus einer fröhlichen, lange versunkenen Welt." When he finally comes upon the mistress of all this enchantment he finds her dressed in "ein himmelblaues Gewand" and reclining "auf einem Ruhebett." The scene which now displays itself to Florio's eyes is reminiscent of the other two festive gatherings which he attended. The gentle movement of people walking to and fro, the overpowering scent of flowers, the fountains, the singing, all gathered together in a lovely swirl of color and light. There is, however, one remarkable difference, a certain pattern which is most striking. Beginning at the focal point, Venus herself, we see that she is attended by one maiden who holds a mirror for her. Others seem to be gathered about her decorating her with roses. At

her feet, "war ein *Kreis* von Jungfrauen auf dem Rasen gelagert (italics mine). "Weiter in der Ferne, wie die Lautenklänge und die Abendstrahlen so über die Blumenfelder dahinglitten, erhoben sich hin und her schöne Mädchen, wie aus *Mittagsträumen erwachend*, aus den Blumen, schüttelten die dunkeln Locken aus der Stirn, wuschen sich die Augen in den klaren Springbrunnen und mischten sich dann auch in den fröhlichen Schwarm" (italics mine). Again there is insistence through repetition; everywhere that Florio looks his eyes encounter the female form. We are told that Florio's "Blicke schweiften wie geblendet über die bunten Bilder, immer mit neuer Trunkenheit wieder zu der schönen Herrin des Schlosses zurückkehrend." It seems as though she were the center of some gigantic flower and the petals were her virgin attendants; or perhaps, considering that she emerged from a pond, we are better instructed in thinking of her as rising from a veritable sea of female flesh and forms. It is my interpretation that Eichendorff combined the two symbols, water and the flower. We know that Venus' realm is "versunken" and Florio has informed us of his search for "ein stilles Glück, das sich vor dem lauten Tage verschliesst und nur dem Sternenhimmel den heiligen Kelch öffnet wie *eine Blume, in der ein Engel wohnt*" (319, italics mine). In other words, the entire complex of "Dichten und Dichtung," the creative process and what is made, is visualized as a sacred flower which "contains" an angelic being. It is as though the poet's purpose were to give form to this image. About 1809 Eichendorff wrote a short poem which says much of the above, but it is also significantly different.[16]

In Das Stammbuch
Der M. H.
Akrostichon mit aufgegebenen Endreimen

Ist hell der Himmel, heiter alle W e l l e n,
Betritt der Schiffer wieder seine W o g e n,
Vorüber Wald und Berge schnell g e f l o g e n,
Er muss, wohin die vollen Segel s c h w e l l e n.
In Duft versinken, bald all' liebe S t e l l e n,
Zypressen nur noch ragen aus den W o g e n,
Herüber kommt manch süsser Laut g e f l o g e n.
Es trinkt das Meer der Klagen sanfte Q u e l l e n.

Nichts weilt. — Doch zaubern Treue und V e r l a n g e n,
Da muss sich blühender alte Zeit e r n e u e r n,
Öffnet die Ferne drauf die Wunder l i c h t u n g,
Ruht dein Bild drin, bekränzt in heil'ger D i c h t u n g. —
Fern lass den Freund nach Ost und West nur s t e u e r n,
Frei scheint er wohl — du hältst ihn doch g e f a n g e n!

(I, 120f.)

This wreath of flowers, actually poems, is sacred and frames an image which is in the immeasurable distance. We must think of the wreath worn by the uninvited guest in "Götterdämmerung" as well as Bianca's wreath which she discards because it was all a lie. Read the first letter in each verse and they spell "Ich bin von Eichendorff"; read the last word in each verse and the spiritual topography of our poet's universe stands out in bold relief. The ocean of existence runs a heavy sea which is filled with reefs, and the sky has many false stars (flowers); woe to the sailor who would quiet the waves for he will sink "in ein Meer von Stille." The ocean is a bottomless depth which drowns the "sanfte Quellen," the fountain of song which expresses nothing more than Florio's "sanfte und hohe Empfindungen . . . und ein stilles Glück." Man has only faithfulness — to God — and longing, and they are the powers which labor to define "die Ferne." And it must be defined because man cannot travel in just any direction; that is like having "gar keine Geschäfte." Of course I am talking about Eichendorff's "nach Hause," the journey to man's "Heimat." And man's native country is most intimately associated with a "Bild," the image of a woman. But this woman remains in "die Wunderlichtung"; she does not come to man nor does she seek him, as is the case with Florio's Venus. Poems are but a wreath for her, and nothing else; she cannot emerge from those "flowers," because she is not in them. She holds on to man so that he may experience freedom. Venus wants to imprison the poet for he is her very life. The last verse of our poem is found (II, 429) in the "Taugenichts" novella. The "Taugenichts" has in his heart the image of the heavenly Venus and Florio's image is the earthly Venus. Let us go back to the final moments of love's deception.

Venus smooths her hair, looks into the mirror and then looks so enchantingly at Florio "dass es ihm durch die innerste Seele ging. —" For the first time, he looks at this image without being reminded of the statue and the eyes of death. The work of the Seducer is almost completed. Night has fallen and the moon shines "zauberisch über die schönen Bilder." Venus takes him by the hand and leads him to the innermost chamber of her castle. Somehow, all the other "Bilder" disappear. We note that they are not referred to as "Masken." This is quite proper; the unreal, the "Bilder," have become persons. Eichendorff never says, "behold Beauty and Truth," but he does suggest that "he who has ears, let him hear." Let man restrain mind and heart with obedience and his ears will be open to the eternal song of praise, the heavenly Alleluia. That is the reason for the mirror symbolism in our story. Florio "sees" only his own yearning, the projection of his own love, the "flower" of his desires. And now Eichendorff exposes the roots of this flower when he tells us that Florio looked at this woman "mit flammenden Augen." Florio cloaks "Poesie" in the characteristics of the Virgin Mary, but she is still only Venus. Human love may seemingly invoke transcendence and transfiguration, but it remains tied to the created with garlands of "desires"; it cannot move man one step toward the heights which are its yearning. The human creature merely deceives himself. This is in strict agreement with Eichendorff's professed faith. Only Divine Mercy stands between man and the darkness of his own light. What we saw in "Jugendandacht" 10:3,4 now occurs in our story. The poem tells us "Sehnsucht muss wachsen an der Tiefe Rauschen/Nach *hellerm Licht* und nach *des Himmels Kunden* .... O Herr!" Florio stands on the edge of the abyss and it is given to him to hear an old, pious song which he had heard in early childhood "und seitdem über den wechselnden Bildern der Reise fast vergessen hatte." Almost the first words that Florio utters in the story are: "Ich habe jetzt das Reisen erwählt." Man must not travel; that is to say, he should not leap from the garden (Romana) or escape from the prison. To be sure, man is not forced to stay; thus we find the verb "erwählen." Florio now wishes to return to the prison, and we can see how the mirage fades into nothingness.

The youth turns to Venus and asks if she recognizes the singer. The kind of song man sings reveals who he is. Venus denies having heard the voice before but she is confused and "schien ordentlich erschrocken." The same reaction was imputed to Donati when he heard the ringing of the church bells on Sunday. Venus now becomes strangely silent, quite the opposite of her previous behavior, and Florio has "Zeit und Freiheit, die wunderlichen Verzierungen des Gemaches genau zu betrachten" (336-37). Time and freedom! The relationship of the vampire and the victim, whereby one gains life as the other loses it, is suddenly interrupted. Florio is free "genau zu betrachten," something he had not done before. And now, because "Gefühl und Phantasie" no longer dominate the mind, the sign of this reality changes. For the first time the flowers are called "ausländisch," their fragrance described as "berauschend" and the movement of light is termed "lüstern." All this applies to "Dichten." At this moment he is suddenly struck by the fact that the women depicted on the wall decorations all look like Venus. And then we read: "Da flog es ihn plötzlich wie von den Klängen des Liedes draussen an, dass er zu Hause in früher Kindheit oftmals ein solches Bild gesehen, eine wunderschöne Dame in derselben Kleidung, einen Ritter zu ihren Füssen, hinten einen weiten Garten mit vielen Springbrunnen und künstlich geschnittenen Alleen, geradeso wie vorhin der Garten draussen erschienen. Auch Abbildungen von Lucca und anderen berühmten Städten erinnerte er sich dort gesehen zu haben." He then explains to Venus that he had dreamed of all this in early childhood and did not think that "das alles einmal lebendig werden würde um mich herum." Florio's words are, "da dachte ich nicht!" Of course not. But now something else moves him to think. "Über den stillen Garten weg zog immerfort der Gesang wie ein klarer, kühler Strom, aus dem die alten Jugendträume herauftauchten. Die Gewalt dieser Töne hatte seine ganze Seele in tiefe Gedanken versenkt, er kam sich auf einmal hier so fremd und wie aus sich selber verirrt vor" (338). This clear, cool stream which is the song of praise, the Hosanna, seems to be the realm or mode of being from which the "Jugendträume" emerge. Looking back at the literal wording of Venus' statement, we see that her image is an integral part of these dreams. Compare this with "Jugendandacht" 1 and it is obvious, from the poet's own imagery, that "Liebe und Andacht" are so delicately intertwined that man may easily mistake one for the other. I can find no other conclusion which accounts for the variables of plot, structure, symbols, and imagery which are encountered in prose and poetry. Because of man's helplessness in this regard, Eichendorff consistently places his heroes in the position of invoking God's mercy. But man must use the resources of mind and heart which are his natural endowment. Thus Florio is depicted as in "tiefe Gedanken versenkt." It is logical, considering the paradoxical nature of Christianity, that a deceptive sinking movement, which elsewhere in our story has a negative connotation, now assumes a spiritually positive meaning. Man is to go within himself, "versenken," and listen to the Truth that can never be found outside himself. And now our young hero is prepared to pray: "Herr Gott, lass mich nicht verlorengehen in der Welt!" No sooner are these words uttered "als sich draussen ein trüber Wind, wie von dem herannahenden Gewitter, erhob und ihn *verwirrend* anwehte" (italics mine). We must read Eichendorff so carefully. The word "verwirrend" is a clear signal that this is more than an ordinary storm which approaches; it is the kind of storm that confuses man and destroys the reality which is the product of his own emotions and imagination. Leontin describes a similar storm: "Wie Gottes Flügel rauschen, und die Wälder sich neigen, und die Welt still wird, wenn der Herr mit ihr spricht! Wo ist dein Witz, deine Pracht, deine Genialität?" (II, 182).

Our young hero is confused because to ask for help is just the first step; it takes as much or more courage to accept it. First a world, literally one's *self*, as we imagine this self, must be destroyed. We were told Florio "[ist] aus sich selber verirrt," his love is "in der Fremde," he is not at home ("Jugendandacht"); but to return means to leave a world that seemed so beautiful, and its song seemed to speak of "alles Liebe, Schöne und Fröhliche" (330) which man could hope for in all eternity. And so he must will the destruction of this world; he must watch as weeds and ruins replace imagined splendor and the snake slithers into the depths. The storm seems to come closer and "der Wind, zwischen dem noch immerfort einzelne Töne des Gesanges herzzerreissend heraufflogen, strich pfeifend durch das ganze Haus und drohte die wild hin und her flackernden Kerzen zu verlöschen." Yes, "herzzerreisend"! With all his heart he had given himself to the love which he had felt to be a pious devotion and which had been the matrix of a lovely poetry. And now that illusion must be destroyed. Suddenly a bolt of lightning illuminates the chamber and Florio is literally taken aback. "Denn es war ihm, als stünde die Dame starr mit geschlossenen Augen und ganz weissem Antlitz und Armen vor ihm." The reader is offered a revealing comparison of the candles and the lightning, two sources of light, and I am justified in saying that the finite and the infinite are contrasted. God and Florio each illuminate a reality. When we are told that the wind threatens to extinguish the candles, we should take this at face value, for Florio almost dies! Remember the death wish expressed in "Götterdämmerung" (313)? As the lightning passes, the room is once again filled with "die alte Dämmerung" and "die Dame sah ihn wieder lächelnd an wie vorhin, aber stillschweigend und wehmütig, wie mit schwerverhaltenen Tränen." The word "Dämmerung" is an exquisitely appropriate term because it is so strikingly neutral; it could mean the dying out or the coming of light. And of course Eichendorff divided the poem "Götterdämmerung" into two parts. The beginning of the story and the events that lead up to the crisis are dominated by the old light, man's own love; the end is under the sign of another light, or we could say another woman who represents another love. But before Florio is freed from the realm of his own desires, this world of the mirror in which all things are but "Bilder" makes one final effort. One is reminded, but only by analogy, of the death that speaks in Goethe's *Erlkönig*, "Und bist du nicht willig, so brauch ich Gewalt."

The world created by Florio's "Phantasie" now seeks his physical destruction. The stone statues advance in frightning silence. The flowers become "buntgefleckte, bäumende Schlangen." Under the influence of the song Venus seems to die, to turn into a statue before his very eyes, and "alle Ritter auf den Wandtapeten sahen auf einmal aus wie er und lachten ihn hämisch an." Venus is dead, and all that is left is the mocking, insane laughter of the other self, the self that is "aus sich selber verirrt" and which has given itself to Evil. Do not forget the poem "Memento"! We may recall "Götterdämmerung" which speaks of Lucifer and the torch which he sometimes inverts, whereupon: "Tiefschauend vergehet/Die Welt und wird stumm." The only light in this innermost chamber of the castle is provided by a few candles held by two monstrous arms extending from the wall. And now these arms seem to move and grow "als wolle ein ungeheurer Mann aus der Wand sich hervorarbeiten, der Saal füllte sich mehr und mehr, die Flammen des Blitzes warfen grässliche Scheine zwischen die Gestalten, durch deren Gewimmel Florio die steinernen Bilder mit solcher Gewalt auf sich losdringen sah, dass ihm die Haare zu Berge standen." The entire scene is a writhing, twisting chaos, the expression of a diabolical hatred which lusts for the human soul and battles in fearful silence to destroy what God had made in His own image. And now our young hero is mortally afraid. The evil which had borrowed the beauty of his own love is unmasked, and he flees in terror from the forces which he had set free. As he passes through the garden he sees the pond and the statue of Venus. "Der Sänger Fortunato, so kam es ihm vor, fuhr abgewendet und hoch aufrecht stehend im Kahne mitten auf dem Weiher, noch einzelne Akkorde in seine Gitarre greifend. —" If this pond, by analogy, is a figure for Florio's soul, the deep from which Venus emerges, it is quite proper that Fortunato should be depicted as sailing on its surface and singing his pious song. But this song, unlike the dance music discussed earlier, touches not just the surface but the very depth's of man's being. That is why Florio prays "Aus tiefster Grund der Seele." Florio keeps running because he fears that Fortunato is nothing more than "ein verwirrendes Blendwerk der Nacht." At this moment one world has been destroyed and the other, as represented by Fortunato, is not yet real to this youth.

As he runs, we are told: "Fernab am Horizonte verhallte nur ein leichtes Gewitter, es war eine prächtig klare Sommernacht." This is the first time since the opening lines of the story that the true season is mentioned; it is summer. But this one line offers another consideration which is of the highest significance. There is a storm in the distance. We recall the wind and the lightning and its function in the crisis just experienced by Florio. Now Eichendorff speaks of a real storm. Why? Because it is a fundamental theorem in our poet's spiritual geometry that the divine and the mundane or the natural and supernatural are not really separated but involved in a mysterious interpenetration which is the foundation of human existence. This is why Fortunato is called a messenger of peace. The same thought is expressed in the short poem which introduces the selection "Wanderlieder."

> Viele Boten gehn und gingen
> Zwischen Erd' und Himmelslust,
> Solchen Gruss kann keiner bringen,
> Als ein Lied aus frischer Brust.

(I, 7)

To be sure, the spiritual world also has a negative component, and Donati is its representative. Thus positive and negative are on a vast continuum and the human being is always involved in a movement toward one or the other. This, as our poet understands it, is the substance of man's spiritual existence, an existence which knows neither compromise nor rest. Man is never neutral! Florio has changed his allegiance and the world is under a different sign. The day before he had visited Donati in his "zierliche Villa," and now it is a humble cottage surrounded by a small garden. As he approaches, a man emerges and sings:

> "Vergangen ist die finstre Nacht,
> Des Bösen Trug und Zaubermacht,
> Zur Arbeit weckt der lichte Tag;
> Frisch auf, wer Gott noch loben mag!"

(II, 340)

The magnificent moon-filled night is now called "die finstre Nacht." But of course! The moon has no light of its own except what is given to it by the sun, and Venus cannot live unless Florio gives her his life and love. And yet, the moon is also an ancient Christian symbol for the Virgin Mary, who has, so to speak, no light of her own, but only reflects the light of her Son. The poem also informs us that the illusion lived by Florio was authored by Evil. This does not contradict the assertion which I have voiced repeatedly, namely, that Florio is responsible for the reality of the deception which almost destroys him. The power of "Gedanken" has been consistently disregarded by critics in interpretations of our poet's works. The Seducer merely panders to the thoughts and dreams of man and cannot compel the human being to accept what is contrary to his will. The poem also suggests that man's work is a praising of the Lord, and that is precisely what Fortunato told Florio at the very beginning of the story.

We might ask ourselves why Eichendorff calls this man, who lives in the very same spot once occupied by Donati's home, a gardener. Why should the poet direct our attention to doves, resplendent in the first rays of the sun, and to a profound peace that hovers like a benediction over this spot? Indeed, who is the gardener of man's soul? Eichendorff tells us that the poet erects the ladder for the reader to climb and we should let our minds surge up toward mystery and impossible truth where proof is no longer needed because love teaches what the mind cannot see. The simplest answer is the absurd truth that this gardener is God. And at this moment our young wanderer says: "Mein Gott! Wo bin ich den so lange gewesen!" Time was lost to this youth, lost in the nothingness of that existence which knows not God. Out of the depths of his own darkness he called for help and the Lord turned His countenance to him. But keep in mind that the pious song was sent first; in other words, out of himself and by himself Florio could not take even that first step. None can come to the Father unless He calls first. That is why God is the gardener of the soul.

When Florio reaches his room he locks himself in and "versank ganz und gar in ein hinstarrendes Nachsinnen." He is filled with but one desire, to die. "In solchem unseligen Brüten und Träumen blieb er den ganzen Tag und die darauffolgende Nacht hindurch" (340). Now suddenly, Eichendorff is very specific about time. Florio came to this enchanted spot, where he had "rebuilt" the temple of Venus, in the late afternoon of the first day. He flees the next morning. That day and the following night he remains buried in his room (341). On the morning of the third day he rises and, in the company of Bianca, her uncle, and Fortunato, he rides into a new dawn. We are told: "Die Morgenröte erhob sich indes immer höher und kühler über der wunderschönen Landschaft vor ihnen." The cool light! Not the wild flame which had been in his eyes nor the fire that destroyed Romana, but a cool flame which does not maim. Is all this really coincidence? Should we not follow Eichendorff's gentle suggestion and be reminded of the words in the Bible, "I shall destroy the temple and rebuild it in three days?" Considering the symbolism of the pond, Florio was that temple in which Venus did dwell. This temple, supported by "jugendliche Gedanken," had to be destroyed so that a man could again be God's temple.

As they ride into the morning, Pietro calls attention to some ancient ruins high up on a hill. "In einer grossen Einsamkeit lag da altes, verfallenes Gemäuer umher, schöne, halb in die Erde versunkene Säulen und künstlich gehauene Steine, alles von einer üppig blühenden Wildnis grünverschlungener Ranken, Heckken und hohen Unkrauts überdeckt. Ein Weiher befand sich daneben, über dem sich ein zum Teil zertrümmertes Marmorbild erhob, hell vom Morgen angeglüht." This "Einsamkeit" is that isolation and alienation to which Florio had committed himself. Particular attention is called to the statement that the statue is enveloped in the flame of the morning sun.[17] Recall what the flash of lightning had done to Venus and then turn once more to the poem "Der Geist," especially the last strophe. "Fröhlich an den öden Mauern/Schweift der Morgensonne Blick,/Da versinkt das Bild mit Schauern/*Einsam* in sich selbst zurück." The spirit, "Der Geist," that looks "mit dem *starren* Sinne" (and Florio's experiences have reduced him to "ein hinstarrendes Nachsinnen") has withdrawn its own love from the created and has not yet learned to "see" with God's love. This describes Rudolf whose "seeing" is a staring "in das wesenlose Meer"; he travels to Egypt, "das Land der alten Wunder," to search for the hidden meaning of all that is because his own "seeing" does not lead to meaning. But Florio is different; he asked for help which was accorded him in the form of a song, a reminder of innocence which is also a part of "Kindheit." Now Fortunato sings the second half of "Götterdämmerung" which instructs the youth on the subject of "Liebe und Andacht." Before moving on to Fortunato's song, we should look again at the last quotation above describing the ancient ruins.

If the reader inspects the passage carefully, he will be struck, as I was, by certain physical laws which our poet blithely violates. We must imagine that the foursome ride along the highway and look *up* at the ruins. Now the reader who has lived in the mountains knows perfectly well that the line of sight does not allow one to see the details which are enumerated. In fact, it is absolutely impossible to see a body of water, a small pond, when one's own vantage point is appreciably lower than the elevation of that pond. In truth, if these people actually see what our poet describes for us, then they have to be located *above* the ruins, the statue and the pond. There can be no other conclusion! Did Eichendorff make a mistake? Or, where are the tall stately trees, the forest, which surround the pond (321)? Did Eichendorff err and forget to include them in the description on page 341? Or again, we are told that Venus leads Florio "in das Innere ihres Schlosses" (336) which we have called the innermost chamber. And yet our poet speaks of Venus standing by a window, of the wind and the lightning which penetrate into this hidden recess of the castle. Is our poet that careless? It would be difficult to find an artist more consciously aware of what he writes and one more unswervingly dedicated to a single purpose. To assume that these are errors because we do not understand would be absolutely unforgivable. These three inconsistencies, I believe, can be understood in terms of the spiritual movement which the novella presents, that is, a rising or a sinking, a moving toward or away from God. The first time that Florio sees the pond we are told it is surrounded by high trees (318). It must follow that this pond cannot be visible from below, from the highway where the four riders are situated. But what if trees are *thoughts* which surround and conceal from the Light above this little pond that is his soul? Eliminate these thoughts, or send them to the heights as our poet says so frequently, and then the pond is visible and the youth can sing "Gegrüsst das Licht." Then the description given on (341) is perfectly in order. From a great height it is possible to see this pond and all the details which the poet mentions. Consider the first two strophes of "Götterdämmerung"; did not Fortunato speak indirectly of a song which carries him up to the clouds and beyond? Does he not say "Wie auf Bergen hoch bin ich/So einsam gestellt/ Und grüsse herzinnig,/Was schön auf der Welt"? And the function of Fortunato's song in the final scenes in the castle — does it not raise Florio from the depths, the pond, into which his ship (318) had taken him? And when he flees, he does not even turn around "bis Weiher, Garten und Palast weit hinter ihm *versunken* waren" (399; italics mine). I think Eichendorff makes it quite clear that Florio arises from the depths of the finite self, the world of "Phantasie und Gefühl" which is energized and given life by his love. And as to the wind and the lightning in the innermost chamber of the castle, we have said that this temple is rebuilt by Florio's love, and the vision, "das Bild," is within him. Consequently, as the song stream penetrates his heart and soul, the flower begins to die. This interpretation accounts for what would have to remain as three unknowns in an otherwise rational and clearly discernible structure. Furthermore, the second half of "Götterdämmerung" provides further imagery which tends to substantiate our viewpoint.

The poem in its entirety contains thirty-six strophes. Eichendorff divided it into two parts, A and B, containing twenty and sixteen strophes respectively and inserted A at the beginning and B at the end of the story. Each part again is divided into two parts: A_1, A_2, and B_1, B_2. A_1 and B_1 provide a summary of what has happened in the story. A_2 and B_2 indicate the further development or movement of events. The reader is urged to look again at the discussion of A at the beginning of this chapter and test my assertion that the poem will be used as an outline. I think I have done this. And now let us look at B_1.

"Von kühnen Wunderbildern
Ein grosser Trümmerhauf',
In reizendem Verwildern
Ein blühender Garten drauf.

Versunknes Reich zu Füssen,
Vom Himmel fern und nah
Aus andrem Reich ein Grüssen —
Das ist Italia!

Wenn Frühlingslüfte wehen
Hold über'm grünen Plan,
Ein leises Auferstehen
Hebt in den Tälern an.

Da will sich's unten rühren
Im stillen Göttergrab,
Der Mensch kann's schauernd spüren
Tief in die Brust hinab.

Verwirrend in den Bäumen
Gehn Stimmen hin und her,
Ein sehnsuchtsvolles Träumen
Weht übers blaue Meer.

Und unterm duft'gen Schleier,
So oft der Lenz erwacht,
Webt in geheimer Feier
Die alte Zaubermacht.

Frau Venus hört das Locken,
Der Vögel heitern Chor
Und richtet froh erschrocken
Aus Blumen sich empor.

Sie sucht die alten Stellen,
Das lust'ge Säulenhaus,
Schaut lächelnd in die Wellen
Der Frühlingsluft hinaus.

Doch öd' sind nun die Stellen,
Stumm liegt ihr Säulenhaus,

Gras wächst da auf den Schwellen,
Der Wind zieht ein und aus.

Wo sind nun die Gespielen?
Diana schläft im Wald,
Neptunus ruht im kühlen
Meerschloss, das einsam hallt.

Zuweilen nur Sirenen
Noch tauchen aus dem Grund
Und tun in irren Tönen
Die tiefe Wehmut kund. —

Sie selbst muss sinnend stehen
So bleich im Frühlingsschein,
Die Augen untergehen,
Der schöne Leib wird Stein.

(II, 342 f.)

It must be apparent that these strophes present precisely what I have indicated — a summary of what Florio has experienced. The words "Frühling" and "Lenz" cannot refer to a season because, as we know, it is summer. It is love that awakens in man and it is love that is responsible for the voices, dreams and songs which lure Venus from the grave. Florio acutally refers to himself as a bird and we find the same imagery above. But the song that his soul (bird symbolism) sings is not a praising of the Lord as Fortunato suggests (307). The resurrection from the grave, the fragrance of flowers, the spring air defined in terms of water symbolism, the waves, Venus always depicted as lächelnd," the fragrant veil which covers Venus ("Jugendandacht") — all these are woven together into that lovely tapestry which came alive for Florio. The last four verses touch upon an observation which I presented before, the fact that Venus lives but to die. She seems to know that her existence has no permanency; the love which she represents no longer reigns supreme as in heathen times. This thought introduces B_2, the last four strophes of the poem.

"Denn über Land und Wogen
Erscheint, so still und mild,
Hoch auf dem Regenbogen
Ein andres Frauenbild.

Ein Kindlein in den Armen
Die Wunderbare hält,
Und himmlisches Erbarmen
Durchdringt die ganze Welt.

Da in den lichten Räumen
Erwacht das Menschenkind
Und schüttelt böses Träumen
Von seinem Haupt geschwind.

Und, wie die Lerche singend,
Aus schwülen Zaubers Kluft
Erhebt die Seele ringend
Sich in die Morgenluft."

(II, 343)

The first line with its "Denn" explains why Venus must die;
one goddess of love has been replaced by another. The last
strophe explains the final disposition or direction of Florio's movement. As we have pointed out, the very first page of the story
reveals that Florio thinks of himself as a lark, but weak "und
vom Winde verweht." The first time that he enters Venus' garden he sees golden birds who flutter back and forth "wie abgewehte Blüten." The movement is exactly the same. Eichendorff
seeks to describe the souls of those who flutter helplessly in
the breeze of an earthly love. The strophes of "Götterdämmerung" which we are now considering inform us that through the
intercession of Mother and Child "himmlisches Erbarmen/
Durchdringt die ganze Welt." Remember the interpretation that
it was divine mercy which sent Florio that pious song, a reminder, a call, which is man's opportunity to exercise his freedom. If man elects to follow this song, then his soul, like a
lark, rises up to greet the new light that is not his. And then
man resides in "den lichten Räumen" and not the innermost
chamber of Venus' castle illuminated only by a few candles, that
is, his own love. Now the soul experiences that magnification
which is the hunger of every man. And this hunger, this yearning, is peculiar to the adventuresome and daring spirit of youth
that has not yet grown old. Christianity is for the young. It is
a law which, in a special manner, asks man to be imprudent,
unwise, selfless. It urges a commitment for which the "old" are
too fearful. That is why one must become a "Taugenichts." In

order to achieve this, it is necessary for the poet to be free. **He must** have in his heart the image of another goddess of love. Florio had strayed far from what poetry, Bianca, should be. **He** is now prepared to come back to the prison. That is why his last song is called "Der Umkehrende." The first strophe, as **we** have seen, is a turning back to God. "Hier bin ich, Herr! Ge-grüsst das Licht!" The second strophe explains his present spiritual condition.

> Nun bin ich frei! Ich taumle noch
> Und kann mich noch nicht fassen —
> O Vater, du erkennst mich doch
> Und wirst nicht von mir lassen!"
>
> (II, 345)

Florio expresses not only his dependency upon God but also his awareness of being in a transitional stage. It is exceedingly important that we recognize this fact. Because Florio's love is no longer "in der Fremde," as the poem suggests, Venus has turned to stone; but now, as we see in "Götterdämmerung" (strophe thirteen), another woman appears and she represents an entirely different goal for love. It would have been pointless for Eichendorff to introduce her if it were not his intention that the Queen and what she stands for should assume some significance in the basic problem of "Liebe und Andacht." Keeping in mind the law of movement, a spiritual movement, it seems indicated that the youth should turn from Venus to the Virgin Mary. But his words, "Ich taumle noch/Und kann mich noch nicht fassen —," suggest that this is but a first step. I believe Eichendorff makes this quite clear. "Mit Wohlgefallen ruhten Florios Blicke auf der lieblichen Gestalt. Eine seltsame Verblendung hatte bisher seine Augen wie mit einem Zaubernebel umfangen. Nun erstaunte er ordentlich, wie schön sie war! Er sprach vielerlei gerührt und mit tiefer Innigkeit zu ihr." The lovely maiden turns to him "in freudiger Demut," and her eyes seem to say, "Täusche mich nicht wieder" (346). She had loved him and he had deceived her. They ride together, and "hinter ihnen versank die Stadt Lucca mit ihren dunkeln Türmen in dem schimmernden Duft." Strange, is it not? The sun has risen but the city of light is in darkness; it is immersed once again in "dem schimmerden Duft" which we encountered in the very first paragraph of the novella. Did it *really* exist, or was it all part of what "Götterdämmerung" (strophe fifteen) calls "böses Träumen"? The answer really is quite simple. That love which is the realm of Venus has always been and always will be an essential constituent of human reality. The vision of Venus is part of every man's "Jugendträume." It is in the nature of flesh to have these dreams. But with the coming of Christianity, love must have another dream; there is now another "Frauenbild" who serves as the goddess of love. If the Queen of Heaven takes man by the hand, and if he follows willingly as a child, she takes him to the Son. And that represents Eichendorff's unalterable conviction concerning the purpose of human existence. Man is a stranger who is always on his way home and Venus cannot guide him there. Because of this, "Das Marmorbild" represents only part of the problem. The last words that Florio utters are addressed to Bianca. "Ich bin wie neugeboren, es ist mir, als würde noch alles gut werden, seit ich Euch wiedergefunden. Ich möchte niemals wieder scheiden, wenn Ihr es vergönnt." He is reborn, the temple is whole again. But the full significance of these words cannot be understood without making one brief comparison. Florio says, "als würde noch alles gut werden" and the last words in "Der Taugenichts" inform us "—und es war alles, alles gut" (434). This cannot be a mere coincidence. Eichendorff suggests to us that the "Marmorbild"-"Taugenichts" stories *really are one,* beginning with Florio's admission that he had decided to travel and ending with the "Taugenichts'" joyous remark: "und gleich nach der Trauung reisen wir fort nach Italien" (II, 434). The difference in this "Reisen" can best be pointed out by a song sung by the "Taugenichts."

"Wer in die Fremde will wandern,
Der muss mit der Liebsten gehn,
Es jubeln und lassen die andern
Den Fremden alleine stehn.

(II, 393)

The expression, "mit der Liebsten gehn," is the heart of the matter. The reader will recall Florio's first song, "Jeder nennet from die Seine/Ich nur stehe hier alleine,/Denn was früge wohl die Eine,/Wen der Fremdling eben meine?" We know which one he meant; he had, so to speak, chosen the wrong woman. Through grace Florio is enabled to turn from Venus and back to Bianca. This ends the movement of events with the hope that everything will yet be "gut." In view of the fact that Eichendorff ends his "Taugenichts" novella with the assertion that all is well, we must conclude that the young hero's "Liebste" is the right woman.[18] This is a simple yet logical organization of the facts available to us. Now, considering that the basic question in the "Marmorbild," story are the words "Ist's Liebe, ist's Andacht/Was so dich beglückt," we are guided to the equation that love is to Venus as reverence is to the Virgin Mary. This type of equation is employed to convey a relationship, and that is precisely what we are concerned with — the relationship between man and the woman who is poetry. "Jugendandacht" was discussed at considerable length and it was demonstrated that the young man in the poem began with thoughts directed toward the Queen; gradually the imagery became more and more erotic, and it was soon apparent that his love had assumed flesh and blood. This process was described with Eichendorff's own words of "Bilder weltlich festhalten." When the individual embraces this error, then the infinite is measured in terms of the finite self; in effect, man gazes at his own image. This is the essential spiritual and psychological structure in "Das Marmorbild." Eichendorff's carefully interwoven imagery is brilliantly organized so that all the threads lead back to Florio. All the imagery that I have discussed, light, water, song, and flower, have Florio as their author; that is, he is the center, "wo alle die Farbenstrahlen, gleich Radien, ausgehen und sich an der wechselnden Oberfläche zu dem schmerzlich-schönen spiele der Erscheinung gestalten" (II, 75). I deliberately selected Friedrich's description of his own creative activity because it describes what Florio has done, that he has been the image maker. The fundamental difference between Florio and the "Taugenichts" is that the former makes images and the latter preserves one. And the image wears the face of that love which fills the heart and mind of the poet.

Notes

1. This expression refers to the Spanish poets, especially Cervantes and Calderon. Their influence upon the young Eichendorff is a demonstrable fact which scholars have ignored.

2. It is of interest to note that the maiden in "Die Zauberei im Herbst," Bertha, is associated with both modesty and brightness. Bianca is graced with the same characteristics. Both names actually mean *shining* or *brightness*. Both women represent the purity of "Poesie" which man may prostitute.

3. But this dance, we must remember, culminates in "Erstarrung." It is the final phase of that movement of love which declares itself independent of God. It is frozen chaos.

4. In the discussion of the tableau vivant (II, 129) I stated that the vast circle of "hoher, traumhafter, phantastisch ineinander verschlungener Pflanzen" were really man's dreams. These "flowers" stand between man and his God. Later we shall see that the flowers grown by the "Taugenichts" must die.

5. The religions which man fashions for himself are indeed "the opium of the people." That is why the Tempter appears wearing a wreath containing the poppy. And in the name of his religions man can create a nightmare of unimaginable brutality and perversion. Human love is so easily adulterated.

6. The young man in "Jugendandacht" wanted to die so that the woman could reward him. Raimund had to kill his "Herzensbruder," so that the woman of his thoughts would be his "auf Erden und in der Hölle." Florio's song will not lead him to heaven but to hell. A rebellious love, centrifugal force, leads down to "Absonderung, Zerstörung und Hass." All this Florio will experience.

7. The first lines of the "Jugendandacht" cycle tell us: "Dass des verlornen Himmels es gedächte,/Schlugen ans Herz des Frühlings linde Wellen." Florio is experiencing this. His are the spring, the waters, the song, and the lost heaven; he is the deep above which the spirit hovers and from which Venus will arise.

8. We should point out that Bianca never sings in the novella. Already he has changed her. The only song in our story which is sad and filled with "Wehmut" is his song.

9. Once again we allow the poet to instruct us in his use of words. Fortunato left Florio a "Gitarre." The song tells he has a "Zither" in his hand. The "Zither" is a Greek instrument. The "Gitarre" was developed much later, in the Christian era. The "Taugenichts" plays a "Geige" or violin which first began to appear in Germany about the middle of the sixteenth century. Eichendorff's intent, I must conclude, is to suggest the heathen nature of Florio's song.

10. It is not nature that remembers, but Florio, and now creation takes up this song of long ago. This, too, was presented in "Götterdämmerung."

11. Venus exists in the circle or on an island. She is also "drüben," on the other side of the river. As Florio runs from the pond, he feels that "die langen, gespenstischen Pappeln" (II,318) reach for him. These trees line the River Styx and Venus is on the other side in the land of the shades, or land of the spirits.

12. The Eichendorff scholar is invited to check the following pattern. Fear, for one of our poet's characters, is always the sign of inner awareness that he has entered a dangerous realm. That which is to be feared is *always* within and is explained for us in the poem "Memento." Eichendorff calls nature, "die Welt," "unschuldig." When nature seems hostile, man has become his own enemy. Fear is like a fever which warns of an illness. And Florio is becoming "ill."

13. The words "rechten Weg" really mean the wrong way, because he is searching for the pond and the statue.

14. Since the beginning of man's existence, this woman, the symbol of a love restricted to the self, has awaited man's awakening call. She would cover man's wound with kisses and cause him to forget that he is not whole.

15. Eichendorff suggests that the world thrives on the very yearning for God whom it denies. In *Ahnung und Gegenwart* we find the following. "Wenn die Schönheit mit ihren frischen Augen, mit den jugendlichen Gedanken und Wünschen unter euch ritt, und, wie sie die eigene, grössere Lebenslust treibt, sorglos und lüstern in das liebewarme Leben hinauslangt und sprosst — sich an die feinen Spitzen, die zum Himmel streben, giftig anzusaugen und zur Erde hinabzuzerren, bis die ganze, prächtige Schönheit, fahl und ihres himmlischen Schmuckes beraubt, unter euch dasteht wie euresgleichen — die Halunken!" (II, 107-108). I repeat this quotation because it is so absolutely fundamental. Man is graced with a generous capacity to believe, love, and trust. When a society perversely exploits this, it has taken a long step in the direction of its own destruction.

16. The last line of this poem states that *she* will keep him her prisoner. This is precisely the same wording which explains the relationship between the "Taugenichts" and his "gnädige Frau." If we were to change the last letters of the poem's title into *H. M.*, then we would have "der heiligen Maria."

17. The statue of Memnon "sings" when the first rays of the sun strike it. The statue of Venus open its lips to sing when Florio's love shone upon it. Now that the sun shines upon her, the mutilated statue stands revealed for what it is: "Die zu Stein gewordene Religion der Phantasie." Venus has no song except what the poet places upon her lips.

18. This does not mean that Bianca *is* the Virgin Mary. Bianca is a pure, simple, unassuming poetry who travels with the poet, disguised as a youth, as he leads her "heim in Waldesprachten" (I, 182; 1807). She must go with him; he cannot stay in her castle.

VI

Taugenichts

Der Wanderande Musikant

1

Wandern lieb' ich für mein Leben,
Lebe eben wie ich kann,
Wollt' ich mir auch Mühe geben,
Passt es mir doch gar nicht an.

Schöne alte Lieder weiss ich,
In der Kälte, ohne Schuh'
Draussen in die Saiten reiss' ich,
Weiss nicht, wo ich abends ruh'.

Manche Schöne macht wohl Augen,
Meinet, ich gefiel' ihr sehr,
Wenn ich nur was wollte taugen,
So ein armer Lump nicht wär'. —

Mag dir Gott ein'n Mann bescheren,
Wohl mit Haus und Hof versehn!
Wenn wir zwei zusammen wären,
Möcht' mein Singen mir vergehn.

3

Ich reise übers grüne Land,
Der Winter ist vergangen,
Hab' um den Hals ein gülden Band,
Daran die Laute hangen.

Der Morgen tut ein'n roten Schein,
Den recht mein Herze spüret,
Da greif' ich in die Saiten ein,
Der liebe Gott mich führet.

So silbern geht der Ströme Lauf,
Fernüber schallt Geläute,
Die Seele ruft in sich: Glück auf!
Rings grüssen frohe Leute.

Mein Herz ist recht von Diamant,
Ein' Blum' von Edelsteinen,
Die funkelt lustig übers Land
In tausend schönen Scheinen.

Vom Schlosse in die weite Welt
Schaut eine Jungfrau 'runter,
Der Liebste sie im Arme hält,
Die sehn nach mir herunter.

Wie bist du schön! Hinaus, im Wald
Gehn Wasser auf und unter,
Im grünen Wald sing, dass es schallt,
Mein Herz, bleib frei und munter!

Die Sonne uns im Dunklen lässt,
Im Meere sich zu spülen,
Da ruh' ich aus vom Tagesfest
Fromm in der roten Kühle.

Hoch führet durch die stille Nacht
Der Mond die goldnen Schafe,
Den Kreis der Erden Gott bewacht,
Wo ich tief unten schlafe.

Wie liegt all' falsche Pracht so weit!
Schlaf wohl auf stiller Erde,
Gott schütz' dein Herz in Ewigkeit,
Dass es nie traurig werde!

4

Bist du manchmal auch verstimmt,
Drück' dich zärtlich an mein Herze,
Dass mir's fast den Atem nimmt,
Streich' und kneif' in süssem Scherze,

Wie ein rechter Liebestor
Lehn' ich sanft an dich die Wange
Und du singst mir fein ins Ohr.
Wohl im Hofe bei dem Klange
Katze miaut, Hund heult und bellt,
Nachbar schimpft mit wilder Miene —
Doch was kümmert uns die Welt,
Süsse, traute Violine!

5

Mürrisch sitzen sie und maulen
Auf den Bänken stumm und breit,
Gähnend strecken sich die Faulen,
Und die Kecken suchen Streit.

Da komm' ich durchs Dorf geschritten,
Fernher durch den Abend kühl,
Stell' mich in des Kreises Mitten,
Grüss' und zieh' mein Geigenspiel.

Und wie ich den Bogen schwenke,
Ziehn die Klänge in der Rund'
Allen recht durch die Gelenke
Bis zum tiefsten Herzensgrund.

Und nun geht's ans Gläserklingen,
An ein Walzen um und um,
Je mehr ich streich', je mehr sie springen,
Keiner fragt erst lang: warum? —

Jeder will dem Geiger reichen
Nun sein Scherflein auf die Hand —
Da vergeht ihm gleich sein Streichen,
Und fort ist der Musikant.

Und sie sehn ihn fröhlich steigen
Nach den Waldeshöh'n hinaus,
Hören ihn von fern noch geigen,
Und gehn all' vergnügt nach Haus.

Doch in Waldes grünen Hallen
Rast' ich dann noch manche Stund',
Nur die fernen Nachtigallen
Schlagen tief aus nächt'gem Grund.

Und es rauscht die Nacht so leise
Durch die Waldeseinsamkeit,
Und ich sinn' auf neue Weise,
Die der Menschen Herz erfreut.

6

Durch Feld und Buchenhallen
Bald singend, bald fröhlich still,
Recht lustig sei vor allen,
Wer's Reisen wählen will!

Wenn's kaum im Osten glühte,
Die Welt noch still und weit:
Da weht recht durchs Gemüte
Die schöne Blütenzeit!

Die Lerch' als Morgenbote
Sich in die Lüfte schwingt,
Eine frische Reisenote
Durch Wald und Herz erklingt.

O Lust, vom Berg zu schauen
Weit über Wald und Strom,
Hoch über sich den blauen,
Tiefklaren Himmelsdom!

Vom Berge Vöglein fliegen
Und Wolken so geschwind,
Gedanken überfliegen
Die Vögel und den Wind.

Die Wolken ziehn hernieder,
Das Vöglein senkt sich gleich,
Gedanken gehn und Lieder
Fort bis ins Himmelreich.

(I, 12)

Verschwiegene Liebe

Über Wipfel und Saaten
In den Glanz hinein —
Wer mag sie erraten,
Wer holte sie ein?

Gedanken sich wiegen,
Die Nacht ist verschwiegen,
Gedanken sind frei.

Errät' es nur eine,
Wer an sie gedacht,
Beim Rauschen der Haine,
Wenn niemand mehr wacht,
Als Wolken, die fliegen—
Mein Lieb ist verschwiegen
Und schön wie die Nacht.

(I, 228)

The full title of our story is "Aus dem Leben eines Taugenichts."
Not all of his life is described, but only a certain part. Considering
that Eichendorff chose to write in the first person, I am inclined
to accept that we have before us something very personal, a rather definitive facet of his own development. In so many poems
and also in the prose works, we find repeated reference to a
woman whom he had seen before. Now she is departed or even
dead, or no longer recognizes him, nor he her; and yet we always find the same insinuation, namely, that she is immeasur-
ably dear to him. It is known that Novalis' experience by the
grave of the beloved was so concrete and palpable that it became the foundation of his poetic existence. Eichendorff's poetry
was given direction by something similar. But there is one difference; whereas Novalis treated this experience openly, Eichendorff concealed his. I have quoted the poem "Lieder" of 1808
in which the poet says:

Maria, schöne Rose!
Wie stünd'ich freudelose,
Hätt' ich nicht dich ersehn
Vor allen Blumen schön.

This early reference to the Queen is clear and unambigous.
But there are scores of poems which critics have ignored because
they have failed to see a pattern in the references. At this
point let us inspect, very briefly, a poem printed in 1831 which
can serve as a point of departure for our "Taugenichts" discussion.

Der Maler

Aus Wolken, eh' im nächt'gen Land
Erwacht die Kreaturen,
Langt Gottes Hand,
Zieht durch die stillen Fluren
Gewaltig die Konturen,
Strom, Wald und Felsenwand.

Wach auf, wach auf! die Lerche ruft,
Aurora taucht die Strahlen
Verträumt in Duft,
Beginnt auf Berg und Talen
Ringsum ein himmlisch Malen
In Meer und Land und Luft.

Und durch die Stille, lichtgeschmückt,
Aus wunderbaren Locken
Ein Engel blickt. —
Da rauscht der Wald erschrocken,
Da gehn die Morgenglocken,
Die Gipfel stehn verzückt.

O lichte Augen, ernst und mild,
Ich kann nicht von euch lassen!
Bald wieder wild
Stürmt's her von Sorg' und Hassen —
Durch die verworrnen Gassen
Führ mich, mein göttlich Bild!

(I, 18-19)

God paints, so it would seem, but if we look closely at the imagery it is more precise to say that he prepares the canvas. All is still grey, and the lark, Eichendorff's dawn-bird, soars toward the heavens and calls out its greeting for a sleeping world. Then Aurora paints! The logic of conventional imagery dictates that the rising sun paints with the colors of the dawn. But that is not what we read. The rays of light are dipped in "Duft" and the universe is painted *with fragrance*. Perhaps the perceptive reader will understand our poet's intent and realize that this is a heavenly fragrance. So the sun, which normally "paints" with light, mixes its colors with a mysterious ingredient, the fragrance of heaven. But wait, how can the *sun* paint, when the title speaks of *Der Maler?* And notice how she, the sun, goes about her labors? The sun is still "verträumt." If this is so, then she can paint only what she dreams. That must be the answer to the enigma of the title; all without realizing it, the sun is the instrument with which God paints. Now he does not paint the ocean, land, or air, as we might expect, but a certain image redolent with heavenly mystery. We recall the words: "Schläft ein Lied in allen Dingen/Die da träumen fort und fort." The poem would instruct us that nature's dream *is* a song. Perhaps the reader will recall the discussion of the tableau vivant, wherein the woman resplendent in light and holding the cross is clearly called man's dream (129). The song which nature dreams and the woman whom man dreams are one. We shall come to this later. Let us return to our poem.

We are told in the second strophe that "ein himmlisch Malen" begins. This reinforces the implication of the word "verträumt"; the painting is done at heaven's command, and Aurora has no real awareness of how she is being used. The second strophe informs us what God has painted: an angel! The logic of the imagery not only encourages but demands that we make a careful distinction. The angel is not visible, is not in the colors; her face cannot be seen in the created, and yet, as the imagery implies, she is a fragrance which is everywhere! And the Queen of Heaven is a rose. She is the angel who is "licht-geschmückt" and graced with heavenly fragrance. Observe what happens as she looks at creation. The entire universe bursts into song and the churchbells ring. We just referred to the song asleep in the created which bursts forth if the poet utters a magic word. The mere appearance of this woman has the same effect. As I discuss the "Taugenichts" I shall suggest that this angel teaches him the magic word, the song which causes the very mountain tops to stand "verzückt." Nature is joyfully frightened, as though royalty had shown itself,[1] but the speaker in the last strophe of our poem reveals a different reaction. Nature can respond only with a song, but the speaker is drawn to her. Actually I should be more precise and say that he cannot look away from her eyes. I remind the reader of the "Jugendandacht" cycle and the Queen who raises the veil "das offen bliebe/Der Augen Himmel in das Land zu scheinen." And three lines further on we read: "Im Angesicht der Stillen Ewigreinen." More than twenty years separate these poems, but the thought

is the same: he sees but her face, that is to say, her eyes which are "ernst und mild." And these eyes belong to "das Bild." This image leads him through the maze of his own cares and hatreds. She is the guiding star and he admits that he cannot be without her. The "Taugenichts" will say of his "schöne Frau" that without her he is a "Null," a "Niemand." Near the end of the story he is asked for the second time where he is going. His answer is evasive because he does not want to reveal "dass ich soeben der schönen gnädigen Frau nachspränge" (II, 402). The entire "Taugenichts" story concerns the pursuit of this woman who is not to be found anywhere, and yet, as "Der Maler" suggests, her fragrant presence is everywhere. We look at one strophe of the song which our hero sings and which is described as "Das Lied von der schönen Frau."

> Wohin ich geh' und schau,
> In Feld und Wald und Tal,
> Vom Berg ins Himmelblaue,
> Vielschöne, gnäd'ge Frau,
> Grüss ich dich tausendmal.

His seeing is a greeting of the Lady. The "Taugenichts" sees what God had wrought with His "himmlisch Malen." And the Father sends our hero into "die weite Welt" to show him "seine Wunder." This woman is God's masterpiece, and the entire universe sings with joy at the splendor of divine grace which renders her the immaculate one. She is the fairest flower of all, but because she is a flower, man's heart may confuse her with "die Wunderblume" whose roots are in the depths and whose fragrance comes not from the Father but from man. Her name is Venus. She, too, is "ein Bild." In "Das Marmorbild" Florio's own "Bild" becomes flesh; in our "Taugenichts" story the fragrant image painted by God is flesh. Therein is found the difference between the earthly and the heavenly Venus; one is fashioned by God's love, the other by man's. One draws man into the depths of the self where her existence finds root, the other draws man to God. One enslaves man and makes of him his own prisoner, the other frees man and induces man to become God's prisoner. Venus is given life by man's (Florio's) love song and the Queen teaches man her love song, the "Magnificat." We began our discussion of the "Marmorbild" story with a brief analysis of the first paragraph; let us return to this on another

level. "Es war ein schöner Sommerabend, als Florio, ein junger Edelmann, langsam auf die Tore von Lucca zuritt, sich erfreuend an dem feinen Dufte, der über der wunderschönen Landschaft und den Türmen und Dächern der Stadt vor ihm zitterte, sowie an den bunten Zügen zierlicher Damen und Herren, welche sich zu beiden Seiten der Strasse unter den hohen Kastanienalleen fröhlich schwärmend ergingen (II, 307). In conjunction with this prose passage we must look again at the song sung by Fortunato just after Florio had seen Venus and Bianca at the ball.

> Still in Luft
> Es gebart,
> Aus dem Duft
> Hebt sich's zart,
> Liebchen ruft,
> Liebster schweift
> Durch die Luft;
> Sternwärts greift,
> Seufzt und ruft,
> Herz wird bang,
> Matt wird Duft,
> Zeit wird lang —
> Mondscheinduft,
> Luft in Luft
> Bleibt Liebe und Liebste, wie sie gewesen!
>
> (II, 332)

The poem is a brief synopsis of the entire novella. Florio meets Bianca at the beginning, changes her into something else and at the end feels as though all will yet be well "seit ich Euch [Bianca] wiedergefunden." When we compare this with the last line of the poem, we can conclude that Fortunato predicts what will happen. Florio's love song, which gave life to Venus, is replaced by another love song, a veritable divine storm, which destroys what the youth hath made. The mirror-world of Venus crumbles as the love which gave it life is withdrawn. Just as the temple is in ruins, so Florio (who *is* the temple) is near death. And what was the substance out of which Florio fashioned his world? We look at the poem and the prose passage and see that it is "Luft und Duft." The poem contains the phrase "Luft in Luft." All returns to the nothingness from whence it came. But this is not completely correct. The novella begins with Florio's admission that his "Freude und Wünschen sind nun auf einmal in Freiheit gesetzt." These same joys and desires, as they find form in poetry, are flowers, the very flowers which the Queen will not accept. They take root in the garden of the soul and are nurtured by the light of man's love. They must die. And yet, if we remain faithful to the logic of our poet's imagery, we are instructed that these flowers, too, have "Duft." This is the "Duft" which "zitterte" above the city of Lucca. It is the same fragrance of which the poem speaks. "Aus dem Duft/Hebt sich's zart." Flowers are poems, and from the essence of these flowers a woman, "Liebchen," emerges and calls him. She is the "Wunderblume," that enchanting poetry which seems to sing of heavenly mysteries, yet is nothing more than the image of man's own love. And thus the questions: "Ist's Liebe, ist's Andacht/Was so dich beglückt?" We now turn to the "Taugenichts" and his love affair with the woman whom he dare not see but who will not let him go as long as he continues to sing the song which she has taught him.

> Das Rad an meines Vaters Mühle brauste und rauschte schon wieder recht lustig, der Schnee tröpfelte emsig vom Dache, die Sperlinge zwitscherten und tummulten sich dazwischen; ich sass auf der Türschwelle und wischte mir den Schlaf aus den Augen; mir war so recht wohl in dem warmen Sonnenscheine. Da trat der Vater aus dem Hause; er hatte schon seit Tagesanbruch in der Mühle rumort und die Schlafmütze schief auf dem Kopfe, der sagte zu mir: "Du Taugenichts! da sonnst du dich schon wieder und dehnst und reckst dir die Knochen müde und lässt mich alle Arbeit allein tun.[2] Ich kann dich hier nicht länger füttern. Der Frühling ist vor der Tür, geh auch einmal hinaus in die Welt und erwirb dir selber dein Brot." —

The opening paragraphs of the twin novellas are exceedingly important because they reveal so much of the problem-mystery which concerns our poet. The "Taugenichts" has come of age and must now work. I have quoted several poems (actually there are many more) which offer the same situation: the child becomes a young man and must go out into the world. "Das Marmorbild" begins in the same fashion. But there are several important differences. Florio, his very name suggesting the world of flowers and the realm of personal joys and desires, is really a good-for-nothing. He even admits it! The "Taugenichts" is the very opposite of what his name implies; he is commanded to work and earn bread. Secondly, it is truly spring, while in the "Marmorbild" story it is summer and Florio lives his own spring. Finally, the "Taugenichts" begins his journey in the morning and Florio is introduced to us in the evening. Everything is reversed. Now let us see how this lad is to earn his bread.

The "Taugenichts" takes his "Geige" (which he plays very well), is given a few pennies by his father, and sets out to seek his fortune, as he says. He has a secret delight in seeing his old friends "rechts und links, wie gestern und vorgestern und immerdar, zur Arbeit hinausgehen, graben und pflügen . . . , während ich so in die freie Welt hinausstrich" (349). These people are working and earning bread but, apparently, that is not what the father had in mind. Furthermore, if we look closely at these words, we sense the adumbration of the circle motif, out to work and back, always the same. It is interesting to observe that his "old friends" take no note of his departure. He is the ideal and joyful example of a theme we have found in scores of poems and prose passages: "I am alone and unknown, a stranger amongst these people." We shall see later that this is indeed true of our hero. As soon as he reaches the highway, he walks along singing his song.

> Wem Gott will rechte Gunst erweisen,
> Den schickt er in die weite Welt.
> Dem will er seine Wunder weisen
> In Berg und Wald und Strom und Feld.

It is almost too obvious! The youth is told to leave by the father and now we read that God sends his chosen ones out into "die weite Welt." No one can prove that the father with whom our "Taugenichts" speaks is God, and yet, is there a more reasonable conclusion? Since before dawn, since the beginning of time, the father has begin working in the mill, Eichendorff's favorite symbol for that aimless, circular existence for which man is the sole measure. Friedrich, as we have shown, "wollte lebendig eindringen," and he soon realized how difficult it is "nützlich zu sein" (II, 165). All this is in reference to helping one's fellow man. How does one accomplish this, this "lebendig eindringen?" By earning bread! If the poet, any poet, would strive to be more than the manifestation of talent or genius, then he must earn bread. Our poem goes on.

> Die Trägen, die zu Hause liegen,
> Erquicket nicht das Morgenrot,
> Sie wissen nur vom Kinderwiegen,
> Von Sorgen, Last und Not um *Brot*. (Italics mine)

Strange, is it not? Our "Taugenichts" passes his friends who stay home, who work hard to earn bread, and now they are called "die Trägen." Critics no longer see our story as the glorification of a romantic repugnance for work, thank heavens. And yet we have read so carelessly. Obviously, the bread of which the above strophe speaks has nothing to do with the bread mentioned by the father. This bread is not earned at home with "graben und pflügen." Furthermore, "zu Hause" cannot mean merely at home. Wherever man lives the sun rises, therefore "zu Hause" is not a place. The "Morgenrot" of which he speaks touches man on the peaks, in a valley, or in a dungeon. "Zu Hause" is the world of the circle, man's own little world, and here he cannot earn bread. It must be earned in "die freie Welt," in God's "weite Welt." If we ask how man gets there, we would have asked the wrong question. In a dream Friedrich is told by the Christ child, if you love me truly then immerse yourself in me and the world is free. Man finds God's "weite-freie Welt" not by going someplace but by being something. The song goes on.

> Die Bächlein von den Bergen springen,
> Die Lerchen schwirren hoch vor Lust,
> Was sollt' ich nicht mit ihnen singen
> Aus voller Kehl' und frischer Brust?
>
> Den lieben Gott lass ich nur walten;
> Der Bächlein, Lerchen, Wald und Feld
> Und Erd und Himmel will erhalten,
> Hat auch mein Sach' aufs best' bestellt!

Now we know what the "Taugenichts" is to be and do. He must be whatever God wills: "Den lieben Gott lass ich nur walten." As Friedrich says, "Was wahr in dir wird sich gestalten /Das andere ist erbärmlich Ding." As he starts out he tells us: "Mir war es wie ein ewiger Sonntag im Gemüte." And why Sun-

day? Because that is the day when man is to praise the Lord.
Nature, as the poem implies, sings its song of praise every day,
because every day is a Sunday. And so the "Taugenichts" is to
sing "aus voller Kehl' und frischer Brust." As long as his every
day is Sunday and he sings his song he will be in God's "freie
Welt" and earning bread. When he stops singing he will be someplace and he will go hungry, for the Lord will turn His countenance from him and he will be without grace. Then, as we
shall see later, he too indulges in "graben." As he strolls
along, he fails to notice the carriage behind him, "weil mein
Herz so voller Klang war." When he does turn around, he observes two ladies who obviously are listening to him. "Die eine
war besonders schön und jünger als die andere, aber eigentlich
gefielen sie mir alle beide" (350). In "Das Marmorbild" the
truth was more concealed; in the "Taugenichts" story everything
is on the surface. Eichendorff reveals the mystery and by making it so obvious he has deceived his readers. Our young hero meets
two women, one older than the other. The tableau vivant and
"Götterdämmerung" inform us that Venus, the older one, was
replaced by the Virgin Mary, the younger one. Eichendorff has
rejected all mystification and confronted the "Taugenichts" with
the flesh and blood representatives of "Liebe und Andacht."
Very much like Florio, he has just started on a journey and
must make a choice. We have discussed Florio's decision and
now discover that our "Taugenichts" is made of the same clay
as all men, for he says that actually both of them, Venus and
Mary, appeal to him. Thus the "Taugenichts" has admitted that
both love and reverence have a certain charm, and the ensuing
conversation continues the fall. The older one comments upon
his singing and the youth replies, " 'Euer Gnaden aufzuwarten,
wüsst' ich noch viele schönere.' Darauf fragte sie mich wieder:
'Wohin wandert Er denn schon so am frühen Morgen?' Da
schämte ich mich, dass ich das selber nicht wusste, und sagte
dreist: 'Nach Wien.' Nun sprachen beide miteinander in einer
fremden Sprache, die ich nicht verstand. Die jüngere schüttelte
einigemal mit dem Kopfe, die andere lachte aber in einem fort
und rief mir endlich zu: 'Spring er nur hinten mit auf, wir
fahren auch nach Wien.' "

What has this young man just done? Eichendorff is both a
good Christian and an excellent psychologist; in the beginning is
the problem. In order to develop an answer I ask the reader to

reflect upon the main theme of this book. Beginning with "Das Zaubernetz," the first poem, we came again and again to the problem and mystery of the woman. I suggested that she is poetry, a woman who "conceals" two faces. In the "Jugendandacht" cycle, "Die Zauberei im Herbste," "Das Marmorbild," and in many other poems, the minstrel gave life to the image of his own love. We should look at part of a poem sung by Victor in *Dichter und ihre Gesellen.*

> Lauten hör' ich ferne klingen,
> Lust'ge Bursche ziehn vom Schmaus,
> Ständchen sie den Liebsten bringen,
> Und das lockt mich mit hinaus.
> Mädchen hinterm blühnden Baume
> Winkt und macht das Fenster auf,
> Und ich steige wie im Traume
> Durch das kleine Haus hinauf.
> Schüttle nur die dunklen Locken
> Aus dem schönen Angesicht!
> Sieh, ich stehe ganz erschrocken:
> Das sind i h r e Augen licht.
> Locken hatte sie wie deine,
> Bleiche Wangen, Lippen rot —
> Ach, du bist ja doch nicht meine,
> Und mein Lieb ist lange tot!
> Hättest du nur nicht gesprochen
> Und so frech geblickt nach mir,
> Das hat ganz den Traum zerbrochen,
> Und nun grauet mir vor dir.
> Da, nimm Geld, kauf' Putz und Flimmern,
> Fort und lache nicht so wild!
> O ich möchte dich zertrümmern,
> Schönes, lügenhaftes Bild!

(650)

For Victor-Lothario-Vitalis, woman or poetry has become a harlot. Florio's Venus artfully manipulates her veil "immer schönere Formen bald enthüllend, bald lose verbergen," until the youth looks at her with "flammenden Augen." Raimund stands "eingewurzelt in flammendem Schauer" as he spies upon his beloved who stands in the pool "und schaute . . . wie verzaubert und versunken in das Bild der eignen Schöneheit, das der trunkene Wasserspiegel widerstrahlte" (979). The same words are found in "Das Marmorbild." In each instance the poet is confronted with "ein lügenhaftes Bild." Man does this to "Poesie" whose name is Bianca; he prostitutes her by making her into something "viel grösser und schöner" (Venus) than she is. The poem is called "Verlorene Liebe." Raimund, Rudolf, Florio, all lost their love, and even Friedrich must undergo that process which forces him to admit: "Die Poesie, seine damalige, süsse Reisegefährtin, genügte ihm nicht mehr, alle seine ernstesten, herzlichsten Pläne waren an dem Neide seiner Zeit gescheitert, seine Mädchenliebe musste, ohne dass er es selbst bemerkte, einer höheren Liebe weichen und jenes grosse, reiche Geheimnis des Lebens hatte sich ihm endlich in Gott gelöst" (226). For Friedrich, her name was Rosa; for Florio, Venus; for Rudolf, Angelina; for Raimund, Bertha. Invariably Eichendorff refers to this love and poetry as "Mädchenliebe." Florio is called "ein träumendes Mädchen" and our "Taugenichts" is mistaken for a girl. This good-for-nothing, a minstrel without peer, makes mistakes, but he is not the victim of "Mädchenliebe." Before we come to the question of his basic error, let us look at another passage which speaks of the image in this poet's heart.

Die Kunst lässt sich nicht abtrotzen oder als Vehikel eines grossen Gemüts von selbst fordern. Was kann man ihr anders geben als sich selber ganz? Sie wird wirklich zur Geliebten, deren blaue Augen, roter Mund ewig keine Ruhe lassen. Im Frühling langt sie aus den duftigen Tälern mit weissen, ganz zarten Armen, um dich nur recht an ihr liebendes Herz zu drücken, das Waldhorn sagt dir, wie sie sich hinter den Bergen nach dir sehnt, die Vöglein und blaue Lüfte lässt sich die Treue viel tausendmal grüssen. In Mondnacht ists, als weinte sie sehr und wollte dir gern ein tröstendes Liebeswort vertrauen. Aber sie kann nicht herüber aus der Ferne zu dir langen. Ja, glaube nur, sie weint auch um dich, sehnt sich auch recht sehr nach dir, deine Lieder bringen ihr auch süssen Schmerz. Liebe nur immer treu und aus allen Kräften deines Lebens, der Himmel bleibt nicht immer verschlossen" (II, 989).

Poetry is a woman. Florio's Venus is a "Wunderblume" or poetry which thrives on his song. Juanna is the very essence of Victor's poetry. She has the same personality characteristics as he has. She is Spanish, and Eichendorff borrowed from the Spanish master Cervantes. Florio in a veiled fashion admits this (307). Like Cervantes, the very young Eichendorff built his art around the principle that ideas must be cloaked in flesh and blood; they could not be abstractions. (I hope to say more of this in a later study.) Raimund admits that the beloved whom he "sees" is "das Fräulein, das alle meine Gedanken meinten" (977). His thoughts became flesh. For all of Eichendorff's poet-heroes we can demonstrate the same pattern. The woman is poetry. But there is another woman who is flesh, an image who does not take her life from the poet. Notice, in the above quotation, that "sie kann nicht herüber aus der Ferne zu dir langen." She is, as one poem calls her, "die Entfernte," yet she is always at hand. She is the woman of the rainbow, the beloved in the "forest" (thoughts) ; she is the one who raises the veil, "die Oberfläche, dass offen bliebe der Augen Himmel in das Land zu scheinen." She holds on to the "Taugenichts" and will not let him go. He sees her everywhere, yet never sees her. She is that other face in poetry; she is the image in his heart, the song on his lips, "die Eine" without whom he would be a "Niemand" and a "Null." Eichendorff's use of language leaves no doubt about the deceptive duality of the image, the woman reflected in poetry. But we can do more than deduce this; Eichendorff actually tells us. The last long passage quoted above, beginning with the words "Die Kunst," was taken from a brief sketch of a novel he intended to write. The title of this work was to be "Marien Sehnsucht." The knowledgeable reader should see in this passage the essential substance of numerous poems as well as the poetry-woman figures in most of the prose works. The Queen seems to be defined in the same terms as Venus-poetry. But Mary, the Queen of Heaven, cannot really walk in the garden with the poet; the minstrel can only pursue her with yearning. Our "Taugenichts" does this. Now let us answer the question: What is it that this young man has just done?

Our young hero has just finished a song which paraphrases the "Magnificat," the overture to Christianity, "Let it be done unto me according to thy Word." "Den lieben Gott lass in dir walten," "Was wahr in dir wird sich gestalten." These verses are taken from "Der Dichter," a poem sung by Friedrich, but the first verse is repeated by the "Taugenichts." The second verse indicates what is to transpire within the ycount poet. The truth is to be formed within him. In Eichendorff we find a deep and profound Catholic wisdom; as the Virgin cooperated with the Spirit so that the Word took form within her, so man is to let the Spirit overshadow him. The "new man" is not of man's making but is "made" by God. Eichendorff voices the same idea in reference to "die Quelle" that "Grundmelodie" placed in each heart and which the poet should let burst forth as it will. And our "Taugenichts" has just declared that he knows songs even more beautiful than the "Magnificat." In Homer's epics, Venus is described as "the ever laughing Dame" and the "Taugenichts" is offered a ride by the older woman, the one who "lachte in einem fort." The younger one, however, shook her head; she rejects him because he, thoughtlessly and foolishly, has already forgotten that he is to earn bread. And now, before the reader forgets the specifics of the imagery in the "Marien Sehnsucht" passage, we should introduce one of those poems which, when viewed from the right perspective, reveals so much of Eichendorff's secret love.

Die Einsame

Wenn morgens das fröhliche Licht bricht ein,
Tret' ich zum offenen Fensterlein,
Draussen gehn lau die Lüft' auf den Auen,
Singen die Lerchen schon hoch im Blauen,
Rauschen am Fenster die Bäume gar munter,
Ziehn die Brüder in den Wald hinunter;
Und bei dem Sange und Hörnerklange
Wird mir immer so bange, bange.

Wüsst' ich nur immer, wo du jetzo bist,
Würd' mir schon wohler auf kurze Frist.
Könntest du mich nur über die Berge sehen
Dein gedenkend im Garten gehen:
Dort rauschen die Brunnen jetzt alle so eigen,
Die Blumen vor Trauern im Wind sich neigen.
Ach! von den Vöglein über die Tale
Sei mir gegrüsst viel tausend Male!

Du sagtest gar oft: Wie süss und rein
Sind deine blauen Äugelein!
Jetzo müssen sie immerfort weinen,

> Da sie nicht finden mehr, was sie meinen;
> Wird auch der rote Mund erblassen,
> Seit du mich, süsser Buhle, verlassen.
> Eh' du wohl denkst, kann das Blatt sich wenden,
> Geht alles gar bald zu seinem Ende.

(I, 233)

Can there be any doubt that the poem and the prose passage speak of the same woman? Compare them carefully. The Queen is the one who yearns for man. This maiden-mother would draw all men to her heart and to her Son. Thus we are informed in the song "Kirchenlied." Notice that the poet is called "süsser Buhle." That is the role played by the "Taugenichts." But already at the beginning of his journey he has, so to speak, left her. Let us see what happens because of his denial. The "Taugenichts" climbs aboard and he is off to Vienna.

> "Wie aber dann die Sonne immer höher stieg, rings am Horizont schwere weisse Mittagswolken aufstiegen, und alles in der Luft und auf der weiten Fläche so leer und schwül und still wurde über den leise wogenden Kornfeldern, da fiel mir erst wieder mein Dorf ein und mein Vater und unsere Mühle, wie es da so heimlich kühl war an dem schattigen Weiher, und dass nun alles so weit, weit hinter mir lag. Mir war dabei so kurios zumute, als müsst' ich wieder umkehren; ich steckte meine Geige zwischen Rock und Weste, setzte mich voller Gedanken auf den Wagentritt hin und schlief ein" (351).

Suddenly it is "schwül," and noon, the sixth hour, grips our wanderer. Just two pages before (and we must assume it is the same day) snow was melting on the roof, and yet the "Taugenichts" now looks at "leise wogenden Kornfeldern." Although he could not have been riding more than a few hours he feels as though his home is "weit, weit" behind him. He thinks of going back, "wieder umkehren," the same word that is the title of Florio's last song, "Der Umkehrende." The story begins in the spring and suddenly it seems summer. "Das Marmorbild" begins in the summer but actually portrays the spring in Florio's heart. Everything is just reversed! Obviously, time and the season are used as indicators of man's spiritual orientation. Much time has passed for the "Taugenichts," a time which has the same

lack of dimension as Florio's experience of time when he asks
"Wo bin ich denn so lange gewesen." It is empty time, and our
"Taugenichts" has already erred three times. He has entered
the same summer in which Florio dwells because both Venus and
the Virgin appeal to him; he does not know where he is going;
and he says he knows lovelier songs than that which says, *Thy will
be done!* And so he falls asleep. But there is a difference between
Florio and the "Taugenichts." Florio had to borrow a musical
instrument from Fortunato. The "Taugenichts" has his own
"Geige" which he secures "zwischen Rock und Veste" close to his
heart. Also, he is "voller Gedanken." This young man thinks!

The carriage does not take him to Vienna but to a castle
where he is employed as "Gärtnerbursche," a position which he
has to accept because he had lost the few pennies which the
father had given him (351). He has lost his wealth because he
knows songs more beautiful than the "Magnificat"! The old gardener does not introduce him to the work of gardening but,
strangly enough, tells him what sort of life he should lead. All
of which the "Taugenichts" promptly forgets. Indeed, it all happens
so quickly, the youth is rather confused: "ich sagte nur immerfort zu allem: Ja, — denn mir war wie einem Vogel, dem
die Flügel begossen worden sind. — So war ich denn, Gott sei
Dank, im Brote. —" (352). The reference to the bird should
remind us of Florio's remark, of feeling like "ein schwaches,
vom Winde verwehtes Lerchenstimmlein." The suggestion is the
same, namely, that neither "flies" as he should. And this reference to bread; is that really what the father had in mind when
he sent him out into "die weite Welt?" I think not! The fact
that our "Taugenichts" is a gardener's apprentice is of more than
passing interest. He says "in dem Garten war schön leben," a
rather unusual expression which insinuates that this is no ordinary garden. Although he must work, the youth also has considerable free time. He enjoys lying on his back, especially
on sultry afternoons, "wenn alles so still war, dass man nur die
Bienen summsen hörte, und sah zu, wie über mir die Wolken
nach meinem Dorfe zuflogen und die Gräser und Blumen sich hin
und her bewegten, und gedachte an die Dame, und da geschah
es denn oft, dass die schöne Frau mit der Gitarre oder einem
Buche in der Ferne wirklich durch den Garten zog, so still, gross
und freundlich wie ein Engelsbild, so dass ich nicht recht wusste,
ob ich träumte oder wachte" (352-53). This is a condensed image

given us in two parts in "Das Marmorbild." Florio tells Venus of his childhood and speaks of lying in the grass, just as the "Taugenichts" does, and in talking with Fortunato he recalls the same scene but speaks of a "zabuerischer Spielmann," a certain spring, that sings of "grosser unermesslicher Lust" (308). This "Spielmann," this spring, appeared as Venus — remember that for Florio, "der ganze Frühling" had become "ein Bild der Schönen" (324). The "Taugenichts" passage above combines all this, but "die schöne Frau" is now "ein Engelsbild." It is clear, as he says, that he is thinking of her. Which *her?* He did meet two of them as he began his journey! But this one is "still, gross und freundlich." With discrete insistence, the "Taugenichts" — we should say Eichendorff — will return to this one woman and offer sufficient details to identify her. Our young hero is unsure when he sees this loveliness as to whether he is dreaming or awake. In this novella, as in the "Marmorbild" story, the dream is to become reality.

Following the paragraph in which he refers to the lady as "ein Engelsbild," the "Taugenichts" sings his first song to her. We recall that Florio's first song was called "Liebe in der Fremde," and this one is entitled simply "Der Gärtner."

> "Wohin ich geh' und schaue,
> In Feld und Wald und Tal,
> Vom Berg' ins Himmelsblaue,
> Vielschöne gnäd'ge Fraue,
> Grüss' ich dich tausendmal."
>
> (II, 353)

Eichendorff parallels the "Marmorbild" structure by allowing the hero to sing only the first strophe. The reason is rather unusual. He happens to be standing by a "Lusthaus" and between the flowers he sees "zwei schöne, junge, frische Augen hervorfunkeln." He stops singing because he is frightened and, without a backward glance, he returns to his work. Florio was often frightened, but he did not listen to his fear. That evening, which happens to be Saturday, our young gardener "stand eben in der Vorfreude kommenden Sonntags mit der Geige im Gartenhause am Fenster und dachte noch an die funkelnden Augen, da kommt auf einmal die Kammerjungfer durch die Dämmerung dahergestrichen" (353).[3] This seemingly harmless statement actually contains a rather serious contradiction. The "Taugenichts" should not prepare himself for Sunday and also think of those sparkling eyes. This inattention and confusion is tantamount to an invitation, and it is heard. The chambermaid has a message. "Da schickt Euch die vielschöne gnädige Frau was, das sollt Ihr auf ihre Gesundheit trinken. Eine gute Nacht auch!" (353). With that, she places a bottle of wine on the window sill and disappears between the flowers and shrubbery. Now which "vielschöne gnädige Frau" is this one? Whoever she is, she offers him wine. And then the "Taugenichts" tells us: "Ich aber stand noch lange vor der wundersamen Flasche und wusste nicht, wie mir geschehen war. — Und hatte ich vorher lustig die Geige gestrichen, so spielt' und sang ich jetzt erst recht und sang das Lied von der schönen Frau ganz aus und alle meine Lieder, die ich nur wusste, bis alle Nachtigallen draussen erwachten und Mond und Sterne schon lange über dem Garten standen. Ja, das war einmal eine gute, schöne Nacht!" We recall that Florio-Bacchus is involved in a scene containing the same factors of wine, woman, and song. The "Marmorbild" situation seems paralleled, but actually our poet has insinuated a significant deviation. The "Taugenichts" does not drink this wine. He stands in front of this "wundersamen Flasche" not really understanding what has happened. He finally bursts into song, singing "das Lied von der schönen Frau" in its entirety and all the other songs that he can remember. Again we could ask, which "schöne Frau" is it that occupies his mind and heart? I think the context suggests that it is not the one who sent him the bottle of wine. The word "wundersam" which describes this wine belongs in the "Marmorbild"-Venus context and is the very opposite of the "Wunder" which God would show him. The song that he sings and his "schöne Frau" have nothing to do with the other beautiful woman who sent him the wine. And yet our friend has erred and must feel the pain of his transgression.

Our "Taugenichts" thinks. He meditates upon such axioms as "eine blinde Henne findet manchmal auch ein Korn, wer zuletzt lacht, lacht am besten, unverhofft kommt oft, der Mensch denkt und Gott lenkt" (353). And then again, when he takes a good look at himself, it seems to him "als wäre ich doch eigentlich ein rechter Lump" (354). If the truth be known, he is bored and displeased with himself. And so, quite contrary to his custom, he gets up very early and goes into the garden.[4]

Da war es so wunderschön draussen im Garten. Die Blumen, die Springbrunnen, die Rosenbüsche und der ganze Garten funkelten von der Morgensonne wie lauter Gold und Edelstein. Und in den hohen Buchenalleen, da war es noch so still, kühl und andächtig wie in einer Kirche, nur die Vögel flatterten und pickten auf dem Sande. Gleich vor dem Schlosse, gerade unter den Fesntern, wo die schöne Frau wohnte, war ein blühender Strauch. Dorthin ging ich dann immer am frühesten Morgen und duckte mich hinter die Äste, um so nach den Fenstern zu sehen, denn mich im Freien zu produzieren hatt' ich keine Courage. Da sah ich nun allemal die allerschönste Dame noch heiss und halb verschlafen im schneeweissen Kleid an das offne Fenster hervortreten. Bald flocht sie sich die dunkelbraunen Haare und liess dabei die anmutig spielenden Augen über Busch und Garten ergehen, bald bog und band sie die Blumen, die vor ihrem Fenster standen, oder sie nahm auch die Gitarre in den weissen Arm und sang dazu so wundersam über den Garten hinaus, dass sich mir noch das Herz umwenden will vor Wehmut, wenn mir eins von den Liedern bisweilen einfällt — und ach, das alles ist schon lange her! So dauerte das wohl über eine Woche. Aber das eine Mal, sie stand gerade wieder am Fenster und alles war stille ringsumher, fliegt mir eine fatale Fliege in die Nase, und ich gebe mich an ein erschreckliches Niesen, das gar nicht enden will. Sie legt sich weit zum Fenster hinaus und sieht mich Ärmsten hinter dem Strauche lauschen. — Nun schämte ich mich und kam viele Tage nicht hin (354).

Much of the imagery is taken directly from the garden of Venus which Florio visits (321 ff.). The meaning, however, is found less in the similarities than in the differences. It is early morn and not high noon. The gold comes not from Florio's "goldne Träume," but from the light of the sun. We see the same trees, "Buchenalleen," but they are nature's cathedral and the atmosphere is "andächtig" as in a church.[5] The birds are very much alive and not like "abgewehte Blüten" (321) as in Florio's dreamgarden. But the most important fact must be deduced indirectly. This beautiful woman sings, as Venus did, but we are not told what her song is. Furthermore, Venus sings Florio's song, "Liebe in der Fremde," but the "Taugenichts" learns his songs from this woman. In other words, the relationship is completely reversed. Venus sings man's love song; but man must learn to sing the Virgin's love song, the "Magnificat"! The sequence of events in the two stories is vaguely similar, yet profoundly different. That is why the garden scene above compares so well with Venus' garden but yet is essentially not the same. Everything is under a positive sign. And yet something is amiss. It all seems so ridiculous; he sneezes and the "liebe schöne Frau" disappears to be replaced by the other one who is described as "recht schön rot and dick und gar prächtig und hoffartig" (355). Just once he believes he sees "die Schöne" hidden behind the drapes. We are reminded of the opening scene wherein the older one offered him a ride while the younger one wanted nothing to do with him. The same thing has happened again! "Sie kam nicht mehr in den Garten, sie kam nicht mehr ans Fenster. Der Gärtner schalt mich einen faulen Bengel, ich war verdrüsslich, meine eigene Nasenspitze war mir im Wege, wenn ich in Gottes freie Welt hinaussah" (355). Why? If we will but reflect, it must be apparent that the "Taugenichts" follows a behavior pattern established by Raimund and Florio; he enters the garden of the beloved and spies upon her. He wants to see! All that our poet is and would be is directed against seeing and directed toward the vision, but a vision which must never assume concrete form. This is "weltlich festhalten." The vision must be lived — but it cannot be possessed. Man must give himself to this vision, and by himself I mean Eichendorff's definition of the whole man, "Glauben, Verstand, Gefühl, Phantasie." The vision toward which he moves is defined by the love which governs his actions. Our "Taugenichts" at this moment is lazy and not earning bread; he does not sing. The entire movement of the story dictates that this is an error, but our poet, via a symbol long unrecognized, tells us that this is wrong. The "Taugenichts" is discovered because a fly causes him to sneeze, and the fly is an ancient symbol for evil! Briefly and bluntly stated, the "Taugenichts" is becoming immersed in a way of life which disregards man's high calling, to love God above else. In his present position, as he tells us himself, he feels like a bird "dem die Flügel begossen worden sind." He is "im Brote," but the bread is not spiritual. The "Taugenichts" even goes so far as to bring "die liebe schöne Frau" into his world; he spies on her and want to see her. It is all tragically improper. He must, through grace, rise to her world, God's "weite Welt," which is a mode of being and not a place. That is why the lady withdraws and will not let him see her, except once, and he is not too sure of that. Our "Taugenichts," however, reveals one characteristic which distinguishes him from Florio: He thinks! He examines himself and his doing and he is disgusted. We have seen this several times and we shall see it again. He who would love the Christ must first and always undergo the painful process of rejecting his own notion of self. "Was wahr in dir, wird sich gestalten,/Das andre ist erbärmlich Ding. —" The "Taugenichts" now becomes fearful that he will be left with his own self, this "erbärmlich Ding."

> So lag ich eines Sonntags nachmittag im Garten und ärgerte mich, wenn ich so in die blauen Wolken meiner Tabakspfeife hinaussah, dass ich mich nicht auf ein andres Handwerk gelegt und mich also morgen nicht auch wenigstens auf einen blauen Montag zu freuen hätte. Die andern Burschen waren indes alle wohlausstaffiert nach den Tanzböden in der nahen Vorstadt hinausgezogen. Da wallte und wogte alles im Sonntagsputze in der warmen Luft zwischen den lichten Häusern und wandernden Leierkasten schwärmend hin und zurück. Ich aber sass wie eine Rohrdommel im Schilfe eines einsamen Weihers im Garten und schaukelte mich auf dem Kahne, der dort angebunden war, während die Vesperglocken aus der Stadt über den Garten herüberschallten und die Schwäne auf dem Wasser langsam neben mir hin und her zogen. Mir war zum Sterben bange — (355).

What we have endeavored to clarify is concealed in the above passage in a delightful bit of bird imagery. He calls himself "eine Rohrdommel" sitting in the reeds. This heron-like bird does not like to fly, prefers the ground, and has nocturnal habits. Combine this with the "begossene Flügel" expression and the fact that Eichendorff deliberately repeats the imagery of Florio's dream experience (316); it must be obvious that the "Taugenichts" has moved toward the danger that Florio experienced. But again there is a difference. This little boat is tied to the shore, and Florio's "Kahn" seems to sail upon a vast ocean of moonlight splendor and then gradually sinks. (The notion of being bound, as though a someone had a firm grip on him, will be encountered later.) Florio had chosen the night; "Taugenichts" belongs to the day, the sun, but, by his own admission, his actions are leading him toward darkness and he is deathly afraid.

Fear of the Lord is the beginning of wisdom. The next scene offers further insight as to why he is afraid.

His reverie is interrupted by approaching voices and laughter.
A group of people including both of his ladies are coming across
the meadow. He is instructed to row them across the pond. And
now we are given a most significant description. "Die schöne
Frau, welche eine Lilie in der Hand hielt, sass dicht am Bord des
Schiffleins und sah so still lächelnd in die klaren Wellen hinunter,
die sie mit der Lilie berührte, so dass ihr ganzes Bild zwischen
den widerscheinenden Wolken und Bäumen im Wasser noch einmal zu sehen war, wie ein Engel, der leise durch den tiefen
blauen Himmelsgrund zieht" (356). Although both of the ladies
are present we are concerned with the one who has a lily in
her hand. This symbol of purity, the Easter flower, identifies
the Virgin. The words "still lächelnd" — one is tempted to think
of the enigmatic Mona Lisa smile — suggest an inwardness,
a withdrawal, as though she really were not a part of the noisy
group. But the passage does suggest a certain activity on her
part which is so gently insinuated that it is easily neglected. If
Eichendorff were concerned solely with the concept of her reflection he could have written the lines as follows. "Die Schöne
Frau . . . sass dicht am Bord das Schiffleins und sah so still
lächelnd in die klaren Wellen . . . so dass ihr ganzes Bild . . . usw."
Our poet deliberately added the fact that she has a lily in her
hand with which she touches the water. Surely this most careful
of artists should not be accused of adding irrelevant embellish-
ment in such an important context. The entire novella revolves
about the identity of these two women and all of the young
man's doing is really an effort to discriminate and select the
right one. Even the most casual reader can see that the "Taugenichts," through his own errors and foolishness, always seems
to pick the wrong one, the older of his "zwei Damen." Why
should the "schöne Frau" touch the water with the lily, the symbol of purity?

If we analyze our passage we detect that its component parts
are drawn from two scenes in "Das Marmorbild." The swan,
boat, and water symbolism come from Florio's dream-vision (316).
The reflection of the woman in the water is taken from the
pond scene (318). Florio sees the marble statue "das dort *dicht*
am Ufer auf einem Stein stand, als wäre die Göttin soeben erst
aus den Wellen aufgetaucht[6] und betrachtete nun, selber ver-

zaubert, das Bild der eigenen Schönheit, das der *trunkene Was-serspiegel . . . widerstrahlte*" (318, italics mine). Venus, like "die schöne Frau," is immediately adjacent to a body of water. Our analysis of the pond symbolism in "Das Marmorbild" suggests that it represents the depths of the self, into which Florio sinks and finds the roots of the "Wunderblume." The light which gives life to the flower is Florio's love song, a love intoxicated with its own splendor. That is why Venus is called enchanted as she gazes at "das Bild der eigenen Schönheit"; it also explains why the pond, the self, is called "trunken." If we now examine these two passages in reference to the word "Bild," a delicate but vital difference gradually becomes apparent. In the "Marmorbild" scene the very structure of the thought insinuates an identity between the image and its reflection. They are one and the same! Eichendorff does not let us forget this in the movement of events. Each time that Florio sees his resurrected Venus he is also reminded of the stone statue until, in the final scene, Venus again turns to stone. This happens because Florio cannot distinguish between "Liebe und Andacht." The purpose of his experiences is to teach him the difference. Turning to the counterpart of this scene in our "Taugenichts" story, we detect a deliberate avoidance of the identity insinuation. The "schöne Frau" does not look at herself, but more significantly, the poet stresses what her reflection seems to be, that is, an angel in the vault of heaven. What she seems to be is the essence of the mystery in this story. If the poet can say to us that a marble statue may be given life by a love song and walk with the lover, could he not also say that the Queen of Heaven will be at the side of the lover who sings the "Magnificat"? I realize that the last line, although really quite logical, seeks to be persuasive and does not offer proof. Let us digress and look at a poem. A cycle simply called "Lieder" which was written in 1808/09 offers pertinent imagery. The cycle contains four poems and I shall discuss them, or their parts, as our subject dictates.

Lieder 1

Frisch eilt der helle Strom hinunter.
Drauf ziehn viel' bunte Schifflein munter,
Und Strom und Schiff und bunte Scheine,
Sie fragen alle: was ich weine?
Mir ist so wohl, mir ist so weh,
Wie ich den Frühling fahren seh'.

Viel' Lenze sitz' ich schon da oben,
Ein Regenbogen steht im Land erhoben
Und durch die Täler, Wiesen, Wogen
Still, wie ein fernes Lied, gezogen,
Schifft immerfort dein himmlisch Bild —
Doch Strom und Schiff nie stille hielt.

(I, 280)

The imagery in the first strophe has been seen in other poems. It is best understood when compared with Romana's song "Frische Fahrt" (I, 9 or II, 124). The second strophe speaks of the Virgin who is intimately associated with the rainbow, the biblical symbol for peace between man and God after the deluge. (See the second strophe of "Kirchenlied" I, 283). This peace is the bridge over the ocean of time and existence which man must traverse and the Virgin is the guide. She is but an image, "ein Bild," but this "Bild" must become alive; she must be a being of flesh and blood and not a mere abstraction. Because the two novellas are so intimately similar yet profoundly different the above also applies to Venus. But this poem suggests a difference. The "Bild" is equated with "ein fernes Lied." I have discussed at great length that this distant song is the eternal "Alleluia" and the Virgin's "Fiat" was the first human note in the overture to salvation, the birth of Christ. In other words, and I repeat myself, whereas Venus *cannot exist* without Florio's love song, the "Taugenichts" is nothing without "das Bild," the song, which the Virgin *is*. The relationship is just the reverse in the two stories. Eichendorff's imagery in "Götterdämmerung" compelled me to introduce the term *inversion*. Florio felt that his movement was toward the Father when, in fact, he gravitated down to the sunken world of Venus. The youth felt that his own love song, "hohe und sanfte Empfindungen," was sufficent energy for his flight (bird symbolism in "Marmorbild") to the Father. The "Taugenichts," on the other hand, never forgets the Virgin's song. The problem in our story is the youth's weakness and foolish assertion at the beginning of the story that he knows other songs which are even more beautiful. But, and this is the heart of the matter, he never forgets her song; he is true to "das Bild," the song, and will be rewarded.

Turning back to our poem we see that the image remains the same even though the stream and the ship (man's life) is always moving. What does this mean? Our "Taugenichts" rows a boat, and the image of the "schöne Frau" appears "wie ein Engel, der leise durch den tiefen blauen Himmel *zieht*" (italics mine.) Such similarity is not accidental; the poet even uses the same verb, "ziehen." We now know why the image is always the same; it accompanies him through life because it sails with him and is always at his side. The prose passage also offers an interesting and important example of the inversion principle. Venus is always associated with water, but the imagery describing "die schöne Frau" leaves us with the final impression that the vision belongs in the sky, "im tiefen blauen Himmelsgrund." The poem suggests the same fact because, although the image is seen in the stream, the Virgin is actually on the rainbow. That is why the fourth poem of the "Lieder" cycle begins as follows:

> Wie in einer Blume himmelblauen
> Grund, wo schlummernd träumen stille Regenbogen,
> Ist mein Leben ein unendlich Schauen,
> Klar durchs ganze Herz ein süsses Bild gezogen.
>
> (I, 282)

Once again we have traced all the imagery back to the heart, to man; the flower, the rainbow, the image are within him. This is the last poem in the "Lieder" cycle and Eichendorff, quite obviously, was not satisfied with the structure of its ideas because he took the same poem, both strophes, and inserted them without change in the "Jugendandacht" cycle, which is a study in the deception of human love. As the last poem in the "Lieder" cycle, it seems to be an acceptable statement because the flower has a reference in the third poem of the cycle. "Maria, schöne Rose!/Wie stünd' ich freudelose,/Hätt' ich nicht dich ersehn/Von allen Blumen schön." Notice that the poet does not use the simple and unambiguous word "gesehen"; he uses "ersehen" which allows us to question the concept of *seeing*. We must let Eichendorff suggest how he wants this word understood. The second poem of the "Lieder" provides some insight.

> Denk' ich dein, muss bald verwehen
> Alle Trübnis weit und breit,
> Und die frischen Blicke gehen
> Wie in einen Garten weit.

Wunderbare Vögel wieder
Weiden dort auf grüner Au,
Einsam' Engel, alte Lieder
Ziehen durch den Himmel blau.

Wolken, Ströme, Schiffe, alle
Segeln in die Pracht hinein —
Keines kehrt zurück von allen,
Und ich stehe so allein.

(I, 280-81)

The speaker in our poem asserts that whenever he thinks of
her, the Queen of Heaven, all despondency is gone and the world
is like a garden filled with ancient songs and angels. But this
garden, "die Pracht," is really a vision of the soul's eternal home
toward which the entire panorama of human existence sails, leaving him once again alone. When man takes his love and pours it
into the sacred vessel of reverence, there are moments when
he experiences the raised veil, "dass offen bliebe/Der Augen
Himmel in das Land zu scheinen." But only for moments, and
then there is, as always, aloneness. And so, the creature, filled
with the echo of the "alten Lieder" and recalling the radiance
of "die Pracht," speaks to his heart.

3

Sei stark, getreues Herze!
Lass ab von Angst und Schmerze!
Steh' auf und geh' mit mir,
Viel Freude zeig' ich dir.

Die Lerchen jubilieren,
Und fröhlich musizieren
Aus grünem frischen Wald
Rings Stimmlein mannigfalt.

Geschmückt mit Edelsteinen,
Die Erd' in bunten Scheinen
Als junge fromme Braut
Dir froh ins Herze schaut.

Im Garten zu spazieren
Die Blumen mich verführen,

> Die Augen aus dem Grün,
> Die Quellen und das Blühn.
>
> (I, 281)

What joys will he show his heart? The speaker has turned from the vision and looks upon a creation filled with song and light. And this world, like a young pious bride, looks into his heart "in bunten Scheinen." This cryptic phrase is a conden‑ sation of "Jugendandacht" 3:1,2. In order that comparison may be facilitated, I quote the strophes again.

> Was wollen mir vertraun die blauen Weiten,
> Des Landes Glanz, die Wirrung süsser Leider,
> Mir ist so wohl, so bang! Seid ihr es wieder
> Der frommen Kindheit stille Blumenzeiten?
>
> Wohl weiss ich's — dieser Farben heimlich Spreiten
> Deckt einer Jungfrau strahlend reine Glieder;
> Es wogt der grosse Schleier auf und nieder,
> Sie schlummert drunten fort seit Ewigkeiten.
>
> (I, 275)

It must be obvious that the poem above seems to speak of the same songs and light that we saw in "Lieder" 3:2,3; but, and the distinction is of the utmost significance, this loveliness is not of the same order as "die Pracht" which "Lieder" 2 describes. In other words, we have two gardens before us; in one the songs and the splendor are of this earth, while in the other the magnificence moves toward the heavens. Now in this context and in reference to the earthly garden, our Eichendorff introduces the word "verführen." If we will glance at the poems of "Lieder" thus far introduced, it is abundantly clear that man is led astray because both gardens are described in terms of song and light; they seem so similar. "Das Marmorbild" comes to a close with Fortunato's observation that "das Andenken an die irdische Lust" releases powers "[die] die alte Verführung üben an jungen, sorglosen Gemütern" (344). Thus the human being is vulnerable because he is wounded; his very yearning for one‑ ness and glorification of the self — to be more than he is — urge him to reject his own contingency and seek fulfillment in the earthly garden. This is Eichendorff's "irdische Lust" which is best described by Romana's song: "Von der Welt kann ich nicht, lassen,/Liebeln nicht von fern mit Reden,/Muss mit Armen warm umfassen! —/Lass mich lieben, lass mich leben!" (138). Recalling Romana's violent death we can grasp the significance of "Lieder" 3:5 in which the speaker asserts that he would be utterly without joy ("freudelos") : "Hätt' ich nicht dich [the Virgin Mary] ersehn/Von allen Blumen schön." Through her man's hopes, joys, and desires are realized. That is why Venus tells Florio to accept the earthly flower and not investigate its roots, the love that gives it life, because "unten ist es freudlos und still." With each garden described above, Eichendorff associates the image of a woman, Venus or the Virgin. We now can see why our poet uses the verb "ersehn." He insists that man's actions reflect an act of the will, a process of differentiation and making a choice. This suggests that man must exercise the power of his mind; he must examine who, what, and why he is. That is why I have described the "Taugenichts" as one who thinks, whereas Florio is governed by "hohe und sanfte Empfindungen." And because our young hero thinks, he has insight into his nothingness and feels the pain of his isolation. This will now cause him to cry bitter tears of anguish.

As he sits in the boat, rowing and looking at "die schöne Frau," it suddenly occurs to "der andern lustigen Dicken von meinen zwei Damen . . . , ich sollte ihr während der Fahrt eins singen." She wants him to sing to her! He is undecided for a moment. "Indem blickte auch die schöne Frau auf einmal vom Wasser auf und sah mich an, dass es mir durch Leib und Seele ging. Da besann ich mich nicht lange, fasst' ein Herz und sang so recht aus voller Brust und Lust" (356). The dynamics of this scene must not escape us. The older one asks him to sing a song to her and the look of the younger one touches his very heart and soul. In effect, young "Taugenichts" is asked to decide between them. Eichendorff carefully stresses the fact that "die schöne Frau" rarely looks at the "Taugenichts" and when she does, it is of the utmost significance. Thus encouraged, he sings.

Der Gartner

"Wohin ich geh' und schaue,
In Feld und Wald und Tal,
Vom Berg' hinaub in die Aue:

Vielschöne, hohe Fraue,
Grüss' ich dich tausendmal.

In meinem Garten find' ich
Viel Blumen, schön und fein,
Viel Kränze wohl draus wind' ich,
Und tausend Gedanken bind' ich
Und Grüsse mit darein.

I h r darf ich keinen reichen,
Sie ist zu hoch und schön,
Die müssen alle verbleichen,
Die Liebe nur ohnegleichen
Bleibt ewig im Herzen stehn.

Ich schein' wohl froher Dinge
Und schaffe auf und ab,
Und ob das Herz zerspringe,
Ich grabe fort und singe
Und grab' mir bald mein Grab."

(II, 356-57)

This song "Der Gärtner" is called "das Lied von der schönen Frau" (353) which the "Taugenichts" started to sing the time that he saw her "wie ein Engelsbild" walking through the garden. Our young hero is a gardener's apprentice and the song about the beautiful lady is called "The Gardener." We have said that the Queen of Heaven teaches him her song; the "Taugenichts" is her apprentice. What must he learn? The garden stands for man's spiritual orientation and the flowers, by definition, are his joys and desires as expressed in poetry. None of these is acceptable to the Virgin. Let us remember the following: Eichendorff has God say, "Meine Lieder sind nicht deine Lieder, Meine Gedanken sind nicht deine Gedanken." He also admits that his own songs are not really what he means because "ewig unereichbar ist das Eine" (I, 94). And what is this one thing which he can never achieve perfectly? It is the song of the Queen, the song of perfect obedience: "Let it be done unto me according to Thy Word." That is why the "Taugenichts" is her apprentice. That is also why his flowers, his joys and desires, must die ("verbleichen"). Man can give nothing to the Father except that love which cannot be compared to any other love. This love must stay within the prison, a heart given to Christ, and must not go in search of another beloved. That is why Florio's song is called "Liebe in der Fremde." Young Florio's final song begins with the words "Hier bin ich Herr! Gegrüsst das Licht." The greeting, as such, is an important theme in Eichendorff's works and worthy of separate analysis. Its meaning is based upon the older and more southern form of German greeting, "Grüss Gott." The other is recognized in God's name; his very existence is a reminder of God. With this greeting two are together in His name and the other is holy. Whatever Eichendorff greets in this manner is raised to the function of mediator; then, and only then, may the created "speak to him" of God. The Queen of Heaven, according to ancient Catholic tradition, stands closest to the Father's throne and to the heart of her Son. To man she speaks of God, and to her Son she speaks of man. For Eichendorff, the dialogue between creature and Creator is best facilitated by the Second Eve. (See "Die Heilige Mutter" I, 313). And thus the "Taugenichts" admits that his very existence, his desires, joys, thoughts, is a greeting of her. In this way they are together in His name; in this way the Mediatrix is asked to intercede that the Lord not turn his countenance from him: "Grüss dich Gott!" But man must pay a price for this. To echo the "Magnificat" is to live the imitation of Christ.

When one looks at the first and last strophe of "Der Gärtner," it seems almost impossible that they should belong in the same song. The "Taugenichts" had been asked to sing a song about "einer vielschönen Frau." The very request embarasses him — "[er] wurde über und über rot" — but he complies. When the song is over the older one of the two ladies gives him a friendly glance and leaves. The younger beautiful lady seems to listen but does not look at him and leaves without saying a word. This scene confronts the questioning reader with certain difficulties which cannot be resolved by the usual concept of the "Taugenichts" as a happy-go-lucky lad with no concern for where he is going. It is a pathetic misinterpretation of a most serious and earnest poet to conclude that he would devote his creative talents to the depiction of a love-sick lad who bursts into tears because his lady fair leaves without a backward glance. Examine all of Eichendorff's works, prose and poetry, and nothing can be found which substantiates such a conclusion. The "Taugenichts" says, "Ich schein' wohl froher Dinge." Indeed, his carefreeness is largely a façade because at heart he is a serious and dedicated young man. The youth feels alone and deserted, the object of mockery, because the love which fills his heart can find no acceptable avenue of expression. The small "Gesellshaft" which descends upon him and asks him to sing represents the society in which he finds himself. He is an interesting oddity, but nothing more. Even "die schöne Frau" seems to disregard him and his love must remain concealed; indeed, it is expressly forbidden to give her his "flowers." But note the third strophe; the word "keinen" can refer only to "der Kranz" and the verb "verbleichen" must apply to the flowers. This leaves two essential components of the wreath, namely "Gedanken und Grüsse." May I stress again that Eichendorff speaks of "irdische und himmlische Blumen," and all joys and desires grounded in the flesh must die. In the poem "An die Dichter," which is addressed to the Virgin Mary, we find the following lines: "O du lieblich Frauenbild!/Willst du bei dem Sänger bleiben? —/Blumen bind't ein streng Geschick: /Wenn die tausend Stimmen singen,/Alle Schmerzen, alles Glück /Ewig lautlos zu verschweigen" (I, 212). This, I believe, says it most clearly. Flowers must be equated with "Schmerzen und Glück," and the poet, Eichendorff's ideal poet, is not called to sing of his human joy and happiness, nor even of the pain occasioned by his existence in the world of man. All these are flowers which must suffer "ein streng Geschick." And that is why those lovely symbols for the transient woven into a wreath by the "Taugenichts" must die. It is obvious that I have equated "verschweigen" in one poem with "verbleichen" in the song "Der Gärtner." Man's thoughts must be a greeting of God, and this alone remains. Let us look again at part of another poem dedicated to the Queen of Heaven, "An die Entfernte," which appeared in 1826 and is probably woven into those thoughts which gave form to the "Taugenichts" story.

> Getrennt ist längst schon unsres Lebens Reise,
> Es trieb mein Herz durch licht' und dunkle Stunden.
> Dem festern Blick erweitern sich die Kreise,
> In Duft ist jenes erste Reich verschwunden —
> Doch, wie die Pfade einsam sich verwildern,
> Was ich seitdem, von Lust und Leid bezwungen,
> Geliebt, geirrt, gesungen:
> Ich knie' vor dir in all den tausend Bildern.

(I, 236)

These paths, the Virgin's and his own, are separated. Eichendorff knows, and says it often enough, that he is incapable of that immaculate thrust into the "heart of God" which is the "Magnificat." The garden of grace, the unconditional surrender of heart to God which Eichendorff experienced as a child, has disappeared from sight. The movement of man's spirit is given in full by the words "Lust und Leid." The withdrawal within initiated by pain and the joyous outward movement which characterizes "Lust" are the twin coordinates upon which man plots his existence. The movement is erratic, but for our poet the line of existence has a reference point which is the guiding star of his love. In the depths and on the heights he has before him one image, that "himmlisch Bild" which we saw in "Lieder" and "Jugendandacht." This same image is presented to us in a song, "Intermezzo," which was written about 1810.

> Dein Bildnis wunderselig
> Hab' ich im Herzensgrund,
> Das sieht so frisch und fröhlich
> Mich an zu jeder Stund'.
>
> Mein Herz still in sich singet
> Ein altes, schönes Lied,
> Das in die Luft sich schwinget
> Und zu dir eilig zieht.

(I, 73)

On the same page (I, 73) we find the last strophe of the poem "Wehmut" which I have quoted before. "Doch wolle nie dir halten/Der Bilder Wunder fest,/Tot wird ihr freies walten,/Hältst du es weltlich fest." The word "festhalten" is repeated for emphasis. For the "Taugenichts," the act of giving his "flowers" to the queen is the equivalent of "weltlich festhalten." When Florio "gives life" to a marble statue, he has involved himself in "weltlich festhalten." As Venus, "die Wunderblume," comes to life Florio is confronted with his own desires and joys; his own love song has taken on flesh and blood and he is lost within himself. Listen to another song and project its implications upon the "Marmorbild" story.

> Blüten licht nun Blüten drängen,
> Dass er möcht' vor Glanz erblinden;
> In den dunklen Zaubergängen,

> Von den eigenen Gesängen
> Hold gelockt, kann er nicht finden
> Aus dem Labyrinth der Brust.
> Alles, alles will's verkünden
> In den Wogen süsser Lust.
>
> (I, 59)

The above thoughts explain why in "Jugendandacht" 1 the cycle of poems which show how the heart transfers its love from the Virgin to Venus must end with the line, "Kein Schmerz, als solcher Liebe Lieb' ertragen." Florio felt the pain of his own love song and our "Taugenichts" feels alone, despised, and so utterly poor. He dare not sing his own song because it is unacceptable; love must remain within the heart. Florio's love is a movement which terminates at that point where he looks at Venus "mit flammenden Augen." He lives the lines: "Von der Welt kann ich nicht lassen,/Liebeln nicht von fern mit Reden,/*Muss im Arm lebendig fassen!/—/*Lass mich lieben, lass mich leben!" (I, 369; italics mine). Florio, the good and pious youth, "[will] lebendig fassen" and the "Taugenichts" also graviates toward the realm of "weltlich festhalten" when he spies upon his "schöne Frau." If even our "Taugenichts" succumbs to the weakness of the flesh, how can Eichendorff expect man, as he puts it in "Memento," to walk "schlicht und gläubig . . . in sichrer Mitte"? The answer is not and has never been acceptable to man who insists upon knowing rather than loving. The last poem in "Jugendandacht" informs us: "O Herr! du kennst allein den treuen Willen,/Befrei ihn von der Kerkerluft des Bösen,/Lass nicht die eigne Brust mich feig zerschlagen!" (I, 279).

It seems that man can never really know; even though his intentions are good, he is easily seduced and led astray. God alone knows whether or not the creature truly intends to pursue the will of the Father or his own. Scattered throughout his works our poet consistently observes that man builds and God destroys in order to teach him. As Friedrich returns to the very point where he began his pursuit of love, we are told, "Sein ganzer damaliger Zustand wurde ihm dabei so deutlich, wie wenn man ein lang vergessenes, frühes Gedicht nach vielen Jahren wieder liest, wo alles vergangen ist, was einem zu dem Liede verführt. Wie anders war seitdem alles in ihm geworden!" (225). The word "verführen" brings us back to the last three lines of the poem "An die Entfernte" quoted above. The poet admits that "Lust und Leid" were a factor in all that he loved, in the songs he has sung and the errors he has committed; and yet the summation of his doing must be understood as a making of "Bilder." The last line of the poem states, "Ich knie vor dir [the Virgin] in all den tausend Bildern." Now let us look again at the first strophe of "Der Gärtner": "das Lied von der schönen Frau." "Wohin ich geh' und schaue,/In Feld und Wald und Tal,/Vom Berg hinaub in die Aue;/Vielschöne, hohe Fraue./Grüss ich dich tausendmal." A comparison with the version on page 353 reveals a variation in the center of the strophe. The third verse does not read "ins Himmelblaue" but "hinab in die Aue." The middle verse of "Jugendandacht" 1 spoke of the same "Himmelblaue" which was a central theme in our discussion. The error into which our young hero was fallen should now be clear. In his search for the "schöne Frau" he neglects to look into the vault of heaven but concentrates his pursuit upon what is *below,* in "Feld und Wald und Tal." This gardener's apprentice is not satisfied with the fragrance of the dawn as painted by "Der Maler," but now plants "ausländische Blumen" in his garden. He stands on the threshhold of "versinken." That is why his song of the beautiful lady ends with the lines: "Ich grabe fort und singe/Und grab' mir bild mein Grab." By changing just one phrase in the entire strophe, Eichendorff reveals the shift of direction in which the "Taugenichts" travels and instructs us that the poet-figure is lost in his own love and has voided the lines: "Den lieben Gott lass ich nur walten." What the youth has failed to do is best seen in the poem "Glückliche Fahrt." "Selig, wer es fromm mag wagen,/Durch das Treiben dumpf und wild/In der festen Brust zu tragen/Heil'ger Schönheit hohes Bild!" (I, 98). At the end of the novella we shall see that this courageous love is imputed to the good-for-nothing.

I digressed from the specific movement of events in the "Taugenichts" story to clarify and stress the importance of what transpires at the end of the first chapter. Our young hero has shown us that he is concerned only with the younger of his "zwei Damen"; he reveals that he is poor in spirit and utterly alone and helpless without her and that her refusal to recognize him reduces him to abject misery. He cries bitter tears of anguish. It is not easy "to earn bread."

The "Taugenichts" is made "Einnehmer." He does not seem to realize it but he has slipped badly from the high resolve of traveling in God's "weite Welt." He meditates and reflects "wie das *vornehmere* Leben doch eigentlich recht bequem sei, und fasste heimlich den Entschluss, nunmehr alles Reisen zu lassen, auch Geld zu sparen wie die andern und es mit der Zeit gewiss zu etwas *Grossem* in der Welt zu bringen." (359, italics mine). Our "Taugenichts" is becoming a philistine! Strangely enough, he was promoted because of "Seiner guten Aufführung und besonderen Meriten" (358). We know, of course, that he is rapidly losing the special merits with which he was graced. As part of his uniform he inherits from his deceased colleague "einen prächtigen roten Schlafrock mit gelben Punkten, grüne Pantoffeln, eine Schlafmütze und einige Pfeifen mit langen Röhren" (358). Again and again our poet warns man to be on guard and awake, "Seid wach und hütet Euch!" The "Taugenichts" begins to sleep the sleep of the busy little world that has no care for the cross and the Mother of Sorrows. When the young man informs us that he had seen his village priest walking about in the same uniform, we should understand this as a severe criticism of the clergy as he knew them. Too many were "asleep" to the desperate need in God's vineyard. Despite all this, the youth can still say: "Inzwischen vergass ich über meinen Entschlüssen, Sorgen und Geschäften die allerschönste Frau keineswegs" (359). Now there is the point of the whole story. Man's nature is wounded and he limps with the infirmity of his own lack of resolve and dedication. But: "O Herr! du kennst allein den treuen Willen!" Our foolish, impetuous youth never forgets "die allerschönste Frau," this most beautiful of all women, will not let him wander too far for his heart is filled with loving reverence.

In the first chapter our hero sings the song "Der Gärtner" and suggests that "im Garten war schön leben" — but he does not have a garden. In the second chapter, now that he is promoted to "Einnehmer," he has his own house and a garden. And this strange lad throws out all the vegetables, and plants "die auserlesensten Blumen" (359). Every evening he picks a bouquet, climbs over the wall which surrounds "den herrschaftlichen Garten," and places it on a stone table. He has no right to be there. This transgression is of the same order of significance as spying upon "die schöne Frau." We shall see that she disapproves. Upon one such escapade he is trapped by her. She approaches on horseback and he does not have time to escape.

> Es war mir nicht anders zumute, als da ich sonst in den alten Büchern bei meinem Vater von der schönen Magelone gelesen, wie sie so zwischen den immer näher schallenden Waldhornsklängen[7] und wechselnden Abendlichtern unter den hohen Bäumen hervorkam, — ich konnte nicht vom Fleck. Sie aber erschrak heftig, als sie mich auf einmal gewahr wurde, und hielt fast unwillkürlich still. Ich war wie betrunken vor Angst, Herzklopfen und grosser Freude, und da ich bemerkte, dass sie wirklich meinen Blumenstrauss von gestern an der Brust hatte, konnte ich mich nicht länger halten, sondern sagte ganz verwirrt: "Schönste gnädige Frau, nehmt auch noch diesen Blumenstrauss von mir und alle Blumen aus meinem Garten und alles, was ich habe. Ach, könnt ich nur für Euch ins Feuer springen!" — Sie hatte mich gleich anfangs so ernsthaft und fast böse angeblickt, dass es mir durch Mark und Bein ging, dann aber hielt sie, solange ich redete, die Augen tief niedergeschlagen. Soeben liessen sich einige Reiter und Stimmen im Gebüsch hören. Da ergriff sie schnell den Strauss aus meiner Hand und war bald, ohne ein Wort zu sagen, am andern Ende des Bogenganges verschwunden (360-61).

Everything he would give to this Lady, even his life. There is in this delightful outburst a charming simplicity, a delightful naiveté, which describes so perfectly the youthful veneration of one's beloved, who has been placed upon a pedestal and must be adored rather than touched. It is exquisitely perfect and absolutely consistent with the words of the poem, "sie ist zu hoch und schön." Our "Taugenichts" could never look at the beloved "mit flammenden Augen." Precisely because his love is chaste she wears his flowers. This youth wants nothing in return and is content to love in secret. The mere vision of the loved one results in "Angst, Herzklopfen und grosser Freude." It would be difficult for a poet to express with greater nicety that lovely fusion of love and reverence which is the uniqueness of our "Taugenichts"-Eichendorff figure. And yet his Lady seems displeased. Her glance is described as "böse und ernsthaft," and while he speaks she does not look at him. We should be reminded that this woman never looks at the "Taugenichts" unless it is to exhort or reprimand. It is not difficult to explain her anger. The "Taugenichts" had been sent into God's "weite Welt," and this good-for-nothing who would sing the "Magnificat" has just decided to become a philistine; he wants to save money and become a someone in this world. Now that is being a "Taugenichts" in a reversed sense; instead of being a fool among men, he is well on the way to becoming a fool before God.

Despite the fact that our young hero has incurred the anger of his lady, and the reason is not clear to him, he is filled with an indescribable joyousness. "Seit diesem Abend hatte ich weder Ruh' noch Rast mehr. Es war mir beständig zumute wie sonst immer, wenn der Frühling anfangen sollte, so unruhig und fröhlich, ohne dass ich wusste, warum, als stünde mir ein grosses Glück oder sonst etwas Ausserordentliches bevor" (351).[8] This reference to spring reminds us of Florio's reaction upon being informed that he might see Venus the next day. It seems that the marble statue had become alive "und von seinem Steine in den Frühling hinuntergestiegen, der stille Weiher plötzlich verwandelt zur unermesslichen Landschaft, die Sterne darin zu Blumen und der ganze Frühling ein Bild der Schönen —" (324). I have endeavored to show that Florio is the author of this spring while for our hero it is something that is given or happens to him. This feeling influences his attitude toward the position of "Einnehmer." As tollkeeper he must keep books and this preoccupation becomes most burdensome.

> Besonders das fatale Rechnen wollte mir nun erst gar nicht mehr von der Hand, und ich hatte, wenn der Sonnenschein durch den Kastanienbaum vor dem Fenster grüngolden auf die Ziffern fiel und so fix vom Transport bis zum Latus und wieder hinauf und hinab addierte, gar seltsame Gedanken dabei, so dass ich manchmal ganz verwirrt wurde und wahrhaftig nicht bis drei zählen konnte. Denn die Acht kam mir immer vor wie meine dicke enggeschnürte Dame mit dem breiten Kopfputz, die böse Sieben war gar wie ein ewig rückwärts zeigender Wegweiser oder Galgen. — Am meisten Spass machte mir noch die Neun, die sich mir so oft, eh' ich mich's versah, lustig als Sechs auf den Kopf stellte, während die Zwei wie ein Fragezeichen so pfiffig drein sah, als wollte sie mich fragen: Wo soll das am Ende noch hinaus mit dir, du arme Nüll? Ohne sie, diese schlanke Eins und alles, bleibst du doch ewig nichts! (361).

My interest in this game of numbers centers on the last three lines. I do not see how we can misconstrue Eichendorff's intention. Man is a veritable zero;[9] his hope resides in the one woman, "diese schlanke Eins und alles," who is the mediator between the creature and the Creator. We must understand our poet in terms of his faith, and for him the Virgin Mary is the co-redemptress. It is she who, in all humility, raises the veil so that the eyes of heaven will shine upon man, that is, so that the Lord will turn His countenance to man. Our "Taugenichts" has been touched by the lily and, consequently, is deeply aware of his own nothingness. This awareness already has caused him to cry bitter tears, but it is also the cornerstone of his joy, for "Sehnsucht muss wachsen an der Tiefe Rauschen /Nach hellerm Licht und nach des Himmels Kunden" (I, 279). This "Tiefe" is the fall from grace which the young man experiences. Our hero now becomes a "Taugenichts" in the worst sense of the word. He sits in front of his house, parasol in hand "und steckte es gegen die Sonne wie ein chinesisches Lusthaus über mich" (369). The reference to the "chinesisches Lusthaus" may remind us of the strange garden and buildings found by Leontin and Friedrich with the figure of a Buddha "als der einzige Bewohner seines unsinnigen Palastes" (248).[10] We may also think of the description of Florio's soul which the morning light cannot touch because it is still in "anderer Macht" (320). All this, considering the values our hero has embraced, means that he might as well be a heathen instead of a Christian. And for this very reason his "schöne Frau" no longer accepts his flowers. For a time he continues to pick bouquets, but each time they are left on the table "und sahen mich mit ihren verwelkten, niederhängenden Köpfchen und darauf stehenden Tautropfen ordentlich betrübt an, als ob sie weinten" (362). We remember the line in his poem "Der Gärtner": "Die (Blumen schön und fein) müssen alle verbleichen." "Verwelken" and "verbleichen," it is all the same; our hero with feet of clay has great difficulty living what he knows, namely, "Die Liebe nur ohnegleichen /Bleibt ewig im Herzen stehn." Because he feels rejected he no longer brings his bouquet to the stone table. "In meinem Garten mochte nun auch das Unkraut treiben wie es wollte, und die Blumen liess ich ruhig stehn und wachsen, bis der Wind die Blätter verwehte. War mir's doch ebenso *wild* und *bunt* und *verstört im Herzen*" (362, italics mine). It seems to me that Eichendorff makes it quite clear; the garden and the soul have gone to seed. The position of the "Taugenichts," his spiritual growth, has become desperate. So Eichendorff tells us, "In diesen kritischen Zeitläuften geschah es denn, dass einmal, als ich eben *zu Hause* im Fenster liege und verdrüsslich in die *leere Luft* hinaussehe, die Kammerjungfer vom Schlosse über die Strasse dahergetrippelt kommt" (ibid, italics mine). What now transpires is the first in a series of incidents designed to show both the faithfulness and foolishness of our hero.

The chambermaid says "die gnädige Frau" will attend a masked ball disguised as "Gärtnerin versteht Er auch recht — als Gärtnerin," and of course she will need fresh flowers. The question, I am sure, is addressed to the reader. Why should the older one of his two ladies go disguised as "Gärtnerin" when it is perfectly clear that the "Taugenichts" is the gardener's apprentice? We know that "die schöne Frau" has rejected his flowers and that the youth has come to a critical period. It would seem that our little would-be Philistine is being asked to enter the service of Venus. Just as Florio "gave" the rose (see poem "Frau Venus") to Venus, so our "Taugenichts" should now give his flowers to this disguised "Gärtnerin." But our hero is perceptive. "Das ist seltsam dachte ich bei mir selbst, man sieht doch jetzt fast keine Blume mehr vor Unkraut —" (ibid). It is odd that "die gnädige Frau" should want "flowers" from a garden that is really nothing more than a weed patch. Furthermore, she needs fresh flowers "zu ihrem Anzuge." We recall of Venus that her maidens are busy "ihre anmutige Gebieterin mit Rosen zu schmücken" (335). Also, Venus' garden, after Florio withdraws the rejuvenating power of his love, turns back into a veritable weed patch.

Venus herself is called "eine Wunderblume," and the youth in "Jugendandacht" 1 seems to gaze into "einer Blume himmelblauen Grund." All this is now brought together in a scene which describes our hero's reaction to the request for flowers. "Nun aber hatt' ich was zu sinnen und mich zu freuen. Sie dachte ja noch immer an mich und meine Blumen! Ich ging in mein Gärtchen und riss hastig alles Unkraut von den Beeten und warf es hoch über meinen Kopf weg in die schimmernde Luft, als zög' ich alle Übel und Melancholie mit der Wurzel heraus. Die Rosen waren nun wieder wie ihr Mund, die himmelblauen Winden wie ihre Augen, die schneeweisse Lilie mit ihrem schwer-

mütig gesenkten Köpfchen sah ganz aus wie sie" (363). It is suggested that the weeds in his garden, the soul, are "Übel und Melancholie." Fortunato, we should remember, calls Donati "einen Renommisten in der Melancholie" (316). These flowers have no business growing in man's garden. We see that "die schöne Frau" is referred to as the lily. And more! All the flowers combined are one flower. We recall that Venus says of herself, "mein Bild dämmert und blüht wohl in allen Jugendträumen mit herauf" (338). The one flower mentioned above is "ein Bild," but rooted in the flesh and blood of man's nature, his heart and soul, is another flower, Venus. Venus tells Florio to accept "die Blumen des Lebens" and not inquire about the roots "denn unten ist es freudlos uns still." The word "freudlos" describes so perfectly what has been happening to our "Taugenichts." That is why when he hears of the request for flowers, and thinking it came from his "schöne Frau," he is, once again, filled with joy. To him, as he says, it is evidence that she still thinks of him. The importance of this must be considered in conjunction with his conviction that without her he is as nothing. And so the hasty refurbishing of the garden-soul. Hear how he speaks as he finishes his labors and stands ready with a basket full of flowers. "Es war ein stiller, schöner Abend und kein Wölkchen am Himmel. Einzelne Sterne traten schön am Firmamente hervor, von weitem rauschte die Donau über die Felder herüber, in den hohen Bäumen im herrschaftlichen Garten neben mir sangen unzählige Vögel lustig durcheinander. Ach, ich war so glücklich!" (363). Yes, he is overjoyed, but now he must learn that he has made a mistake.

The "Taugenichts" takes his flowers and waits under a tree. He waits and waits and she does not come, so he decides to climb the tree "um wieder im Freien Luft zu schöpfen" (364). The tree, we should note, is Eichendorff's "Jakobsleiter" and a place of refuge, especially for the "Taugenichts." Our hero, unlike Florio, does not attend dances and masquerades; they should not be a part of his way of life. As he waits he feels ever more alone and is sure his lady has forgotten him and his flowers. "Und so geht es mir überall und immer. Jeder hat sein Plätzchen auf der Erde ausgesteckt, hat seinen warmen Ofen, seine Tasse Kaffee, seine Frau, sein Glas Wein zu Abend und ist so recht zufrieden; selbst dem Portier ist ganz wohl in seiner langen Haut. — Mir ist's nirgends recht. Es ist, als wäre ich überall eben zu spät gekommen, als hätte die ganze Welt gar nicht auf mich

gerechnet —" (364).[11] Again he suffers the temptation of wishing to be like other people who belong in this world. He finds it so difficult to accept his otherness, to live with the full burden of what he actually desires, that is, to be His prisoner through her. Florio was called, but he heard only the echo of his own love song; our "Taugenichts" was chosen, touched by the lily, and he resists like a foolish child.

And then, as he philosophizes to himself, she appears. But what a disappointment! When she takes off her "Larve" he sees that is is "die andere *ältere* gnädige Frau" (365, italics mine). After recovering from the initial fright, he feels fortunate "dass ich mich hier oben in *Sicherheit* befand" (italics mine). Now he worries and is even angry at what might ensue "wenn nun die liebe schöne Frau die Blumen abholt." The older lady converses with her maid, Rosette (rose symbolism), voices her annoyance, and finally leaves. The "Taugenichts" is left alone in his treetop hideaway and listens to the music. "Wie ich mich soeben zurechtsetzte, um der schönen Serenade zuzuhören, gingen auf einmal oben auf dem Balkon des Schlosses die Flügeltüren auf. Ein hoher Herr, schön und stattlich in Uniform und mit vielen funkelnden Sternen, trat auf den Balkon heraus, und an seiner Hand — die schöne junge gnädige Frau, in ganz weissem Kleide, *wie eine Lilie in der Nacht,* oder wie wenn der Mond über das klare Firmament zöge" (366, italics mine). Once again our poet uses his conventional signal, the dash, to introduce a thought of special significance. The "Taugenichts" tells us that *his* "schöne Frau" appears. She is the night, the lily and the moon, all of which are conventional symbols for the Virgin Mary. (If the word *night* as a reference to the Queen is unfamiliar, it is instructive to look at the poems "Einsiedler" [I, 299] and "Marienlied" [I, 317]). Note that the lady merely walks out upon the balcony, but our poet expands the imagery by suggesting that the moon travels across the heavens. The insinuation of a transcending significance is suggested by the passage which follows. "Ich konnte keinen Blick von dem Glanze verwenden, und Garten, Bäume und Felder gingen unter vor meinen Sinnen, wie sie so wundersam beleuchtet von den Fackeln hoch und schlank dastand und bald anmutig mit dem schönen Offizier sprach, bald wieder freundlich zu den Musikanten herunternickte. Die Leute unten waren ausser sich vor Freude, und ich hielt mich am Ende auch nicht mehr und schrie immer aus Leibeskräften Vivat mit —"

(366). Just looking at her seems to draw him up toward the heavens, which is just the opposite of what Florio experiences with Venus. And do the people not seem to greet a queen?

This moment of exquisite joy is followed by a sinking despair as the night wears on and his lady does not come for the flowers. He now realizes that it was really the older one of his "zwei Damen" who wanted the flowers. Our "Taugenichts" concludes that "die Schöne gar nicht an mich dachte und lange verheiratet ist, und dass ich selber ein grosser Narr war" (367). And now follows one of the more significant passage which differentiates so decisively between Florio and our hero. "Alles das versenkte mich recht in einen Abgrund von Nachsinnen. Ich wickelte mich, gleich einem Igel, in die Stacheln meiner eignen Gedanken zusammen: vom Schlosse schallte die Tanzmusik nur noch seltner herüber, die Wolken wanderten einsam über den dunkeln Garten weg. Und so sass ich auf dem Baume droben, wie die Nachteule, in den Ruinen meines Glücks die ganze Nacht hindurch." The "Taugenichts" thinks; he examines his conscience, and his thoughts are like pin pricks into mind and heart. He knows that he should not give flowers, his own thoughts and desires, to the Virgin. He has behaved like all flesh and blood by entertaining thoughts of being a someone, of finding his happiness through what can be touched and possessed. He was chosen to enter God's "weite Welt" and to earn his bread; but instead of complying he has tarried along the way and starved his own soul.

Wrapped in his own painful thoughts he falls asleep. As the dawn breaks and the morning rays strike his breast, he awakens and something has changed. "Da richtete ich mich in meinem Baume auf und sah seit langer Zeit zum ersten Male wieder einmal so recht weit in das Land hinaus, wie da schon einzelne Schiffe auf der Donau zwischen den Weinbergen herabfuhren, und die noch leeren Landstrassen wie Brücken über das schimmernde Land sich fern über die Berge und Täler hinausschwangen" (367). Suddenly the world has expanded and the highway soars up from the earth toward the source of light. In "Morgengebet" we read: "Die Welt mit ihrem Gram und Glücke/Will ich, ein Pilger, frohbereit/Betreten nur wie eine Brücke/Zu Dir, Herr, über'n Strom der Zeit" (I, 284). As our young hero contemplates this mystic landscape another association is made. "Ich weiss nicht, wie es kam — aber mich packte da auf einmal wieder meine ehemalige Reiselust: alle die alte Wehmut und

Freude und grosse Erwartung. Mir fiel dabei zugleich ein, wie
nun die schöne Frau droben auf dem Schlosse zwischen Blumen
und unter seidnen Decken schlummerte, und ein Engel bei ihr
auf dem Bette sässe in der Morgenstille. — Nein, rief ich aus,
fort muss ich von hier, und immer fort, so weit als der Himmel
blau ist!" Two things have happened simultaneously, and it is
difficult to distinguish between cause and effect. The return of
his "ehemalige Reiselust," the desire to walk in God's "weite
Welt," coincide with thoughts of "die schöne Frau." Once again
the veil is raised and the light penetrates "der müden Brust/Mit
seiner strengen Kühle." In just one moment now this light will
touch the heart-strings and the youth will burst into song.

As an outward sign of his emancipation he hurls his basket
of flowers into the air and takes keen delight in seeing them
flutter to the ground. He goes home, pausing frequently at various places where he had seen or thought of her. The little house
is just as he had left it. "Das Gärtchen war geplündert und wüst,
im Zimmer drin lag noch das grosse Rechnungsbuch aufgeschlagen,
meine Geige, die ich schon fast ganz vergessen hatte, hing verstaubt an der Wand. Ein *Morgenstrahl* aber aus dem gegenüberliegenden Fenster fuhr gerade blitzend über die Saiten. Das gab
einen rechten *Klang in meinem Herzen*. Ja, sagt' ich, komm nur
her, du getreues Instrument! Unser Reich ist nicht von dieser
Welt! —" (II, 368, italics mine). In this brief passage we have
the summation of his activities as gardener, tollkeeper, and what
he is really supposed to be, the new troubador, the singer whose
every note is in praise of the Lord. He had forgotten that he
was to earn bread by singing, and the violin is dusty from lack
of use. The imagery clearly tells us that the song is in his heart,
and this heart which he now must "play" sings of a love beyond
compare. Has our "Taugenichts" not told us often enough that he
does not belong in this world, that he is a misfit? From the very
beginning, when he first meets his "zwei Damen," the Queen is
annoyed with him because he has been trying to find his place here,
because he foolishly rebels at being "poor." This he has been
taught in the first two chapters, and now he is prepared to
leave "Rechnungsbuch, Schlafrock, Pantoffeln, Pfeifen und Parasol
liegen und wanderte, arm wie ich gekommen war, aus meinem
Häuschen und auf der glänzenden Landstrasse von dannen." All
this is "Plunder" and belongs to this world; the "Taugenichts"
must be absolutely poor so that the world can have no hold

on him. That is why Eichendorff again resorts to the bird symbolism. When the youth first came to this castle and found his bread, he felt like a bird "dem die Flügel begossen worden sind" (352). Now as he leaves he is somewhat sad "und doch auch wieder so überaus fröhlich, wie ein Vogel, der aus seinem Käfig ausreisst" (368). The highway points to heaven, into the light, and can be traveled only by those who have wings. And now, like the dawn-bird, he again sings his song.

> Den lieben Gott lass ich nur walten;
> Der Bächlein, Lerchen, Wald und Feld
> Und Erd' und Himmel tut erhalten,
> Hat auch mein Sach aufs best' bestellt!

Yes, it is the same song that we heard at the very beginning; but not quite! Our poet altered one word and thus changed the sign of the entire universe. The second chapter ends as our hero sings just the last strophe of "Der frohe Wandersmann." When we compare this strophe with its counterpart on page 350, we see that the poet has deliberately changed a verb. In the third verse the original formulation is "will erhalten" and the final version reads "tut erhalten." The poem was written in 1817 and later purposely altered. Reflecting upon what our hero has experienced between the singing of these two songs, we see that the significance of the change may be expressed as follows: That which God would want to do, he now does. Only man stands between the Divine Will and its implementation. The "Taugenichts" has finally understood the correct version of the "Magnificat," "Let it be done unto me according to Thy word" and has become one of literature's loveliest examples of those who are poor in spirit. But, it might be objected, the first and last verses remain unchanged and these two lines speak clearly of obedience and divine providence. Of what significance are the second and third verses in this spiritual equation? Let us look somewhat more carefully at "Der frohe Wandersmann."

God sends his chosen ones into "die weite Welt" in order that they might see "seine Wunder." Only the indolent sit at home and are not quickened by the morning-red. A literal interpretation of "zu Hause" is not meaningful in this context because the dawn's light could touch man anywhere. This staying at home, because it is associated with "Kinderwiegen," must mean that the movement of a man's love has terminated with woman and his life is filled with care and the search for bread. This is man's "kleine Welt." This theme that man, through his love for woman, may become a prisoner and disregard the command to love God above all else is given us in the poem "Sommerschwüle."

> Die Nachtigall schweigt, sie hat ihr Nest gefunden,
>   Träg ziehn die Quellen, die so kühle sprangen,
>   Von trüber Schwüle liegt die Welt umfangen,
>   So hat den Lenz der Sommer überwunden.
>
> Noch nie hat es die Brust so tief empfunden,
>   Es ist, als ob viel' Stimmen heimlich sangen:
>   "Auch d e i n Lenz, froher Sänger, ist vergangen,
>   An Weib und Kind ist nun der Sinn gebunden!"
>
> O komm, Geliebte, komm zu mir zurücke!
>   Kann ich nur deine Hellen Augen schauen,
>   Fröhlich Gestirn in dem verworrnen Treiben:
>
> Wölbt hoch sich wieder des Gesanges Brücke,
>   Und kühn darf ich der alten Lust vertrauen,
>   Wenn ew'ger Frühling will bei L i e b e bleiben.
>
>   (I, 99-100)

The above imagery and thoughts will not be meaningful unless we recall Fortunato's words to Florio, "Jeder lobt Gott auf seine Weise, . . . und alle Stimmen zusammen machen den Frühling" (307). The minstrel in our poem is fearful that the particular spring which is initiated by God's grace in the heart of man may have deserted him. The beloved whom the poem addresses is the Virgin through whose eyes heaven's grace shines upon man. The thought that this mysterious "Geliebte" might be the muse of poetry is denied by the imagery. Our poet wants his song to echo the "Magnificat" for only then will it be his bridge to heaven. Let us not forget the song, "Andre haben andre Schwingen,/Aber wir, mein fröhlich Herz,/Wollen grad' hinauf uns singen,/Aus dem Frühling himmelwärts!" (I, 267). His songs, because they praise the Lord, are his wings. The poem tells us that if she will but stay with him he would dare to keep on singing. This is "sich bewahren wollen," the poet who wants to use his talents in the service of his God. And yet it is a fearful venture because God has said, "Meine Lieder sind nicht deine Lieder." Our Eichendorff is afraid that his songs may speak only of his "Lust und Leid" and neglect the God on high. That is why, as the last line tells us, he prays that eternal spring may always be a part of love. In other words, it is only through grace, "ew'ger Frühling," that man can use the power of love so that his doing will conform to God's will. And for this, man needs the Queen Mother, "die schöne Frau."

The third strophe of the first song sung by our "Taugenichts" states that all of creation sings the praises of the Lord and, consequently, why should man do otherwise? This brings us to the last strophe with the variations "will erhalten" and "tut erhalten." In both instances the entire universe is the object of the verb "erhalten." If we now look at the first strophe of "Der Gärtner," which our "Taugenichts" actually sings twice, it would seem that it describes the same vast panorama, that "weite Welt" into which the "Taugenichts" is sent. Our young hero also tells us that his "gehen und schauen" is, in effect, a greeting of the "viel-schöne, gnädige Frau." But in the very next strophe he speaks of his garden, and no further reference is made to "Bächlein, Ler-chen, Wald und Feld,/Und Erd' und Himmel" which is God's "weite Welt." What has happened? We recall Florio's song "Liebe in der Fremde" (317), in which he speaks to the maiden on the other side of the river and feels sure she will recognize "den Sänger an den Gruss." Our "Taugenichts" gravitates toward the same isolation from God's world as we saw in "Das Marmorbild." In the first two chapters he does not live the words "Den lieben Gott lass ich nur walten." He assures Venus that he knows songs which are even more beautiful. He wants to possess things and *be* someone. He spies upon his Lady and thus shows that he wants her image in his heart to assume flesh and blood. He wants to see. That is why "die ältere Dame," Venus, sees in his behavior a greeting of her. She suspects that he may listen to cupid's emissary, portrayed by Rosette, who flits about "Und laden, was fein,/Als goldene Träume/Zur Königin ein."

Look again at the last strophe of his song "Der Gärtner" found on p. 357. It is a perfect description of his behavior during the first two chapters. I stated at the beginning of my discussion that the "Taugenichts," like the friends he left at home, will in-dulge in "graben." In his poem he admits it: "Ich grabe fort und singe/Und grab' mir bald mein Grab." All his doing, thus far, is equated with digging a grave. In many respects Eichendorff *is*

the "Taugenichts." Up until the year 1806, our poet, with seemingly pious intent, had indulged in a form of poetry, a use of imagery,
which he then recognized as being an effort to glorify the self
through "Poesie." All of the poems in the Cotta-Bauman edition
are dated no earlier than 1807. From that year on Eichendorff
becomes his own critic and a formidable opponent of the Romantic "Gefühl und Phantasie." It is not the purpose of this volume
to describe this in detail. But aside from the analysis of imagery,
I offer one surprising bit of evidence for this assertion. In the
"Paralipomena zur Zauberei im Herbste" which in many ways contains more of the "Marmorbild" structure than of the "Zauberei"
story, note the following directions. "Er [Alessandro] rüttelte
sich an allen Gliedern, gab seinem Rosse rasch die Sporen und
sang mit heller Stimme:/: Hier das Lied: Hier bin ich Herr!
etc. - :/" (IV, 1482). Now this is the first verse of the song
which Florio sings in precisely the same situation. The song
is called "Der Umkehrende." Our edition states that this song
was first printed in 1819. That is quite correct because it first
appeared in "Das Marmorbild." However, it obviously was written about 1807-08, the very period when Eichendorff began to
take issue with Romanticism. Also, in order that the full significance of this may be grasped, one must recall the full import
of the words "Der Umkehrende." The Marmorbild story concerns
a poet who goes in one direction and then returns, as we said,
to the prison. On the very first day that our "Taugenichts" begins
his journey, and after he had accepted the ride from Venus,
he feels a compelling urgency to return, "umkehren." But before
he does he must shed tears of anxiety, experience the pain of
aloneness, feel utterly disgusted with himself and examine his
conscience. When he realizes and accepts his poverty then he is
ready to travel again toward God's "weite Welt."[12] The "will
erhalten" has been changed to "tut erhalten" because he is
no longer an "Ein-nehmer" and he discarded his "flowers."

Our hero leaves Vienna and sets sail for Italy. The "Portier"
had once told him: "Italien ist ein schönes Land, da sorgt
der liebe Gott für alles, da kann man sich im Sonnenschein
auf den Rücken legen, so wachsen einem die Rosinen ins
Maul, und wenn einen die Tarantel beisst, so tanz man mit un-
gemeiner Gelenkigkeit, wenn man auch sonst nicht tanzen gelernt
hat" (369). So he wishes to embrace an existence where God takes
care of everything — that paraphrases his song. Two further

features characterize this land, dancing and — I was going to say wine[13] — a fruit from which the wine has been drawn, raisins.[14] And how does one get to this promised land? I should point out that at the beginning he did not know where he was going; now he has a goal, but he does not know the way. In such straits one just walks in faith, "ohne an die verschiedenen Wege zu denken, auf der Strasse fort, die mir eben vor die Füsse kam" (369). To be sure, one does not select the most pleasant path, which was Friedrich's initial error (II, 17). It is not long and he decides to rest under an apple tree. "Ich war recht fröhlich im Herzen, die Vögel sangen über mir im Baume, ich dachte an meine Mühle und an den Garten der schönen gnädigen Frau, und wie das alles nun so weit, weit lag — bis ich zuletzt einschlummerte" (370). Again Eichendorff injects a rather awkward reference to time. We know that he has just left the castle and garden, yet it seems that all this is far behind him. We cannot escape the conviction that the vision of "die schöne Frau" in the garden is something that happened long ago. He finally falls asleep and has a dream.

Da träumte mir, als käme diese schöne Frau aus der prächtigen Gegend unten zu mir gegangen oder eigentlich langsam geflogen zwischen den Glockenklängen, mit langen weissen Schleiern, die im Morgenrote wehten. Dann war es wieder, als wären wir gar nicht in der Fremde, sondern bei meinem Dorfe an der Mühle in den tiefen Schatten. Aber da war alles still und leer, wie wenn die Leute Sonntags in der Kirche sind und nur der Orgelklang durch die Bäume herüberkommt, dass es mir recht im Herzen weh tat. Die schöne Frau aber war sehr gut und freundlich, sie hielt mich an der Hand und ging mit mir und sang in einem fort in dieser Einsamkeit das schöne Lied, das sie damals immer frühmorgens am offenen Fenster zur Gitarre gesungen hat, und ich sah dabei ihr Bild in dem stillen Weiher, noch viel tausendmal schöner, aber mit sonderbaren grossen Augen, die mich so starr ansahen, dass ich mich beinah gefürchtet hätte. — Da fing auf einmal die Mühle, erst in einzelnen langsamen Schlagen, dann immer schneller und heftiger an zu gehen und zu brausen, der Weiher wurde dunkel und kräuselte sich, die schöne Frau wurde ganz bleich, und ihre Schleier wurden immer länger und länger und flatterten entsetzlich in langen Spitzen, wie Nebelstreifen, hoch am Himmel empor;

> das Sausen nahm immer mehr zu, oft war es, als bliese
> der Portier auf seinem Fagott dazwischen, bis ich endlich
> mit heftigem Herzklopfen aufwachte.

This dream is an excellent example of Eichendorff's usual technique; the dream presents the confusion in the hero's soul and, at the end, the external world is woven into the symbolic fabric. In fact, this is the basic structure of the "Taugenichts" novella which presents, in flesh and blood, man's relationship with love's ideal and then concludes with the reality in which man must live. Our hero falls asleep thinking of the "schöne Frau" who now appears in his dream. It seems, at first, that she appeared from below, a clear reference to "Jugendandacht" and the Virgin, who "schlummert drunten fort seit Ewigkeiten." Then he corrects himself and sees her emerging from the ringing of the churchbells, the call to worship God! The scene shifts, suggesting a regression in time, to his native village. Here the woman takes him by the hand and walks with him, singing her song. But suddenly, in the same sentence, the poet returns us to the castle scenes and the pond. He sees her image in the water, but this face is far more beautiful and looks at him "starr" with "sonderbaren grossen Augen." This contradicts the description of her appearance given before (350) and evokes the usual imagery associated with Venus. As our "Taugenichts" begins to embrace the values of this world the image becomes ever more frightening. It should be clear to the reader that our poet has introduced the adumbration of Florio's "Marmorbild" experience. The "Portier," who assumes the role of Fortunato in the first two chapters, plays his instrument and awakens the youth who is caught in the purposeless movement of the wheel.

As it happens, the noises he had heard in his dream come from a farmer who chases him off his land. So he commends himself to God, plays his violin and moves on. Toward evening he approaches a village where one and all are just sitting about doing nothing. Our "Taugenichts" plays and all dance. He refuses money but accepts a glass of wine from a pretty maiden. And once again the lad is open to temptation. The little coquette lures him on and gives him a rose, which he accepts. She asserts that he plays very beautifully. Venus, at the beginning of the story, had made the same observation. But this time our hero replies: "das ist so eine Gabe Gottes" (374). He has learned much but is still a weak little man. The maiden goes on to say that her father is rich and likes music. At this juncture and before matters could proceed, a humorous and seemingly arbitrary altercation in the village creates such an uproar that the maiden flees. But the thought is already in his heart. "Mir aber ging mancherlei im Kopfe herum. Die Jungfer, die mir vorhin die Rose geschenkt hatte, war jung, schön und reich — ich konnte da mein Glück machen, eh' man die Hand umkehrte. Und Hammel und Schweine, Puter und fette Gänse mit Äpfeln gestopft — ja, es war mir nicht anders, als säh' ich den Portier auf mich zukommen: 'Greif zu, Einnehmer, greif zu! Jung gefreit hat niemand gereut, wer's Glück hat, führt die Braut heim, bleibe im Lande und nähre dich tüchtig.' In solchen philosophischen Gedanken setzte ich mich auf dem Platze, der nun ganz einsam war, auf einen Stein nieder, denn an das Wirtshaus anzuklopfen traute ich mich nicht, weil ich kein Geld bei mir hatte" (375). Obviously, the Venus temptation still has its power. But a "Taugenichts" blessed with God's gifts is not ordained for such happiness. As he reflects in this fashion he suddenly thinks of "die schöne Frau" at home in her castle and how unimportant and alone he is. He is brought close to tears. Whenever this lad thinks of what the world can offer him he feels alone and thinks of her. The movement of events is such that, whenever he is tempted and about to stray, he is distracted and guided. It seems that "die schöne Frau" will not let him go.

Thus preoccupied, he hears horses approaching and immediately thinks of robbers. He recalls stories he had heard in early childhood and how he had always wanted to experience "eine solche Geschichte" (376). And then he observes to himself "Da hatt's ich's nun auf einmal für meine dummen, frevelmütigen Gedanken! —" (376). This thought seems to fit the context and yet it is out of phase. The words "dumm, frevelmütigen, Gedanken" are charged and do not fit the situation. The term "frevelmütig" can apply only to such thoughts as "die Braut heimführen, im Lande bleiben, sich tüchtig nähren" (375). This would be a fatal spiritual error properly described by the verb "freveln." And now our "Taugenichts" seeks to extricate himself by climbing a tree, "die Jakobsleiter." As it happens, he remains partially visible because his legs hang down from the limb. A voice calls out, "Wer ist da?" To this, our impossible young man responds with his famous "Niemand." It seems so droll and absurd and yet it is a carefully selected answer. We recall the little game with numbers which he plays as "Einnehmer." He calls himself "eine arme Null," and "Ohne Sie, diese schlanke Eins und alles [the Virgin Mary], bleibst du doch ewig nichts" (361). This is now the sum and substance of his wisdom. Unless the Queen raises the veil so that God's light may shine into man's heart, the human creature is a *no one*. Man may be a king upon earth but he must first become a beggar, a "Niemand," if he wants to wander in God's "weite Welt." Our poet offers the reader the ancient and unacceptable paradox of Christianity: if you would be first, then seek to be the last. The "Taugenichts" is pressed into service as a guide by these "robbers" even though he has not the faintest idea of the road to take. And this, too, is a lovely touch; a good-for-nothing with the worldly wisdom of a child leads others.

It is not necessary to discuss the details of his experiences, although each event contributes to our understanding of this individual. He actually finds the village for which the "robbers" are searching; is deserted by them for reasons he does not understand; is provided with a full purse as well as a horse and carriage which stops only long enough for meals. The beggar lives like a king but rides in a closed carriage. He has no chance to stray because he is a veritable prisoner. And so he should be; the prisoner of a love that would not let him lose his way. He is brought to a castle where everyone thinks he is a girl. A young would-be-monk even falls in love with him. (Remember that Florio is called "ein träumendes Mädchen!") The young man is not what people think he is! For a time he enjoys living like a prince and then he becomes quite "melancholisch." "Die Glieder gingen mir von dem ewigen Nichtstun ordentlich aus allen Gelenken, und es war mir, als würde ich vor Faulheit noch ganz auseinanderfallen" (393). Once again, he is plagued with doing nothing as during his "Einnehmer" existence. And then, one day, while seated "im Wipfel eines hohen Baumes, der am Abhang stand" (393), he hears the sound "eines Posthorns" and this sound reminds him of a song he used to sing at home.

> Wer in die Fremde will wandern,
> Der muss mit der Liebsten gehn,
> Es jubeln und lassen die andern
> Den Fremden alleine stehn.

Was wisset ihr, dunkele Wipfel,
Von der alten, schönen Zeit?
Ach, die Heimat hinter den Gipfeln,
Wie liegt sie von hier so weit!

Am liebsten betracht' ich die Sterne,
Die schienen, wenn ich ging zu ihr,
Die Nachtigall hör; ich so gerne,
Sie sang vor der Liebsten Tür.

Der Morgen, das ist meine Freude!
Da steig' ich in stiller Stund'
Auf den höchsten Berg in die Weite,
Grüss dich, Deutschland, aus Herzensgrund!

(II, 393)

The poem was written about 1817, at a time when Eichendorff lived in the north and may well have been filled with longing for the warmer and more compatible south. It does not seem unreasonable to equate "die Fremde" with the rather incompatible north. And yet, he has been married just two years and now has a child. Who is this "ihr"? Who is the beloved before whose door the nightingale sings? To whom does this young married man sing love songs? Now put this song into the context of our story. Our "Taugenichts" has gone into "die Fremde." He knows that he is a stranger wherever he goes and has felt the pain of aloneness. He has been tempted, but has never really allowed his love to wander "in die Fremde." He will have none other than "die schöne Frau." And now, because he has been faithful, he will be rewarded. It all begins with the sound of the "Posthorn," the call to be up and away; indeed, "Es war, als wenn mich das Posthorn bei meinem Liede aus der Ferne begleiten wollte" (393). And there is good reason why this song and the "Posthorn" belong together. Our "Taugenichts" is about to receive a letter "von — meiner schönen Frau, . . . 'Es ist alles wieder gut, alle Hindernisse sind beseitigt. Ich benutzte heimlich diese Gelegenheit, um die erste zu sein, die Ihnen diese freudige Botschaft schreibt. Kommen, eilen Sie zurück. Es ist so öde hier, und ich kann kaum mehr leben, seit Sie von uns fort sind. Aurelie' Die Augen gingen mir über, als ich das las, vor Entzücken und Schreck und unsäglicher Freude" (394). Look at what Aurelie says and compare it with the thoughts in the projected novel, "Marien

Sehnsucht," especially the lines: "In Mondnacht ist's, als weinte sie sehr und wollte dir gern ein tröstendes Liebeswort vertrauen. — Ja, glaube nur, sie weint auch um dich, sehnt sich auch recht sehr nach dir, deine Lieder bringen ihr auch süssen Schmerz." The Queen of Heaven expresses her careful and loving yearning for man. And that is the mystery and truth our poet would have man contemplate: Heaven cares! Thus the "Taugenichts" cries, "nun ist's je klar, sie liebt mich ja, sie liebt mich!" (394). But that is not all. Note the sequence of events. He feels as though he would dissolve in his own laziness, and then he hears the sound of the "Posthorn," the call to travel. He now sings his song called "Heimweh." In other words, so desperate is man's plight that he must be reminded of his homesickness. He forgets! He cannot remember that he is loved, is called, and the reason is always the same. He fears that the "Hound of Heaven" will reduce him, make him less than he is, demand a price which his own sense of excellence will not allow him to pay. Man becomes immersed in the "pond-of-self" (Florio) or in the stream of time, and puts Him out of his mind ("Bäume aushauen"). He hides the sword. So pitiful is the creature that heaven must remind him he is wounded. In the presence of Fortunato, Florio feels "heimatlich zumute" and the "Posthorn" reintroduces "Heimweh" into the heart of our "Taugenichts." We shall see in a moment just what images fill his mind as his heart experiences homesickness. In a letter not intended for him, his lady, "die Eine," tells him "es ist alles wieder gut." The last words in the story are "es war alles, alles gut!" Florio's final words are "Ich bin wie neugeboren, es ist mir, als würde noch alles gut werden, seit ich Euch wieder gefunden" (346). When the poet, in three different contexts, uses essentially the same phrase it behooves us to see this as a pattern. The final description of Bianca tells us she "sah recht wie ein heiteres Engelsbild auf dem tiefblauen Grunde des Morgenhimmels aus" (Ibid). These words should be familiar because they depict "die schöne Frau" (356). Florio's final experiences are condensed for us in two strophes of "Götterdämmerung" Part II.

Sie selbst muss sinnend stehen
So bleich im Frühlingsschein,
Die Augen untergehen,
Der schöne Leib wird Stein.

> Denn über Land und Wogen
> Erscheint, so still und mild,
> Hoch auf dem Regenbogen
> Ein andres Frauenbild.
>
> (II, 343)

The first strophe above refers to Venus, the second to the Virgin. The latter is the one Eichendorff wants us to think of when he has Florio say to Bianca, "seid ich Euch wiedergefunden." I point to this, and would have the reader consider it carefully, because Florio's words seem to suggest that we have involved our-selves in a contradiction. The evidence could indicate that Bianca is the Virgin. In fact, past Eichendorff criticism would see this novella as a Venus-Maria problem. There is a correctness in this position. However, from the very beginning Florio has left the "prison" and we cannot speak of a conflict between the spiritual forces represented by Venus and the Virgin, but rather that Ven-us seemed to be the Virgin, that eros seemed to be agape,[15] that what came from below seemed to come from above. Now that Florio has learned this, his poetry must be divested of what it should not express. And thus Bianca, "Um ungehinderter rei-sen zu können und zugleich alles Vergangene gleichsam von sich abzustreifen" (345), now wears "Knabentracht." She is what Frie-drich speaks of, "Die Poesie . . . seine damalige, süsse Reisege-fährtin" (226). Bianca, an immaculate poetry which reflects his "Andacht," is a companion who rides with him toward the inef-fable light of the perfect day. That is what our poet would want us to "see" when he speaks of "das blühende Mai-land" (346), the land of eternal spring, even in the summer. And now our "Taugenichts" approaches that "experience" for which the end of "Das Marmorbild" is but a beginning. His behavior in the first two chapters are termed "Hindernisse" in the letter. They are set aside because the young man has demonstrated his purity of heart. And so his lady Aurelie tells him to re-turn.[16] Why is she called the sun? Let us look at another poem, "Der Winzer."

> Es hat die Nacht geregnet,
> Es zog noch grau ins Tal,
> Und ruhten still gesegnet
> Die Felder überall;

Von Lüften kaum gefächelt,
Durchs ungewisse Blau
Die Sonne verschlafen lächelt'
Wie eine wunderschöne Frau.

Nun sah ich auch sich heben
Aus Nebeln unser Haus,
Du dehntest zwischen den Reben
Dich von der Schwelle hinaus,
Da funkelt' auf einmal vor Wonne
Der Strom und Wald und Au —
Du bist mein Morgen, meine Sonne,
Meine Liebe, verschlafene Frau!

(I, 204)

Criticism, strangely enough, has shown little concern for the names our poet gives his characters nor the titles of his poems. A "Winzer," a gardner who "grows" wine, labors in the vineyard. "Das Lied von der schönen Frau" which our "Taugenichts" sings is called "Der Gärtner," and he works in the garden as an apprentice. Look at the poem "Der Maler" and compare it with the last strophe above, especially nature's reaction as the angel or the sun, "Verschlafene Frau," appears. Also compare "Der Winzer" with "Heimweh," particularly in the last strophe. This "wunderschöne Frau" is his morning, is his joy. And the "Taugenichts" stood in the garden and spied upon his "verschlafene Frau." Above all he receives a letter from Aurelie, and the Queen of Heaven is described as clothed in the sun; she is his "Morgen, Sonne, liebe verschlafene Frau." All this is part of a decipherable pattern which with our poet delicately and discreetly paints the image of the Virgin Queen. The imagery also suggests that the "Taugenichts" is a "Winzer" who labors in the vineyard, and it is written that the Master invited all to work in his vineyard. (Remember that our good-for-nothing is to earn bread by singing.)

And now that he has heard from his lady — we should point out that throughout the entire novella she never *speaks* to him except with her eyes — he is once again prepared to travel. Does he return to the castle as the letter seems to suggest? Of course not! His "schöne, gnädige Frau" lives in Rome, the Rome of his childhood: "Wenn ich dann an Sonntagsnachmittagen vor der Mühle im Grase lag und alles ringsum so stille war, da dachte ich mir Rom wie die ziehenden Wolken über mir, mit wundersamen Bergen und Abgründen am blauen Meer und goldnen Toren und hohen glänzenden Türmen, von denen Engel in goldnen Gewändern sangen. —" (398-99). In this Rome he will find his lady, in the heavenly city, and nowhere else. But we would call attention to the interesting relationship suggested by the words "Wolken" and "denken." If we now turn to "Das Marmorbild" we will find a different definition of the word "Wolken." The scene occurs in the middle of the novella just after Florio had seen both Bianca and Venus at the dance. Bianca tells him, "Es ist gar seltsam, so plötzlich aus der lauten Lust in die weite Nacht hinauszutreten. Seht nur, die Wolken gehn oft so schreckhaft wechselnd über den Himmel, dass man wahnsinnig werden müsste, wenn man lange hineinsähe; bald wie ungeheure Mondgebirge mit schwindligen Abgründen und schrecklichen Zacken, ordentlich wei Gesichter, bald wieder wie Drachen, oft plötzlich lange Hälse ausstreckend, und drunter schiesst der Fluss heimlich wie eine goldne Schlange durch das Dunkel, das weisse *Haus* da drüben sieht aus wie ein stilles *Marmorbild*" (333, italics mine). It is truly amazing to observe how mysterious and provocatively suggestive this man can be. A stream that is like a golden snake, the green-golden snake that slithers down the ruins of the castle, the green-golden jewelry worn by Donati and Venus, the fact that Florio feels like a wave in a stream — all these factors are identifying features. In the next poem even the title is significant, we are told:

Die Nachtblume

Nacht ist wie ein stilles Meer,
Lust und Leid und Liebesklagen
Kommen so verworren her
In dem linden Wellenschlagen.

Wünsche wie die Wolken sind,
Schiffen durch die stillen Räume,
Wer erkennt im lauen Wind,
Ob's Gedanken oder Träume? —

Schliess' ich nun auch Herz und Mund,
Die so gern den Sternen klagen:
Leise doch im Herzensgrund
Bleibt das linde Wellenschlagen.

(I, 211)

Once again — because it is fundamental to my thesis — attention is called to the ambiguity inherent in the poet's imagery. The Queen of Heaven is called "die heil'ge Nacht," but the night of our poem is remarkably different, "ein stilles Meer." It is the ocean of human time and existence and our involvement is given by the words "Lust und Leid und Liebesklagen." With all this, as "Jugendandacht" informed us, the poet must remain "stumm verbunden." That is why lips and heart must remain closed. From these "waters" the night flower would emerge just as Venus, "die Wunderblume," rises from the sea. The flower must not grow; desire must not assume form though it whispers sweetly in the depths of one's heart. If we look at the second strophe we see that Eichendorff has given us a formula, "Wünsche = Wolken = Träume." Bianca points to this and suggests that this is the substance of Florio's reality. Where did Florio's reality come from? We were told that the quiet pond had been transformed "zur unermesslichen Landschaft." In the novella it is "der stille Weiher" and in the poem "Die Nachtblume" it is "ein stilles Meer," but both are "Lust und Leid und Liebesklagen." These are the "waters" from which Venus emerges. It is written that the Spirit of the Lord hovered above the deep and then creation followed. Man made in the image of his God seeks to do the same. For man, this deep is a personal existence structured by a love which seeks but its own will. Richard Alewyn in his brilliant analysis states, "Es gibt kein seelisches und kein sittliches, kein soziales und kein religiöses Verhältnis, das sich ihm nicht unwillkürlich in Raumwerte umsetzte, das Bewusstsein der Zeit nicht ausgeschlossen" (43).[17] In other words, and to use my own terminology, everything experienced by our poet can be reduced to a common denominator: "Raum." Why should this be so? Remember that our poet sees two antagonistic forces in man's spiritual universe, centripetal and centrifugal forces. One is defined by him as "Liebe" and the other we have interpreted as love. The human potential to love, when it seeks its own will, is centrifugal force; when it seeks the will of God it becomes one with centripetal force. We insist upon this because Eichendorff's thoughts clearly embrace the belief that man cannot turn to the Father unless the Father draws him. Perhaps the above will be of greater significance when we read Alewyn's assertion that "Eichendorff's Landschaft ist reiner Raum, *aus nichts gemacht als Bewegung*, der konsequenteste Versuch, reinen Raum in der Dichtung darzustellen" (italics mine) .[18] This is absolutely correct because our poet would structure the movement of love, God's and man's. Just as human love may seek to merge with the will of God, so may it also gravitate toward denial and become one with the Luciferian rejection. This, I submit, is the key of which Alewyn speaks.[19] The entire spectrum of the poet's emblematic language is carefully designed to conform to this basic principle. He is a spiritual geometer who defines the dimension of man's love. We choose this term *dimension* deliberately because it brings us to an aspect of "Raum" which Alewyn also discusses, however briefly. "Man wird finden, dass, man darf wohl sagen *ausnahmlos* alle unerquicklichen oder bedrohlichen Begebenheiten und Verhältnisse geschlossene Räume zum Schauplatz haben. Wenn sie sich nicht geradezu in Zimmern oder sonst innerhalb von Gebäuden abspielen, dann gewiss in Tälern oder Schluchten, in Gebüschen oder in der Tiefe des Waldes. Es ist leicht zu sehen, dass diese Naturschauplätze mit dem Innenraum eine Eigenschaft gemeinsam haben, nämlich *die Enge*" (italics mine) .[20]

I have used, without distorting them, Alewyn's thoughts concerning "Landschaft" and have arrived at that position which is a fundamental theorem in this work. What Alewyn calls "die Enge" and die "Weite" (the term is admittedly borrowed from Eichendorff) , I call positive and negative reality. The basic purpose, and that is exactly the word which must be used, of our poet's creativity is to structure human existence in God's realm or in its own. That is precisely what Florio and the "Taugenichts" experience. That is why a pond, the *deep* of "Lust, Leid und Liebesklagen," can become a seemingly infinite landscape. Alewyn adds one further phrase which we must use in this context; he speaks of "erlebter Raum." In this sense, Eichendorff's use of "Raum" tells us whether the individual involved in a particular context experiences God or self; I should like to say, *lives* God or self. This is the cornerstone of Christianity, the stone which was rejected, and Eichendorff builds upon it. That is why there is no "Verhältnis, seelisch, sittlich, sozial und religiös," to use Alewyn's words, which is not given in terms of space. Always and everywhere our poet is concerned with this microcosm and macrocosm, human love which rises to agape or sinks to denial. Again, I use these words with deliberate intent, because the direction of movement is significant in Eichendorff's thinking. It enables him to insinuate the principle of deception. It is possible, as in the case of Florio, to feel that "die Enge" is "die Weite," and to believe that his sinking into the "waters" is a rising — "Nimm, Vater, mich auf!" To such an extent can man be deceived by "Wünsche wie die Wolken sind." It is as though man were a sun and from the "waters" could draw into being the paradise (garden) which is the hunger of his soul. But the city is secular and the castle a heathen residence raised for man's pleasure and glory. The "Taugenichts" sees another city, a city which he created in his thoughts and in which there lives a maiden-woman-mother, "die schöne Frau." He steps out of the forest and there it is. The following quotation makes it obvious that it is not really visible. All is seen with mind and heart directed at an inner vision that is never concretized; for if it were, then Florio and the "Taugenichts" would be one. And precisely because this city, which is like a wisp of fog, is called a sleeping lion which is invisible, we can say with authority that the lion is a reference to Christ and not the lion who is awake and prowls about the land seeking its prey. In this "Bild" Eichendorff shows us God's Kingdom and then says it is not *here* but *there*. "Das Meer leuchtete von weitem, der Himmel blitzte und funkelte unübersehbar mit unzähligen Sternen, darunter lag die heilige Stadt, von der man nur einen langen Nebelstreif erkennen konnte, wie ein eingeschlafener Löwe auf der stillen Erde, und Berge standen daneben wie dunkle Riesen, die ihn bewachten" (399). This picture needs only the angels with the flaming swords and it could be called God's kingdom. But before the "Taugenichts" may enter the holy city he must pass, symbolically as it were, through the world of Venus.

> Ich kam nun zuerst auf eine grosse einsame Heide, auf der es so grau und still war wie im Grabe. Nur hin und her stand ein altes verfallenes Gemäuer oder ein trockener wunderbar gewundener Strauch; manchmal schwirrten Nachtvögel durch die Luft, und mein eigener Schatten strich immerfort lang und dunkel in der Einsamkeit neben mir her. Sie sagen, dass hier eine uralte Stadt und die Frau Venus begraben liegt, und die alten Heiden zuweilen noch aus ihren Gräbern heraufsteigen und bei stiller Nacht über die Heide gehn und die Wanderer verwirren. Aber ich ging immer gerade fort und liess mich nichts anfechten. Denn die Stadt stieg immer deutlicher und prächtiger vor mir herauf,

und die hohen Burgen und Tore und goldnen Kuppeln glänzten so herrlich im hellen Mondschein, als ständen wirklich die Engel in goldnen Gewändern auf den Zinnen und sängen durch die stille Nacht herüber (ibid).

The word "Denn" explains why nothing disturbs him. This young man walks toward his vision of the eternal city where his beloved dwells. And because his mind and heart have concern only for her, the intrusion of the heathen world is presented in terms of the humorous and ridiculous. Everything which Florio treats with soul-destroying seriousness is given a ludicrous turn in our story. Venus "courts" him, but he simply does not understand. She gives him roses, sings to him, arranges a tryst through Rosette the chambermaid, and appears to him in a house that has been vacant for years; in short, the complete spectrum of the "Marmorbild" structure is invoked to deceive him, but the "Taugenichts" is a fool. The chambermaid is thoroughly disgusted with him and concludes "du trittst dein Glück ordentlich mit Füssen." — "Aber," erwiderte ich, "ich meinte die Gräfin aus Deutschland, die schöne gnädige Frau." — "Ach," unterbrach sie mich, "die ist ja lange schon wieder in Deutschland, mitsamt deiner tollen Amour. Und da lauf du nur auch wieder hin! Sie schmachtet ohnedies nach dir, da könnt ihr zusammen die Geige spielen und in den Mond gucken, aber dass du mir nicht wieder unter die Augen kommst!" (415). And here is the root of the confusion: He always had his "schöne gnädige Frau" in mind. This obsession is gently and delightfully mocked when he mistakenly thinks that he had recognized her "an den kleinen, geschwinden Füsschen" (400). But this is really quite logical; he had said, "Wohin ich geh' und schaue,/—/Vielschöne, hohe Frau,/Grüss' ich dich tausendmal." And is this not the essense of the words, "deiner tollen Amour?" It is indeed a mad love, from the world's viewpoint, a love that has learned to reject the values of this world, because its kingdom is not of this world. Our "Taugenichts" had said this to his "Geige," and we see that the chambermaid suggests that he and his beloved can play the instrument together. Our poet dearly loves to conceal his precious truth in such seemingly irrelevant remarks. After all, it is his conviction that man was created to play the heart-instrument in praise of the Lord.

In the "Taugenichts" he has given us an ideal Christian, the "magister ludi," "ein Bild," which we should become in flesh and blood. It so happens that our hero spends just one day in Rome, and his only accomplishment is to have his picture painted. A painter friend of his has decided to include him in a scene which is highly suggestive and instructive for our understanding of the "Taugenichts" and his secret love. The painter shows him his canvas and,

> Auf dem Papier war bloss mit grossen schwarzen Strichen eine alte Hütte gar künstlich abgezeichnet. Darin sass die Heilige Jungfrau mit einem überaus schönen, freudigen und doch recht wehmütigen Gesichte. Zu ihren Füssen auf einem Nestlein von Stroh lag das Jesuskind, sehr freundlich, aber mit grossen, ernsthaften Augen. Draussen auf der Schwelle der offnen Hütte aber knieten zwei Hirtenknaben mit Stab und Tasche. — "Siehst du," sagte der Maler, "dem einen Hirtenknaben da will ich deinen Kopf aufsetzen, so kommt dein Gesicht doch auch etwas unter die Leute, und will's Gott, sollen sie sich daran noch erfreuen, wenn wir beide schon lange begraben sind und selbst so still und fröhlich vor der Heiligen Mutter und ihrem Sohne knien wie die glücklichen Jungen hier —" (403) .

Our "Taugenichts" is to be immortalized as a simple shepherd kneeling before the Virgin and Child. The picture of man kneeling before a woman is used rather frequently by Eichendorff. Of special interest in our passage is the thought that, if God wills, future generations may find joy in the contemplation of this scene. Here, once again, we find Eichendorff's personal justification for his existence as an artist. This same thought we have found in the poem "An die Freunde" (I, 179), but its deepest expression is found in the poem "Dichterlos."

> Für alle muss vor Freuden
> Mein treues Herze glühn,
> Für alle muss ich leiden,
> Für alle muss ich blühn,
> Und wenn die Blüten Früchte haben,
> Da haben sie mich längst begraben.

(I, 95)

Many of Eichendorff's "Chiffern," the elements of his secret language, are found here: joy, the flame, suffering, the flower, and the heart of the poet, "Das Herz der Welt"! The poet knew that no one understood him; he was alone with his love. And yet he knew that this aloneness would not last. His poetry is the garden and the "Bilder" are the "Blüten." Others will walk in "his garden" and see the flowers; perhaps they will bear fruit and the poet will have been the instrument of God's will. That is precisely why the martyrs who died for their God are "des Dichters echte Brüder" (32). We are told, "mitten in der Täuschung den grossen, herrlichen Glauben an das Bessere festzuhalten und die andern mit feurigen Armen emporzuheben, das gab Gott nur seinen liebsten Söhnen" — (74). And surely our "Taugenichts" must be viewed as such a son. God has shown him special favor and sent him into "die weite Welt." We remember that Friedrich and Florio do not know where they are going, and even the "Taugenichts," at the beginning of the story, admits an uncertainty as to his destination. But our young hero has learned. His painter friend asks what he is doing in Rome. "Da wusste ich nun nicht gleich, was ich sagen sollte, denn dass ich soeben der schönen gnädigen Frau nachspränge, mocht' ich ihm nicht sagen. 'Ich treibe', erwiderte ich, 'mich selbst ein bisschen herum, um die Welt zu sehn' —" (402). Here is a clear and simple statement of purpose. The "Taugenichts" is in pursuit of "die schöne Frau," but he is not going to tell anyone. Without really knowing where to look for her he had gone to Rome, the golden city of his dreams. Of course, he did not find that Rome. The last paragraph of the eighth chapter tells us what he did find. "Ich nahm mir nun fest vor, dem falschen Italien mit seinen verrückten Malern, Pomeranzen und Kammerjungfern auf ewig den Rücken zu kehren, und wanderte noch zur selbigen Stunde zum Tore hinaus" (416). Italy is false! This provocative thought is most interesting. Let us look at the first two strophes of "Götterdämmerung" II.

> Von kühnen Wunderbildern
> Ein grosser Trümmerhauf',
> In reizendem Verwildern
> Ein blühender Garten drauf.
>
> Versunknes Reich zu Füssen,
> Vom Himmel fern und nah
> Aus anderm Reich ein Grüssen —
> Das ist Italia!

(II, 342)

In Italy he did not find the fair lady, "die Eine," without whom he would be a veritable nothing. We must remember that the "Taugenichts" is a minstrel, a singer who plays his violin-heart. He is dedicated to a pursuit of "die schöne Frau," and in Italy he finds the older one, Venus. Florio travels to Lucca, Italy, where Bianca "becomes" Venus. Otto, in "Dichter und ihre Gesellen," wanders to Italy and marries Annidi, the living emblem of his poetry. Eichendorff offers more evidence than this, but the point should be clear; he decries the influence of Italy upon the poetry and aesthetics of his period. Its splendid "Wunderbilder" are called "ein grosser Trümmerhauf" upon which thrives a garden defined by two significant words, "verwildernd und blühend." Clearly, this process cannot refer to the eternal cycle in nature, but the circle motif of human existence when the garden of the soul grows but the flowers of earthly desires. This is the realm of Venus, the kingdom of the dead, because love is not obedient to the Father. All this is summarized for us by the words "versunkenes Reich." However, his criticism does not stop there. Italy is also a greeting "aus andrem Reich." What Italy or Rome has to say must be understood by the ear and the "Wunderbilder" speak to the eye. That Truth and Beauty which concern our poet cannot be seen. As we saw in "Jugendandacht" the spring of man's own love is but a reminder, a greeting from heaven, and the beauty of all that is must be a greeting from what eye hath not seen nor ear heard of. Eichendorff deliberately seeks to be a messenger of good news. He knows that what he intends "ist ewig unerreichbar" but he gives us "Bilder," imperfect images of transcendant Beauty. Like a man in a concentration camp he draws pictures of the home that fills his heart with longing.

> Ein Himmelstrahl fällt schweifend auf die Wand,
> Da rührt's lebendig sich in allen Bildern. —
> Dem Auge scheint's ein lieblich bunter Tand —
> Doch wer der lichten Heimat recht zu eigen,
> Dem wird der Bilder ernster Geist sich zeigen.

(I, 94)

And so the "Taugenichts" leaves the false Italy where he found a Rome which, like the city of Lucca, is the home of Venus. The minstrel who would sing of mysteries cannot stay in a kingdom where only man's genius is venerated and what God hath wrought remains neglected. All this, I should remind the reader, must be understood in terms of what this art meant to Germany. It does not describe the image for whom the "Taugenichts" is searching. She has left Italy and so he now must search elsewhere. The ninth chapter opens with a poem.

> Die treuen Berg' stehn auf der Wacht:
> "Wer streicht bei stiller Morgenzeit
> Da aus der Fremde durch die Heid'? —
> Ich aber mir die Berg' betracht'
> Und lach' in mich vor grosser Lust
> Und rufe recht aus frischer Brust
> Parol' und Feldgeschrei sogleich:
> Vivat Österreich!"
>
> Da kennt mich erst die ganze Rund',
> Nun grüssen Bach und Vöglein zart
> Und Wälder rings nach Landesart,
> Die Donau blitzt aus tiefem Grund,
> Der Stephansturm auch ganz von fern
> Guckt über'n Berg und säh' mich gern,
> Und ist er's nicht, so kommt er doch gleich,
> Vivat Österreich!

(II, 416)

The "Taugenichts" comes "aus der Fremde," from heathen Italy, and is challenged by the faithful guardians of another land. He is not the least disturbed because the confrontation with the sentry means that he is approaching his destination. With joy in his heart he utters the password, but a password which is also a call to battle. It seems suggested that the same word whereby one gains admittance to the new land is also a banner for which one lives and dies. And this singular and all-embracing term is simply "Vivat Österreich." Or is it? Somehow this does not fit the context. Looking at the second strophe we see that his greeting has a remarkable effect. As these words are uttered, the entire region responds as though he were now recognized. And that is the function of a password. "Liebe in der Fremde" ends with the line, "Und kennt den Sänger an den Gruss." The short poem "Wünschelrute" states that the world will begin to sing if man will utter "das Zauberwort" and in "Der Maler," as well as other poems, the earth sings with joy when the face of the queen "appears"; all this is part of a pattern. If our equation is valid then it must follow that "Vivat Öster- reich" serves as "das Zauberwort" in the above poem. We can then conclude that "die ganze Rund' " recognizes him because the "Taugenichts" sings that eternal song of praise which is "asleep" in nature. The created, all the things that are, "look" to man as their spokesman; he speaks for the universe because only the lips of man can sing the glorious notes of a love that is free and yet obedient. To the Christian there can be but one word which may serve as both "Parol' und Feldgeschrei"; it is the one name above all names, Christ. After all, and now we climb the ladder which Eichendorff demands of the reader, "Österreich" can mean the Eastern empire, the Orient which is but another name for Christ, the light of the world. In other words, our young hero comes "aus der Fremde" and is about to enter another kingdom where his Lady dwells.

As our hero sings the last strophe he finds himself accompanied by three musicians. It seems they had joined him in song in the hope of receiving some small reward for their efforts. The "Tauge- nichts" denies that he is a musician, asserting that he is an "Einnehmer" just returned from Rome who "seit geräumer Zeit nichts mehr eingenommen, so habe ich mich unterwegs mit der Violine durchgeschlagen" (417). Now that he is going home, he paraphrases the last words spoken to him by the father, "geh auch einmal hinaus in die Welt und *erwirb dir selber dein Brot*" (349, italics mine). Of course he earns his bread by playing the violin, the instrument whose kingdom is not of this world. The response by one of the musicians is more significant than we realize. "Bringt nicht viel heutzutage!" (ibid). After all, who cares if your song glorifies the Lord? Let us not forget, as I have pointed out, all that the "Taugenichts" represents includes the feeling of being "verlassen von der Welt." Now, in the ninth chapter, he comes among his own kind, those who care. It is appropriate that these musicians should be students; indeed, it seems that they are studying for the priesthood. I cannot discuss the implication of this without offering a rather long excerpt from the conversation that now takes place. Our "Taugenichts" is asked if he is also "ein Studierter," to which he replies that he had never had the money to fulfill this desire.

"Das tut gar nichts", rief der Waldhornist, "wir haben auch weder Geld noch reiche Freundschaft. Aber ein gescheuter

Kopf muss sich zu helfen wissen. Aurora musis amica, das heisst zu deutsch: mit vielem Frühstücken sollst du dir nicht die Zeit verderben. Aber wenn dann die Mittagsglocken von Turm zu Turm von Berg zu Berg über die Stadt gehen, und nun die Schüler auf einmal mit grossem Geschrei aus dem alten finstern Kollegium herausbrechen und im Sonnenscheine durch die Gassen schwärmen — da begeben wir uns bei den Kapuzinern zum Pater Küchenmeister und finden unsern gedeckten Tisch, und ist er auch nicht gedeckt, so steht doch für jeden ein voller Topf darauf, da fragen wir nicht viel danach und essen und perfektionieren uns dabei noch im Lateinischsprechen. Sieht der Herr, so studieren wir von einem Tage zum andern fort. Und wenn dann endlich die Vakanz kommt, und die andern fahren und reiten zu ihren Eltern fort, da wandern wir mit unsern Instrumenten unterm Mantel durch die Gassen zum Tore hinaus, und die ganze Welt steht uns offen."

Ich weiss nicht — wie er so erzählte — ging es mir recht durchs Herz, dass so gelehrte Leute so ganz verlassen sein sollten auf der Welt. Ich dachte dabei an mich, wie es mir eigentlich selber nicht anders ginge, und die Tränen traten mir in die Augen. — Der Waldhornist sah mich gross an. "Das tut gar nichts", fuhr er wieder weiter fort, "ich möchte gar nicht so reisen: Pferde und Kaffee und frisch überzogene Betten, und Nachtmützen und Stiefelknecht vorausbestellt. Das ist just das Schönste, wenn wir so frühmorgens heraustreten, und die Zugvögel hoch über uns fortziehn, dass wir gar nicht wissen, welcher Schornstein heut für uns raucht, und gar nicht voraussehen, was uns bis zum Abend noch für ein besonderes Glück begegnen kann." — "Ja," sagte der andere, "und wo wir hinkommen und unsere Instrumente herausziehen, wird alles fröhlich, und wenn wir dann zur Mittagsstunde auf dem Lande in ein Herrschaftshaus treten und im Hausflur blasen,[21] da tanzen die Mägde miteinander vor der Haustür, und die Herrschaft lässt die Saaltür etwas aufmachen, damit sie die Musik drin besser hören, und durch die Lücke kommt das Tellergeklapper und der Bratenduft in den freudenreichen Schall herausgezogen, und die Fräuleins an der Tafel verdrehen sich fast die Hälse, um die Musikanten draussen zu sehen." — "Wahrhaftig", rief der Waldhornist mit leuchtenden Augen aus, "lasst die an-

dern nur ihre Kompendien repetieren, wir studieren unterdes
in dem grossen Bilderbuche, das der liebe Gott uns draussen
aufgeschlagen hat! Ja, glaub' nur der Herr, aus uns werden
gerade die rechten Kerls, die den Bauern dann was zu erzäh-
len wissen und mit der Faust auf die Kanzel schlagen, dass
den Knollfinken unten vor Erbauung und Zerknirschung das
Herz im Leibe bersten möchte" (419-20).

The "Taugenichts" and these future priests must live with the
feeling of being "verlassen von der Welt," and they must learn
to do this with joy. In addition, both play the instrument and
sing their song in honor of God and for the other. Remember,
wherever the "Taugenichts" plays, people dance, and the purpose
of the dance is to destroy the configuration of empty habits
(373-74). Studying has precious little to do with books; one learns
from "das grosse Bilderbuch" fashioned by God, that is, the created. Friedrich tells Romana to look at the created and observe
how it obeys God. This reference to nature must be understood
in terms of the word "Bild." What anything means to man depends
entirely upon what man thinks himself to be. St. Francis of Assisi addressed the created as brother and sister because this expressed his sense of oneness with the All and his utter dependency
upon God's Law. In this way he affirmed his love for that Love
which generated the universe, and the entire cosmos was a "Bild"
of this Love. This "Bilderbuch" contains the secret language,
"Chiffern, Hieroglyphie," which is the song that is asleep and
awaits the liberating utterance of man's magic word. Eichendorff's
minstrel and his concept of the priest are taught by the same
grace and both convey what they have learned to their fellow
man, with this difference: the priest points to the Word and the
poet sings of the Word's image in the world. It is not enough
to be "verlassen" by the world; one must also be poor. The
priest and the minstrel should possess nothing, not even earthly parents, and embrace the cardinal rule imposed by Francis of
Assisi. Whatever man possesses is an impediment — the letter
from Aurelie had spoken of "Hindernisse" — if he is to enter
the service of the Master and sing the song of Our Lady. What
is demanded of the priest is also imposed upon the minstrel.
They are brothers — in law. This spiritual relationship is suggested in a most devious manner by our poet. It seems that one
of the musicians has an uncle at a certain castle. As it happens,
our "Taugenichts" is on his way to this castle and the uncle is

none other than the "Portier," the very same man whose niece the "Taugenichts" is going to marry.

The subject of marriage brings us to the final scenes in our story. In *Ahnung und Gegenwart*, Leontin comes upon a small castle nestled in an isolated valley surrounded by a forest of evergreens. He is moved to call out: "Wie *fürchterlich schön*, hier mit einem geliebten Weibe ein ganzes Leben lang zu wohnen! Ich möchte mich um alle Welt nicht verlieben" (80, italics mine). How strange to speak of the seemingly idyllic as frighteningly beautiful. And yet, in the poem "Sommerschwüle," the mintrel fears that spring is over, for "An Weib und Kind ist nun der Sinn gebunden." It is apparent that "sich ver-lieben" could be dangerous because love, which energizes man's flight toward his God, may be trapped in the created. The very first song sung by the "Taugenichts" speaks of "die Trägen, die zu Hause liegen"; their life revolves about "Kinderwiegen" and "Not um Brot." In view of all this, it becomes rather embarrassing when Eichendorff has our hero rush home to get married. It seems so out of character, as though the final chapter were a contradiction of all that the "Taugenichts" seemingly represents. But our hero clearly speaks of himself as "der verlorene, glückselige Bräutigam" (424). Furthermore, we have insisted that our good-for-nothing "met" Venus and the Virgin Mary at the very beginning of the journey. Both appealed to him! It seems that the youth will marry Venus or the Virgin. The movement of events in the novella instructs us that the "Taugenichts" is not interested in the older of his two beautiful ladies; it follows then that he will marry the Queen. But this is absurd. Our Eichendorff structured the final events in such fashion so that the resolution of the mystery would be readily apparent. He does not marry his "schöne, gnädige Frau" but someone else!

In the tenth chapter the "Taugenichts" returns to the castle. He is greeted by "ein Duften und Schimmern und Jubilieren von allen Vöglein" and even "die vergoldeten Wipfel neigten sich im Abendwinde" (427) as though they were bidding him welcome. He is the lost bridegroom, and it seems that everyone had been waiting for him. This brings us to an interesting observation. He had left the castle because he thought his "schöne Frau" had been promised to someone else. He returns because of a letter intended for someone else. During his trip through Italy he is thought to be someone else. He constantly encounters the older of his two ladies because he is looking for someone else. This *someone else* is the basic theme in the composition; it suggests the song we should hear and the image we should see. And yet, by design, it is exquisitely concealed because this someone else, in truth, cannot be seen or heard. It is a vision, just as Rome is nothing more than "ein Nebelstreif" (399). Our youth has been invited to a wedding feast, a very special celebration. Before one can join the other guests certain requirements must be fulfilled. That is why, just before he jumps over the garden wall, our "Taugenichts" hears a song, a reminder of what is needed.

> Schweigt der Menschen laute Lust:
> Rauscht die Erde wie in Träumen
> Wunderbar mit allen Bäumen,
> Was dem Herzen kaum bewusst,
> Alte Zeiten, linde Trauer,
> Und es schweifen leise Schauer
> Wetterleuchtend durch die Brust.
>
> (II, 427)

Be still and know that I am God! That is the first requirement. Take a wife, buy a farm, become involved in this or that; all speaks insistently and loudly to the heart and mind. Man does not even hear the invitation, the silent greeting brought by the entire universe. He who has ears, let him hear. But first be silent; that is why the first verse has a colon. Then you will hear the song and feel the light in your breast. Nature sings as though in a dream because this is the song that is asleep in all things. Eichendorff has told us many times that this song is heard by only a certain kind of poet, one who refrains from singing merely of his own "Lust und Leid." Our "Taugenichts" is such a minstrel, the new troubadour who sings for others and earns bread by playing the heart-instrument. Florio's song was heard by Venus, and he too was invited to a wedding feast. Quickly now, so as not to detract from what our "Taugenichts" experiences, let us review a few salient features of Florio's "Marmorbild Erlebnis." He meets Bianca and then dreams of sailing upon a vast ocean and the sails of his ship are "schwanenweiss." The sirens emerging from the waters all look like Bianca. Then he changes her into something else. That night he finds the pond and the statue which seemed to have emerged from the waters. His song gives her life and she becomes his all. In the final scenes he sees her in the castle which is supported by "jugendliche Gedanken." Maidens are busy enhancing her beauty with roses; strange cavaliers and their ladies wander among the rose bushes. Venus is constantly busy with this and that, and is never still. Wreathed in roses, she occasionally glances at him, "dass es ihm durch die innerste Seele ging." And now let us look at another picture, a picture which should and must bear striking resemblance to the "Marmorbild" scenes.

The young man jumps from the wall and runs toward the song. "Als ich nun zwischen den letzten Rosensträuchern hervortrat, blieb ich plötzlich wie verzaubert stehen. Denn auf dem grünen Platze am Schwanenteich, recht vom Abendrote beschienen, sass die schöne gnädige Frau, in einem prächtigen Kleide und einem Kranz von weissen und roten Rosen in dem schwarzen Haar, mit niedergeschlagenen Augen auf einer Steinbank und spielte während des Liedes mit ihrer Reitgerte vor sich auf dem Rasen, gerade so wie damals auf dem Kahne, da ich ihr das Lied von der schönen Frau vorsingen musste." (427-28). This description combines two "Marmorbild" scenes: when Florio first sees the statue by the pond and his meeting with Venus in her castle (318 and 335). But our "Taugenichts" is not rooted to the spot as he sees his lady by the swan-pond resplendent in the rays of the evening sun and surrounded by roses. We have before us what at one time was a favorite subject for painters, "Maria im Rosenhag."[22] Unlike Venus, this lady is quiet; Eichendorff calls her "die Stille." Here, as throughout the story, she is depicted with downcast eyes. The mirror, always associated with Venus, is gone and their are no ladies in waiting. She is alone; as another poem instructs us she is "Die Einsame" (I, 233). Thus far we have seen the vision, "das Bild," which is in the mind and heart of our good-for-nothing. This image must be a living being for our hero. And yet Eichendorff cannot let the process move toward "weltlich festhalten" because this would repeat Florio's error. At the same instant that the heavenly Venus appears almost as in a dream, she must also disappear. Three times Eichendorff tells us that the vision is gone, and the first "withdrawal" is given us in the "Rosenhag" picture quoted above. The "Taugenichts" tells us that this is the same woman who had been in the boat with him.

In the description on page 356, she is an angel in the depths of heaven who holds in her hand a lily with which she touches the pond. This I have explained. Looking at the passage on page 428, we see that this lady holds not a lily but a riding crop. The notion of an error on the part of our poet must be rejected because he goes on to say, "gerade so wie damals auf dem Kahne." Eichendorff has the "Taugenichts" say, in effect: "See, it is the same woman." But Eichendorff wants the reader to understand that this cannot be. He points to this deviation with such deliberate intent that we would be foolish to call this a mistake. Furthermore, it is only the first step in a carefully structured withdrawal of the lady as flesh and blood.

Our hero is given but a moment to enjoy this heavenly beauty and then it is interrupted. His lady notices him, gives a cry, and her companion who had been singing the song claps her hands three times — it is as though all had been prepared for his coming and this was a prearranged signal — and

> Wir bringen dir den Jungfernkranz
> Mit veilchenblauer Seide,
> Wir führen dich zu Lust und Tanz,
> Zu neuer Hochzeitsfreude.
> Schöner, grüner Jungfernkranz,
> Veilchenblaue Seide.
>
> (II, 428)

Perhaps the reader will remember the discussion of "Jugendandacht" 6, especially the last strophe.

> Kann unser Lied auch nie den Lohn erwerben,
> Dass hier mit eignem, frischen Blumenkranz
> Uns endlich kröne nun die Wunderschöne! —

The youth of the above poem would find the beloved in the light-filled colors of existence, and the "Taugenichts" sees her in the fragrance used by "Der Maler." Her presence is felt, like the scent of heavenly flowers, but she is not seen. That is why she disappeared when the "Taugenichts" spied upon her under the window. But even though he had to endure separation he kept the image in his heart, kept on singing her song, and now he is rewarded. The bridal wreath which is given him is held together "Mit veilchenblauer Seide." In his song "Der Gärtner" (and remember the discussion of the poem), the second strophe tells us,

> In meinem Garten find ich
> Viel Blumen, schön und fein
> Viel Kränze wohl draus wind ich,
> Und tausend Gedanken bind' ich
> Und Grüsse mit darein.

The unassuming little violet has long been a symbol of faithfulness, Eichendorff's "Treue." This is the equivalent of his "Gedanken." Flowers he cannot give her, but she will accept his faithful thoughts. This faithfulness is returned because she did not let him go but instead — and the story revolves about this — she actually calls him back. More of this in a moment. The mystery of being faithful concerns a garden and Eichendorff weaves this into the context. The little girls who had danced about appeared out of the roses. This parallels the "Marmorbild" structure where beautiful maidens, as though awakening from midday dreams, "erhoben sich . . . aus den Blumen." (335). Of course, we must not miss the significance of the insinuation that these female figures seem to arise from the flowers while the little children burst forth from them. As their dance is suddenly arrested, we are told: "Die kleinen Mädchen öffneten nun den Kreis und standen auf einmal wie verzaubert alle unbeweglich auf einem Beinchen, während sie das andere in die Luft streckten und dabei die Blumengirlanden mit beiden Armen hoch über den Köpfen in die Höh' hielten" (428-29). This, in the truest sense of the word, is "ein Bild." This picture disappears from the story and no further reference is made to it. But we have seen it before in *Ahnung und Gegenwart*. I have in mind Romana's reference to her mother's warning that she should not leave the garden, a garden that is "fromm und zierlich umsäumt mit Rosen, Lilien und Rosmarin. Die Sonne scheint gar lieblich darauf und lichtglänzende Kinder sehen dir von ferne zu und wollen dort zwischen den Blumenbeeten mit dir spazierengehen" (124). This is the pious garden of love, purity, and faithfulness where angels would walk with man. Romana escapes and her love destroys her; our hero is drawn back to it. And now it is explained what had happened to him.

"Die Liebe — darüber sind nun alle Gelehrten einig — ist eine der couragiösesten Eigenschaften des menschlichen Herzens, die Bastionen von Rang und Stand schmettert sie mit einem Feuerblicke danieder, die Welt ist ihr zu eng und die Ewigkeit zu kurz. Ja, sie ist eigentlich ein Poetenmantel, den jeder Phantast einmal in der kalten Welt umnimmt, um nach Arkadien auszuwandern. Und je entfernter zwei getrennte Verliebte voneinander wandern, in desto anständigern Bogen bläst der Reisewind den schillernden Mantel hinter ihnen auf, desto kühner und überraschender entwickelt sich der Faltenwurf, desto länger und länger wächst der Talar den Liebenden hinten nach, so dass ein Neutraler nicht über Land gehen kann, ohne unversehens auf ein paar solche Schleppen zu treten. O teuerster Herr Einnehmer und Bräutigam! obgleich Ihr in diesem Mantel bis an die Gestade der Tiber dahinrauschet, das kleine Händchen Euer gegenwärtigen Braut hielt Euch dennoch am äussersten Ende der Schleppe fest, und wie Ihr zucktet und geigtet und rumortet, Ihr musstet zurück in den stillen Bann ihrer schönen Augen. — Und nun dann, da es so gekommen ist, ihr zwei lieben, lieben närrischen Leute! schlagt den seligen Mantel um euch, dass die ganze andere Welt rings um euch untergeht — liebt euch wie die Kaninchen und seid glücklich!" (429).

I shall take from this passage no more than is needed for my present purpose. Love is a magic carpet which conceals the lovers. In this sense, its function must be equated with the "Zauberberg" of which Florio is warned by Fortunato. But there is an important difference. By entering the "Zauberberg" Florio sinks into the sunken realm of Venus. Under the mantle of love our "Taugenichts" is together with his "schöne Frau" and rises until "die ganze andere Welt rings um euch [he and his beloved] untergeht." The "Taugenichts" thus enters "ein unermessliches Revier" (I, 154), while Florio almost drowns in the pond, in "dem Labyrinth der Brust." The insinuation that our young hero enters God's "weite Welt" is conveyed by the quality of extension imputed to this mantle — it seems to cover the earth. Remember that she is also under this mantle, and then recall the song, "Der Gärtner," our hero sings: "Wohin ich geh' und schau . . . Vielschöne, gnädige Frau./Grüss' ich dich tausendmal." His seeing is a greeting but not a seeing of her. In Rome the young man is

asked what he might be doing there and he conceals the fact
that he is in pursuit of his lady. The above passage tells us
that a certain someone has a firm grip on his coattails and would
hold him secure even though he wandered "bis an die Gestade
der Tiber." In other words, if she did not hold on to him, he
could not pursue her. I have pointed out several times that only
when the "Taugenichts" thinks of her is he inspired to travel.
His very freedom is grounded in the fact that he is her prisoner.
This is the very opposite of Florio's "Marmorbild" experience.

This love makes all men equal. With this statement Eichendorff informs the careful reader that the heavenly Venus is a
living image in the heart of the "Taugenichts." How is this so?
Throughout the entire story, the young man seemingly is in love
with his "gnädige Frau," a countess. Consequently, the suggestion
that love destroys "die Bastionen von Rang und Stand" appears
to imply that a commoner, the "Taugenichts," is about to marry
nobility. This is of the same order of significance as the fact
that a lily is now a riding crop. The truth of the matter is that
the maiden he married is a commoner. She is not "die Eine"
without whom he would be "ein Null," a "Niemand." His one and
only must remain an image in his heart. What does the poem
"Der Gärtner" say? "Die Liebe nur ohnegleichen/Bleibt ewig im
Herzen stehn." This is the problem-mystery which I have made
the essential thread in this book because it is presented again and
again in prose and poetry: the poet's love takes on form, becomes
flesh and blood; the human creator creates in his own image
and sings his own song, and the beloved is Venus, a projection
of his personal joys, desires, and pain. That is why the poem "Das
Gebet" tells us:

> Du seltner Pilger, lass dich warnen!
> Aus ird'scher Lust und Zauberei,
> Die freud- und leidvoll dich umgarnen,
> Strecke zu Gott die Arme frei!

> (I, 302)

This passage offers the third, incontestable reference to the
delicate "withdrawal" of the Queen which Eichendorff must effect. We read that the "Taugenichts" could wander at will, and
the small hand of his "gegenwärtigen Braut" would nevertheless keep a firm grip on him. And who is his present bride?
The "Taugenichts" at this precise moment in the story still thinks

"die gnädige Frau." She is in his mind and heart, in the same sense as Raimund says, "das Fräulein, das alle meine Gedanken meinten" (977). The "Taugenichts," too, says this. I have tried, throughout this book, to emphasize the significance of "Gedanken." Eichendorff does not embrace the notion, "I think, therefore I am," but rather, the idea that man tends to become what he thinks.[23] But thoughts are dead unless implemented, and it is love that gives them life. Love gives direction to man's doing, and the intellect merely illuminates the previously selected path. In our story, the Queen "holds on" to the youth and does give direction to his doing; she helps him implement the words of his song, "Den lieben Gott lass ich nur walten." And now, because he has tried to sing her song, he will be rewarded.

> "Darum bin ich dir gewogen,
> Darum wird dein Haupt geschmückt,
> Weil der Strich von deinem Bogen
> Öfters hat mein Herz entzückt."

Of course, the Queen does not sing this song. Throughout the entire story "die Stille" never utters a word. Although she teaches the "Taugenichts" his song — he "hears" her sing — we, the readers, must not be party to this communication. This is the mystery of love and grace which defies all artistry and can be insinuated only indirectly. To render the mystery concrete is an error, a "Gelüst" which Rudolf senses as he stands before the works of Albrecht Dürer and Michelangelo. They fill him with a desire "das Unaussprechliche auszusprechen, das Undarstellbare darzustellen" (274). Victor-Lothario-Vitalis calls this tendency in his poetry "Die Blocksberge seiner Phantasie." And precisely because Eichendorff rejects this dangerous compulsion on the part of the poet to create "einen fertigen Himmel," he prefers the simple lines of the sketch which outline and suggest but leave it up to the reader to labor with the poet and complete the vision. This brings me to the final thread of internal evidence for what I have called the "withdrawal" of the Queen. She cannot really be flesh and blood for man but must remain a living image in the heart. This is the perfect reversal of the process demonstrated in "Das Marmorbild" where love turns a statue which represents an idea or thought into flesh and blood.

Our hero is told that the Lady would draw him back "in den stillen Bann ihrer schönen Augen." But I have repeatedly called

attention to Eichendorff's insistence that "die gnädige Frau"
is depicted with downcast eyes and rarely "looks" at the "Taugenichts" unless it is to express her displeasure or to admonish him.
We recall "Jugendandacht" 1 where "die Stille, Ewigreine"
raises the veil "dass offen bliebe/Der Augen Himmel in das Land
zu scheinen." In my discussion of these lines I pointed to the
danger inherent in the verse which follows closely after the
above lines, "Im Angesicht der stillen Ewigreinen." In the "Taugenichts" story the Queen never seeks a confrontation with the
youth; he always encounters her by accident, and when he tries
to see he already has fallen into error. As a consequence, the
above reference to her eyes cannot be taken literally; Eichendorff however, and in accordance with his standard technique,
weaves this remark into the concrete movement of events. The
"Taugenichts" does seem to get married to the lady whom he
had been pursuing. And now I must quote the lines which categorically reject the conclusion which critics have always accepted. The girl in question is the proper person to identify herself.
"Aber was nennst du mich denn Gräfin?" — Ich sah sie gross
an. — "Ich bin ja kar keine Gräfin," fuhr sie fort, unsere gnädige
Gräfin hat mich nur zu sich aufs Schloss genommen, da mich
mein Onkel, der Portier, als kleines Kind und arme Weise mit
hierher brachte" (434). It must be obvious that this little orphan
is not the woman whom he saw walking in the garden, "so still,
gross und freundlich wie ein Engelsbild," (353), nor the woman
with the lily whom he saw reflected in his pond "wie ein Engel,[24]
der leise durch den tiefen blauen Himmelsgrund zieht" (356).
The reader is asked to compare this line with "Jugendandacht"
2. Nor can she be the same "gnädige Frau" who in a dream
walks hand in hand with him "bei meinem Dorfe an der Mühle"
— in other words, his past childhood — or who seems to rise
"zwischen den Glockenklängen." Furthermore, she cannot be
"diese schlanke Eins" without whom he — "du arme Null" —
would remain "ewig nichts" (361). It might be argued that the
last item is untenable because his little orphan maiden tells
him, "Siehst du . . . das weisse Schlösschen, das da drüben im
Mondschein glänzt, das hat uns der Graf geschenkt, samt dem
Garten und den Weinbergen, da werden wir wohnen" (433, italics
mine). This hardly sounds as though he would be a nothing.
Now observe his response. He promises to change clothes and
"gleich nach der Trauung reisen wir fort nach Italien, nach Rom,

da gehen die schönen Wasserkünste, und nehmen die Prager Studenten mit und den Portier" (434). Our young man, by conventional standards, is a strange bridegroom. He would take with him the entire "Sippschaft," and is not at all interested in being alone with his bride. He does not want to live in "das Schlösschen" because the minstrel commissioned to earn bread by singing of "der Gloria des Maien" cannot be an "Einnehmer." After all, if this had been the formative idea in Eichendorff's mind, to show how a good-for-nothing manages to acquire "Hab und Gut," then this novella must be viewed as a complete contradiction of everything our poet wrote and lived. Indeed, the first song our youth sings speaks of "Die Trägen, die zu Hause liegen." The "Taugenichts" must wander — and toward Rome, the Rome of his childhood dreams. He now can do this with impunity, for it is written in his song, "Heimweh": "Wer in die Fremde will wandern/Der muss mit der Liebsten gehn." The road to Rome is always through "die Heide" and the Christian, our poet insists, needs the hand of the Queen who is mother to all children. And thus Eichendorff brings to a conclusion what had been a hope at the end of the "Marmorbild" story. The "als würde noch alles gut werden" has been changed to "und es war alles, alles gut!"

The "Taugenichts" story is an exquisitely conceived and brilliantly executed example of the ideal toward which our poet constantly strives; a work of art which demonstrates the interpenetration of two realities — God's and man's. Man is not alone; indeed, the poem "Wunder über Wunder" tells us that man lives in "ein unermessliches Revier" in which he is "das grösste Wundertier" (I, 154). Note, once again, the parallel. Florio creates his "unermessliche Landschaft" and does not realize that this is unnecessary. That is why the same poem goes on to say, "Was du begreifst, mein Freund, ist doch nur Plunder." Man need not search the earth nor the distant stars for a better garden; he runs away from himself only to find the same old self again. And thus Rudolf, in speaking of his past, remarks, "Das Ziehen in den blauen, lieblichen Tagen über grüne Berge, Täler und Flüsse rollt sich noch jetzt blendend vor meiner Erinnerung auf, wie ein mit prächtig glänzenden, wunderbaren Blumen gestickter Teppich, auf dem ich mich selbst als lustige Figur mit buntgeflickter Narrenjacke erblicke" (271). This "Teppich" is that word which is also called "ein Vorhang, an dem unsere Gedanken, gleich

Riesenschatten aus einer andern Welt, sich abarbeiten" (182). In other words, man is a glorious creature who exists, in truth, in one "Revier," while his thoughts are constantly directed toward the other. Precisely because he is a stranger here, as Eichendorff says, he tries to create "die alte Heimat" in a foreign land fashioned of his "Lust und Leid und Liebesklagen."

Notes

1. Precisely the same pattern is found in the "Taugenichts" novella. When the "junge gnädige Frau," who is really no more than the niece of one of the servants, appears upon the balcony, everyone is utterly beside themselves with joy.

2. The father seems to suggest that the son should help with the work. The son should be "about his father's business." In doing his work he is to earn bread. That, really, as the essence of the problem-mystery: How is the minstrel to earn bread?

3. Again I must stress "Gedanken." Raimund's thoughts are directed toward a certain woman. Florio sings a song to the girl on the other side of the river, and these thoughts are a greeting which identify the poet. And now the "Taugenichts" thinks of sparkling eyes, the very eyes which had frightened him not long ago.

4. The pre-dawn moments are perhaps the most precious moments in Eichendorff's day. It is the time of the lark who rises to greet the sun. The fact that the "Taugenichts" has been sleeping late shows his lack of concern for earning "bread."

5. In the "Taugenichts" story these trees are referred to as "Buchenalleen," whereas for Florio they were called "Buchenhallen." The first time that Florio sees the statue Eichendorff already suggests that it is in a temple, "Halle." And this temple, we are told, is supported by "jugendliche Gedanken." Such are the details one must observe if one would understand the poet.

6. Another significant deviation must be noted. This woman, "die gnädige Frau," does not seem to arise from the waters, as is the case with Venus. She sits with the "Taugenichts" in the boat, a word Eichendorff always uses to refer to man's life. Thus, she is part of his life. To say it in another way (and this statement is frequently repeated in the novella), he always thinks of her. Also, compare this scene with the passage (II, 75), where the poet must be like a pond (mirror) "um den Himmel in sich aufzunehmen."

7. Notice that, once again, the "woman" appears "zwischen . . . den Waldhornsklängen." This time, however, the woman does not sing; there is no "Waldhornslied" as in Raimund's experience.

8. Florio says that spring became "ein Bild der Schönen." Upon seeing his "gnädige Frau," the "Taugenichts" feels that spring is near. But it is summer. In other words, she is his spring, while Florio was Venus' spring. All is reversed!

9. The "Taugenichts" speaks of himself as "du arme Null." Clearly we must not conclude that man is nothing. The Father so loved his creatures that he sacrificed his Son for man. The expression shows us that the "Taugenichts" understands his fall from grace. His position is becoming precarious.

10. I have deleted from this book a chapter of perhaps 50 pages which discusses "das Bild." Only some of the ideas have been woven into this edition. The quotation is taken from the description of a journey taken by Leontin and Friedrich in Ahnung und Gegenwart." In the midst of a dense forest they come upon a complex of buildings which are totally uninhabited. The only evidence of movement or life is portrayed by the figure of a Buddha which just rocks back

and forth. I decided to delete my lengthy discussion of this scene because it concerns social criticism rather than our subject, the poet and his song.

11. I have long felt that this thought describes the attitude of literary critics. The "Taugenichts" is "der neue Troubadour" who is the champion of the Heavenly Queen. He is her knight who fights for her and wears her favor. We find it difficult to understand this figure from another age. (Read "Die Schärpe," I, 232).

12. The song, "Der frohe Wandersmann," was written in 1817 just two years after Eichendorff's marriage. He now has a wife and child. Already he fears that all of his thoughts will be governed by the problems of supporting a family. The poem, "Sommerschwüle," expresses this fear. He begs the beloved to return, for it is in her bright eyes that he "sees" the stars which are his "Wegweiser." In her "presence" he can trust his inborn desire and need to sing of the love which he feels. Remember that Florio's spring becomes "ein Bild der Schönen" who is Venus. But eternal spring comes only through the Mediatrix, "die Geliebte." The Queen of Heaven is his secret love. She is the "Wunder" of the "weite Welt."

13. Eichendorff's frequent and enigmatic use of the term *wine* raises it to the status of an emblem. Wine is always associated with "Verführung." Just as the fragrance ("Duft") of the "flower" is the spirit of poetry, so wine seems to be the spirit of that love which "fills" the poem. Eichendorff says that art is "ein von Gott bestimmtes Gefäss himmlischer Wahrheiten. Aber gebt diesem entweihten Gefässe, bevor sie es ganz zerschlagen, den ursprünglichen Wein des Lebens wieder." And this wine is then defined as "jene grosse tiefsinnige Weltansicht, welche, indem sie das Diesseit an das Jenseit knüpft, aller irdischen Erscheinung eine höhere Bedeutung, Wahrheit und Schönheit verleiht" (IV, 859).

14. The "Portier," a caretaker or doorman, is an ambiguous figure. Like the sleeping servant in "Das Marmorbild" who lets Florio escape into the night, he is the conscience of the "Taugenichts," which he ignores and even "throws out" when it suits him. By suggesting that the youth go to Italy, he leads him astray. His words reveal the contradiction. The "Taugenichts" must not lie on his back; he is to earn bread. In the preparation of raisins, the ripe grape is cut from the vine. Consequently, it is impossible to say that raisins *grow*; the thought even implies that the vine is bare. In other words, the nourishment is illusory. In the same sense, whenever the "Taugenichts" wishes to be somebody, he actually becomes less than he should be. This "being somebody" is also an illusion. Furthermore, raisins were probably introduced from Greece, just like the Greek maiden in "Das Marmorbild." The Tarantula is a symbol for human passions. The "Taugenichts" must not dance to their sting, but dance the dance of life. Thus the words of the "Portier" are a contradiction. Italy is really false and no longer a place where God takes care of everything. The Greco-Roman thrust in art and its influence upon Germany is viewed as spiritually negative. This conviction runs through Eichendorff's works. Only the rare poet can withstand and overcome the temptation of Venus.

15. The word *agape* has a very pertinent definition. Among primitive Christians it was a love feast. It was observed with prayers and songs. It ended with the holy kiss. The reader is asked to inspect the "Marmorbild" passage (II, 310), beginning with "Es war

ausgemacht . . . . " In the novella, the love feast refers to a human love which has forgotten "Andacht."

16. In the novella proper, Aurelie is not his "schöne Frau." The latter is never given a name. I took the liberty of using the name because his beloved is like a sun to him. The poem speaks of this.

17. Richard Alewyn, "Eine Landschaft Eichendorffs," in *Eichendorff Heute,* ed. Paul Stücklein (München: Bayerischer Schulverlag, 1960), p. 43.

18. Alewyn, p. 42.

19. "Eine Erschliessung der räumlichen Symbolik würde den Schlüssel zu Eichendorffs Geheimnis liefern und ihn als einen Dichter erweisen, der mit keinem zu vergleichen ist" (Alewyn, p. 43). The concept of "Raum" is defined as the movement of love in my book. As man has less and less physical space upon our earth, he must learn to give the other that love which affords him the "spiritual" space so necessary for existence and growth. If we do not learn this, we shall have anarchy or tyranny.

20. Alewyn, p. 16.

21. When a poet departs from a conventional pattern, it is always of significance. Both Florio and the "Taugenichts" experience the agony of the sixth hour when darkness covered the earth, but in this passage the lameness of the soul has been exorcised by the ringing of church bells. The musicians play so that all will dance. Because they play, people do not succumb to "Trägheit."

22. Martin Schongauer (1430-1491) painted Madonnas who were always true-to-life figures, quietly introspective, gentle, and poetic. I have in mind the altarpiece in the church of St. Martin Comar, Augsburg.

23. Man tends to "become like" the object of his thoughts toward which his love is directed.

24. This angel, the woman with the lily, and the vision in the window have dark brown hair (II, 354), while the girl he will "marry" has black hair. The same detail concerning the hair distinguished Venus from Bianca in "Das Marmorbild."

Epilogue

I selected the poem "Verschwiegene Liebe" as an introduction to the "Taugenichts" chapter because it is one of Eichendorff's last poems and yet it seems to say what I have discerned in the novella itself. The poem speaks of a secret love. "Die Nacht ist verschwiegen . . . Mein Lieb ist verschwiegen/Und schön wie die Nacht." I understand this to mean that "my love (the object of my love) is secret, silent, discreet, and beautiful as the night." The poem "Marienlied" contains the line: "O Maria, heil'ge Nacht!" (I, 317). She is the woman of the night, and yet she is always associated with the rising and setting of the sun, when the sky is the color of redemption's blood and water. In the following poems I would like the reader to think of the "Taugenichts." The two-poem cycle, "An die Entfernte" (I, 236; 1826) was printed just two years after the "Taugenichts" novella had been published. In the first strophe we should visualize the good-for-nothing sitting with his "Braut" in the rose arbor.

An Die Entfernte

1

Denk' ich, du Stille, an dein ruhig Walten,
An jenes letzten Abends rote Kühle,
Wo ich die teure Hand noch durfte halten:
Steh' ich oft sinnend stille im Gewühle,
Und, wie den Schweizer heim'sche Alphornslieder
Auf fremden Bergen, fern den Freunden allen,
Oft unverhofft befallen,
Kommt tiefe Sehnsucht plötzlich auf mich nieder.

Ich hab' es oft in deiner Brust gelesen:
Nie hast du recht mich in mir selbst gefunden,

Fremd blieb, zu keck und treibend dir mein Wesen,
Und so bin ich im Strome dir verschwunden.
O nenn drum nicht die schöne Jugend wilde,
Die mit dem Leben und mit seinen Schmerzen
Mag unbekümmert scherzen,
Weil sie die Brust reich fühlt und ernst und milde!

Getrennt ist längst schon unsres Lebens Reise,
Es trieb mein Herz durch licht' und dunkle Stunden.
Dem festern Blick erweitern sich die Kreise,
In Duft ist jenes erste Reich verschwunden —
Doch, wie die Pfade einsam sich verwildern,
Was ich seitdem, von Lust und Leid bezwungen,
Geliebt, geirrt, gesungen:
Ich knie' vor dir in all den tausend Bildern.

(I, 236).

As in the novella, whenever he thinks of her, even in the midst of chaotic action, he is suddenly filled with "Sehnsucht." But in the second strophe with its line, "Nie has du recht mich in mir selbst gefunden," we are suddenly transported to the final scenes in the "Marmorbild" story when Florio observes, "er kam sich auf einmal hier so fremd und wie aus sich selber verirrt vor" (II, 338). That is why the young man in our poems says, "Und so bin ich im Strome dir verschwunden." The identification of this "dir" is clearly given in the last line of the strophe: "Ich knie vor dir in all den tausend Bildern." For Eichendorff, these words could apply to only one woman — the Queen of Heaven. He admits that they have gone their separate ways, and "In Duft ist jenes erste Reich verschwunden." This is the kingdom for which man searches, and the poet has given us a "Himmelsleiter," as he calls his poetry. It is the dream of man's true goal. The second poem of this cycle dedicated to "die Entfernte" concludes with the following strophe.

Und im schönen Garten droben,
Wie aus Träumen erst gehoben,
Sah ich still mein Mädchen stehen,
Über Fluss und Wälder gehen
Von der heitern Warte oben
Ihre Augen licht und helle,
Wann der Liebste kommen werde. —

Ja! da kam die Sonne schnelle,
Und weit um die ganze Erde
War es morgenschön und helle!

(I, 238)

In the discussion of the poem "Treue" (I, 94; 1819), I deliberately deleted the last strophe, because I wanted the reader to see it in this context.

So wachse denn und treibe fröhlich Blüte,
Du kräftig grüner, deutscher Sangesbaum!
Rausch nur erfrischend fort, mir ins Gemüte
Aus deiner Wipfel klarem Himmelsraum!
Du aber, wunderbare, ew'ge Güte,
Die mir den Himmel wies im schönen Traum,
Erhalt auf Erden rüstig mir die Seele,
Dass ich, wo's immer ehrlich gilt, nicht fehle!

There can be no question that the "ew'ge Gute" is the "Mädchen" in the poem "An die Entfernte." Heaven "was shown" to this poet in a dream, and he spent his life giving us "Bilder" of his vision. She is the one who lifts the veil "dass offen bliebe /Der Augen Himmel, in das Land zu scheinen." But this is a labor of love, and man must do his share, "Denn Gott ist freilich schon an sich barmherzig, aber nur dann, wenn unsere Liebe der Seinigen entgegenkommt, gleichsam eine Gemeinschaft der Liebe, *Liebe um Liebe*" (IV, 1071, italics mine). This statement is absolutely fundamental. It enables us to see a pattern in his use of emblems and deduce the noetic structure in his works. With these words, Eichendorff formally states what his imagery would convey to us. There are only two spiritual forces in man's universe: God's love and his own. And this is not the thought of an old man. Christ told Friedrich: Liebst du mich recht, so gehe mit mir unter, und die Welt ist frei." Give your love to me — "Liebe um Liebe." Total, unreserved surrender to the flaming heart of love is the ideal. And the man who would reject all selfish and thus pointless use of freedom is a warrior.

Nennt mir die Palme eures hohen Strebens!
Bequeme Rast ist nicht des Lebens wert,
Nach Ruh sehnt sich die Menschenbrust vergebens,
E r k ä m p f t will sein, was hoher Sinn begehrt.

Ein Krieger bleibt der grössre Mann zeitlebens,
Er kämpf' mit Rede, Büchern oder Schwert,
Und rechter Friede wird nur da geschlossen,
Wo jedem Streiter seine Palmen sprossen.

(I, 151)

The poem "Der Dichter" (I, 211) summarizes much of what we have gleaned from the poet's imagery. It is the word, given him by God, which resolves the conflict and fashions the rainbow, the symbol of peace. He is the instrument which introduces eternal spring. But in order for him to sing the song which man needs to hear, the woman must stay with him. The flowers (poems) which speak of his personal pain and happiness must be entombed in silence. If the poet persists in this endeavor then he follows the pattern of behavior imputed to the Virgin Mother. She suffered in silence. But so great is her love for such a man (see "Marien Sehnsucht") that she would like to appear to him — "Möcht dem duft'gen Kelch entsteigen." (This same imagery, but with a negative connotation, we have seen in "Jugendandacht" and "Das Marmorbild.") She cannot really arise from the flower-poem, thus the word "möcht." The woman of the night is the source of light and the inspiration of his songs. There is so much he would like to tell her! With her he would wish to spend the night (the night of his own darkness) until the morning star, the Christ, appears.

Nichts auf Erden nenn' ich mein
Als die Lieder meiner Laute,
Doch nenn' den, der freud'ger schaute
In die schöne Welt hinein!
Alles Lebens tiefste Schöne
Tun geheimnisvoll ja Töne
Nur dem frommen Sänger kund,
Und   d i e   Freude sagt kein Mund,
Die Gott wunderbar gelegt
In des Dichters Herzensgrund.
Wenn die Welt, so wild bewegt,
Ängstlich schaut nach ihren Rettern:
Über aller Nebel Wogen
Wölbt Er kühn den Friedensbogen,
Und, wie nach verzognen Wettern,

Rauscht die Erde wieder mild,
Alle Knospen Blüten treiben,
Und der Frühling ist sein Haus,
Und d e r Frühling geht nie aus. —
O du lieblich Frauenbild!
Willst du bei dem Sänger bleiben? —
Blumen bind't ein streng Geschick:
Wenn die tausend Stimmen singen,
Alle Schmerzen, alles Glück
Ewig lautlos zu verschweigen.
Doch bei kühlem Mondenblick
Regt ihr stiller Geist die Schwingen,
Möcht' dem duft'gen Kelch entsteigen.
Sieh, schon ist die Sonn' gesunken
Aus der dunkelblauen Schwüle,
Und zerspringt in tausend Funken
An den Felsen rings und Bäumen,
Bis sie alle selig träumen.
Mit den Sternen in der Kühle
Blühn da Wünsche, steigen Lieder
Aus des Herzens Himmelsgrund,
Und ich fühle alles wieder:
Alte Freuden, junges Wagen!
Ach! so viel möcht' ich dir sagen,
Sagen recht aus Herzensgrund,
In dem Rauschen, in dem Wehen,
Möcht' ich fröhlich mit dir gehen,
Plaudern in der lauen Nacht,
Bis der Morgenstern erwacht! —

(I, 212)

Der Einsiedler

Komm, *Trost der Welt, du stille Nacht!*
Wie steigst du von den Bergen sacht.
Die Lüfte alle schlafen,
Ein Schiffer nur noch, wandermüd',
Singt übers Meer sein Abendlied
Zu Gottes Lob im Hafen.

Die Jahre wie die Wolken gehn
Und lassen mich hier einsam stehn,

Die Welt hat mich vergessen,
Da trat'st du wunderbar zu mir,
Wenn ich beim Waldesrauschen hier
Gedankenvoll gesessen.

O Trost der Welt, du stille Nacht!
Der Tag hat mich so müd' gemacht,
Das weite Meer schon dunkelt,
Lass ausruhn mich von Lust und Not,
Bis dass das ew'ge Morgenrot
Den stillen Wald durchfunkelt.

(I, 299; italics mine)

There is only one "night" which could be called "Trost der Welt."
The poem refers to the woman of the rainbow who prays "dass
sich rings die Stürme legen." Hers are "die treuen Augen, himmelblauen" ("Die Heilige Mutter," [I, 313]), and she intercedes for
"ihre Kinder und' der Schiffe Trümmer" (ibid.) The poet reveals
his secret when he says in the second strophe, "Da trat'st du
wunderbar zu mir." She comes to him from the mountain peaks,
and in her "presence" he finds a measure of rest "von Lust und
Not." With her he would stay until the eternal day dawns.

Erwartung

O schöne, bunte Vögel,
Wie singt ihr gar so hell!
O Wolken, luft'ge Segel,
Wohin so schnell, so schnell?

Ihr alle, ach, gemeinsam
Fliegt zu der Liebsten hin,
Sagt ihr, wie ich hier einsam
Und voller Sorgen bin.

Im Walde steh' und laur' ich,
Verhallt ist jeder Laut,
Die Wipfel nur wehn schaurig,
O komm, du süsse Braut!

Schon sinkt die dunkelfeuchte
Nacht rings auf Wald und Feld,
Des Mondes hohe Leuchte
Tritt in die stille Welt.

Wie schauert nun im Grunde
Der tiefsten Seele mich!
Wie öde ist die Runde
Und einsam ohne dich!

Was rauscht? — S i e naht von f e r n e! —
Nun, Wald, rausch von den Höh'n,
Nun lass Mond, Nacht und Sterne
Nur auf und untergehn!

(I, 225; 1826)

Be silent! Concentrate on this silence. Insist that the songs of other poets ("Vögel") and your own thoughts ("Wolken") be but messengers who send your greetings. And then the night, a different night because it is "dunkelfeucht," seems to sink away, revealing the moon, "Des Mondes hohe Leuchte." The imagery is imperious in its insinuation, because it is followed by the line, "Tritt in die stille Welt." This verb, "treten," was used in the poem "Der Einseidler." "Da trat'st du wunderbar zu mir." In that same poem she "appeared" after the line, "Die Welt hat mich vergessen." In the present poem we read: "Wie öde ist die Runde/Und einsam ohne dich." The appearance of the moon, the effect of its appearance, is not described in terms of light but of sound: "Was rauscht?" At her approach the song seems to burst forth from the "Höh'n." The last two verses of the poem are most important, because here we find another reference to the moon. The poet wants us to be cognizant of a vital difference. It makes no difference if "Mond, Nacht und Sterne/. . . auf und untergehen," as long as he feels the presence of "Des Mondes hohe Leuchte," "Die süsse Braut." She is the bride of heaven. Remember that the "Taugenichts" is "der verlorene Bräutigam" and his "gnädige Frau" is the bride. The moon is a symbol for the Queen of Heaven. But, as always with Eichendorff, we must be careful. Let us look at another bride.

Der Alte Held

(Tafellied zu Goethes Geburtstag 1831)

"Ich habe gewagt und gesungen,
Da die Welt noch stumm lag und bleich,
Ich habe den Bann bezwungen,

Der die schöne Braut hielt umschlungen,
Ich habe erobert das Reich."

"Ich habe geforscht und ergründet
Und tat es euch treulich kund:
Was das Leben dunkel verkündet,
Die heilige Schrift, die entzündet
Der Herr in der Seelen Grund."

"Wie rauschen nun Wälder und Quellen
Und singen vom ewigen Port:
Schon seh' ich Morgenrot schwellen,
Und ihr dort, ihr jungen Gesellen,
Fahrt immer immerfort!"

(I, 92)

The poem contains five strophes, but I quote only the first three which "have been placed" upon Goethe's lips. I am concerned primarily with two verses. "Ich [Goethe] habe den Bann bezwungen,/Der die schöne Braut hielt umschlungen." There can be no question that the word "Braut" refers to "Poesie." All of Eichendorff's poets pursue the bride. As long as she remains a bride, the poet is "safe." Should she become his, then he dies. In Eichendorff's work, poetry is a woman to be loved and she returns the same love with which the poet courts her. It is Eichendorff's perspective that all poets are lovers. Let us look at another poem.

Die Riesen

Hoch über blauen Bergen
Da steht ein schönes Schloss,
Das hütet von Gezwergen
Ein wunderlicher Tross.

Da ist ein Lautenschlagen
Und Singen insgemein,
Die Lüfte es vertragen
Weit in das Land hinein.

Und wenn die Länder schweigen,
Funkelnd im Abendtau,
Soll manchmal dort sich zeigen
Eine wunderschöne Frau.

Da schworen alle Riesen,
Zu holen sie als Braut,
Mit Leitern da und Spiessen
Sie stapften gleich durchs Kraut.

Da krachte manche Leiter,
Sie wunderten sich sehr:
Die Wildnis wuchs, je weiter
Je höher rings umher.

Sie waren recht bei Stimme
Und zankten um ihren Schatz
Und fluchten in grossem Grimme,
Und fanden nicht den Platz.

Und bei dem Lärm sie stunden
In Wolken bis an die Knie,
Das Schloss, das war verschwunden,
Und wussten gar nicht wie. —

Aber wie ein Regenbogen
Glänzt's drüben durch die Luft,
S i e hatt' indes gezogen
Neue Gärten in den Duft.

(I, 325)

The poem was printed in 1837, and, as in so much of Eichendorff's works, reveals his criticism of Romanticism. In this instance the bride is "die wunderschöne Frau," the Queen of Heaven. The minstrel's song will soar only so high, and her garden is beyond his reach. Note that her garden is "in den Duft," the very same fragrance with which "Der Maler" (God) has painted her face upon the canvas of creation. Only a "Taugenichts" can "find" her garden and castle. But it is only in a dream, as it were, for he must spend his life traveling toward the Rome of his childhood dreams. Only then will he really see her. Two years after the "Taugenichts" novella was finished, Eichendorff gave us another poem which also speaks of the woman and her house.

Sonette

1

Es qualmt' der eitle Markt in Staub und Schwüle,
So klanglos öde wallend auf und nieder,

Wie dacht' ich da an meine Berge wieder,
An frischen Sang, Felsquell und Waldeskühle!

Doch steht ein Turm dort über dem Gewühle,
Der andre Zeiten sah und bessre Brüder,
Das Kreuz treu halten seine Riesenglieder,
Wie auch der Menschlein Flut den Fels umpspüle.

Das war mein Hafen auf der weiten Wüsste,
Oft kniet' ich betend in des Domes Mitte,
Dort hab' ich dich, mein liebes Kind, gefunden;

Ein Himmelsbote wohl, der so mich grüsste:
"Verzweifle nicht! die Schönheit und die Sitte
Sie sind noch von der Erde nicht verschwunden."

2

Ein alt Gemach voll sinn'ger Seltsamkeiten,
Still' Blumen aufgestellt am Fensterbogen,
Gebirg' und Länder draussen blau gezogen,
Wo Ströme gehn und Ritter ferne reiten.

Ein Mädchen, schlicht und fromm wie jene Zeiten,
Das, von den Abendscheinen angeflogen,
Versenkt in solcher Stille tiefe Wogen —
Das mocht' auf Bildern oft das Herz mir weiten.

Und nun wollt' wirklich sich das Bild bewegen,
Das Mädchen atmet' auf, reicht aus dem Schweigen
Die Hand mir, dass sie ewig meine bliebe.

Da sah ich draussen auch das Land sich regen,
Die Wälder rauschen und Aurora steigen —
Die alten Zeiten all' weckt mir die Liebe.

3

Wenn zwei geschieden sind von Herz und Munde,
Da ziehn Gedanken über Berg' und Schlüfte
Wie Tauben säuselnd durch die blauen Lüfte,
Und tragen hin und wieder süsse Kunde.

Ich schweif' umsonst, so weit der Erde Runden,
Und stieg ich hoch auch über alle Klüfte,

Dein Haus ist höher noch als diese Lüfte,
Da reicht kein Laut hin noch zurück zum Grunde.

Ja, seit du tot — mit seinen blüh'nden Borden
Wich ringsumher das Leben mir zurücke,
Ein weites Meer, wo keine Bahn zu finden.

Doch ist dein Bild zum Sterne mir geworden,
Der nach der Heimat weist mit stillem Blicke,
Dass fromm der Schiffer streite mit den Winden.

(I, 251-53; 1826)

The essential thought in the first poem is a severe criticism.
Humankind is a vast stream which encircles the cross, and yet
this haven stands in a vast desert. Water is in the desert, yet it
cannot produce life but even seems bent upon destruction. This
is the work of man when he forgets his God. The last two strophes
counterbalance the despair and speak of a beauty which is the
subject of the second poem. The poet clearly tells us that he
wants us to see a picture. The second strophe may be compared
with what the "Taugenichts" sees in the tenth chapter (II, 427-
428). This is "Maria im Rosenhag." The picture, "das Bild," seems
to assume life, and gives him her hand as a promise that she
will never leave him. And what was the "Taugenichts" told?
It makes no difference where he goes "das kleine Händchen Euerer
gegenwärtigen Braut hielt Euch dennoch am äussersten Ende
der Schleppe fest, und . . . Ihr musstet zurück in den stillen
Bann ihrer schönen Augen" (II, 429). Again I emphasized the
word *gegenwärtig* because at that moment she was his "gnädige
Frau," and not the waif whom he "marries." The last strophe of
the second poem repeats what we have seen in many other contexts. The moment she is with him the world is filled with
light and love. Of course, and I want the reader to be clearly
aware of this, the thought of Venus seems to have the same
effect upon Florio.

The third poem repeats, but in a slightly different form, the
final scenes of the "Taugenichts" story: the withdrawal of the
vision. We note again that her home is so high that his song
cannot reach her. The most confusing thought is the phrase in
the third strophe: "Ja, seit du tot." Everything depends upon
the personal and unique definition of the poet's words. Eichendorff tells us:

Trennung ist wohl Tod zu nennen,
Denn wer weiss, wohin wir gehn, —
Tod ist nur ein kurzes Trennen
Auf ein baldig Wiedersehen.

(I, 265)

The first verse in the third strophe of the poem "An die Entfernte" reads: "Getrennst ist längst schon unsres Lebens Reise." And precisely because they are "separated," she is "dead," and, as the third strophe suggests, he cannot find a path to follow. But this sense of helplessness is mitigated and even voided by the last strophe. The "Mädchen" who seemed to come alive in the second poem is a "Bild" which is now his star. The star points home. And the word "Blicke" is a gentle insinuation that the star is really her eyes. (Again we recall the experience of the "Taugenichts" and the eyes of the maiden who would not let him get lost.) The first strophe of "An die Entfernte" also states that he was permitted to hold her hand. But these moments when he senses her fragrant presence are rare. That is why the story of the good-for-nothing was called "Aus dem leben eines Taugenichts." It is really the story of his yearning ("Sehnsucht") for the ideal of a Christian love which she represents and which man, the poet, so seldom achieves. Eichendorff's poetry is like a sine curve. It soars to the light, like a lark, and then sinks into the depths of despair. There is much more of Brentano in this poet than we have realized. Indeed, every God-seeker, especially the mystic, is frequently overpowered and almost crushed by the darkness of his aloneness. In scores of Eichendorff's poems I find the feeling: "O God, my God, why hast Thou forsaken me?" And yet the pain of being forsaken, this torture of a dark nothingness, is also the bedrock of his glorious love song. And that is a basic difference between Florio and the "Taugenichts." The former would embrace death to find the beloved, and the "Taugenichts," although he feels that his own foolishness is digging his grave, refuses to succumb.

Von allen guten Schwingen,
Zu brechen durch die Zeit,
Die mächtigste im Ringen
Das ist ein rechtes Leid.

(I, 80)

Ich möcht' in den tiefsten Wald wohl hinein,
Recht aus der Brust den Jammer zu schrein,
Ich möchte reiten ans Ende der Welt,
Wo der Mond und die Sonne hinunterfällt.

Wo schwindelnd beginnt die Ewigkeit,
Wie ein Meer, so erschrecklich still und weit,
Da sinken all' Ström und Segel hinein,
Da wird es wohl endlich auch ruhig sein.

(I, 52)

Wie oft wollt' mich die Welt ermüden,
Ich beugt' aufs Schwert mein Angesicht
Und bat Dich frevelhaft um Frieden —
Du wusstet's besser, gabst ihn nicht.

(I, 298)

Gestürzt sind die goldnen Brücken
Und unten und oben so still!
Es will mir nichts mehr glücken,
Ich weiss nicht mehr, was ich will.

Von üppig blühenden Schmerzen
Rauscht eine Wildnis im Grund,
Da spielt wie in wahnsinnigen Scherzen
Das Herz an dem schwindligen Schlund. —

(I, 284-85)

The notion that Eichendorff, as man and poet, rested comfortably and securely in his faith is a myth fabricated by generations of careless readers. Faith in God and the determination to love God above all else are the gifts of true freedom, and for these man must fight every day. Each day is a new battle and the outcome is always in doubt. The Christ did not come to bring man, a truly Christian poet, peace. Eichendorff fought and suffered for his freedom, which is synonymous with peace, when the latter is properly understood. Like the knights of another age, he rode forth to slay the dragons that hold men in bondage. And as was the custom in those days, he wore a favor given him by his secret love.

Die Schärpe

Mein Schatz, das ist ein kluges Kind,
Die spricht: "Willst du nicht fechten:
Wir zwei geschiedne Leute sind;
Erschlagen dich die Schlechten:
Auch keins von beiden dran gewinnt."
Mein Schatz, das ist ein kluges Kind,
Für die will ich l e b e n und fechten!

(I, 232; 1815)

For her he would live and fight. While others sleep he sings his songs and calls: "Wachet auf, wacht auf, wacht auf!" (I, 292). In the same poem we are told that each night the Lord "makes his rounds" seeking His own, but everywhere he finds "Tür und Herzensgrund verschlossen." Sadly He turns away and remarks: "Niemand ist, der mit mir wacht. —" These words are taken from the gospels. On the night of his betrayal, Christ agonized in the garden as he contemplated the chalice filled with man's rebellious love. He returned to his sleeping disciples and asked: "Could you not watch one hour with me?" And this is what Eichendorff the poet would seek to do, watch with his Lord. As the God on high woos man with his love, so our poet seeks to rouse man with his love song and remind him of home.

Allgemeines Wandern

Vom Grund bis zu den Gipfeln,
Soweit man sehen kann,
Jetzt blüht's in allen Wipfeln,
Nun geht das Wandern an:

Die Quellen von den Klüften,
Die Ström' auf grünem Plan,
Die Lerchen hoch in Lüften,
Der Dichter frisch voran.

Und die im Tal verderben
In trüber Sorgen Haft,
Er möcht' sie alle werben
Zu dieser Wanderschaft.

Und von den Bergen nieder
Erschallt sein Lied ins Tal,

Und die zerstreuten Brüder
Fasst Heimweh allzumal.

Da wird die Welt so munter
Und nimmt die Reiseschuh'
Sein Liebchen mitten drunter
Die nickt ihm heimlich zu.

Und über Felsenwände
Und auf dem grünen Plan
Das wirrt und jauchzt ohn' Ende —
Nun geht das Wandern an!

(I, 9-10)

And who is this "Liebchen" who secretly nods her approval of his efforts? Could she be anyone other than the Heavenly Queen who watches over her children? Eichendorff, the spiritual Pied Piper, seeks to do her work and sings her song: "Let it be done unto me according to thy Word."

I should like to close with three poems. The first two have the same title, "Entschluss." Man must make a decision. Nothing so destroys the productive energy of a nation or an age as the lack of a clearly defined goal. Man was made to do, and if he does not know why, or to what he should commit himself, he sinks into apathy or gives himself to a senseless explosion of passion which always embraces destruction. In our age, the twentieth century, the word *peace* is an utter perversion. The outrageous and blind violence which characterizes our era is but the symptom of a more serious illness which has always been the ground of man's suffering. At first glance, the two poems do not seem to be related or speak of the same subject. But this is not so. The first poem tells us that whatever we wish to achieve, we must first risk. If you would labor for freedom, then restrain your own. If you would see love grow in the human community, then give it to God and He will return it to all. If you want peace, then accept the blind fear of the other, which usually manifests itself as hostility. But it takes courage to fight in this way. And we are all cowards. It is not that we lack good will, but we fail in audacity. We have not dehumanized ourselves — the term is void of content and essentially stupid, because whatever man does is within the potential of his human nature; the problem is that we have become like sheep without a shepherd.

Entschluss

Gebannt im stillen Kreise sanfter Hügel,
Schlingt sich ein Strom von ewig gleichen Tagen,
Da mag die Brust nicht nach der Ferne fragen,
Und lächelnd senkt die Sehnsucht ihre Flügel.

Viel' andre stehen kühn im Rossesbügel,
Des Lebens höchste Güter zu erjagen,
Und was sie wünschen, müssen sie erst wagen,
Ein strenger Geist regiert des Rosses Zügel. —

Was singt ihr lockend so, ihr stillen Matten,
Du Heimat mit den Regenbogenbrücken,
Ihr heitern Bilder, harmlos bunte Spiele?

Mich fasst der Sturm, wild ringen Licht und Schatten,
Durch Wolkenriss bricht flammendes Entzücken —
Nur zu, mein Ross! Wir finden noch zum Ziele!

(I, 138-139; 1814)

Entschluss

Noch schien der Lenz nicht gekommen,
Es lag noch so stumm die Welt,
Da hab' den Stab ich genommen,
Zu pilgern in's weite Feld.

Und will auch kein' Lerch' sich schwingen,
Du breite die Flügel, mein Herz,
Lass hell und fröhlich uns singen
Zum Himmel aus allem Schmerz!

Da schauen im Tale erschrocken
Die Wand'rer rings in die Luft,
Mein Liebchen schüttelt die Locken,
Sie weiss es wohl, wer sie ruft![1]

Und wie sie noch stehn und lauschen,
Da blitzt es schon fern und nah,
All' Wälder und Quellen rauschen,
Und Frühling ist wieder da!

(I, 16-17; 1835, italics mine)

Then what are we lacking? We have become insensitive to pain. No, more than that. We fear it, hide from it, declare it anathema. I speak of that pain which the spirit suffers. If the body ignores the pain which it feels, then it may die. If the spirit rejects the suffering which life imposes then a nation and a civilization will die. We are in desperate need of men who have the courage to sing of that Love which eternally invites man's love. Germany may have poets whose sheer genius transcends the excellence of Eichendorff, but it does not possess a more important poet. No other German poet, with the possible exception of Novalis, had such respect and love for the dignity and high promise of man's ultimate destiny. No other poet had such a deep and penetrating awareness of man's nature and the gift of love which moves secretly, silently, gently, and yet with supreme authority. Eichendorff was utterly optimistic. The foundation of the heavenly kingdom is anchored in creation (I, 102). The edifice soars beyond man's vision and he gives us "Bilder" of that splendor, freedom, dignity, and beauty which fills the heart with yearning. But man, here and now, must labor to beautify the "house" prepared by the Father. Man is the instrument whereby this work is to be accomplished. Nothing unnatural is asked of man. The human creature pursues and labors for the dream of his love. But what is his secret love? Will he succumb to the siren song of the Great Whore which his love has created or will he let love soar, like an eagle, into the heart of the sun? What will man remember and what will he forget? Will he listen to the pain and anguished cry which is the child in every man? Or will he remain silent, alone, and united only by fear and greed which always sing the song of death, the song of *denial?*

Zeichen

So Wunderbares hat sich zugetraten:
Was aus uralten Sagen
Mit tief verworrener Gewalt oft sang
Von Liebe, Freiheit, was das Herz erlabe,
Mit heller Waffen Klang
Es richtet sich geharnischt auf vom Grabe,
Und an den alten Heerschild hat's geschlagen,
Dass Schauer jede Brust durchdrang.

Was für ein Klang in diesen Tagen
Hat übermächtig angeschlagen?
Der Völker Herzen sind die Saiten,
Durch die jetzt Gottes Hauche gleiten!

(I, 137-38; 1812)

Notes

1. Florio's song, "Liebe in der Fremde," is addressed to the maiden, "jenseits überm Fluss,/Du lauschest wohl und hörst's vom weiten /Und kennst den Sänger an dem Gruss." The song identifies the "woman" who is the poet's love. In our poem, the minstrel's pain initiates a song of joy which invites all others to join him in his flight. His song is a call to the Queen, "dass offen bliebe/Der Augen Himmel in das Land zu scheinen." Then it is spring!

Eichendorff: The Spiritual Geometer was printed by the letter-press method on 60-pound wove finish Mead Publishers' Suede Book paper, and casebound in a matte finish Interlaken vellum bookcloth by the Benton Review Publishing Company, Fowler, Indiana. The typeface used for the text was Baskerville, and the chapter headings are of Bulmer. The dust jackets were printed by offset lithography on 50-pound cover weight Warren's Lusterkote by the Owen Litho Service, Spencer, Indiana. Artwork was by Moroni St. John, Purdue University designer, and editorial and production supervision were by Diane Dubiel, assistant university editor.